FRENCH DISCOURSE ANALYSIS

'This is an excellent and much-needed introduction to French Discourse Analysis which should attract a great deal of interest amongst sociologists and discourse analysts.'

Norman Fairclough, *Lancaster University*

'A very ambitious, constructively controversial treatment of a so far little known tradition of discourse analysis that shares the concerns with indexicality, reflexivity and context of current Anglo-American work in Linguistic Anthropology and Sociolinguistics. Recommended reading for anyone interested in gaining insights into the conflicting discourses that mark the intellectual history of the field.'

John J. Gumperz, *University of California, Berkeley*

Why is French Discourse Analysis so important to Sociology and Linguistics?

French Discourse Analysis derives from Michel Pêcheux's attempts to develop a linguistic method for promoting Althusser's theory of ideology. Between the 1960s and the present, this body of work has moved closer to the post-structuralism of Michel Foucault. In this book, Glyn Williams draws together current debates in linguistics and social theory, and provides the first study in English of the principles and theories of French Discourse Analysis.

Williams outlines how the enunciatative linguistics of Benveniste and Culioli serves as the basis for a language-based method that corresponds to the theoretical force of post-structuralism. He guides the reader through the general history of structuralism and post-structuralism before covering the different stages in the development of French Discourse Analysis between 1965 and the present. Key contributors to the field are referred to throughout. The nature and detail of the method is outlined and the relevance of the approach for social and linguistic theory is debated.

Glyn Williams is Director of the Research Centre Wales and Reader in Sociology at the University of Wales, Bangor. His previous publications include *Sociolinguistics: A sociological critique* (1992).

FRENCH DISCOURSE ANALYSIS

The method of post-structuralism

Glyn Williams

London and New York

First published 1999
by Routledge
11 New Fetter Lane, London EC4P 4EE

Simultaneously published in the USA and Canada
by Routledge
29 West 35th Street, New York, NY 10001

Typeset in Bembo by Keystroke, Jacaranda Lodge, Wolverhampton
Printed and bound in Great Britain by Mackays of Chatham plc, Chatham, Kent

British Library Cataloguing in Publication Data
A catalogue record for this book is available from the British Library

Library of Congress Cataloguing in Publication Data
Williams, Glyn
French Discourse Analysis: The method of post-structuralism/Glyn Williams.
Includes bibliographical references.
1. French language—Discourse analysis. 2. Poststructuralism.
I. Title.
PC2434.W55 1998
440.1'41—dc21 98–13943

ISBN 0–415–18940–3

I ELLIW HAF
Fy nghariad a'm cymar.

CONTENTS

ACKNOWLEDGEMENTS

During the time when I have been learning about FDA, visits to France have been supported by both the British Council and the ESRC. I am grateful to both institutions. It is inevitable that the personal interest in FDA which covers more than twenty years has spawned a number of close and enduring friendships. I owe a debt of gratitude to these friends from whom I have learnt so much. Martin Clarke made several useful corrections to the manuscript. Bernard Conein and Françoise Gadet have been kind enough to read and comment on the manuscript. Such good friends should not be held responsible for my mistakes! There was also Pierre Achard. His tragic, early departure has left a void. At the time of his death he was reading the manuscript with the intention of helping to improve the contents. His intelligence and generosity will be sorely missed.

INTRODUCTION

This book is about a particular phase in recent French intellectual work as it relates to what is termed critical and cultural theory. It covers the period since 1960 and focuses upon ideas which have had a profound influence, not only upon intellectual activity across a range of disciplines, but also on politics. Under the label of post-structuralism this body of work has tended to focus upon the contribution of a relatively small number of highly prolific authors – Deleuze, Derrida, Lacan, Foucault and Althusser. Whereas post-structuralism has become something of a catch-all with reference to French intellectualism, leading to disagreement about whose work should be included within its confines, its effects have been far-reaching. Post-modernism in some respects has drawn upon post-structuralism (Boyne and Ratansi, 1990:10). It became fashionable in Anglo-American circles following the publication of *The Postmodern Condition*, written in 1979 and published in English in 1984 by Lyotard, who, hitherto, tended to be a relatively marginal figure within post-structuralism in France. Without wishing to enter a debate, I view the two as distinctive problematics which share a particular orientation towards modernism. This book is not about post-modernism.

The emergence of post-structuralism as an alternative to Enlightenment materialism has led to a polarisation between idealism and materialism, leading to strong feelings on either side about the validity of their respective positions. The idealist camp proclaims a kind of triumphalism in which it is claimed that the age of Enlightenment and all that it entails is at an end, the decentring having undermined the rationalism upon which it was premised, while the consequence can only be that the essence of truth is denied. The opposition rises to the bait. Norris (1996:xiv) has recently vehemently argued that the consequence of the emergence of post-modernism is 'a failure – or a downright refusal – to conceive that science can actually make progress in attaining a more adequate (causal-explanatory) grasp of real-world occurrent objects, processes and events'. During (1990) on the other hand claims that the unease with post-structuralism in some circles is merely a re-presentation of Burke's detestation of French 'men of theory'. This is reiterated in a recent review of the impact of French ideas on British culture (Appignanensi, 1989), a

1

collection which betrays a limited knowledge of what is at stake, while displaying a clear antipathy towards even the few notable names which have had some impact on the subject at hand.

Not that this kind of ethnocentrism characterises the work of the more sophisticated commentators such as Norris, far from it. What is interesting is that such a dogmatic position is accompanied by departure from the customary insistence upon objectivity so that it becomes a manifestation of an overlap between explicit political agendas and science. In this respect it is reminiscent of the *philosophes* of the eighteenth century who made little attempt to conceal their political objectives of state formation and political change in pursuing their philosophical discourses. In this respect it can be claimed that sociology has its origins in political science. Whereas Marxism developed as an explicit manifestation of this political agenda, much of the rest of social science has sought to deny any such interest in the name of objectivity, even refusing to recognise the political materialism that is embedded in its concepts. The recent political events and the emergence of neo-liberalism as the dominant discourse within a global economy mean that Marxism is challenged from two quite different directions, the one challenging its claim to truth through reason, and the other challenging the entire relevance of reason.

It is clearly evident that this debate cannot be resolved in that it is a debate about the very elements that are central to any resolution – the nature of 'truth' or 'reality'. In this respect it is the kind of futile debate that can only lead to polemic rather than resolution. None the less, it is an important debate in that it does oblige each side to adopt a reflexive orientation towards their respective positions. What is usually missing is the detail of the post-structuralist argument and a familiarity with the intellectual context of its development. Consequently, the debate tends to focus upon the preconstructed elements of post-structuralism and/or on their consequences. This book seeks to overcome this weakness by taking the reader through the general history of structuralism and post-structuralism before focusing upon the work which sought to apply the relevance of decentring to the study of ideology, and then introducing the linguistic nature of discourse analysis. It seeks to redress attitudes such as those of Jackson (1991:119), who claims that '"discourse" is a woolly notion, part of the point of which is to avoid doing linguistics'. Eagleton (1991:196) does take an interest in French Discourse Analysis (FDA), but merely accuses its practitioners of 'solemnly labouring the obvious, wheeling up the big guns of linguistic analysis to dispatch the inconsiderable gnat of a dirty joke'. His lack of interest in the relationship between language and ideology is encapsulated in the claim that such diverse theoretical orientations to discourse as those found in the work of Coulthard, Labov, Halliday, Hodge, Kress and Fowler derive from FDA! J.B. Thompson (1990) makes no direct reference to FDA in his survey of ideology. This is characteristic of the tendency for anti-foundationalist orthodoxy to ignore linguistics (Norris, 1996:35). Such silences and glosses appear, increasingly, to be a manifestation of a desire to fix the debate at a certain point around the issue of modernism/non-modernism, while simultaneously ignoring the central elements which would clarify the debate. It is even claimed to lead to a rift between post-structuralists and linguists that derives from the limited understanding of the concerns of the latter among the former (Graham, 1992; Pavel, 1990; Norris, 1996). However, it is equally clear that most linguists are ignorant of the relevance of linguistics for post-structuralism, and in particular of the work of FDA, where the overlap between the two interests is most complete. It is hardly surprising that the two camps stand on different ground.

An exception to this omission is the work of Fairclough (1992), who has sought to take charge of this body of work. However, even here, there are glaring omissions, particularly with reference to enonciative linguistics, which, in many respects, is the cornerstone of FDA. None the less Fairclough has been among the few linguists who have sought to take on board socio-political issues and the relevance of linguistics for such issues. His work encompasses both Marxism and the work of French linguists to an extent that is not evident among the Hallidayan linguists such as Hodge and Kress.

In some respects FDA emerged from a dissatisfaction among Marxists seeking to come to terms with the nature of ideology and the value of 'content analysis' for textual analysis. The tendency for content analysis to treat verbal material as simple conveyors of information clashed with a view which claimed that texts should not be understood as transparent representations of the social subjects which they were claimed to reflect. Thus, in a very general sense, FDA derives from the philological tradition of textual reflection, but in a more specific sense it derives from structuralism and post-structuralism, which, in turn, drew upon Russian formalism. As such it draws upon Saussurean linguistics, the philosophic work of Foucault, the psychoanalysis of Lacan and Althusserian Marxism. It would be a mistake to regard it as a body of work that pertains to linguistics or sociolinguistics, at least according to the way these fields usually tend to be defined and demarcated. It is this range of involvement that is the challenging aspect of coming to terms with FDA. As a sociologist I have had to come to terms not only with orthodox linguistics but also with enonciative linguistics. Given the manner in which post-structuralism spans disciplines while focusing upon language and the subject, this process of spanning intellectual territory that is marked by disciplines is becoming increasingly evident. It is hoped that this book will serve as a relatively gentle introduction to the relationship between the social and the linguistic as conceived of in FDA.

The tension alluded to above between hermeneutic and idealist approaches to the social construction of meaning runs across the entire scope of FDA from its origins to the present. A brief overview of the orientations of some of the contributing names referred to in the preceding paragraph is illustrative. In this respect it is particularly important to focus upon the work of Althusser, whose ideas spawned the emergence of FDA, with his student Michel

Pécheux taking on the task of exploring the implications of Atlhusser's seminal work on ideology. Yet, to restrict it to this purist linearity would be to ignore both the eclectic nature of French intellectualism and the extent to which French Marxists and post-structuralists drew upon their respective intellectual inspirations, and also the extent to which post-structuralism was of significance in the formulation of FDA.

In some respects this overlap between Marxism and post-structuralism parallels the 'Nietzschean' ideas of the later work of both Horkheimer and Adorno. It makes us aware that Western modernism has always expressed the tension between idealism and materialism. At specific historical conjunctures it has surfaced in an explicit polemic, as in the debates that have encompassed the works of Nietzsche, Heidegger and Foucault at specific points during the past hundred years.

Althusser refused to base Marxism on the consciousness of the human subject, replacing the post-Hegelian philosophy of 'praxis' with an epistemological orientation. Epistemology coincided with Marxist philosophy and constructed the conditions of a scientific discourse as ideology, leading Althusser to 'read' *Das Kapital* as an event in the history of science. He refuted the economic reductionism which, for him, plagued much Marxist thinking. Following Gramsci, he claimed that the economic order only acts on the social formation indirectly. It meant that the various instances of the social whole were capable of being autonomous and effective. Such views had far-reaching implications. The direct functionalist link between the economic order and ideology was broken, allowing ideology to be conceived of autonomously. Similarly, the conception of ideology both as a conspiratorial entity which operated against the interests of the masses, and as the converse of science, was brought into question. It was the departure of such ideas from what were taken to be Marxist orthodoxies which created tensions and disputes within the French Communist Party (PCF). It also led to an argument for a method for the study of false consciousness by reference to a thesis on the relationship between consciousness and conscience wherein psychoanalysis, Marxism and structuralism all played a role. It involved viewing ideology as focusing upon the unconscious, and it involved the mechanism whereby the individual was welded into the social by 'constituting' individuals as subjects. This was the link to the decentred subject of post-structuralism.

Althusser himself was not interested in the methodological aspects of such a study, and showed little interest in linguistics. He was, of course, aware of the relative autonomy which structuralism had allocated to language, priority being given to the laws of language rather than to socio-economic factors. He was also aware that it was claimed that linguistics had also experienced an 'epistemological break' that served to reveal the ideology that legitimised its scientific status. Consequently, linguistics was in a position to serve as the basis for developing a methodological framework for a truly scientific discourse analysis. It was this task which fell to Michel Pécheux, leading to the development of FDA.

The work of Foucault has a different grounding, one based upon the idealist refutation of Cartesianism. In refuting positivist notions of method and truth, his work was neither hermeneutic nor epistemological but, rather, sought to develop a challenge to the received knowledge of the normative order by undermining the principles whereby it was established. The very cornerstones of Enlightenment thought – the power of reason, the inevitability of progress or the central role of humankind in determining its own destiny – were reconceived as means of social and political control. This thrust of Foucault's work clearly overlaps with the Althusserian concern with ideology, even if they do derive from different problematics.

A central element of Foucault's work is the concept of discourse as the point of entry to a concern with language and the linguistic. There is a concern with the various signifying practices that relate to alternative truth-claims. Again we recognise that Foucault himself was, for one reason or another, unwilling to pursue the linguistic dimension even though he wrote extensively about the shifting nature of language as an object, and linguistics as a discipline. Language differs from discourse and the two involve different approaches to language. Language pertains to the organisation or structure of any particular language, and is studied by reference to a variety of models which treat the same linguistic phenomena differently, often focusing upon specific elements or processes. Discourse, on the other hand, involves the subjective and social play of 'enonciation'. The English term 'statement' does not correspond to the French term *énoncé*, which relates to the process of 'enonciation' or the production of a statement. Thus when Foucault referred to 'enonciative modalities' he was not referring to the propositional content, but, rather, to the status and institutional setting of that statement. For this reason, I will refer to 'enonce' and 'enonciation' and the respective terms that constitute the conceptual framework of what is known as enonciative linguistics.

Orthodox linguistics is very much a product of modernity and, as such, tends to involve the centred rational subject as dipping into the resources of language in order to convey a meaning which is created and controlled by that individual subject. Semantics becomes the study of this process and the associated negotiation between rational actors. Evidently, a perspective which conceived of the social by reference to the decentred subject has to relate to a conception of linguistics which is similarly decentred. This does not mean refuting the essence of syntax or the manner in which language is structured so that the possibilities of meaning are developed. What it does mean is paying attention to the manner in which the infinite possibilities of language are transposed into meaning as the effect of discourse without the orthodox emphasis upon the centred subject. That is, it involves focusing upon a social construction of meaning which does not rely upon the centred subject as the explanandum of that construction. Within this context discourse becomes 'the use of language in practical situations, envisaged as an effective act, and in relation to the collection of acts (both language and non-language acts) of which it is a part' (Achard, 1993:10). This is not far removed from

Benveniste's (1966) understanding of discourse as 'the phrase, an indefinite creation, variety without limit, it is the life of language in action . . . with the phrase, one leaves the domain of language as a system of signs, and one enters another universe, that of language as instrument of enonciation, where the expression is discourse'. The effects of discourse rely, not on the rationality of the human subject, but on the system of language, while also leaving room for the interpretative disciplines, each of which might have a distinctive perspective on the role which language acts play in the phenomenon under scrutiny. Discourse does not pertain to the same properties of language as those which are of relevance to the linguist. Also, discourse occupies a different theoretical and methodological place with reference to its object of study.

The objects of relevance for the application of FDA are texts or enonces which are produced within an institutional frame that constrains enonciation. Furthermore, these enonces or texts are never 'new' entities, but are inscribed in a forceful interdiscourse which fixes the historic, social and intellectual stakes. That is, any enonce is conditioned by prior discourse which influences the meaning that the enonce is capable of achieving. It involves presupposi-tions which operate upon the enonciative structure. We draw on the past in the way we use language, we use notions that not only derive from the past but which bear structured relationships with other notions, subjects and objects. They carry a complex and relatively stable structuration which retains value for a social collectivity, and which has a specific functioning within a discursive field. Thus, subject places are, to an extent, pre-defined, and the enonciateur occupies a specific place in relation to other subjects and objects which give a structure known as the 'discursive formation'. Such places determine what can and must be said by such an enonciateur.

The particular brand of linguistics drawn upon in order to facilitate FDA is known as enonciative linguistics. What enonciative linguistics strives to reject is the equation of enonciateur/enonciataire with locuteur/locataire (speaker/hearer), partly in order to avoid the problem of the centred subject. Language displaces these relationships and expresses interaction, not in any innate, pre-formed way, but as a feature constructed into language. As such it embodies three interrelated arguments: the 'enonciateur', 'enociataire' and the one-person (I, you, it; me, him, her; here, there, elsewhere; self, other, foreigner; etc.). This social deixis, involving person, time and space, is the means whereby discourse is able to operate in social reality. These dimensions are integrated into a zero point of origin for its enonciation – the 'I-here-now'. They can be integrated into two kinds of operation – one which designates an alternative place of enonciation (you-there-then), and the other that operates alternative spatial points of designation that lie outside the existing field (she/he/it, elsewhere, once upon a time). These are the marks of discourse that designate the nature of the interaction. Additionally there are the modalities, the other relevant dimensions of discourse. This model of enonciation is also capable of generating opposition and neutralisation. Thus, for example, neutralisation occurs when 'we' takes the meaning of both 'I' and 'you', thereby marking a reference to a value that neutralises the I/you opposition. Within any interpretation these various markers in a text operate together with the enonciateur and locuteur's knowledge of customary practice in operating that part of the discourse which is 'free' in the sense of it not revealing any relevant deictic marks or modalities. That is, in any speech-act both the enonciateur and the locuteur must take account of the place they assume in the interpretation of the existing situation. It is these places into which the individual is interpolated by taking in charge the discourse through becoming actively involved in the speech-act.

The constraining aspect of discourse involves the manner in which enonciation is always confronted by that which it cannot say, by that which cannot be said from the subject place that the enonciative marks help to establish. Meaning now becomes something other than the conception of orthodox semantics involving the stable and homogenous projection of what a rational human subject wishes to say (Collinot and Mazière, 1997). Whereas orthodox linguistics refers to the unstatable in terms of the impossible (the agrammatical of syntactic linguistics), discourse analysis refers to the unenonciable by reference to what cannot be stated from a determined place. As a consequence, meaning is always shifting. Despite the relationship between what can be said and the constraining force of what has already been said, there remains a space for creativity, both in terms of language and in terms of interdiscourse.

Foucault's overriding concern with the normative now assumes a specific relevance. Given that there is no reality external to discourse, and since the social only exists in and through language, it is not possible to distinguish between the social and linguistic norm. The task of the analyst is to make the norm explicit, and thereby to destroy its status as a norm. It is here that the work of Foucault and that of Michel Pécheux, the predominant force in FDA, overlap. They shared a concern with the power of the normative as the common factor which is imposed on all knowledges of a specific historical epoch, and the manner in which it absorbs earlier knowledges.

It needs to be emphasised that enonciative linguistics draws upon the long history of deixis, a field which has been around at least since the time of Nicolas de Cusa, and has linked with different conceptions of language (M. Clarke, 1997). It linked with the mathesis of Classical Greece. Two paths open up from De Cusa. On the one hand, it was argued that God is within everything as the *priori* first cause of creation. With Descartes this leads to the claim that everything is given beforehand through motion, and humankind must abstract the dimensions of any object through a geometric operation of thought. Deixis pertains to such spatial dimensions. On the other hand, the *posteriori* accepts humankind's estrangement from God. By the time of Hobbes and Locke mathesis is denied to humankind, who is cut off absolutely from nature. Objects cannot be given to humankind externally through motion, the essential number of things cannot be known. Rather, everything that is, must be spoken into being in the form of a word. Perception becomes the domain of the geometric and, thereby, of the deictic. By the mid eighteenth century the necessary opposition between I and you is established and society becomes conceived of as something which happens between I and you. Where, in the seventeenth century, the subject was subordinate to the truth of his/her discourse, s/he became the source of that discourse by reference to a compendium of needs, fears and desires (Pécheux, 1982:29). New philosophies of subjectivity and theories of knowledge emerge, giving a new function for language.

Post-structuralism directs itself against Husserlian phenomenology and the centred subject which it posits. Yet both Husserlian modernism and post-structuralism derive from the *priori* and *posteriori* paths which emerge from scholasticism. Husserl effectively merges these two distinct paths and, in so doing, makes post-structuralism itself possible. His phenomenology descends from the Port Royal thesis, it retains the seventeenth-century opposition between necessary and contingent but superimposes the objective/subjective distinction upon it. Enonciation is at the centre of the new configuration.

This debate evidently relates to the relationship between language and reality. For Husserl consciousness was associated with reflection, the former, in the form of the subject, being the zero point or origin of representations. As such the 'I' begins its journey from the 'here' as zero point to 'there', allowing the 'I' to look back on itself as the 'I' there, which is also other. This is the structure of the reflective moment, and the space between them is the space of objectivity. For Heidegger, on the other hand, it made no sense to speak of language and reality or being as separate realms, the terms 'reality' and 'being' would not refer except within language. It was Benveniste who took this phenomenological structure and transposed it into the social. In the decentring the 'I' and 'you' cease to be the beginning and the end. The social space of experiencing emerges – discourse – within which subjects are positioned, and which determines their position.

The social is made explicit in the work of Wittgenstein and Bakhtin. Wittgenstein's language play involves a practice of interpretation that resolves ambiguity. As such it involves a practical relationship between the locuteurs and their enonces. That is, the practices within which language is placed cannot be reconstituted starting from that which is said. For Wittgenstein it involved conventions which are incapable of being made explicit. From a sociological perspective, each sector of life can be viewed as a play of language. Bakhtin's dialogism relates to the claim that the structure of enonces does not indicate the language play in which they are implicated. Through the notions of polyphony and dialogism he refuted both the form of idealism wherein the meaning of words mysteriously exists outside of their use, and a psychologistic position. An enonce only achieves meaning as a result of a multitude of language plays.

Meaning is the consequence of a practical confrontation of social groups around signification and language play. It is the product of open option as the interior of discursive organisation, organising points of view, practices and interests. Meaning is the site of struggle.

The above constitutes the body of work which this book seeks to address. In so doing it assumes a specific structure. Chapter 1 addresses the manner in which both sociology and linguistics derive from a particular historical conjuncture during which Enlightenment philosophy was deployed to construct a social science. However, this was not a neutral, objective science, but one which was employed for specific political purposes. This allows us to recognise both disciplines as discourses, the essential starting point of any attempt to suggest a different orientation towards society and language. It serves to outline the critique of modernism addressed by post-structuralism. Chapters 2 and 3 build on this initial chapter in presenting an overview of structuralism and post-structuralism. Emphasis is placed on those whose work laid the basis for the emergence of FDA, most notably Saussure, Lacan, Althusser, Foucault and Culioli. Chapters 4 and 5 are devoted to an overview of the main developments and trends in FDA between the early 1960s and 1985. The first of these two chapters focuses on the Althusserian thrust of the early work, with its specific focus upon ideological analysis. Chapter 5, on the other hand, discusses the shift away from the materialism of the early work, towards the idealism associated with the work of Foucault and Deleuze, the confrontation with technical problems and the steps taken to circumvent them.

It was inevitable that an approach which began with the assumption concerning the decentring of the subject would, in time, be obliged to consider the relationship of orthodox linguistics to this issue. If sociology was to be seen as a discourse, and philosophy as a discourse premised on the false proposition of rationalism, resorting to orthodox linguistics in search of a method suitable for the analysis of discourse must be akin to employing a discourse to analyse discourse. Chapter 6 discusses this issue while also focusing upon the manner in which its resolution, via the adoption of enonciative linguistics, has led to encompassing the work of Bakhtin and Wittgenstein. It seeks to show how enonciative linguistics is distinctive from orthodox linguistics.

This focus on the linguistic continues in Chapter 7 with a discussion of issues surrounding the lexical. It allows a consideration of some of the technical issues associated with the analysis of meaning within FDA. It involves a focus on the paraphrase and on the lexical items which organise them.

In an introductory survey such as this one it is not possible to cover the breadth of methodological practices associated with FDA. None the less, an attempt is made in Chapter 8 to demonstrate what a preliminary approach would strive to achieve. This is undertaken by contrasting the way in which two practitioners – Achard and Bonnafous – have applied the principles of FDA to specific corpus.

Finally, Chapter 9 seeks to draw the preceding chapters together by considering the implications of FDA. It considers the implications for the study of ideology, for both orthodox sociology and linguistics, for modernism, and specifically, for the sociology of language.

1

MODERNISM AND THE PHILOSOPHY OF LANGUAGE

The recent surge of interest in what is termed post-structuralism among Anglo-American academics has tended to relate to the post-modern thesis. As such it tends to draw post-structuralism out of its original context and gives it quite different terms of reference. Simultaneously, the focus rests on theoretical concerns, with the methodological aspects by and large being confined to literary analysis, an interest which often tends to ignore the theoretical. Yet, in French intellectual circles post-structuralism carries quite a different momentum, usually unrelated to, and antithetical to, Lyotard's post-modernism (Lyotard, 1984). In recent years, it has contributed to an area of study which is referred to as French Discourse Analysis (FDA). As the word 'analysis' would imply, the emphasis is very much on the methodological, yet it does not ignore the theoretical concerns. In some respects perhaps it can be regarded as one aspect of the methodological side of post-structuralism. As such it is an interest which, by and large, has thus far escaped the attention of the Anglo-American intellectual community. Given the history of FDA, which will be discussed below, a useful starting point is the very modernism that is denied by post-structuralism. This can then serve as a background to the emergence of structuralism and, subsequently, post-structuralism.

Modernism

As the term post-modern implies, the current debate in the social sciences involves modernism and the Enlightenment. Modernism involves the affirmation that the essence of being human pertains to a world governed by natural laws which are capable of discovery through reason, laws to which reason itself is submitted. It identifies the people, the nation, as a collective humankind which constitutes a social body which also functions according to natural laws. During the Enlightenment it was claimed that these natural laws would replace what was regarded as forms of organisation and irrational domination which derived their legitimacy from recourse to revelation or superhuman decision. Modernism came to be understood as the diffusion of the products of rational, scientific, technological, administrative activity. Instrumental rationality came

11

to be deployed at the core of a type of activity, as a function of its integration into a general vision, based on its contribution to a holistic societal project. God was to be replaced at the centre of society by science, leaving religion as the prerequisite of private life. Intellectual activity was treated as objective and was to be protected from political propaganda and religious belief, while the impersonality of the legal system guaranteed protection against nepotism, clientism and corruption. Since administration was not to be the instrument of personal power, public and private life had to be separated. Evidently, modernism was a struggle for the establishment of a new ideological order against the pre-existing form. This involved the creation of a rationalist image of the world which integrated humankind with nature, microcosm in macrocosm, a view which rejected all forms of dualism of body and soul, of the human world and the transcendental.

The Enlightenment, reason and philosophies of language

There is a tendency for sociologists to ignore pre-nineteenth-century social philosophy. This tendency is associated with the claim that modern sociology began with the work of Comte, whose biological analogy served as the basis for a supposedly scientific approach to the study of society. As a consequence there is often an ignorance of the Enlightenment and how it generated an essentially different perspective on the world from what existed previously. The current post-modern debate which seeks to add a new phase to the evolutionary perspective on time and space has at least obliged sociologists to focus attention on modernism and its origins. This, in turn, involves a scrutiny of the Enlightenment and all that it entailed. This is not to suggest that a critique of the Enlightenment is in any way new, as a mere scrutiny of the writings of Nietzsche, Horkheimer, Benjamin and Adorno, whose work carries considerable emphasis in contemporary sociology, will attest. None the less it is relevant that this interest has once again surfaced among sociologists.

The philosophers of the seventeenth century rejected the Aristotelian argument that human and physical behaviour was intelligible only to the extent that it could be seen as contributing to an overarching purpose. As a consequence there emerged a separation of humankind and the physical universe. Objective reality became identified with matter and a law-governed physical world, while humankind became a subjective, mental, being. It is hardly surprising that the study of humankind was restricted to the study of the human mind. When an attempt was made to apply the empirical methods of physics to a science of mind during the eighteenth century, the focus was on the psychological rather than the social condition.

Be that as it may, there remains a great deal to know about the manner in which the Enlightenment shaped subsequent developments in what became the social sciences. I have sought to demonstrate elsewhere how Enlightenment thought on language ran parallel to Enlightenment thought on society (G. Williams, 1992). What I would like to do here is to focus upon the particular philosophy of language which derived from this particular historical conjuncture, while also outlining the main principles of modernism, since the issues discussed in this book constitute a direct challenge to modernism. In this respect we must distinguish between modernity, which involves the manner in which rationalisation serves the interests of society, displacing sentiments, customs and beliefs which are labelled 'traditional', and modernisation, which is the practice of which this modernity is the agent. The Western ideology of modernity is referred to as modernism.

A modernist reading sees the traditional role of philosophy since the time of Descartes as being the foundation of rationalist conceptions. It involved an attempt to develop a fundamental ontology, or an account of the essential structure of reality. This was attempted via a reflection on first principles, conceptual analysis or other *a priori* means. The Cartesian proof of the uniformity of the laws of nature, and the claim that this uniformity had existed since the beginning of time, and would persist in the future, was an important construction since it related to the claim that the development of scientific knowledge would lead to the rational control of the social and natural environment constructed by humankind. Central to this objectivity was rationality, but it also involved a dedication to the pure knowledge of philosophy and science. Primacy was given to intellect and knowledge. The link between philosophy and intellect on the one hand, and science and knowledge on the other, related to the claim that knowledge was cumulative. Thus science would involve a growth of a knowledge which derived from intellectual ability or reason. Linking this cumulative view of knowledge with the claim for the constancy of the laws of nature led to the belief that new knowledge was superior knowledge. It was but a short step to the claim, not only that progress was conceivable, but that it was inevitable. From the time of Leibniz the progressive development of knowledge was seen as natural and normal. It was held that it was in the nature of human knowledge to progress constantly, cumulatively and surely. This rationalistic argument made progress through knowledge not merely desirable, but inevitable. However, reason was not merely related to scientific and technical activity, but to the government of people and to the administration of things. Society was seen as an order, as an architecture based on calculation, and reason became the instrument of creative order. Indeed, reason was reified to become the agent of all development, with history being seen as a structure with a direction that was governed by reason, a direction which dispelled tradition and particular allegiances in favour of the State, which was the epitome of modernism.

There is a very clear case for arguing that sociology emerged as the 'science' based on rationality which made the case for the progress of reason as the basis for general progress and happiness in the name of the State. In so doing it argued against social and cultural forms which were regarded as irrational, labelling them as 'traditional' in serving specific interests. In this respect the current distaste for modernism on account of its link to States which are seen to be oppressive and intolerant flows over into a critique of sociology and its identification as an ideological discourse which, over more than 150 years, has become accepted as the unquestioned 'science' of society. As such it is a feature of modernist ideology, striving to legitimise the belief in the union of humankind and nature, a sociologism which is the central element of the modernist vision. It involves an image of society as collections sharply defined by frontiers, as the recognised sources of authority, as organs associated with the application of laws and as a conscience of belonging. As such it has supported a distinctive form of oppression against all that exists outside of these confines, involving the various elaborate dualisms of twentieth-century sociology – modern/traditional, community/society, mechanical solidarity/organic solidarity, ascription/achievement, normative/ethnic. Thus struggles internal to society, especially where they focus upon a resistance to the existing State order, are interpreted as atavistic resistances of the irrational to the progress of reason. A nation or a social category is obliged to choose between universalist modernity and destruction, and the preservation of an absolutely different culture on the one hand, and what can be construed as a gross lie on the other, if they are not to conform to the interests and stratification of domination. All of this is the creation of struggle for modernity against its precursor, and, more than anything, in relation to the associated goal of establishing and consolidating the Absolutist State. Following the Enlightenment the rejection of all revelation and of all moral principles created a void which was replaced by the idea of society based on the concept of social utility. Charity became solidarity, conscience became respect for the law, humankind became little more than the citizen as an ideal form wherein the individual's private life is dedicated to the common good.

The idea of a common good was transformed by the emergence of the Absolutist State which assumed its proper rights and interests as foremost. This defence of rights separate from, and independent of, a politics founded entirely on reason involved the transformation of the ancient dualism of Christianity into the philosophy of the subject. It was Locke, in striving against the Absolutist Monarchy, who separated the individual and society. The individual had a God-given ability to determine her/his own life, to direct her/his own actions, this constituting the liberty of the will. By the first half of the eighteenth century it was claimed that 'primitive people' lived according to the law of nature, civilised people controlled nature, which was transformed through work and which gave the right to personal property. Thus the community passed to forms of individual property which affected the way in which law protected the individual rather than the community.

It can be claimed that both Hobbes and Locke gave natural rights an economic interpretation which was directly opposed to orthodox political reasoning, arguing that the rights of conquest gave a complete discontinuity between the state of nature and social organisation. This led to the founding of political society on the free decisions of individuals, on a contract or on trust, leading to a ruling by consent through the will of the majority rather than via the general will which was meant to protect individual rights. This, in turn, led to Locke's conception of the citizen who was independent, and to the construction of community which benefited from the transfer of individual rights to a sovereign authority, a transfer which implied the involvement of all bound together through a strong element of trust. The triumph of reason of the State led to the idea of a popular sovereignty, where the reason of the State involved the condition of the liberty of its citizens and the participation of the individual in public life. It also led to the absolute authority of the State founded on contract, general will or the revolutionary uprising of the people. For Hegel, the individual was devoid of objectivity, truth and morality, unless integrated as a member of the State, since it was the destination of individuals to lead a collective life. That is, egoism should not be allowed to overrule the collective interests represented by the State. The nation was not akin to the State but to the people, the general will which was expressed through law, which was the instrument of legality and individual rights. Where the seventeenth- and eighteenth-century philosophers reflected on order, peace and liberty, the period between the end of the eighteenth century and the beginning of the present century witnessed a preoccupation with transforming natural law into a collective will. Its focus was State nationalism.

The eighteenth century sought to replace the arbitrary of religious morale with a knowledge of the laws of nature. However, since humankind did not divorce itself from living in accordance with nature, it was insufficient to appeal to the reason in nature. Society was to replace God as the principle of moral judgment as well as being an object of study, a principal of explication and of the evaluation of conduct. It was seen as a source of values, the good being at the service of society, and the bad being that which foils social integration and its efficacy. Thus the individual was to submit to the interests of the collectivity. It is hardly surprising that social science was born as a political science.

Rousseau held the belief that the social order was created by individuals who submitted to the general will, which was expressed in the form of the social contract. Similarly Diderot opposed individual passions to the general will in a way which was to become the essence of the evolutionary argument in which the civilising role of Christian culture controlled human passion, a line of argument that was to dominate nineteenth-century anthropology. For Rousseau and Diderot social order was not meant to involve anything other than free human decisions based on the principle of good and evil; it was not a manifestation of some predestined order established by God or nature. For Hobbes the imperative was the foundation of the political order and his work lacks any conception of social actor or social relations. On the other hand, his work does confront the idea of political order, but lacks the reference to culture and society of Toqueville. In contrast to Diderot, both for Hobbes in the seventeenth century, and for Rousseau in the following century, social order derived from free decisions which, in turn, were the expression of a general will. This general will could not defend the interests of the majority, nor could it be applied to the general problems of society. Rather, it existed as a natural order within which humankind was inserted. The social contract gave rise to a new form of sovereignty which was society itself.

In a sense Rousseau's sovereignty can be equated with Durkheim's *conscience collective* as the origin of all society, defining all the principal functions of society, and evaluating the conditions by their positive or negative contribution to social integration, and by the capacity of institutions to control personal passions and interests. Durkheim inherited this position following a protracted period of historicism involving the evolutionary perspective, with society being represented as a field of social conflicts between present and past, interest and tradition, public and private life. In many respects there is an overlap between the *conscience collective* and its expropriation as the fulcrum of the modern state as the will of a nation. Thus we look to Rousseau for the source of the grand model of social life, with a correspondence of system and actors at the centre of institutions and socialisation. Being human no longer involved a creature created by God in his image, but rather, it involved a social actor defined by roles as channels attached to status, which led to the smooth functioning of the social system, with good and evil being distinguished on the basis of the contribution to the survival of the social body. In the French case the Revolution and the associated emergence of the Absolutist State involved the passage from *universitas* to *societas*, replacing the divine by the political as the expression of the sacred in social life. This principle was taken to its extreme in identifying the nation with reason and civilism with virtue.

Not that things were remarkably different in Britain, where the English philosopher Locke argued that understanding did not give form to things, whereas reflection, based as it is on sensation, did. Thus he argued that thought lacks any transcendental guarantee and becomes purely an instrumental reason. Nature was imprinted in humankind by desire, and by the resultant happiness which derived from the acceptance of natural law. Both the categories of nature and of reason had the function of uniting humankind with the world.

In contrast to most seventeenth-century philosophers, Rousseau did not see war and the threat of death as the driving force which led humankind to seek social order and to wish to transfer rights to some absolute sovereignty, but rather he saw inequality as the basis for the founding of a political order in opposition to civil society. For Rousseau the appeal to a general will was based on the struggle against inequality. Thus, in a sense, Rousseau can be seen as anti-modernist and communitarian. Indeed, he saw community as the opposition of society writ large, where unity is threatened by the division of labour and the quest for profit. In this respect his views on community differ from the conceptions which, after Condorcet, tended to relate the community to the State. Rousseau thought in terms of a popular sovereignty incarnated in the national State and this led him towards a very Hegelian analysis of the State where he recognised the contradiction between the natural order and the social order. His proposed solution to this contradiction was the construction of a social communication founded on intuitive knowledge and truth and the reversal of social contradictions. Voltaire's argument that modernity leads to a rational social order was not accepted by Rousseau, who claimed that the individual was the repository of nature in opposition to the State, and he argued in favour of the idea of popular sovereignty in the service of reason. Thereafter the critique of modernism was not based on an appeal to personal freedom, nor to a collective tradition against power, but rather he appealed to order against disorder, to nature and to the community against private interests.

Neither Rousseau nor Kant chose to oppose happiness and reason, or reason and nature, and they also rejected the stoicist reduction of virtue as an epicurean illusion according to which virtue constitutes the quest for happiness or the good life. In this sense theirs was not a philosophy of progress. The Kantian morality was based on reason, where communication is established between humankind and the universe. He shared with Rousseau the total submission of the individual to the general will which constructs a society which is both voluntarist and natural, thereby assuring communication between the individual and the collectivity in founding the social link necessary for the guarantee of liberty. In this respect Kantian morality links with Rousseau's politics.

This leads to a consideration of objectivity and truth. For Descartes there existed an order of the world created by God which was capable of discovery. The existence of God cannot be discovered from an observation of the world since this merely confused two orders – the order of the body and the order of the soul. The fact that I have the idea of God does not prove that God exists, it is the idea of God that demonstrates the existence of God. Thus the detachment of immediate experience from opinions which permit reason to operate leads the human spirit to discover the laws of nature created by God, and humankind to define its proper existence as that of the creature created by God in his image, where thought is the mark of divine influence. This is the basis for what Horkheimer called objective reason, which opposes subjective reason.

Thought is defined separately from any transcendental guarantee, it is detached from God and becomes a purely instrumental reason. This kind of dualism was central to Hegel's argument where he seeks to interiorise difference within thought, making it the basis of reality while sublimating difference into self-realisation. Thus, for Hegel, truth 'is . . . the bacchanalian revel where not a member is sober; and because every member no sooner becomes detached than it *eo ipso* collapses straightaway, the revel is just as much a state of transparent unbroken calm' (Hegel, 1966:105). Reality destroys itself by reference to a process through which identity is restored, this time at the conscious level. The starting or zero point of philosophical thought – being

– is unconscious, inarticulate and indeterminate. However, when the primordial self-identity is disrupted by its negation in difference, it is transformed into becoming, thereby making being a form of self-knowledge. It is here that self-consciousness is separated from objective reality. This, in turn, is negated, leading to the comprehension of the process as a whole. Thus, it is recognised that the external relations of essence exist outside of the self-consciousness of being as the Absolute Idea. Mind and reality are two separate entities, whereas the 'truth is the whole' (Hegel, 1966:81).

It is no surprise that this perspective on the scientific transformation and control of nature was adopted by those European philosophers of the eighteenth century who argued that the social environment could be controlled and understood on the same principles as the natural environment. This view is characterised by Condorcet's claim for the progress of the human mind. A feature of this 'progress' was the need to constantly define and redefine 'modernity'. If progress relied upon the systematic application of reason in the form of the physical and mathematical sciences in order to increase human control of nature, then its realisation produced an ever-changing world, a world whose description relied largely upon the comparison of past and present. Modernity was the present and contrasted with what had already gone – not merely the past, but tradition.

The importance of the human mind and the associated quality of reason in this argument is clear. The Enlightenment promised a rational organisation of social life associated with which was universal moral and intellectual self-realisation. It was a universal human reason which was the basis for assessing whether or not particular social and political tendencies were progressive or not. Indeed, the goal of politics was the very realisation of reason in practice. In this respect the Enlightenment argued forcefully for a process whereby all rationality was to be measured by reference to a single standard. This intellectual monism is most clearly expressed by Kant, who argued not only in favour of a single human reason, but also, and as a consequence, for a single true system of philosophy based upon specific principles (Kant, 1946:5). It is this claim which establishes philosophy as a 'grand narrative' which the postmodernists reject.

Condorcet's seminal contribution to the debate referred to above was far-reaching. It involved a claim for unending human progress, a discourse on the human mind, and a focus upon social and cultural history which emphasised the concept of civilisation. This evolutionary perspective was not new, indeed it dated back at least to the seventeenth-century work of Leibnitz. Condorcet emphasised that the progress of civilisation lay in the human mind. He adopted a comparative perspective on society and culture, arguing for a temporal association between progress and social complexity through to a condition labelled civilisation. This was the forerunner of a theme which dominated the proto social sciences during the nineteenth century. The title of Condorcet's bench-mark was *Progress of the Human Mind*, a clear indication of his emphasis upon the importance of reason in the development of civilisation. Despite seeking to apply the principles of the Enlightenment as they referred to science in his study of society, Condorcet, as well as his followers, established social evolution through a typological schema which emphasised the progress of society through a series of 'types of society'. In this respect Condorcet treated history as science, even though his method differed from the demographic and statistical emphasis of science. This was compatible with faith in science as a guide to shaping the social sciences.

For Condorcet it was reason that animated science and its application, and it was also reason that commanded social adaptation, whether it involved collectivities or individuals. It was he as much as anyone who was responsible for consecrating the State in the name of social order. Reason was treated as the converse of the arbitrary and violence, and reason, being rooted in the very nature of the State, was related to right. As a consequence of this harnessing of reason by the State, humanity, living in accordance with a law proclaimed by the State, advanced accordingly into a condition of abundance, liberty and the good life, with legal rationality being the basis of the market economy in the construction of modern society. The liberation of controls and of traditional forms of authority contributed to the good life but did not guarantee it – this was the role of a centralised organisation of production and consumption. The triumph of reason was the basis for claiming this correspondence between a scientific culture and an ordained society of free individuals. It alone established a correspondence between human action and social order. Local customs or tradition were opposed to the rationalisation of production and universal social order and the State of rights. Superimposed upon the theory of evolution involving inevitable progress was the claim that the most recent form was held to be the closest to perfection, which was the end phase of evolutionary progress. Other forms were treated as the antithesis of this perfection. Thus the labelling of social forms as modern and traditional merely served to denigrate that which they described, through the comparison of two forms which both existed at the same moment in time, making them, at least in terms of time and space, equally modern. Thus the force of reason is implicated in the struggle against tradition and the arbitrary as the basis of unreason.

The domination which derived from the equation of the State and reason was exercised liberally, even though in an authoritarian way, addressing the freedom of the subject, but in a context where each submits to the interests of all, whether the totality involves the enterprise, the nation, society or reason itself. The whole was equated with the State itself, an abstract notion which was there to serve the interests of all. As such, this duality of the whole could not deny any altruistic claim.

The idea of progress was linked with the spirit of a people (*Volksgeist*) by Herder, a pupil of Leibniz. Thus reason and nation were linked much in the same way as was implied in the Durkheimian notion of national culture, where the State itself was not the only basis for the creation of the *conscience collective*.

This denies the usual tendency to create a distinction between the German inclination to see the nation as a community of destiny and the French idea that rested on the concepts of free choice and national sovereignty opposing the tyranny of royalty.

Within modernism the divine subject outside of humankind was replaced by the human subject which, under specific conditions, was capable of reasoning. This shift brought about the rupture of person as a list of social roles and of particular individualities, giving a restless conscience of self and a will of freedom and responsibility. The rationalist world replaced the universe which linked humanity and the divine, the world of magic and enchantment, by the reason of the subject, rationalisation and subjectification. Rationalism became thought of as humanism, involving a conscience and piety which was opposed to the arbitrary anti-humanism of the divine. The subject and reason cohabited in the human being, with the result that human experience was reduced to thought and instrumental action. It was Descartes who freed the world of sensations and opinions, treating humankind as a thinking being in his philosophy of the subject and existence. The worlds of nature and of God were separated and the will of the world was no longer discoverable through God but in the 'I', the subject. It is claimed that it was Descartes who argued for the union between thought and personal existence, the liberty of humankind being an expression of the triumph of reason over belief. However, it can also be said that there is another interpretation of Descartes' work wherein thought can only occur through the encounter with the world, and it is through this encounter that the self comes into existence.

Within pre-modernism, humankind submitted to impersonal forces or destiny, which were beyond human control and human action, and could not conform to any known order. The world was created by a divine subject and was organised according to rational laws. This correspondence between the divine subject and a natural order was associated with the separation of order of objective knowledge and the order of rational laws. As modernity developed, the subject and the object became increasingly separated. Indeed, modernity is defined by the efficacy of instrumental rationality, by the mastering of the world that is made possible by science and technology. It is this that leads to the modern idea concerning the emergence of the human subject as both free and as creation. Rationalism and subjectivism go to together. Whereas in pre-modernism knowledge of the person was separate from a knowledge of nature, in the same way that action was distinct from structure, in modernism the person is viewed as 'true' or existing in the same way as nature as well as being the object of an objective knowledge and the subject and subjectivity.

The claim that the creation of the world involved rational laws, and the belief that intelligence involved the thoughts of humankind, were brought together and the subject was often depersonalised in being reduced to reason itself. Reason and the subject crossed, conscience and science were linked, leading to a renouncing of the subject in the name of scientific triumph. Thus modernity triumphed with science, albeit that the human condition is ruled by conscience. Simultaneously, the subject was associated with the appeal to freedom and the claim that the individual had control over his/her own actions and situation. The subject became the will of the individual to act and to be recognised as an actor. Where pre-modernity involved human beings searching for wisdom in a world where they was crossed by impersonal forces within a context of destiny, in modernity this is replaced by a world which involves submission via social integration; the worker, the student, the soldier partici-pates in collective work. To become an actor of one's personal life is to be an agent of collective work. Modernity triumphs when humankind shifts from being part of nature to the recognition that nature resides in the human. The actor no longer conforms to a place occupied in a social organisation, but is capable of modifying the material and social environment within which s/he is placed.

This tendency for modernism to construct an image of the social world in terms of preconceived understandings of human behaviour and its relationship to rationality carried over into its understanding of the role of language in society. Indeed, as we shall see, it can be argued that it is not merely sociology but also linguistics and sociolinguistics which have been constructed on the edifice of modernism.

Language

Inevitably, at a practical level, modernism penetrated the political realm via a form of language planning. The denigration of what did not conform with the unity of the absolutist State in France was found in the creation of French as the language of reason, in association with the conscious goal of eliminat-ing all other languages within the Republic (Calvet, 1984). In Britain the same process of denigration was allied, during the nineteenth century, with a suspicion of language and a concern about its revolutionary potential. The desire to control the population of the State was complicated by the existence of languages other than English, and forceful arguments were made about the desirability of eliminating such languages. This attempt to legitimise the dominant language as the sole language of the populace was based on the claim for a link between particular languages and the process of reasoning, a claim which replaced the pre-modernist Babel thesis concerning the hier-archical nature of languages deriving from divine proximity. The classical languages, Greek and Latin, were taken as the model of rational language, and attempts were made to model the 'modern' languages of the State on these classical languages within a process of language standardisation (R. Balibar, 1985). This is the source of the current division of languages into classical, modern and those languages labelled as patois, Celtic, etc. which are grouped as a residual classification based on their incapacity for inclusion as languages of reason.

21

The nationalisation of French involved the transfer of the exercise of the legitimate language to the national collectivity (R. Balibar, 1985:147), the nation being defined as coterminous with the State. Democracy did not involve extending the practice of political principles to the various language groups which existed within the State's territory, but, rather, to ensuring that every citizen understood French, the language of reason and democracy! This was the goal behind the creation in 1789 of an elementary textbook which was to be employed by all children living in France. It should not be surprising that the driving force behind this particular enterprise was Condorcet!

However, it is the evolutionary argument which epitomises the manner in which Enlightenment thought influenced the philosophy of language. The distinction between human and animal life rested upon the human capacity for reason, and the ability to communicate. The early debates on the origins of language stressed the role of reason, and its link to language in human development. For Condorcet one of the dividing forces of humankind was the distinction between language and mind. While recognising that all humans had language, he claimed that not all humans had the capacity for reason. Language and reason were separate entities, and the importance of reason for his evolutionary claims allowed him to place those humans who had the capacity for reason above those who did not in the drive for progress. This is explicit in the manner in which French became the language of reason in post-Revolutionary France, eliminating all other languages to a position outside of reason, as patois.

Drawing upon the earlier work of Condorcet and Rousseau, Herder argued that mind and anatomy were independent, and that it was speech which 'alone awakens slumbering reason' (Herder, 1966:124). What he was referring to was his claim that while lower animals had minds, and were capable of giving expression to their sensations, none of them displayed even a rudimentary language. This is perfectly consistent with the evolutionary argument, for what is missing in the pre-human form lies in the relationship between mind, language and reason. For Herder, speech relied on the capacity of the human brain, this in turn depending upon the human's upright stance. Thus 'human reason is the creation of humans' (Herder, 1966:264). What he was seeking to establish was the propensity of all humans to reason. However, even though all humans by definition possess language, this does not, of necessity, mean that they also have reason, merely the capacity for reason. It is this position which allows the social differentiation of social evolutionism to appear. Herder held that a crucial ingredient of language was '[a *Volks*] organisation and mode of life', language and tradition being inherited, thereby giving continuity to the changing history of each *Volk*. His anti-essentialist stance allowed him to explain cultural differences even if he did rely on environmental determinism.

What is clear in this argument is that language and mind are separate. Without such a separation the evolutionary argument flounders through an inability to justify the essential distinction between the achievement of different societies, a justification that is crucial for the evolutionary argument for a species which shares the gift of language and relies on reason to foster its progress. Thus we must have, not only the separation of language and reason, or of speech and mind, but also differing propensities for reason, determined by society and/or culture.

This is not to suggest that the separation of language and mind was a consequence of the evolutionary argument. On the contrary, such a separation of language and mind was a feature of the predominant philosophy of language at least from the time of Gregory of Nyssa. More recently, for Bacon, all human knowledge derived from sense impressions such that the individual subject was the source of its own thought. Language is thereby linked to reason through the rationality of the human subject. Furthermore, the human subject is held to be capable of manipulating language as a means of self-expression. That is, language is flexible, having the capacity of a variety of forms of expression.

Associated with this view of language and thought is another claim that derives from the seventeenth century – the empiricist concept of knowledge which we have already touched upon with reference to Hegel. This involves the idea that knowledge rests on the relationship between subject and object. The products of knowledge, the concepts which derive from it, already exist in reality as its essence. This means that the subject of knowledge only has to seek the essence of things in an informed way in order to discover it beneath the surface of appearances. It is this structure of the real which is divisible into the essential form and the non-essential surface which makes knowledge possible.

One consequence of the separation of language and thought, even though their interdependence persists, is a focus on the question of meaning. Of course, the empiricist conception of knowledge maintains that the human subject expresses its relationship to real objects through language. However, there remains the issue of whether what is referred to is the surface form or the essence. Furthermore, there is the issue of how such meaning is conveyed in and through language.

However, there is yet another issue to be confronted in the separation of language and thought. If we invoke the relationship between the individual and society in the discussion, we arrive at the conclusion that the social precedes language. In the same way as language is a form of individual self-expression, if that individual is a social being, then language becomes an expression of the social. Language reflects society. Discourse intervenes between thought and reality. That is, there is a social reality that exists independent of thought, but which is capable of expression in language. Thus the relationship between language and society is unproblematic, since language is merely an overlay, or mirror, of society. This begs as many questions about the nature of the social as it does about the relationship of the social to society.

Callinicos (1982:114) points out that the epistemological doctrine of realism of analytical philosophies of language constitutes a form of materialism. Its main elements conform to what has been discussed above:

- Sentences are true or false by virtue of the state of the world rather than that of human knowledge.
- Thought reflects rather than constitutes the world.
- The unobservable entities posited to explain the observable behaviour of things exist independently of thought.

The first element amounts to the correspondence theory of truth – the correspondence of reality and thought. Truth is objective truth. The second derives from the first, with objective truth, as expressed through language, being subordinated to the claim that thought itself, in the form of some Absolute Idea, is the true reality. Realism in this sense involves that which can be independent of thought. The third involves a rejection of instrumentalism as we find in the work of Weber, and indeed most sociologies, where ideal types do not relate to a claim for their existence since they are conveniences which facilitate the work in hand. Realism would claim that the understanding of behaviour, for example, does not amount to a superficial observation, but rather involves a comprehension of the hidden structures of which it is a manifestation.

This particular doctrine clearly fits into the philosophy of language which treats language as a reflection or expression of reality or truth. It is the central concern of orthodox sociolinguistics. As I have argued elsewhere (G. Williams, 1992), most sociolinguists operate on the assumption that a social structure actually exists. It is this structure which organises the social behaviour of individuals, of which speech behaviour is a part. The social therefore exists prior to, and, to an extent, independent of language and thought. Yet it is conveyed through language, even if only in so far as the social identity of the individual is expressed in and through language. As a consequence, if the social is reflected in language, then it is the sociolinguist's work to investigate which aspects of speech correspond to which objects of the social. Perhaps it is the phenomenological orientation of conversation analysis which conforms least to this doctrine in that, to an extent, it does not take social structure for granted as a pre-existing source, but rather claims that this structure appears only in interaction. However, even here there is a degree to which the structure which does emerge in interaction precedes language.

Outside of the confines of orthodox sociolinguistics the Doctrine of Reason is also evident in the limited amount of work on language undertaken within the Marxist framework. The predominant difference between these two camps lies in the nature of the social. Callinicos (1982:115) claims that the realist doctrine is entirely consistent with the writings of Marx himself. For Marx 'The ideal is nothing but the material world reflected in the mind of man, and translated into the forms of thought' (Marx, 1976a:102). It is echoed in Lenin's claim about the relationship between reality and the mind: 'matter is a philosophical category denoting the objective reality which is given to man by his sensations, and which is copied, photographed and reflected by our sensations, while existing independently of thought' (Lenin, 1947:116). For Marx, while the social world undoubtedly existed, it was to be known only by the process of acting upon and transforming it. The structural forms of capitalism included a propensity for crises which Marx held was the driving force of change, including revolutionary change.

However, it is with reference to the concept of ideology that the issue of language and truth is most evident in the Marxist writings on language. There is an implicit claim that truth is concealed by ideological forces to the extent that a false consciousness prevails. This false consciousness is expressed through language, again with reason and language being treated as separate entities. Thus we have a series of false beliefs in relation both to reality and to the true, scientific knowledge of that reality being expressed. This is linked with the claim that illusions produced by the 'historic life-processes' serve the interests of the ruling class since they obscure the contradictions of a class society. This second claim does not relate to the truth or falsity of ideological discourse, but rather to the institutionalisation of class power. None the less, the net effect is the concealment of the contradictions that are implicit in capitalism and which ensures that the overthrow of the capitalist order is not guaranteed by the workings of the economy.

Yet there is a faith that language somehow contains the truth, a truth which relevant analysis can reveal, this being the basis of hermeneutics. If we return to the proposition discussed above, that thought and language are interdependent, we are led to the position that the study of ideology focuses upon a theory of meaning, involving how meaning is produced and reproduced. It is here that the focus upon discourse emerges. Our preceding discussion would imply that such a discussion, from a Marxist standpoint, would insist that meaning be interpreted in terms of the separation between thought and language, with the latter being merely the conveyor of thought, and with reality lying outside of the linguistic. As we shall see, this is merely one argument and such a stance does result in the generation of specific problems for Marxist linguistics. I will develop this point in Chapter 4.

A more focused approach to a Marxist study of language involves the claim, not unlike that found in conversation analysis, that meaning, rather than being the product of linguistic structures, resides in specific contexts of speech. Such a context, as in orthodox sociolinguistics, includes the social context. Thus the Marxist perspective on society is seen as the base upon which meaning is allowed to be constructed. That is, a non-discursive structure pre-exists, influences and determines the discursive. Once again language is held to reflect society, except that the society in question is discussed within the Marxist social philosophy. Language becomes an expression of a social structure which is premised upon the contradictions, conflicts and antagonisms of the capitalist economic order. In this respect there is a similarity to the work of speech-act theorists in that meaning is determined by the intentions, recognised or unrecognised, of the speaker.

Discourse

The modernists discussed above gave attention to the issue of discourse. Thus, for example, the eighteenth-century grammarians sought to rationalise the Franco-Latin construction in accordance with an idealised logic which gave prominence to discourse (R. Balibar, 1985:119). All subordinate propositions related to a principal whereby all the words of the proposition related to the subject. Thus, according to this logic, all verbal processes are organised around the principal subject, who in Balibar's words became 'the grand master of ceremonies'. This meant that this principal subject, in a real situation, became the representative of the sovereign. This, in turn, survived the Revolution, with the president taking the speech in the name of the Assembly in the same way as the master of ceremonies took the name of the king, a process which was inscribed in a verbal process involving the Assembly's power to meet and freedom to deliberate. Of course, at the end of the eighteenth century there did not exist any idea of grammar in terms of *coordonner* and *subordonner*.

Contemporary linguistics has inevitably inherited the modernist philosophy. Chomsky considered language to be based on the competence of the speaker. To cite merely one example, the generative model is conceived of as able to engender the infinite collection of possible enonces. The object of linguistics is the intuition of the locuteurs. The model is verified if they accept the produced enonces, with the structure which the model attributes to them. The centred rational subject is held to choose that which reflects a norm or which sustains a particular model of competence from among a series of possibilities.

It is hardly surprising therefore that a variety of contemporary approaches to the study of language encompass discourse analysis, and it is imperative that we distinguish these approaches from FDA on the basis of their entrenchment in modernism. While many forms of discourse analysis are strictly linguistic in context, being motivated by concerns about descriptive linguistic adequacy, our concern is with the sociolinguistic forms of discourse analysis, maintaining that the social is never absent in discourse. The particular philosophy of language discussed above, and its relation to the social, has generated a number of forms of discourse analysis. This should not be surprising if we adopt a broad view of discourse as spoken and written language practices, since the scope for theoretical standpoints which account for the existence and variation in such practices is broad. J. B. Thompson (1984:99) has outlined the properties common to most of the modernist forms of discourse analysis. He claims that they deal with 'natural' language, either in terms of speech or written text, the focus being on the organisational rather than on grammatical structure. They also involve a concern with linguistic units larger than the sentence, with the interconnectedness of utterances. Finally, they relate the linguistic analysis to some perspective on the social, which tends to be the explanatory variable.

Within these perspectives, for the transactionalists, discourse tends to be treated as the product of rational action by appeal to orthodox sociological principles. Thus, for example, Sinclair and Coulthard (1975) analysed classroom behaviour in terms of transactions and exchanges, focusing upon the opening and closing of exchanges and the operations between them. The function of any statement is understood in terms of the pragmatic involvement within the exchange, involving what they refer to as tactics. What they were striving to establish were the interpretative rules which derive from the linguistic forms of sentences in association with situational factors. It is assumed that dialogue involves systematic properties, and these they seek to uncover and describe. Explanation resides in the pragmatic effect of rational human action.

It often appears as if the ethnomethodologists who operate within the conversation analysis framework have appropriated the term discourse analysis for their own exclusive use. This is mainly a result of the tendency not to be specific about the theoretical side of the enterprise. Ethnomethodology derives from a reaction to the mechanical nature of structural functionalism, which ignored what ethnomethodologists feel is the importance of the creative role of the individual actor. The phenomenological input relates to the claim that the only reality that is of relevance is that in the mind of the actor. Thus discourse is something that is constantly created and re-created by interacting subjects rather than in relation to any predetermined social structures. Discourse is again characterised by negotiation among rational actors.[1]

One of the central aspects of conversation analysis is intersubjectivity, in which the actors involved subjectively interpret the context of interaction as it proceeds. This avoids the problem of the pre-formed subject whose interaction is a function of its social position. It involves a distinctive form of Kantianism which focuses upon the social and in which intersubjectivity is a substitute for the transcendental subject. There is, within this intersubjectivity, a tacit agreement on the rules of language, this being an essential prerequisite for effective communication. The focus is on natural language rather than on formalised language, and the assumption is made that it is an agreed-upon truth-condition which gives meaning to a sentence. This form of realism is also holistic in the sense that meaning is established by seeking to trace the manner in which patterns of intersubjectivty are developed.

The hermeneutics of Habermas (1979) offers an example of discourse analysis by a Marxist, even though many would argue that his work deviates fundamentally from Marxist theoretical principles. Callinicos (1982:142) has referred to that which Habermas himself calls 'formal pragmatics' or 'universal pragmatics' in terms of communication-intention. In this respect it resembles the work of speech-act theorists who claim that the meaning of an expression is determined, either by the intention of the speaker, or by those conventions associated with speech-acts of that sort.

Habermas distinguishes between 'communicative action' involving language and culture, and 'instrumental action' which involves the labour process as determined by instrumental rationality. This of course approximates to the Marxist distinction between superstructure and infrastructure, with language being a feature of the former. In a sense he relates back to the principles of the Enlightenment even though this involves reference to Fichte's claim that reason is a feature of the drive for human emancipation, with language as the *sine qua non* of that emancipation. Habermas argues that, this being the case, the universal nature of language as the basis of human communication is an expression of an intention of universal and unrestrained consensus. It is society which thwarts this consensus. The modernist thrust of his argument is evident.

Habermas' discussion of discourse hinges on this faith in the liberating force of language. His work often involves an eclecticism which appears to contradict his purported Marxism in that the work of many of those whom he cites is the antithesis of Marxism. He draws on speech-act theory. In so doing he seems to reject the Kantian claim that utterances are generated and experiences constituted (Habermas 1979:24). Habermas appears to share with conversation analysts a faith in the speech participant's desire for cooperative action, with speech-acts involving validity claims which are a manifestation of a desire to be understood, and the intention of telling the truth sincerely and appropriately. Indeed, his statement to the effect that the objective of a speech-act is 'to bring about an agreement that terminates in the intersubjective mutuality of reciprocal understanding, shared knowledge, mutual trust and accord with one another' (Habermas 1979:3) is remarkably close to the ethnomethodological position. It is a position which claims that society is constituted by communication, with other forms of social action, including conflict, being a consequence of the striving for mutual understanding. It is the relations of production, in their relationship to values and norms, which generate the social integration and unity of a social life-world, this being expressed in the speech-act.

While this position seems to contradict the fundamental assumptions of Marxism, Habermas claims that viewing society as communicative action counteracts Marx's mistaken claim that society is akin to instrumental action. Habermas' position seems to be that liberation does not rely on a denial of class antagonism, but rather will occur through education, a distinctively liberal stance.

The usual rebuttals of a communication-intention theory such as that proposed by Habermas take several forms. If the meaning of expressions relies on the conditions of utterances, it is impossible to account for the same words occurring in an infinite variety of sentences and speech-acts. Furthermore, it is not possible to attribute meaning to intentions without simultaneously interpreting speech, since intentions, beliefs and words must be interpreted simultaneously. Such views should be familiar to those conversant with speech-act theory.

Of course the work of Habermas is only one among many Marxist theories of discourse. Recent work (cf. *inter alia* Hodge and Kress, 1988) has tended to move closer to the theoretical issues of FDA by focusing upon the issue of signification and ideological discourse, the claim being that 'ideologies . . . find their clearest articulation in language' (Kress, 1985:29). Some of this work draws upon the contribution of Halliday (1978, 1985), who sees discourse as one aspect of a threefold division of language, the other two being phonology and lexico-grammar. The focus is upon the semantic/pragmatic components of alternative descriptive formulations, albeit that it is an approach which departs from the logico-formalist tendency of linguistics, with its subjectivist notion of individual creativity as the necessary precondition of language, in claiming that the assumption of individual creativity is inadequate with reference to semantics. An attempt is made to relate the social functioning of language to the manner in which language constructs meaning. The more recent work of Hodge and Kress has moved still closer to FDA and it does contain reference to French literature – rather than the exclusively Hallidayan influence of the earlier years, where the emphasis was on the relationship between grammatical structure and linguistic function. However, their best-known work still tends to adhere to the claim that function is transformed into intelligible communication via grammar, such that studying the grammatical structure of a language throws light on social relations and contexts of language use.

In a manner reminiscent of deixis, they strive to establish relations between objects and events in grammatical statements. Thus they refer to a transactional model where one entity causes an action which affects another entity; a non-transactional model where a single entity is related to a process; and a relational model where a relation between two entities occurs without action. On the other hand, the relational model involves either the equatives, where relations between nouns are 'equative', or the attributive, where the relational model establishes relationships between nouns and qualities in an attributive way. These are drawn together to give the schema of syntagmatic models shown in the diagram on page 30.

This model serves to classify events while affecting their causal inter-pretation. Transactionals will display a clear relationship between two nominals, whereas non-transactionals display an immediacy and indeterminacy which portrays the situation as strange and other-worldly. Thus a number of forms are associated with effects of meaning with, for example, relexicalisation affecting control through the one-way flow of meaning or plurality giving a degree of imprecision lacking in singulars.

The objective of this work is to establish the overlapping relationship between linguistic and social analysis. They seek to demonstrate how our

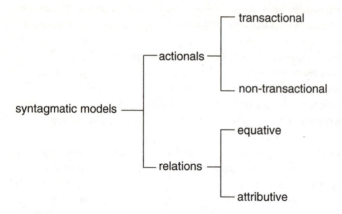

understanding of the world is shaped by language, while also implying that this includes unequal social relationships which relate to these language processes and are affected by them. They seek to go beyond the mere analysis of transactions by positing explanatory relationships associated with social groups which are claimed to pre-exist the actual discourse that is produced. In this respect, even though much of their work has a relevance to FDA, they remain firmly entrenched within the modernist camp. I shall have more to say on critical linguistics below.

There is one further approach to discourse analysis which must be mentioned, that proposed by the French linguist Emile Benveniste. In many respects it was Benveniste who laid the ground for post-structuralism. In many respects his work was orthodox and it is the limited amount of his work which pertains to enonciation that is seminal in developing a break with structuralism. Certainly he was the most prominent of the French linguists writing during the 1950s and 1960s, during which time he established a close rapport with those who developed post-structuralism, most notably Lacan, and his *Problèmes de linguistique générale* had a profound influence on French sociolinguistics in general. Although Benveniste's perspective on discourse will be discussed more fully below, it is perhaps appropriate to briefly mention that perspective in concluding this first chapter.

Benveniste's main concern was with what might be termed the 'linguistics of *parole*' (Pécheux, 1982d:6). Achard (1986:10) contrasts his emphasis with that of the speech pragmatists who emphasise the conscious subject as the driving force of enonciation, and how the effects which take place 'in language' directly influence interlocution. In Benveniste's work primacy is given to communication and this leads to a consideration of rhetoric and poetics, of style as deviation, transgression, disruption, etc. and, to a certain extent, to viewing speech as a play between interlocuteurs. His understanding of discourse is perhaps most evident in the distinction which he made between *histoire* as a story of history and *discours*. He noted the distinction in French between the *passé simple*, which is reserved for writing, and the *passé composé*, which is reserved for speech. Commentators had placed this difference in an evolutionary context, claiming that the *passé simple* was in the process of disappearance. In contrast Benveniste claimed that, rather than being a past tense, the *passé simple* was, in fact, the 'present of *récit*'. This form is characteristic of the historical enonciation which, in French, is almost exclusively a written genre. Benveniste used the term 'discourse' to contrast with *récit*:

> the historian never says 'I', nor 'you', nor 'here', nor 'now', because he never borrows the formal display of discourse, which consists of the address of the personal relation I, you.
>
> (Benveniste, 1966:105)

Thus, for Benveniste, discourse was a broad phenomenon. He saw all enonciation as involving a speaker and an audience, the first seeking to influence the second in some way. The diversity of oral discourse involves all of the genres of address involving the speaking subject and is organised on the category of person. The distinction between historical accounts and discourse does not correspond to the difference between the written and the spoken. The discourse is written as much as it is spoken. When the historian reproduces the speech of a person, or him/herself intercedes, a different temporal system, that of discourse, is introduced. Such observations laid the ground for developing a typology of discourses structured by their enonciative form.

This view of discourse was elaborated by others (Culioli, Simonin-Grumbach) to refer to the ensemble of genres which are examined in terms of the stabilised constraints of enonciation. The historical genre represents the extreme wherein all of the functions of anchorage of the discourse are suspended. Discourse now becomes a speech–act characterised by a specification of marks of enonciation. Thus each work has a series of enonciative constraints, this being the basis of discursive genres. However, there is, in addition to the linguistic domain, an interest in the social conditions of its use. Simonin-Grumbach (1975) offers an exhaustive list of the operators of enonciation, placing emphasis upon discourse relations, something that was implemented by Voloshinov as early as 1929 (Achard, 1987:12). This emphasises the point that discourse appears in the enonciations without the speaker being the direct source of that discourse. Thus the link between the 'I' and the 'you' or 'him/her' involves social relations a great deal richer than the verbal form of referential functions would suggest. The concrete analysis of discourse involves more than the linguistic markers, and includes the implicit in discourse. This point will be developed in Chapter 6, when the topic of intertextuality involving how one text immediately serves to implicate another text as party of the same discourse will be explored.

31

Conclusion

This chapter has served as an introduction in the sense that it has allowed me to outline the basic arguments and assumptions associated with modernist thought which post-structuralism and FDA reject. I have sought to argue that the founding fathers of sociology inherited this modernist discourse. Thus Durkheim inherited the political philosophy of the seventeenth and eighteenth centuries, with the emphasis on the triumph of historicism and the representation of society as a field of social conflict between interests and tradition, between public and private life. His *conscience collective* drew heavily on the ideas of Hobbes in being the basis of a sociology which defined the principal functions of society in terms of its positive or negative contribution to social integration, and in terms of the contribution of institutions to controlling the interests of individual desire. In common with Hobbes, he saw the individual as inherently egoistic and violent, and argued that it was only a social contract, and the idea of justice, which could create sufficient barriers against the forces of destruction. Thus, society, in the form of a basic social order, replaced God within the modernist discourse and, in a sense, the current dilemma is that the idea of society itself is being undermined and displaced. The classic affirmation according to which moral and social judgments are the means of maintaining and reproducing cultural values, social norms and mechanisms of socialisation, associated with Durkheim, Parsons and Habermas, is under question.

However, the crisis may be even more profound. Clearly, there is a very strong argument in favour of the view that sociology, far from being a neutral, objective discipline, has developed as a feature of an argument which serves to consolidate the existence of the State. Not the particular form which the State should assume, which many of sociology's detractors claim is its preoccupation, and which many sociologists take to be their concern, but rather the very existence of the State. The statism that is inherent in the historicism of social evolutionism merely serves to denigrate non-conforming social forms, which, as a consequence, are labelled as atavistic, traditional and primordial. Minorities, whether they are based on gender, culture or nationalism or even some other form of minority dimension, are treated as deviants from some unspecified, normative order which aligns with the interests of the centralised State. One suspects that the lukewarm reception which post-structuralism and post-modernism have received in some sociological circles relates to their threat to the individual political activities of those who are deeply involved in the activities of constitutional statist parties. Conversely, it is no surprise that those who have been most responsive to these perspectives and critiques are to be found among the disenfranchised groups in society – the women confronted by subordination despite their 'achievements', the blacks who will always be black, the gays struggling against being labelled deviant and the minority nationalists who, despite being confronted by the tyranny of the majority, persist in their belief in the State.

2

STRUCTURALISM

Having discussed in the opening chapter the basis of modernism and the manner in which it focuses upon a conception of rationality which involves the thinking subject as a creative entity, I would like to devote this chapter to a consideration of the field of structuralism, which had such a profound impact upon French intellectual thought following the second world war. For many, structuralism was a method, a specific way of approaching and rationalising the data belonging to a particular field of enquiry. For others, including Lévi-Strauss, it involved a quest for a structure in the form of the universal properties of the human mind. Some of those who have been labelled 'structuralists' have objected to being thus described, with those such as Foucault regarding such labelling as a breach of principles of intellectual freedom. At times one comes to the conclusion that some so-called 'structuralists' subscribe to a form of universalism whereas others can be called relativists, yet they all appear under the same heading. As we shall see in the discussion of the work of Saussure below, the key idea of structuralism is that language constitutes a system. The term structure replaced that of system as a consequence of the influence of Gestalt and Husserlianism on the Prague Linguistics Circle, and this is the source of the term structuralism (Gadet, 1989b:141). Gadet (1989b:31) has recently sought to tidy up this academic conceptualisation by proposing that structuralism should be distinguished from what she terms an 'enlarged' or 'generalised' structuralism which derived from a desire to distinguish this structuralism from the preceding existentialism. Thus the essential feature of structuralism resides in Saussure's emphasis on structural linguistics. This must be distinguished from the other uses of the concept — what Gadet calls the 'restrained' structuralism of semiology, which derives not merely from Saussure's work but also from that of Jakobson and Hjemsler, and an 'enlarged' structuralism, with its highly philosophical focus.

In some respects the starting point of both structuralism and FDA must be the work of Ferdinand de Saussure, although in other respects the contribution of Frederick Nietzsche cannot be ignored. Saussure was a Swiss linguist working at the turn of the century. Even though his published work is not voluminous, most of it being in the form of the posthumous publication of his university lectures, his influence has been far-reaching. It is important to emphasise that this failure to publish the work for which he became important has led to a tendency for others to elaborate some of his ideas, ideas which remained unrefined in their published form. His work contains several contradictions and many of the problems of structuralism can be located in these contradictions. As I will seek to show, the most important aspect of his work in so far as FDA is concerned is the manner in which he breaks the distinction between thought and language, thereby leading to the formation of a distinctive philosophy of language, distinctive that is from that of modernism. This is the basis of what Pêcheux has called the Saussurean break (Haroche, Henry and Pêcheux, 1971).

However, this should not imply that he deviated in any way from his ultimate aspiration of building a science of language. He claimed that the study of grammar was based on logic but that it lacked a scientific approach, mainly because of its preoccupation with rules for distinguishing between 'correct and incorrect forms' deriving from Greek and Latin antiquity, linguistics thereby becoming a normative discipline separate from actual observation (Saussure, 1972:1f., 3,1). The route to making 'general linguistics' a 'true science' was by supplying the theoretical and methodological framework hitherto missing (Saussure, 1972:82f.). The concrete object of linguistic science was the social product deposited in the brain of each individual (Saussure, 1972:23). However, whereas the other sciences worked with pre-given objects, he argued that in linguistics it was what he called the viewpoint which created the object (Saussure, 1972:8)!

Pêcheux (1982a:6) created an interesting typology of language and philosophy in which he distinguished:

1   the logico-formalist tendency of the Chomskyan school from
2   the historical tendency within which he included at least the variationist trend in sociolinguistics and
3   the linguistics of *parole* which includes discourse analysis.

He made the point that the second is linked to the first in a rather obvious way, even though most sociolinguists react strongly to the Chomskyan denial of the relevance of the social. But, as we have already seen, the third can also be linked to the first through analytic philosophy. This domination of the Chomskyan school can be broken by emphasising the relationship between 2 and 3. That is, discourse analysis can be seen as a feature of sociolinguistics, understood not as a sub-discipline of linguistics, but of sociology. Certainly there is a need to consider the manner in which language structure, variation and use interact within the socio-cultural environment. In pursuing such a goal it is essential to establish the distinction between *langue* and *parole*, and it is in this respect that the work of Saussure is crucial.

Sign and signifier

What Saussure broke with was the orthodox concept of language which derived from the Enlightenment and which is exemplified in the work of the Port Royal school, Locke and Condorcet among others. To recap, there are two fundamental elements to this conception of language. First, that language is merely a gloss on what exists outside of discourse. Thus the meaning of a word is held to be the object outside of language to which it refers – the relationship between sense and reference. In many of the associated philosophies of language it is claimed that the mind mediates between the world external to language and the spoken word. This results in the claim for a structure of representation wherein ideas are the signs of things and words the signs of ideas. Thus the nature of the signs which make up language depends upon their relation to things which lie outside of language or discourse. The second element involves the guarantor of this relationship between language and the world. It is here that the subject enters the stage. The human subject is claimed to be a rational being in full control of his/her consciousness who assigns meanings to words and ensures their correct usage. Following Cartesian logic, the subject is allocated primacy in that orders of thought and of the world are constructed by the subject.

Within orthodox sociolinguistics (G. Williams, 1992) most writers conceive of the subject as a free entity, rational and conscious, who is able to manipulate language in order to express his/her being in the form of identities, roles, related to social structure. The main basis for this manipulation is claimed to be a desire for co-operation and a drive for self-improvement. In accordance with the philosophy of individual liberalism, the subject becomes the primary force for social order and advancement. Consequently, language merely reflects the social order within which the rational subject conducts his/her attempt to establish harmonious relationships with others and to insure self-improvement.

Saussure was strong in his criticism of those who regarded language merely as a naming process, with lists of words corresponding to the things that they named. He criticised the assumption that ready-made ideas existed before words, and stressed that a name could be both vocal and psychological in nature. In contrast he claimed that 'the linguistic sign unites not a thing and a name, but a concept and a sound–image' (Gadet, 1987:30). The sound–image was sensory in nature, being a 'psychological imprint of the sound, the impression that it makes on our senses'. The linguistic sign becomes a two-sided psychological entity consisting of concept and sound–image, which are intimately united, whereas hitherto 'sign' referred simply to the sound–image. He then proceeded to replace the concept and sound–image by the terms signified (*signifié*), the mental representation of the meaning, and signifier (*signifiant*), or the 'psychological imprint of the sound' respectively. This served to indicate the opposition that separates them from each other as well as from the whole of which they are parts. Gadet emphasises (1987:32–33) that 'There is a bond in which both signified and signifier are created, in a sign'. They should never be thought of as separate. This bond simultaneously defines an order of language separate from reality and posits language as the bond between sound and idea. In treating linguistics as part of semiology, Saussure was emphasising the centrality of the sign for the study of language:

> Semiology would show what constitutes signs, what laws govern them
> ... Linguistics is only part of the general science of semiology;
> the laws discovered by semiology will be applicable to linguistics, and
> the latter will circumscribe a well-defined area within the mass of
> anthropological facts.
>
> (Gadet, 1987:33)

Yet signs were distinct from symbols, which were not arbitrary in that 'there is the rudiment of a natural bond between the signifier and the signified' (Gadet 1987:35). Language is then a system of signs whose equilibrium is permanently assured by social functioning. That is, the study of language is essentially a social phenomenon.

In referring to the sign as the entirety which derived from the association of the signifier and the signified, Saussure did not merely state that the bond between the signifier and the signified was arbitrary, but that the linguistic sign was arbitrary. The fundamental issue is the relationship between a concept and that to which it refers. Thus the sound 'tree' is tied to the concept of tree rather than to the object in the real world that comes under that concept. In making this link he was seeking to overcome the tendency to separate language and thought, and he claimed that:

> Language can be compared with a sheet of paper: thought is the front
> and sound the back; one cannot cut the front without cutting the back
> at the same time; likewise in language, one can neither divide sound
> from thought nor thought from sound.
>
> (Saussure, 1972:65–66)

The process of signification related to the movement from sound-image to concept and back; it is impossible to divide sound from thought, or thought from sound. Gadet has indicated that this relates to two fundamental questions: what is the relation between what is heard (sound), and what is understood (meaning), and what is the relation between language and reality?

What Saussure did here was to suppress the relationship between thing and word in traditional language philosophy. In so doing he consciously raised the issue of agency in the production of meaning. Language was no longer a stock of things waiting for a stock of labels to give them their designation. The suggestion that ideas sometimes exist prior to language and are conceivable without its intervention was no longer tenable. That is, he refuted the claim that there was a real world out there waiting to be designated by the use of language. In his words:

> Without language (*langue*), thought is a vague, uncharted nebula. There are no pre-existing ideas, and nothing is distinct before the appearance of language (*langue*).
>
> (Saussure, 1972:111)

He arrived at this conclusion in the knowledge that different languages have a varying number of concepts for an entity – where one language may have a single concept, another might have three. That is, languages do not divide up reality in the same way; what occurs is a division whose precise form is not determined by the material substance of reality. The bond between signified and signifier is arbitrary for the linguist, but not for the speaking subject who is subjected to it in that 'the community . . . is bound to the existing language' (Saussure, 1972:90). In this respect it is independent of the will of the speaker for whom it is necessary. Saussure stated: 'I mean that it is unmotivated, i.e. arbitrary in that it actually has no natural connection with the signified' (Saussure, 1972:69).

As Gadet (1987:37) indicates, there are two senses in which the sign is 'arbitrary'. First, it is an extra-linguistic reality that determines the conventional; second, it is unmotivated, that is, it is established by reference to other signs. Saussure emphasised the second, treating it as a specifically linguistic field. The linguistic arbitrariness which he referred to is underlined by the linearity of the signifier, the phonic signifier being linear in the sense that it unfolds in time, and the graphic signifier being linear as a consequence of its unfolding in space. However, there is a restriction on arbitrariness since language is ruled to some extent by logic.

As a consequence of the arbitrariness of the sign, there is no more reason for a sign's persistence than for it becoming something else, or changing. Consequently, language both changes and persists. The sign as a legacy of a prior epoch is resistant to deliberate modification. There are a number of reasons why this should be the case. First, there being no rationale for the sign being what it is, the linguistic community has no reason to prefer any other alternative. Second, given the large number of signs which constitute any given language, it is unrealistic to consider a vast change in signs over a short period of time. Third, since signs, taken together, constitute an intricate system, the alteration of a single component affects the entire system. Fourth, in a normative argument, he claimed that since language is of relevance to all speakers of a particular language, there will be a tendency towards conservation. On the other hand, mutability applies – there is no example of a language which has not been subject to change. Transformative factors always result in a modification of the relation between the signifier and the signified.

He stated that thinking of the signified as remaining stable, as in the orthodox approach, with only the signifier being affected, is to persist in a nomenclative conception of language. Even though the mutability/immutability derives from the arbitrariness of the sign, and ultimately from the existence of language as a social institution, it is not like other social institutions. Claiming that other social institutions involved elements which were founded upon some natural relation or other, he indicated that 'language is limited by nothing in the choice of means' (Gadet, 1987:41). That is, there is nothing to prevent any series of sounds being associated with any idea.

Saussure had one further thing to say about the arbitrariness of the sign. In his discussion of etymology he stated: 'to explain means to relate to known terms, and in linguistics, to explain a word is to relate it to other words, for there are no necessary relations between sound and meaning' (Saussure, 1972:189). Thus linguistics has been entirely divorced from a claim for reality and has become the study of the internal organisation of the order of signs, to explain signs through signs. This in turn leads to a consideration of his emphasis upon difference.

First of all it is necessary to refer to Saussure's understanding of language system or structure as it has become known within structuralism. In referring to language as a system, Saussure was concerned with the internal study of language without reference to any extraneous explanatory principles. A system might be in equilibrium at any moment in time but, since languages change, there is both the synchronic and diachronic element to language. In reality, of course, since language is always changing, synchronic states cannot be observed. Thus synchrony was akin to a Weberian form of ideal type which allows the theoretical definition of an abstract system. It refers to everything a speaker has at his/her disposal for speaking, it is only synchronic facts which are accessible to the speaker's awareness, and a synchronic fact has the capacity for creating signification.

Signs were held to be the key to the separation of distinctive ideas that is necessary in order to give order to thought (Saussure, 1972:133). Furthermore, the sum of word-images within the individual mind within which forms were associated through their meanings was the basis for the social bond that constituted language (Saussure, 1972:13,165). This was the kind of mentalist approach reminiscent of Durkheimianism which linguists were later to reject. None the less, it did lead to a consideration of the knowledge of speakers as involving a level of which they are not conscious (Saussure, 1972:47). Thus a language might not be complete in any speaker but 'exists perfectly only within a collectivity', being located in the collective mind of speakers where 'logical and psychological relations form a system' (Saussure, 1972:14,99f.). This was relevant for the synchronic approach, while a diachronic analysis was essential in studying the relations which link together successive terms not perceived by the collective mind, but substituted for each other without forming a system (Saussure, 1972:99f.).

Diachrony, on the other hand, refers to what has changed in a language or languages, and it assumes a secondary place for Saussure, who went so far as to see what he called language 'evolution' as the transition from one synchrony to another, as a series of stages. Yet the problem this has for functionalism did not arise since, for him, change never supervenes for functional reasons, and in this respect it is profoundly anti-teleological (Gadet, 1987:51). However, the system is not the sum of pre-existing elements, but the work of the relations that constitute the elements: 'Language is a system whose parts can and must all be considered in their synchronic solidarity' (Gadet, 1987:87).

Having insisted that signification depends upon the relations holding between the units that constitute language, Saussure discussed these relations in terms of value, claiming that signification depends upon value. Much as in economic transactions, a word can be exchanged for something dissimilar, an idea, while it can also be compared with something of the same nature, another word. Thus its value is not fixed since it can be 'exchanged' for a given concept, that is, it has this or that signification. However, it is also necessary to compare it with similar values, with other words that may stand in opposition to it. The content of a word is fixed by the concurrence of everything that stands in opposition to it. In claiming that signification depends upon value, he was stating that the link between sound-images and concepts rests on the relations within the two series of the signifier and the signified. However, a word of caution is necessary here. It is clear that Saussure did not pursue the economic metaphor and that this reference is not to the economic metaphor. His initial preoccupation was with the metaphor of time but he appears to make a causal reference to the economic, which, of course, was a primary concern at the time he was teaching.

What was being emphasised here was that the important thing in the word is how it can be distinguished from all others, since it is differences that carry signification. Indeed, he proceeded to claim that in language there are only differences, while adding that there are only differences 'without positive terms' (Saussure, 1972:120), thereby implying that difference is not a primordial quality. That is, whether one is referring to signified or signifier, there are neither sounds nor ideas in language which exist prior to, or independently of, the linguistic system. Every term is a complex site of differences, and language consists of two parallel and interdependent series, the signifiers and the signified. Both of these series are constituted by the relations between the elements of language, sounds and concepts respectively, these relations being produced by difference.

Evidently Saussure's emphasis upon the importance of language as a system was what led him to claim priority for *langue* over *parole*. *Langue* he treated as a sort of norm, being 'the set of linguistic habits which allow an individual to understand and to be understood' (Saussure, 1972:19), and which organises terms on the basis of their relations and of the priority of synchrony – the relationships constituting language at any one moment in time – over diachrony.

39

Signification relies on the terms of the language, which are the totality of the materials for signifying, and it is institutionalised through the creation of values associated with these terms. It derives from the relationship between signifier and signified. His principle of difference established the sign as 'the counterpart of other signs of language'. The meaning of every term is circumscribed by oppositions. When two similar things are compared – a sign with another sign – the relation, as we have seen, gives rise to a value. Signified and value must overlap in signification. Thus, rather than meaning deriving from pre-existing ideas, values derive from the system.

Langue and *Parole*

Saussure seems to have claimed that in separating language (*langue*) from speaking (*parole*) he was simultaneously separating what is social from what is individual, and what is essential from what is accessory and more or less accidental. However, there are different ways of interpreting his remarks on *langue* and *parole*. None the less, let us pursue the line of argument of this particular claim. Thus, whereas language was a collective and homogeneous phenomenon, speech was active, individual and heterogeneous (Saussure, 1972:13,15). The social for him involved a Durkheimian social bond, and he saw language as a specific form of social bond, being a storehouse filled by the members of a given community through their active use of speaking (*parole*), as a sort of contract between members of a community. But language was a potential, for it was never complete in any single speaker, it existed perfectly only within a collectivity. This is a view reminiscent of Habermas' claim for communication. Neither was it a function of the speaker, but was rather 'a product that is passively assimilated by the individual, whereas speech is an individual act which is divisible into the way in which a speaker expresses his/her own thoughts by employing the language code through combinations on the one hand, and the psychophysical mechanism which allows him/her to exteriorise those combinations' (Saussure, 1972:18). As if emphasising the principle of difference, Saussure pursued a series of oppositions between *langue* and *parole* which Gadet (1987:66) summarises as follows:

Langue	*Parole*
social	individual
essential	incidental
passively registered	act of will and intelligence
psychological	psycho-physical
sum of imprints in each brain	sum of what people say
collective model	non-collective

This, of course, is the culmination of Saussure's attempt to establish his own position on linguistics, which, in studying the manner in which its object is determined, he saw as a part of semiology. On a grand scale Saussure's objective was to establish a 'science that studies the life of signs within society' (Saussure, 1972:16). The object of linguistics, which was only a part of that general science (Saussure, 1972:17), was *langue* as a formal system. As such, it was the organising principle of a discipline as opposed to some reality of linguistic facts. Thus, it constituted a special system within the mass of semiological data, and its true nature could only be discovered via a consideration of what it held in common with the other semiological systems (Saussure, 1972:17). A consideration of the way in which a discipline orders facts relies on the distinction between *langue* and *parole*. *Langue* is treated as a social fact in being the faculty of language that is peculiar to humans. In treating it as such, he sought to divorce it from all that lay outside of its system, from all the external causes and determinations that may act upon language. *Langue* becomes 'a system that contains its own arrangement' (Saussure, 1972:22). As we have already seen, this meant separating linguistics from any discussion of an external reality, and this includes the prevalent idea that thought exists independently of *langue*. The signified is not anterior to the signifier. *Langue* becomes established as a principle of heterogeneous facts that make up language (Gadet, 1987:66).

As the oppositions between *langue* and *parole* presented above make clear, not only is *langue* a social institution, being a norm in the sense of being 'a collection of necessary conventions' (Saussure, 1972:9), but it is also a system of signs, a system with its own arrangement which 'is a self-contained whole and a principle of classification' (Saussure, 1972:9). Gadet (1987:67) rightly raises the issue of the nature of the relationship between the sociological and the semiological. There is no doubt that the semiological perspective was central to the study of language, and in an important way. Since language was a system of signs it was the basis for the development of a science of signs (Culler, 1976: 90). Such a science would have the objective of making explicit the convention on which the discipline rests. Since human actions or productions convey meaning, through the manner in which they function as signs, and since signs imply the existence of system, then signifying practices are considered as languages. But language is merely one aspect of semiological systems. Yet it was treated as *le patron général* of semiology, and, as such, was to be the model for semiology.

Gadet (1987:67) indicates that two arguments have been proposed for the relationship between the semiological and the sociological. First, that because *langue* is a system of values, being a normative system, it is not subject to individual innovations. As such it functions as a social institution. The sociological follows from the semiological. Alternatively, since arbitrariness derives from the social nature of language, *langue* thereby becomes a system. The semiological follows from the sociological. As she indicates, the sociological definition was characteristic of the turn of the century, whereas the semiological definition serves as the starting point for what she calls 'modern linguistics', for it allows the development of the abstract study of *langue*.

If, as is implied, the linguist has access to language through *parole* rather than *langue*, it is clear how many of Chomsky's ideas owe an allegiance to Saussure. Achieving an understanding of *langue* does not derive from direct observation because of its abstract nature, a nature which gives form to *parole*. Saussure claims that *langue* 'is passively assimilated by the individual' (Saussure, 1972:14), involving neither premeditation nor reflection. *Parole* on the other hand is 'an individual act . . . wilful and intellectual' (Saussure, 1972:14). However, there does seem to be a link between them since *langue* is 'a storehouse filled by the members of a given community through their active use of *parole*, a grammatical system that has a potential existence in each brain' (Saussure, 1972:13–14). What seems to be implied here is that it is social practice that feeds the memory, which then contributes to the 'system', which is visible in its effects. As Gadet has indicated (1987:69–70), there is a tension here between memory and creativity, and she attempts to avoid the static context of the link between the functioning of *langue* and memory. In many respects the problem seems to derive from Saussure's attempt to separate the individual from the social, much in the same way as this became problematic for Durkheim in his development of the *conscience collective*. There appears to be a freedom allocated to the individual which is constrained by the nature of *langue*, which is a system that constrains through its normative nature. Much as Durkheim saw society as the basis of social order, placing constraints on individual freedom, so Saussure saw *langue* as the basis of a linguistic order which fetters the individual freedom of *parole*. In this respect it is akin to Chomsky's 'rule-governed creativity'.

The mechanisms of *langue* operate at the level of discourse or the linearity of the spoken chain. It is assumed that there is a complex mechanism which ensures the functioning of the combinations that are words, both in their systemic potential and their linear realisation. There is some mechanism which links *langue* with the observable – with *parole*. This is assured by what Saussure calls syntagm, or the order of linearity, and the associative, or the order of the system.

In the linear chain the elements maintain relations of contiguity, and word order is an important feature of this. It is these linear relations that Saussure calls syntagmatic, syntagm referring to any linguistic sequence when it is open to analysis. Referring back to Saussure's claim that in language there are only differences, it is useful to recognise that he added reference to groupings, at which point he was referring to syntagmatic organisation. The sentence is an obvious example of one such grouping. There are also associations which Saussure refers to as the manner in which a word recalls other words with which it has relations, these relations being termed associative relations. They are presented as facts of memory. The speaking subject can not only make these associations, but can also come to terms with their mechanism; they can know the character of the relation.

The two spheres of linearity and association come together in a complementary form in the production of the spoken chain: 'The syntagm can only be produced if we are aware of all the differences or oppositions the group of associations may present' (Gadet, 1987:82). In pursuing this line, Saussure offered a rudimentary indication of how meaning is constituted in *langue*. A form is selected not because it signifies what the speaker wishes to say but on the basis of a much more complicated process, one based on differential: 'In reality the idea evokes not a form but a whole latent system that makes possible the oppositions necessary for the formation of the sign' (Saussure, 1972:130). The sign, it would seem, exists at the intersection of a number of associative series. However, there is no discontinuity between words and the sentence, as in the distinction between syntax and lexicology, since the principle applies at the most complicated level. He thereby reaches the conclusion that the entire linguistic system is to be understood in terms of the interplay between syntagmatic and associative relations. What this, in turn, implies, is that the speaking subject does have a knowledge of grammar. However, the distinction between *langue* and *parole* precludes the kind of phenomenological insistence on subjectivity, and *langue* is treated as involving additional information possessed by the linguist through his/her knowledge of the history of the relevant language. The meaning of a word 'is fixed because it is surrounded by analogues which make the partial meaning visible by furnishing a series of new units inferior to the word' (Saussure, 1972:83). Saussure goes further in claiming that these units are not accessible merely to the analyst, but also to the speaker who recognises their significance.

Creativity, in the relationship between *langue* and *parole*, rests on the concept of analogy, a concept which led him to an awareness of the speaker's incomplete conscious knowledge (Saussure, 1972:167). By 'analogy' he means that there is a model which is regularly imitated, and as such it is rule-bound. It leads to the creation of a new form which is substituted for an earlier form. *Langue* contains the potential for its own creation in that the speaking subject, operating through *parole*, employs the resources of language in creating innovations which are fed back into *langue*:

> Creative activity will simply be a combinatory activity – the creation of a new combination. But a combination created out of what materials? They are not given from outside; *langue* must derive them from itself. This is why the first act of analysis was required: *la langue* spends its time interpreting and decomposing the contribution of previous generations in order to combine the new constructions with the subunits thus obtained.
>
> (Quoted in Gadet, 1987:93)

The *langue/parole* distinction is confirmed, but with *langue* changing through *parole*, with speakers intervening in a process of language through analogy. Despite being an innovative process, it was remarkably conservative, since analogy always drew on what was referred to as 'old materials' (Saussure,

1972:172). This, of course, is the key link between collective memory and creativity.

There is an obvious subtlety in *langue* if we consider its use by speakers:

> If the mass of forms which make up *la langue* for each individual simply retained a chaos in their heads, *parole* and *la langue* alike would be inconceivable. The necessity of classification, of some order, is an a priori necessity even in the absence of psychology.
>
> (Quoted in Gadet, 1987:94)

As Gadet (1987:94) notes, the initial idea of the sign as a simple bond between signifier and signified has been displaced by a far more complicated mechanism wherein the sign summons up an infinite chain of associations. There is an infinite play in *langue* which can be investigated through the use that speakers make of it. It is this that leads to the link between *langue* and the unconscious.

One of the things which confused Saussure was the abundance of anagrams in texts. He came to the conclusion that they were not intentional and therefore lay outside of *langue*. This in turn meant that the signifier had to be credited with a materiality, and there was an infinity to *langue*, and that the subject was not the master of *langue*. He came close to suggesting that not every thing concerning *langue* is explained by *langue*. He was on the verge of opening a way to the unconscious. Yet his refusal to pursue this issue meant that his main focus remained with the manner in which meaning was produced.

Influences

In the conclusion to her invaluable book, Gadet has undertaken an excellent survey of the extent to which the ideas of Saussure have been incorporated in the work of those who followed him and who, it is claimed, live on his legacy. The most widely publicised of these developments of Suassure's ideas was structuralism, which was associated with non-linguists who delved into the field much later than their counterparts in linguistics. Our interest in such developments is much narrower than those of Gadet, and will be restricted to the work of those from which FDA derives. What will become evident is Gadet's claim that: 'If "Sausserian linguistics" still constitutes a model, it is certainly not as the strict application of a method, but in a broader and less rigorous sense' (Gadet, 1987:112).

Saussure's work was taken on board by the Moscow Linguistics Circle, but this was followed by a pronounced anti-formalist period under the influence of Marxism. The main thrust of the criticism was that Saussure's ideas were fundamentally anti-humanist, partly as a consequence of the absence of the centred, rational subject in his work. None the less, it was the Moscow Circle which first sought to unravel the 'structural laws' of linguistics and poetics. Roman Jakobson was the key link between the Moscow Circle and the Prague

Linguistics Circle, which was established in 1926, followed by the Copenhagen Linguistics Circle, which was set up in 1931, and the Linguistics Circle of New York, which was founded three years later. There was considerable overlap and interchange between the activities of these different Circles, and the work of French linguists, most notably Benveniste, was incorporated in their activities.

It is from these activities that structuralism derived. Yet within the various Circles there were other influences. Thus, for example, the Prague Circle drew on the phenomenology of Husserl, while Russian formalism turned to Gestalt psychology, among other sources. Indeed, Gadet (1987:121) argues that Husserl's claim for the intentional nature of consciousness was highly influential, and involved the claim for introspection on the part of a pre-formed, conscious subject.

In one respect it is the work of Benveniste which is most influential because of his profound influence on studies of language in France in general. Gadet (1987:132) regards him as 'genuinely a structuralist, a continuator of Saussure'. He was involved in the transition from the idea of a language system to that of structure. Yet, despite the tendency to base his work on Saussure, there were numerous innovations in his work. His focus upon the speaking subject and on enonciation involved the study of specific elements within behaviour. The study of these 'indexical' units overlaps with the work of Austin and Jakobson.

Benveniste's focus upon the subject within a structuralist framework involved an interest in the problem of the relationship between the *langue* as a system of signs, and the manner in which *langue* as an instrument of communication was put into action through enonciation. Thus the linguistic aspect of *langue* as a system of signs was linked with the linguistics of discourse in which the speaking subject was master of his/her speech (*parole*), the presence of which can be analysed as a system of traces. Thus traces of the enonciation are to be found in the utterance and are linguistically analysable. His important contribution was his focus on the speaking subject and the idea of the subject of the enonciation, this being in line with the general dismay of sociolinguists at Saussure's lack of interest in *parole*.

Comment must also be reserved for Jakobson, if only because of his influence on the work of Lévi-Strauss, who played such an important role in the early development of many working in FDA, and to a different degree on Lacan. Gadet (1987:145) regards Jakobson as the fundamental link between Saussurean linguistics and the human sciences. While claiming the work of Saussure as his inspiration, Jakobson did undertake a critical interpretation of Saussure's work, the most basic critique involving a challenge to the conception of an object specific to linguistics. He modified the idea of the arbitrariness of the sign towards a claim for a motivation of the bond between signifier and signified. Similarly, he queried the linearity of the signifier through a phonemic analysis. He rejected the *langue/parole* division, and also that of synchrony and diachrony. He preserved the two axes but developed them into a marked/unmarked opposition, these in time being replaced by metaphor and metonymy. The entire emphasis shifts to what is termed external linguistics, involving the manner in which the socio-cultural framework of language and history relates to the internal structure of language, making this, to a great extent, the link to the work of Lévi-Strauss. Jakobson's innovations included the idea of functions of language, which derived originally from the distinction made by the Russian formalists between ordinary language and poetic language, and which eventually came to refer to the variable nature of factors of communication. His main point of perseverance with Saussure involved the concept of difference, which he felt was the point of access to the system.

It is clear that the Saussurean legacy which is claimed for the human sciences has been subject to profound modification, and it might be useful to consider the specific aspects which have played a significant role in the development of FDA. Undoubtedly the most important and far-reaching aspect is what is referred to as the decentring of the subject. Within the social sciences there has been a tendency to see causality as associated either with the rational human subject in full control of his/her consciousness, a view carried to its extreme in rational choice theory, or with some supra-individual structure, be it the Marxist infrastructure or the Durkheimian *conscience collective*. This has involved a claim for a reality or 'truth' which can be encountered by considering how 'valid' knowledge is possible. In this sense most theories of society are epistemological, in the sense that epistemology claims that knowledge can be identified and known. Objectivity in sociology rests on the claim that there is an approximation between the discourse in question and 'truth', with 'truth' implying a correspondence between reality and thought. Evidently, if objective knowledge is denied, then the discipline of epistemology is undermined.

The central assumption here is that there is an immediate, direct, intuitive contact between subject and object and that this is the basis of our knowledge of the world. This means that our knowledge consists of objects that are discussed in discourse; that is, objects and discourse are two separate entities. In the sociological quest for truth it becomes a question of which of the competing theories gives the closest approximation of reality. Sociological criticism often involves evaluating theories in terms of a 'but given such and such an example it is evident that the world is not really like that and therefore this theory will not suffice'. An external world is taken for granted. Clearly a central issue in the discussion of epistemology is the relationship between subject and object, and epistemology remains concerned primarily with how the subject can have a knowledge of the object, that is, the subject is taken for granted as the origin and justification of knowledge. We have already seen how this is evident in the orthodox philosophies of language, where language is treated as a reflection of either the social or of thought. Ideas are the signs of things and words the signs of ideas. Language as a collection of signs rests on the relation to extra-linguistic phenomena. It is the conscious, thinking subject that gives meanings to words and insures that they are correctly employed. Language contains consciousness.

It should be evident how the work of Saussure has a revolutionary effect upon this general perspective of human creativity. It does so in two respects: first, that the sense of a word or sentence no longer resides in anything external to language; and second, the human subject is not the source of meaning. This evidently demands a fundamental reassessment of semantics, one which Pécheux (1982a:39) refers to as locked in substantialist and subjectivist illusions involving the relationship between a set of scientific statements on the one hand and conversation on the other. As Jameson (1972:32) emphasises, Saussure constantly related one sign to another rather than relating a word to a thing. Language has an internal coherence rather than being a system of symbols which relates to external phenomena being symbolised. In this respect language is autonomous. On the semantic level, meaning no longer resides in individual words or sentences, but in the relations that constitute language, difference being an important feature of such relations. This being the case, how can the subject be the source of meaning in the orthodox sense of being the guarantor of the relation between word and object? The human subject can no longer be the secure foundation of thought and the world – it has been decentred with reference to explanatory objectives. As we shall see, the subject becomes the creation of certain relationships which are prior to and beyond it.

As a consequence of shifts in the philosophy of language and the associated decentring of the subject, the work of a number of French social philosophers who drew upon this insight has been lumped together under the heading of post-structuralism. This is rather unfortunate since there are significant differences from one author to another, even if they do have a great deal in common. Indeed, several of those regarded as post-structuralists object to being so labelled (Henry, 1990:14). None the less, it is from this broad group of social philosophers that FDA has emerged, and it is important to be specific about which theoretical aspects of post-structuralism pertain to FDA.

The reference point of post-structuralism is the structuralism in the work of Saussure, that is, his structural linguistics, which led to what Gadet (1989:2) refers to as a *structuralisme généralisé*, rather than the structure or institutional orders of anthropology. Interestingly, this advent of structuralism into the human sciences emerged at a time when linguistic structuralism, confronted by generative grammar, which challenged some of its postulates, and by the emergence of enonciative linguistics, was undergoing a crisis. Anderson (1983) argues that post-structuralism represents a dissolution of 'structure', but before we consider the relevance of this claim, let us look at the breadth of the work that it encapsulates.

Lévi-Strauss

It is the anti-humanism of Lévi-Strauss that is generally regarded as characteristic of early structuralism. Saussure claimed that equal importance should be applied to signifiers and signified, thereby rejecting the orthodox distinction between the word and the object that it is meant to denote. It was the Prague Circle which recognised the need to abandon the concept of system in favour of the concept of structure. Whereas systems can be open, structure cannot. Significantly the Prague Circle never used the term 'system'. Rather they related structure to Gestalt, while accommodating an external philosophic relationship. This structural conception of language was extended by Lévi-Strauss to encompass the social world. In so doing he accorded primacy to signifiers over signified, so that meaning became a matter of the inter-relationship of words. However, it was much more than this since it claimed to uncover deep mental structures which were held to exist in humans, and which manifested themselves at the material level in social structures. Again what we have here seems to be a reappearance of the thought/language separation, with social structure replacing language. This Cartesian rationalism emphasises the structures of thought rather than the emotional. This development should not be surprising given that Saussure shared with Durkheim the ideological opposition of the individual and society, and in this respect Lévi-Strauss was merely pursuing the Durkheimian concern with the *conscience collective*. What he was striving to uncover were the unconscious psychological patterns that motivate human behaviour. None the less, his importance and his relevance for FDA lie in his being the first to adapt Saussurean linguistics to the social sciences. In so doing, his goal was that of making anthropology scientific by modelling it on structuralist linguistics.

The fundamental claim of Lévi-Strauss' early work is that society is constructed on the incest taboo, which obliges the exchange of persons – for Lévi-Strauss it was men who exchanged women – which, in turn, created a social structure of which the nuclear family was merely a part. Society was based upon three main forms of exchange: the economic, based on the exchange of goods; the exchange of women, according to specific rules which constitute the kinship structure; and the exchange of verbal messages, which is responsible for culture. In seeking to uncover the relationship between the various parts of existing structure without recourse to any historical basis for explanation, Lévi-Strauss was elaborating the approach of synchronic linguistics. He thus abandoned any attempt to achieve a factual description and concentrated on mental representations of 'reality'. Yet in many respects his work represents a continuation of the modernist vision in which society is constituted by unconscious mental representations shared by members of that society, and which contain an inherent logic which holds priority over the social and the individual order. The individual is projected into the system in generating individual subjectivities, while society becomes the processing of social behaviour by the mental system. In this respect it represents the form of Kantianism which preceded the work of Lacan, Althusser and Foucault. Indeed, Lévi-Strauss himself accepted the description of his work as a Kantianism without the transcendental subject.

It was Roman Jakobson who introduced Lévi-Strauss to Saussure's structural linguistics. It was by drawing upon Saussure's work and Troubetskoy's phonological work that Lévi-Strauss sought to discover algebraic structures and groups of transformations within the different kinship organisations. Lévi-Strauss explicitly discusses how he looked to Jakobson for a solution to the difficulties which he had encountered in recording the languages of central Brazil, but emerged from his lectures with something quite different in the form of the revelation of structural linguistics (Lévi-Strauss, 1976). However Lévi-Strauss also incorporated Jakobson's own model of phonemic analysis, which sought to show that the structure of any language follows a binary path of parallel constructions to the *langue/parole* and signifier/signified distinctions of Saussure's work. The claim is made that it is the basic propensity of the human mind to build logical categories by means of binary contrast. For Lévi-Strauss such oppositions were the basis of most, if not all, socio-cultural phenomena. However, in recognising the manner in which he drew on the linguistic work of Jakobson, it should be emphasised that Lévi-Strauss' subsequent analysis was far more sophisticated and innovative than, for example, the simple appropriation of the technique of componential analysis from linguistics into American cultural anthropology during the 1960s. Indeed, it is evident that his concern was with the entire discipline of anthropology and how it was devoid of the scientific rigour that was so evident in its sister discipline of linguistics (Lévi-Strauss, 1963:69). In this respect it was an attempt to convert the humanities into a scientific discipline.

As I have suggested, the linguistic input in Lévi-Strauss' work derives as much from the Prague Circle as from Saussure. Indeed the work of Jakobson, Karcevski, Troubetzkoy, Bally and Sechehaye, the last two being the editors of Saussure's work, all contributed to the emphasis on Saussureanism as involving the description of language as a system (Gadet, 1989a:5). However, it was Jakobson who drew together Russian formalism and the Saussurean emphasis. He was also instrumental in the formation of the Linguistic Circle of New York, in the first number of whose journal, *Word*, Lévi-Strauss was a contributor. This focus of his insight involved the principle of distinctive feature contrasts in which the systemic nature of the set of phonological contrasts employed by each system is not a simple linear catalogue of the significant sounds, but, rather, consists of the network of oppositions in which binary groupings of sound differences take their position in a multi-dimensional space. Thus the infinite variety of sounds is reduced to a small number of systems of contrasts. This discovery of the deeper structure underlying surface appearances led to Lévi-Strauss' claim that such a structure similarly underlay the social order.

The implications of the work of Lévi-Strauss are far-reaching. He focused upon the study of an 'unconscious infrastructure' rather than on its conscious manifestations; there emerged an emphasis upon the relationship between terms or items, rather than upon the terms or items themselves; general laws in the form of universal invariant relationships were to be exposed; and concrete systems in terms of specific cases were to be demonstrated in preference to more abstract theorising. Clearly there is a wide-ranging theoretical and methodological enterprise involved here, a range which coalesces in a form of idealism which focuses on mental representation. To a certain extent it can be claimed that his main concern was with how the mind organises data, focusing on the study of representations of structures in the mind.

Lévi-Strauss' debt to Saussure involves an attempt to link the latter's postulate of a dynamic relationship between the components of every linguistic sign, that is, between *langue* and *parole* and between signifier and signified, with Jakobson's model of phonemic analysis. Lévi-Strauss was convinced that structural linguistics would revolutionise the social sciences, largely because it allowed for the discovery of general laws, and for the discovery of a system. He asserted that the phonetic method of Jakobson could not be transposed to anthropological analysis without being refined to allow for the fact that what is established at the micro level would be invalid at the macro level. The example which he employed was that of kinship terms, which are terms of address which designate kinship relations. These, he claimed, would vary from one society to another. Even though there may be differences between systems of nomenclature and those of social organisation, Lévi-Strauss claimed that all such systems are alike, in that they are all symbolic. Consequently, neither phenomena nor kinship systems can be explained through observation alone, but must also be seen as sets of symbolic relationships. On the macro level such symbolic relations exist between languages and cultures, and in some societies they converge in myths which are structured in a similar manner across cultures, much as languages are structured in Jakobson's framework. It is important to recognise that this reflects a general concern with the universal in anthropology, which, as a discipline, differs from sociology in its universalist orientation about the condition and nature of humankind. It is also important to recognise the claim that kinship relations effectively obey rules that are analogous to those of language, but do not obey the rules of discourse.

Saussure's concern with establishing semiology as a science which studied the relationship between signs and the social led Lévi-Strauss to propose that the signification of a social sign is the effect of differential relations to other signs, and by analogy to other social systems; and, in the last instance, by analogy, to the totality of productions of what he called the 'unconscious spirit' (Lévi-Strauss, 1963:37). In this respect he was drawing upon Saussure's concept of the articulation of signs, which claims that meaning is in itself as amorphous as sound, which is why anything that intervenes between them must be cognisant of the schematisation of the articulation, which allows a perceptible sound to be related to a non-sensitive signification. In so doing he placed this conceptualisation within an explicitly Marxist superstructural context involving the relationship between praxis and practices, claiming that they were separated by a conceptual scheme involving material and form as structures. Frank (1989:128) argues that Lévi-Strauss' application of this conception to myth, emphasising linguistics rather than kinship relations or social structure, served as an inspiration for Foucault's work on discourse. The point which Frank emphasises here is the manner in which myths are linguistic forms at the same time as they are speech events, or what he referred to as statements of discourse (Lévi-Strauss, 1963:230).

Lévi-Strauss sought to demonstrate that myths are constituted in the same way regardless of culture. In itself this was not a new theme, as the work of Raglan (1956), Stith Thompson (1953), Propp (1958) *inter alia* attests. What was novel in Lévi-Strauss' approach was the manner in which he employed the Saussurean distinction between *langue* and *parole* in order to account for how events which seemingly belong to the past are constituted in myths of the present. To these two elements he added a third – 'the gross constituent unit' as the meaningful combination of two or more words in a sentence. Jakobson had focused upon binary oppositions between consonants and vowels, and between contradictory relationships, such as the differences between the emotive and conative aspects of a speech event. Lévi-Strauss similarly assumed a similarity between myth and language, in that contradictory relationships can be seen as similar, providing they are self-contradictory in a similar way. Evidently, he was unable to discover or produce a 'true' version of any myth, but had to analyse all versions of any particular myth. That is, even if he saw myth as a social entity he could not break it down into reality/falsehood distinctions. What he did was to reduce each myth into short sentences or constituent units which were capable of producing a functional meaning only when combined with other such units into 'bundles of relations' which would account for the two-dimensional aspect of revertible time and non-revertible time. Together they constituted the primary elements of most myths. He was then able to produce a three-dimensional picture of myth based on the arrangement of its constituent units (Hawkes, 1977:34–49).

This analytical procedure had to be undertaken for all versions of every myth by organising two-dimensional charts in three-dimensional order in order to be able to read diagonally. He claimed that if all known myths were thus charted there would emerge a structural law of myth.

Lévi-Strauss then sought to elaborate the analyses by reference to parallels between the transition from nature to culture on the one hand, and changing customs on the other. Thus, for example, food was no longer eaten raw, but cooked. Further contrasts involved a series of transformations and oppositions, some appearing remarkably complicated and marginal to the main objective of discovering unconscious structures. The transformation from the raw to the cooked related to a series of oppositions which sought to explain the common ingredients of myths.

Lévi-Strauss' work represented his rejection of phenomenology and existentialism, with their emphasis on subjectivity as the converse of 'true' thought. He claimed that history was reconstituted each time a myth was retold in that the past is recalled. The past becomes part of the present and the orthodox theories of progress and evolution are discounted – history exists within an interplay of mental structures that occur at a specific 'moment'. In his view it could not be claimed that 'men (sic) make history', but rather that history possessed its own irreducible dialectic or intelligibility. The humanist tendency to see history as the product of collective human action was, in Lévi-Strauss' mind, akin to the role of myth, being a repetition of the error of the Cartesian *cogito*, history being treated as if it provided access to a self-validating truth. Yet his assumption that there exists an unknown but discoverable structural order which directs society was reminiscent of Durkheim's *conscience collective*.

One of the criticisms levelled against Lévi-Strauss' work was made by Sartre (1964). He asserted that even though Lévi-Strauss claimed an affinity with Marxism, his concern was with cultural transformation rather than causality. As we shall see, this is a recurring problem in the brand of discourse analysis which relates to ideology through recourse to a linguistic analysis which implies a decentred subject, but which persists in the claim to be Marxist. It involves the unwillingness to divorce the superstructure from the infrastructure.

Perhaps the importance of Lévi-Strauss' work lies in his insistence on the primacy of the signifier over the signified, for it is this which has led to the claim within FDA that the process of the production of meaning does not reside in a signified external to language as Marxism would insist. This primacy means that the subject cannot any longer treat words as things which stand for his/her thoughts. It was Lévi-Strauss' belief that language contained an abundance of signifiers which can contribute to the infinite production of new meanings. The superabundance of the signifier relative to the signified is responsible for notions such as *mana* which exists in certain societies and which

> represent an undetermined value of signification, in itself devoid of sense and therefore susceptible to receive any sense, whose unique function is to overcome a gap between signifier and signified.
>
> (Lévi-Strauss, 1950:xlix)

He called these notions 'floating signifiers'. Furthermore his emphasis on the priority of the signifier illustrates his understanding of society as a symbolic order governed by the laws of language. He specifically states that the social is the same reality as language and in that sense it is autonomous (Lévi-Strauss, 1950:xxxiii).

It is also important to recognise the fact that Lévi-Strauss claimed that myths were closed collections of phrases which constitute a linguistic event, even if it is not an event in which the sequences can be extracted from their temporal context. It was the linearity of signs and, initially, that of the collection of phrases, which gave each signifying elements its temporal indice. This observation led him to claim that there were three levels to language – *langue*, *parole* and discourse. Myths share with the linguistic system that property which leads to their elements having value or a meaning not in themselves but in virtue of the relationships between them. That is, they constitute a structure. Myths as discourse are structures composed of transphrastic units which distinguish them from *langues*. Recognising the various constitutent parts or units of language and of the relationships between them led him to gross constitutive units. It is in this respect that he recognises the 'linguistics of discourse'. It led Barthes (1966) to suggest the need for a new form of linguistics based on the study of discourse.

By the 1950s Lévi-Strauss' work had become extremely influential, but it was the work of Lacan during the early 1950s which introduced Saussurean principles into psychoanalysis, and from there into social theory. Lacan thus followed Lévi-Strauss in departing from essentialism and moved towards the field of cultural enquiry. However, as we shall see, Lacan's work has much more relevance for the concept of the subject than anything which Lévi-Strauss produced. Yet both of them shared the claim that structures of meaning can be constructed – Lévi-Strauss by reference to how the phoneme in itself is meaningless, but achieves meaning in relationship to other units of the same kind; and Lacan, as we shall see, by reference to the structures of human consciousness. Surprisingly, whereas Lacan's work heralded a shift away from structuralism, Lévi-Strauss, despite relinquishing his scientific claims, persisted with the theme of structuralism.

Lacan

One who derived a great deal of his earlier work from Lévi-Strauss and Jakobson was Jacques Lacan (Gadet, 1989a:34). Saussure is clearly evident in his work where he alludes to a form of structuralism. He was a structuralist in the sense that while he was interested in the analysis of the psychological condition of individuals, he was also deeply involved in the operations performed by the human mind in general. Certainly his theoretical work referred to the functioning of the human psyche in general in a form of meta-psychology. His main concern was to deny that interpretation of Freud which insists that psychoanalysis unearths unconscious, repressed, biological instincts, that a biological base underlies conscious experience.

However, we should not lose sight of the fact that, whereas in this chapter we link Lacan with Lévi-Strauss, Jakobson and Saussure, his work also pertains to the anti-humanism associated with Althusser and Foucault, where the transcendental subject is abandoned. Lacan was profoundly influenced by Hegel and Heidegger, indeed he attended the lectures of Kojeve, whose work on Heidegger had such an important influence in France during the 1930s. However, Lacan's psychoanalysis is not a humanism, there is no emphasis upon the autonomous, self-conscious human subject which contains knowledge, experience and emotion, or which bears a relationship to the social environment which can be evaluated in terms of creativity and self-recognition. The orthodox interpretation of Freud is an expression once again of Enlightenment thought, in the form of a faith in the humankind/nature dichotomy, with the achievements of humankind in the form of culture and civilisation obscuring the biological tendencies. Thus, civilisation served as a veneer which overlay the basic tendencies, and it was claimed that Freud had managed to penetrate that veneer through his psychoanalytic work. It was this interpretation which Lacan rejected.

Lacan had a profound influence on Althusser, and it can be claimed that Althusser's 'return to Marx' merely echoes Lacan's own 'return to Freud' – an attempt to rescue the respective authors from the misreadings of their respective followers. Lacan argues that the human experience is characterised by lack and separation. A child is born as an entirely dependent being which is transformed into a human subject – the unconscious is the record of that transformation. A decisive stage in such a transformation is the Oedipus complex, and its successful resolution leaves the person firmly lodged in the symbolic order. Echoing Lévi-Strauss, Lacan maintained that the symbolic order is the order of both language and society. According to his re-reading of Freud:

> Freud's discovery was that of the field of the effects in the nature of man and of his relations to the symbolic order and the tracing of their meaning to the most radical agencies of symbolisation in being.
>
> (Lacan, 1977:64)

Evidently such a view results in the denial of the Freudian concepts of instinct and sexuality in their biological context.

The two central concerns which enter into the re-reading of Freud are desire and absence. Resolving the Oedipus complex involves an acceptance of the lack at the very heart of the child's being, this lack being symbolised by the phallus, which the female child does not possess and which the male child can be deprived of by the father. Desire is Lacan's equivalent of Freud's *cogito*, whereas instincts are referred to in terms of drives. However, these drives do not represent the completeness of a biological need suppressed by civilisation as in the work of Freud. Rather, since sexuality is caught up in the fundamental lack at the centre of human existence, it is realised through the operation of the drives, even if they are partial drives with reference to the biological finality of sexuality. Desire on the other hand is to be distinguished both from biological need and from demand. Demand derives from man's inherent incomplete nature, and can never be entirely satisfied since it relates back to the original unity with the mother. Lack becomes constitutive of both sexuality and the drives, it induces organic need. Given that sexual drives are partial, being shattered by a basic incompleteness, desire becomes the means whereby the subject seeks to gain the recognition of the Other. That is, throughout its existence the subject will strive to make up for its fragmentation through recognition by 'another self-conscious', primarily the mother. This perpetual struggle, for Lacan, can only take place within language.

Lacan's reference to language involved the claim that the unconscious answers to language. This he deduces from a scrutiny of Freud's early reference to hypnotism, where it was claimed that it worked through verbal suggestions, there being a continuation link between the hypnotic trance and waking verbal suggestions. In the example of the hypnotised subject who eats a lemon, s/he does so not because of a transformation of the visual image of the fruit through hypnosis but because, through prompting, s/he *interprets* it as an apple and this in spite of the taste buds. That is, the interpretation overrides the biological. Furthermore, hypnosis can generate a long-term restructuring of the unconscious, the interpretative connection being effective beyond the hypnotic state. Such an implant can be effective in correcting neuroses because the neurotic depends upon a myth which speaks to him/her. It comes from the outside, being 'the discourse of the other' (Lacan, 1978:27). As Callinicos (1982:38) has indicated, this is reminiscent of Hegel's account of the dialect of master and slave in his *Phenomenology*, where he insists that self-consciousness depends upon the existence of other subjects. Lacan saw that the intersubjective relations which are the basis of self-consciousness depended upon the symbolic order of language and society. The link with language is made explicit:

> desire is an effect in the subject of the condition that is imposed in him
> by the existence of the discourse to make his need pass through the
> defile of the signifier.
>
> (Lacan, 1978:264)

The perpetual struggle for recognition by 'another self-conscious', most notably the mother, can only occur within language, which is the framework within which self-consciousnesses exist and relate to one another. Its effects are to be found in the unconscious, hence his claim that the unconscious is structured like a language, and that the unconscious is the discourse of the Other.

The transformation of the subject into a self-conscious member of society involves repressions which do not allow him/her access to the record of that process that is secreted within him/herself. As a consequence, the subject is decentred, with the result that its meaning lies not in the self-certainty of the *cogito*, but in the other scene where it speaks. Linguistics is the means whereby it can be understood since, if the unconscious is structured in the same way as language, by the same laws as those discovered in the study of language, then the unconscious can be recovered. It is here that he reaches for, and transforms, Saussure.

Given that the subject cannot lie within self-consciousness, the orthodox approach to language, wherein the rational thinking subject is responsible for the link between thought and reality, through the representation of external reality in language, is no longer conceivable. Thus Lacan must adopt a different approach to language, one in which the subject is decentred, no longer being capable of contact with reality. The existence of the subject in the subconscious has to be captured, and this done by employing the tools offered by linguistics, since the subconscious is structured like language. The linguistics he resorts to is Saussurean linguistics. Furthermore, his claim that intersubjective relations were crucial for the attempt to recover the self-conscious led him to relate this striving to the symbolic order of language and society which was shared by the subject and the Other, thus being the basis of intersubjectivity. Herein lies his claim that 'the unconscious is the discourse of the Other'. However, the forming of the subject as a self-conscious member of society involves various repressions which serve to remove her/him from access to any record in her/himself of that very process. The subject is incapable of recapturing its true self in the unconscious and must fall back on an existence within the self-conscious. Its only encounter with the unconscious is in the gaps, the ruptures, the slips of the tongue and the fragmented discourse of the dream which Freud (1973) referred to in *The Interpretation of Dreams*; it is here that the subject speaks.

Lacan's use of Saussure is by no means orthodox. Sounds and signifiers do not stand for things, rather, the signifier becomes constitutive of *langue*,

> the synchronic structure of the language material, in so far as in that structure each element assumes its precise function by being different from the others; this is the principle of distribution that alone governs the function of the elements of the language at its different levels . . .
> (Lacan, 1977:126)

The signified, on the other hand, consists of a diachronic set of discourses which exist in a historical relationship to the first network. Thus signifier and signified are not seen as parallel series, their relationship being determined by the differential relations between the series, but rather the signifier is welded onto *langue* and synchrony, while the signified is welded onto *parole* and diachrony. This means that the signifier does not represent the concept towards which the signifier points, since it now represents the uses to which language, in all its differential relations, is put.

Both Saussure and Jakobson claimed that language has two dimensions and Lacan accepts this. The first dimension is the paradigmatic, which enables the substitution of one word for another, while the second is the syntagmatic, which allows the combination of words to form a sentence or series of sentences. It was, of course, Jakobson (1963:63) who related these to the two features of poetry and rhetoric – metaphor and metonymy. Lacan draws on this insight to demonstrate the way in which the latent content of the dream, which for him constitutes repressed thoughts, is transformed into a different manifest content in Freudian dream-work. Paradigm/association/substitution/metaphor is one pole of language with which Lacan assimilates condensation – the process whereby different meanings are drawn together to occult a censored thought; while syntagm/combination/metonymy is the other pole with which he assimilates displacement, or the transposition of one term for another. The net effect is to transform language into a never-ending play of substitutions and combinations of signifiers, a play which denies the possibility of a safe resting place for any signifier: 'No signification can be sustained other than by reference to another signification' (1978:97). Thus signification involves the reference of one signifier to another, rather than in linking signifier and signified. Meaning is now produced, not by the signifier indicating the signified, but in the production of other meanings through the metaphoric and metonymic relations of the signifier with other signifiers. This sliding of the signifier relates to Lévi-Strauss' idea of the floating, signifier wherein re-ordering of the relations between signifiers and the production of new meanings are made possible. It is the mechanism whereby Lacan is able to conceptualise the manner in which dream-work occults, distorts and trans-forms meanings. Desire is assimilated to metonymy, involvement in the symbolic nature of language results in the permanent loss of unity with the Other. By passing through the defile of the signifier, need becomes desire, the endless process of displacement that is characteristic of metonymy. A parallel between the openness of language and humankind's incompleteness is created.

The most obvious consequence of this approach was that it undermined orthodox psychoanalysis, which claimed that its objective was to re-engage the patient with reality. But reality is undermined by the significance of a word deriving not from its associations, but from the fact that it is uttered by a subject. By undermining the entire issue of the subject's relationship with reality, that objective was dismissed. In asserting the primacy of the signifier over the signified, Lacan was returning to Freud's discussion of the 'talking cure' within which it was claimed that analysis was a never-ending process of revealing new layers of meaning within the unconscious.

As we have seen, the decentring of the subject involved an entire re-orientation of the philosophy of language. Rather than language being a reflection of thought, or even of society, as the Cartesian model would imply, for Lacan language is thought. Indeed language, culture and society are no longer seen as human creations, a consequence of humankind's attempt to shape his/her world. With humankind absent as creator they become 'the voice of no one', an impersonal circuit into which everyone has no choice but to be integrated. The only line of contact with Cartesian formulations is that humankind is socialised into language, culture, and society; but, as we have seen, it is a conception of socialisation far removed from the orthodox. Humankind is no longer a free entity or controlling force. The traditional oppositions between humankind and society, between culture and society, become redundant. The laws of culture and society are stabilised in language. The subject has to be discovered within discourse.

There is a recognition that language itself has a history in Lacan's work, new concepts being introduced into language throughout history. This is a theme we shall return to in discussing Foucault's work. Thus history becomes a process within which new ideas and new symbols inevitably come into existence. There is, of course, nothing new in this claim, it is found in the work of Marx and Hegel, but whereas they seek to explain this phenomenon, Lacan leaves aside any explanation. Indeed the absence of the centred subject makes explanation difficult.

Lacanian literary analysis treats literature, and thereby the text, as an instance of the symbolic structures which determine the patterns of conscious and unconscious thought, as an integral part of the symbolic order whose laws it shares. There is a repetition of symbolic reference systems, established literary models and narrative methods, as well as a variety of voices, often in contradiction or conflict, which are borrowed from extant ideologies and the forms of everyday speech. It cannot represent or reflect reality, but merely constitutes itself as a self-referential system so that 'language speaks of itself, its forms and its objects' (Macherey, 1978:58). It involves silences, much as in Althusser's sense of reading. The role of the analyst is to discover how such silences obscure the text's unconscious and to display the conflicts among the text's diverse voices.

It has been noted that Lacan did not preach any party ideology (Bannet, 1991:42), nor did he offer a solution for the subject in its position. In this respect his work can be seen as a cry against statist politics, and this anarchist strain can be found in a number of authors regarded as post-structuralist. In a sense this should not be surprising given that the decentring of the subject undermines the very basis of State legitimation. In this respect it is some distance removed from the Marxists and minority nationalists whose suspicion of the State is restricted to the existing form of State apparatus which will be replaced by an alternative form of State.

Lacan described society in terms of a 'culture of hate', involving a constant social struggle for power and prestige. It is the subject's imaginary identification with the Other without, and the Other within, that is responsible for this human condition of aggressiveness and destructiveness. The subject interjects images of others in establishing idealised self-images before re-projecting the self-image onto others. Conformity with the subject's idealised self-image leads to falling in love, a narcissistic investiture. More often the interpersonal relationships are based upon rivalry, competition and alienation. Since it is through identification with another that the subject grasps itself as an ego, another with more complete satisfaction is seen as a threat, as someone who deprives the subject of what s/he sees as his/her own. This can involve a deprivation of self-image. The aggressive tension of rivalry is integrated into every aspect of the functioning of mankind's imagination. In modern society it is all-pervasive, existing in humankind's exploitation of humankind, and in the struggle for power and prestige.

This begs the question of where social order, the ability to coexist, derives from. For Lacan it derives from the way imagination is overlaid by language because language is the basis of civilisation. The acquisition of language represents the introduction of law and harmonisation: 'the law of mankind is the law of language' (Lacan, 1966:150). This claim is premised on three grounds. First, words give permanence and regularity to human perceptions, which are otherwise transient. In an argument reminiscent of Locke, he argues that objects are perceived fleetingly by the imagination, whereas language allows objects to be present even in their absence: 'The word is a presence of absence which allows absence to be named' (Lacan, 1966:155). 'I' fixes the subject, making it permanent, and since language is a system of paired oppositions, with 'I' being known in reference to 'you', the coexistence of 'I' and 'you' is embodied in language as 'we' or 'us', thereby being a law of humankind.

Second, language is a pact among people. He states that although signifiers are constantly shifting, a 'signifier' can only name an object if people agree that it does. Yet he simultaneously insists that language is a completely arbitrary phenomenon, with different peoples agreeing to use different sounds to signify objects:

> Naming constitutes a pact by which two subjects agree at the same time on the recognition of the same object. If human subjects did not first name the major species (as in Genesis), if subjects did not agree on this recognition, there would be no world, even perceptually, which could be sustained for more than an instant.
>
> (Lacan, 1978:202)

Third, Lacan claims that there can be no law which is not embodied in language. He rejects the idea of a natural or intuitive law. This stance is reflected in the knowledge that who is permitted access to whom in human society relies on the availability of language for a descriptive intergenerational kinship system which gives each individual a clear position within it. Language fixes identities and relationships, marks taboos and operates the pact, all as a symbolic order.

This symbolic order facilitates human coexistence in allowing subjects to transcend the imaginary alienation referred to above, but in so doing it generates two further alienations. First there is the alienation from reality. As we have already seen, language does not coincide with reality in the orthodox Cartesian sense. Rather it is a self-referential system which, because of the particular means of signification, can generate connotations which are remote from human experience. Language involves 'an original murder of the thing' (Lacan, 1981:226). Language does not reflect reality, but creates it: 'It is the world of words which creates the world of things, which are first confused in the *hic et nunc* of everything in its becoming' (Lacan, 1966:155). As such it creates a cloak over nature and reality to the extent that they become invisible.

The second alienation derives from the impersonal order that is language. The subject's understanding and identity is no longer his/her own creation, but the product of that impersonal order external to the subject. While making exchanges between subjects possible, it simultaneously predetermines the nature of these exchanges. The subject is no longer a controlling authority. Naming procedures generate a position for the subject in the symbolic order, within culture and society. It is in this symbolic order that the subject's sexuality is determined:

> The subject finds his place in a pre-formed symbolic mechanism which lays down the law for sexuality. And this law no longer permits the subject to realise his sexuality except on the symbolic plane. This is the meaning of the Oedipus.
>
> (Lacan, 1981:191)

Whatever we are is predetermined by the possibilities of the symbolic order. Furthermore, language is allowing and confining. It allows the subject to state and thereby to recognise her/his desires and imaginary experiences, but these can only be expressed and recognised in terms of the concepts and words already in language. That which has not already been 'created' by words is repressed. The structure and significations of the symbolic order which exist beyond the subject, prior to it, and independently of its existence and experience, also lie beyond the real world of objects. Language determines the shape and content of thought; language is thought.

This order of language and things generates conformity and denies the existence of the individual so that 'the collective and the individual are the same thing' (Lacan, 1978:43). Furthermore, what we say and do is clearly governed by language, rather than being the product of the free, independent subject. This enslavement of the subject means that the orthodox view of a subject expressing him/herself through language is rejected; rather, language expresses itself through humankind. Signification may derive from the relation among signifiers in language, so that the meaning of words becomes apparent from their usage in different contexts, but meaning is not the consequence of the rational subject consciously manipulating signifiers. Drawing upon Lévi-Strauss, Lacan claims that this symbolic order also rests in the unconscious, which he conceives of as a mechanism which repeats that which has been repressed. Clearly the conscious subject is a slave of the symbolic order, whereas the unconscious is a slave of symbols which function according to their own peculiar laws. The conscious subject may ensure the transmission of the symbolic order, thereby guaranteeing its reproduction and ensuring historical continuity, but the unconscious subject does likewise. Thus 'the collective and the individual are the same thing' and the unconscious I 'the discourse of the Other'.

However, the conscious and the unconscious cannot speak simultaneously. Indeed they are in constant struggle for priority. The resultant alienation is inescapable. While the ego is an alienated form of being, it is essential if the subject is to have any form; the subject's desire is alienated and realised in the Other. Language alienates humankind from reality, but it allows them to create their own world, a world of culture and society. Without language, intersubjectivity, and thereby communication and co-existence, are impossible. The idea of the subject as a unique, independent sovereign ego was a creation of the Enlightenment. It has become a slave of an all-pervasive social mechanism which rules him/her through the manipulation of language. Interjecting the various social philosophies which sought to convey some semblance of humanity, Lacan claimed that there is no difference between exploiter and exploited, since they are both equally subject to the economy as a whole. There is no future golden age as the Enlightenment doctrine of progress has claimed, there is only a resignation to the status quo.

Conclusion

The important work of Lacan, his *Ecrits*, was published in 1966, the same year as the publication of Foucault's *The Order of Things*. In the previous year Althusser had published both *For Marx* and *Reading Capital*, and in the following year Derrida published no fewer than three books. When we recognise that the initial thrust of FDA came with the publication of Pécheux's work on content analysis and the theory of discourse in 1967, and perhaps from Achard's work on science and ideology in the same year, the association becomes clearer.

It is evident that the work of Saussure gave rise to the structuralism that is so evident in the work of Lévi-Strauss and Lacan. The former derived the Saussurean influence from Jakobson, attempting to employ linguistic principles in developing a new approach for anthropology. Lacan similarly drew upon Saussure's concepts in seeking to rewrite psychoanalysis. Both of them can be said to present a position in which the mind enters the social world constructed from structural codes which are claimed to define society. Thus, there is some basis for considering Lacan's consideration of Freud's Oedipal phase side by side with Lévi-Strauss' claim that the incest taboo is the driving force of human culture. Lévi-Strauss' culture is akin to Lacan's symbolic, with language playing a central role in both. In this respect they reject the human/nature opposition of modernism.

Culler (1976:76) makes the following perceptive observation concerning how language involves the unconscious:

> I know a language (in the sense that I can produce and understand new utterances, tell whether a sequence is in fact a sentence of my language, etc.) yet I do not know what I know. I know a language, yet I need a linguist to explain to me precisely what it is that I know. The concept of the unconscious connects and makes sense of these two facts and opens a space of exploration. Linguistics, like psychology and a sociology of collective representations, will explain my actions by setting out in detail the implicit knowledge which I myself have not brought to consciousness.

In a move reminiscent of Lévi-Strauss, he proceeds to draw the work of Freud, Saussure and Durkheim together by linking the rules of language, societal norms and the mechanisms of a psychical economy.

In some respects structuralism is a label which suggests more than the literal quest for universal properties since it invariably leads to the labelling of individuals as members of this or that school of structuralism. Among those who reacted to being labelled in this way was Michel Foucault, who objected to being called a structuralist because of his reluctance to be pinned down to a determinate position along the ideological or intellectual spectrum. Indeed this is entirely understandable when one considers the eclectic consequences of many of Foucault's ideas, and his comments about the modernist creation of disciplines at the turn of the nineteenth century. In many respects it is easier to think of Foucault as a relativist whose main concern is with the shifting dimension of thought in history, and of the implications of such shifts for society. Yet there is no denying that his work, at least in its early stages, constitutes the general thrust that was evident in what has become known as post-structuralism. Similarly the work of Althusser, despite its explicit link to Marxism, also displays a continuity with the work discussed in this chapter. For example, it is from Lacan that Althusser derived his structural theory of the subject, a theme which was of crucial importance to his overall thesis. The influence of Althusser and Foucault on FDA was paramount and much of the history of FDA revolves around the tensions which derived from the differences between their respective positions. A consideration of their respective works is essential.

3

POST-STRUCTURALISM

Gadet (1989a) makes the point that while Lacan shares the decentring of the subject with Althusser and Foucault, the latter two share a distinctive position in that they do not seek to directly integrate the work of Saussure into their respective perspectives.[1] She adds that in their work the structuralist qualification is metaphoric. She advocates that their work be thought of in terms of a structuralism within human sciences rather than having a direct reference to structuralist linguistics. Structuralism strictly defined – as deriving from Saussurean linguistics via the work of Jakobson and Hjemslev – has had little influence on their work. This is explicitly expressed in the 1968 edition of Althusser's *Lire le Capital*, and is also implicit in Foucault's work. However, we should recognise that the division between structuralism and post-structuralism refers to the orientation towards language and the subject (Henry, 1990). For structuralists such as Barthes or Lévi-Strauss the transferal of the concepts of linguistics without fundamental re-elaboration leads to the retention of the idea of human nature as a specific object and as an explanatory principle (Gadet, 1989a:35). In this respect structuralism remains entrenched in Enlightenment philosophy. The post-structuralists, and here Lacan is located side by side with Althusser and Foucault, reject such a conception of subject, and their 'anti-humanism' involves the abandonment of the modernist position involving the transcendental subject, leading to what Ricoeur (1974) refers to as a form of 'Kantianism minus the transcendental subject'. This is not sufficient a reason to label their position as post-modernist. Yet, as we shall see, Althusser's adherence to the Marxist problematic does raise questions about the extent to which he lies outside of the modernist paradigm.[2]

Having thus clarified the shift to post-structuralism and its relationship to Saussurean linguistics, I would like to consider the work of Althusser and Foucault, who played such a seminal role in the emergence and development of FDA. However, before proceeding to a consideration of their work, it is necessary to consider influences other than those associated with the philosophy of language, and specifically the influence of Gaston Bachelard and Georges Canguilhem, both of whom played a central role in the moulding of the burst of intellectual activity in France during the 1960s.[3] They were particularly important in that their theory of science was the basis on which

Althusser sought to establish the scientific nature of Marx's later work, and, in many respects, it is the work of Bachelard and Canguilhem which is the basis of the similarity between the work of Althusser and Foucault (Lecourt, 1978). Their neo-positivist and anti-empiricist influence on the history, epistemology and philosophy of science argued against the disassociation of epistemology and the history of science, while also refuting the claim that science was a process of continuous progress.

Bachelard and the philosophy of science

The contribution of the historian of science Gaston Bachelard to post-war French social science is little recognised outside of France. His ideas have been important in the production of two concepts generally associated with others – the epistemological break and the problematic of a science. Both of these concepts, through the influence of Althusser and Foucault, have constituted important contributions to the development of FDA.

Bachelard's main concern, one which is evident when the concepts of epistemological break and problematic are placed side by side, was with how new theoretical discourses relate to the formulation of new questions, this requiring either a new vocabulary adequate to these new questions, or the use of existing terminology to express the new questions, this severely modifying and changing the vocabulary in expressing the heuristic. His work, among others, has contributed to the critique of the eighteenth-century programme of establishing a social science on the model of the natural sciences. The view of science common to empiricists and anti-naturalists which involves the accumulation of isolated facts, or require quantification methods for its own dynamic, has been undermined, and the focus has shifted to the importance of the elaboration of the concepts which precede and guide empirical research. For Bachelard, philosophies of science were both effects of innovations in science and obstacles to further advance. Furthermore, as Machado (1989:16) emphasises, he rejected the universalism of science based upon universal validity, focusing rather upon local or regional features of scientificity.

Perhaps the clearest link between Bachelard's ideas and those of the post-structuralists is in his claim that the identity of a theory lies not in the intentions of the theory's author, nor in any specific presuppositions which the theory involves, but in its structure. That is, science has no object outside its own activity. Knowledge, working on its 'object', does not work on the real object, but on a peculiar raw material which might be termed ideology, intuition or representation, the scientific concept being the outcome of the process. It is this that has led to the claim that science constitutes merely another discourse, unrelated to the epistemological quest for truth and reality, a claim which Norris (1996:170) suggests derives from a misreading of Bachelard's work, which sought to distinguish between two realms of thought – pre-scientific and scientific. The point I wish to pursue here is the importance of Bachelard's work for Althusser's science/ideology distinction and for Foucault's emphasis upon the epistemological break. This will be followed by a consideration of how these sets of work, in turn, influenced FDA.

Clearly there is an anti-rationalist bent to Bachelard's ideas which some (Benton, 1984:24–25) have taken to involve a struggle between common sense and objectivity. More important from our point of view is Bachelard's claim that theoretical concepts cannot be changed or modified piecemeal, but that change must involve the entire theoretical system if breakthroughs are to be made. The reason for this is that the concepts and problems of the theoretical structure cannot be identified apart from their position in the totality. Not only are concepts within the structure interdependent, but they determine what problems can be presented while excluding other problems.

The emergence of a new structure does not involve the disappearance of what has been displaced. There remain 'epistemological obstacles' which restrict scientific development. They include natural and common-sense tendencies of thought – 'animism', 'realism', and also philosophies which link scientific innovations to natural tendencies of the mind. Such philosophies may appear as universal, but pertain only to phases of the history of each science. Furthermore, any philosophy must negate all previous philosophies in order to survive. It must not establish a fixed ontological system which will obstruct further transformation. Evidently science carries its own internal dynamic which is open ended.

Bachelard explicitly rejects empiricism and realism in his claim for a self-generating scientific practice. This leads to a denial of scientific objectivity as the correspondence between the concepts of theory and some external reality which is independent of theory.

Canguilhem on science as discourse

Bachelard's successor at the Sorbonne in 1955 was Georges Canguilhem, who continued his predecessor's work on the philosophy of science. He also continued the work which they shared on what Deleuze (1989:189) refers to as 'sociopolitical research on the modes of rationality in power'. In his work on the epistemology of medical knowledge (Canguilhem, 1966) he investigated the notion of norm, and sought to demonstrate the fragile relationship between the rational and the irrational, in a manner characteristic of Nietzsche, and, subsequently, Foucault. In so doing he pursued Bachelard's claim that it is not possible to discover the origin of a norm, and in this respect his work preceded the recent concern of the sociology of deviance. More importantly he heralded the current focus on the demise of modernism, rejecting the evolutionist nature of progress, especially with reference to the relationship between science and reason.

In his work on the construction of medical knowledge Canguilhem opposed a Nietzschean perspective in favour of a directly historical discourse in which he investigated the conceptual and institutional configurations which render possible any delimitation of the norm or the pathological. In so doing he rejected the Hegelian dialectic and the associated idea of historic progress, claiming that science was responsible for creating and supporting both ideas. In developing such arguments he crossed disciplinary boundaries in order to retrieve the epistemological coherence of a specific period of what he called the transversal break. It was from this concept of the transversal break that Foucault develop the concept of episteme, which was a central pivot of his book *Les mots et les choses*, a work which Canguilhem favourably reviewed in 1967. This is merely one example of the direct influence which his work had on that of Michel Foucault. Indeed, Foucault refers specifically to Canguilhem in his condemnation of the French media for ignoring an entire body of important work in their insistence on pursuing the importance of Lacanian psychoanalysis.

By questioning the place of discourse in the constitution of ideas Canguilhem realised a fundamental displacement of the traditional approach to research on origins. In this respect he touched upon the establishment of a correlation between discourse and the institutional space which allowed its emergence and which constituted its condition. This work on the conditions of enonciation of scientific knowledge was the founding axis of Foucault's work on the clinic, punishment, etc., all of which reflects a refusal to recognise the distinction between science and non-science, between science and ideology. This led Canguilhem to describe Foucault's work as being entirely unconcerned with the norms of scientificity (1967:612). Foucault in turn credits Canguilhem with developing a displacement in French history of science by refusing to discuss science in terms of continuity and development, while reshaping the theme of discontinuity and revolutions, thereby forcing a focus upon the relationship between discursive and non-discursive practices.

Clearly Canguilhem broke with the cumulative conception of scientific progress, claiming that the internal frontiers of scientific knowledge involved an incessant displacement, and a successive re-shaping. Thus the history of science was not a programmatic elucidation of a progress of truth, understood as the progressive unwinding of truth; rather, it involves aponies and reverses. 'For Canguilhem, error is the permanent risk around which the history of life and becoming human is wrapped' (Foucault, 1985:14). Through his research on the constitution and validation of concepts he discussed the relationship between the elaboration of knowledge of diverse sciences and that which, in their institutional reality, is social. He also had an influence on Althusser: on the one hand in his setting the ground for the attempt to revive Marxist concepts, and on the other in his reflection on the pathological status of science and the validity of concepts.

His contribution to the Lacanian break was through his anti-psychologism. He sought to deconstruct psychology in order to show that its knowledge was not cumulative, and in so doing he revealed the incompatible paradigms which it contained. It was this which led to the anti-history in Foucault's archaeological approach. He also took an ethical stance in asking whether psychology was working for science or for the police. His work was a mix of questioning of social order, history of science and moral consciousness, and there is little doubt about the importance of his influence in French intellectual circles at the end of the 1950s.

Althusser's anti-humanism

Bachelard's ideas were fundamental for the development of the work of Luis Althusser, one of his students. In turn, Althusser's work was influential not only for the development of FDA but also for general Marxist arguments in France during the 1960s. His primary objective was to establish Marxism as the scientific discipline, while simultaneously undermining the canons of orthodox science. This is the direct link to Bachelard's history of science and the critique of the modelling of the social sciences upon pure science. Althusser argued that humanist Marxism had to be abandoned in favour of scientific Marxism, which was to be established by recourse to epistemology and the philosophy of science. Thus Marxist concepts had to be authenticated as 'scientific', or they had to be rejected as ideological. Thus his work involved a denial of phenomenological and existentialist Marxism.

It is in the rejection of humanist Marxism, which Althusser regarded as Marxism's prehistory, that he resorted to Bachelard's ideas concerning the epistemological break which facilitated the transition to scientific Marxism. Althusser argued that Marx's early work, which focused upon the alienation of the human subject in the capital–labour relation, was ideology and not science. The transition to his scientific work required an epistemological break which occurred with the writing of *The German Ideology* and *Thesis on Feuerbach*. Since history was a process without a subject, and since the subject is constitutive of ideology, viewing the relations of production as a series of places occupied by subjects served to transform the ideological nature of early Marx into the science of his later work. Clearly this is an important development in that it moves away from some of the functionalist positions associated with much Marxist argument.

The concept of problematic is a highly influential development in that it refers to the co-existence of incompatible theoretical schemes in a single text, while also referring to what underlies and determines the questions posed and answers given in any text. More importantly, perhaps, it leads to a discussion of what questions can and cannot be asked. It is a step towards developing a particular technique of text analysis since it involves a distinctive technique of reading. This should not be surprising, and Althusser's theory of reading rests on a denial of the empirical epistemology in which the meaning of a text is immediately accessible – it simply has to be read.

In developing the concept of problematic Althusser was emphasising that theory was not a manifestation of social interests nor of the superstructure but, rather, it had its own autonomy. Theory is a thought process with its own laws which no reference to the real process of society or history can invalidate or justify. As such, he suggested that the production of theory was describable within the same terms as economic production. Thus he proposed a Generalities I or the raw materials of theoretical practice which involved the pre-existing theoretical discourses from which the discourse in question begins. These included concepts, whether they be scientific or ideological concepts. He added:

> By practice in general I shall mean any process of transformation of a determinate given raw material into a determinate product, a transformation affected by a determinate human labour, using determinate means (of production).
>
> (Althusser, 1969:166)

The Generalities II refers to the labour – the means and forces of labour – the axiomatic and methods of a science. It involves the set of questions, often unstated and implicit, which imposed its general unity or problematic on the discourse in question. Generalities III is the end product – the knowledge that is produced by the action of Generalities II on Generalities I.

It should already be evident that for Althusser the process of knowledge takes place entirely in thought. The thought-object of a discourse must be distinguished from its truth-object – it is the features of Generalities I that constitute the thought-object. This anti-empiricism claims that the raw materials of science already exist in a conceptual or propositional form.

The distinction between science and ideology is also important for the Althusserian project. Each has a different problematic. The scientific problematic is open and capable of infinite discovery. On the other hand the problematic of the ideological discourse is limited, so that predetermined answers result from predetermined questions. This is an important point for FDA – how a problematic determines what can be said, what kinds of questions can be presented, and what kinds of solutions derived. It is an orientation we shall return to in our discussion of Foucault's conception of power. What it underlines is Althusser's adoption of a structuralist position which he distinguishes from that of Lévi-Strauss while emphasising its anti-historicism.

Yet his retention of a conception of science implies that he simultaneously accepted that it is possible to escape from the closed world of the ideological. But in so doing he rejects the empirical claim that the scientific nature of knowledge rests on the relationship between subject and object. Theoretical discourses can only be validated by reference to their internal criteria and not by reference to some external conception of knowledge or reality. Thus we have the following statement:

By what mechanism does the process of knowledge, which takes place
entirely in thought, produce the cognitive appropriation of its real
object, which exists outside thought in the real world?

(Althusser, 1968:56)

His answer is to seek guarantees for the scientificity of theory external to
that theory. However, as I have already indicated, this is not possible because
of the claim that knowledge rests on the relation between real objects and
thought-objects, between subject and object. This approach, which is
characteristic of all bourgeois philosophy, must therefore be rejected because it
is ideological. Thus, for Althusser, the issue of ideology resides in the subject/
object relationship.

It is essential that we pursue the Althusserian conception of ideology because
of the extent to which it has played a central role in the development of
FDA, which, for some of its practitioners, became a form of ideological deconstruction. His understanding of ideology relates to Spinoza's distinction
between knowledge of imagination and knowledge that derives from concepts
of ideas that are theoretically elaborated (Norris, 1991). In this respect it is
important to recognise that Althusser saw Spinoza as opposing Hegel. Also,
Spinoza's distinction of knowledges bears no little relevance to the desire
to separate the proto-philosophical work of the eighteenth century from the
explicitly political objective of State formation towards the end of that century,
thereby disentangling proto social science from political practice, the former
being that which, through the use of reason to discover reality, leads to the
inevitable development of the good life. Thus, he emphasised that theory
was impossible unless it could break with received ideas and beliefs. This in
turn bears some relationship to Spinoza's suspicion of language in his claim
that 'natural' language is a source of confused or inadequate ideas, capable
of correction via conceptual critique. Indeed, such a position is akin to the
French faith in languages of reason through standardisation and language
planning, a central feature of the formation of the nation-state, and it is difficult
not to conceive of Althusser's goal as a re-explication of the eighteenth-century
French drive for a rational society and polity in the name of Marxism.

It would appear that for Althusser ideology is an essential feature of all
societies:

Ideology (as a system of mass representation) is indispensable in any
society if men are to be formed, transformed and equipped to respond
to the demands of their conditions of existence.

(Althusser, 1969:235)

The 'empiricist conception of knowledge' (Althusser, 1968) Althusser locates
in the religious claim for appearance as a manifestation of God's presence.
During the seventeenth century this idea is transformed, while retaining the

basic idea that the results of knowledge exist as its essence. All that is required in order to discover this essence is to look beneath the surface. This complicity between subject and object is produced within ideology. Thus he describes the production of ideology in terms of how the formulation of a problem is a manifestation of the generation of a solution which already exists outside of the process of knowledge; it allows the solution to recognise itself. In this respect knowledge becomes the recognition of a difference between essence and phenomenon inscribed in the real. The issue of recognition relates to that of causality. While:

> Ideology is a matter of the lived relation between men and their world . . . In ideology men do indeed express, not the relation between them and their condition of existence, but the way they live the relation between them and their conditions of existence: this presupposes both a real relation and an 'imaginary', 'lived' relation. Ideology then, is the expression of the relation between men and their 'world', that is, the (overdetermined) unity of the real relation and the imaginary relation between them and their conditions of existence. In ideology the real relation is inevitably invested in the imaginary relation, a relation that expresses a will (conservative, conformist, reformist or revolutionary), a hope or a nostalgia, rather than describing a reality.
>
> (Althusser, 1968:233–234)

For both Spinoza and Althusser reality is a matter of lived experience so that it is not possible to remove undesirable beliefs through an appeal to reason. Rather, an appeal to criticism or theoretical practice can work on the given materials of ideology in order to produce a knowledge or adequately theorised concepts by reference to ideology and how it operates. Thus modes of existence should be weighed against immanent criteria in relation to their 'possibilities', in liberty, in creativity without any appeal to transcendental values.

The importance of Spinoza vis-à-vis anti-humanism pertains to his opposition to Hobbes and the manner in which this leads to a novel conception of society. According to Hobbes, norms were imposed on society by the State as laws in order to protect humankind against itself, in order that the right to life be sustained. That is, humankind was essentially divisive and aggressive, their existence being premised upon the emotive, and its link to the instinctive, associated with the state of nature. The civilising force was a society which derived from reason and rational calculation, a society constructed out of calculation and goodwill from which a doctrine of civil rights in harmony with an administrative State can emerge. It involved a voluntary transfer of power on the part of all members of the social body in creating a sovereign power, recovering, through its own calculation, the instinct of domination relevant to all humankind in the form of an absolute obligation. This idea of the transcendence of the norm led to the disitinction between the law of nature and natural law as sovereign law, something that was staunchly rejected by Spinoza, who rejected the distinction between the state of nature and the state of society. Spinoza maintained that within society it is always nature which continues to operate in putting the same laws and passions into play. Without nature the meaning of laws would turn against itself, putting in place the dialectic of a counter-power. Thus power is not necessarily defined by reference to domination. To live in society according to norms does not mean that the law of nature has to be replaced by a law of reason. Rather, the goal is one of managing and regulating the relations of force which determine all inter-individual relations through a free and necessary play of effects. Hobbes was preoccupied with establishing an anthropological politics based upon a theory of human passion which allows releasing the fear of death, which he saw as the fundamental motivation which determined all the actions of human-kind and which gave law its fundamental principles, leading to the juridicial conception of power. For Spinoza, on the other hand, this could only lead to the development of a nature that was totally opposed to *the* nature, leading him to develop a natural theory of emotions in general, claiming that everything, including human beings, is immersed in nature, where they follow its laws, of which they themselves are the expression. Norm derived from necessity and not from imposition, and law takes its force of being from the substance.

It is hardly surprising therefore that for Althusser it is through ideology that the individual becomes a feature of the social world:

> The category of the subject is only constitutive of all ideology in so far as all ideology has the function (which defines it) of 'constituting' concrete individuals as subjects.
>
> (Althusser, 1971:159)

That is, the subject can only appear as a feature of ideology, and therefore cannot pre-exist it. Ideology is not conceived before the act, it is the act. It becomes the system of representations through which people live out their relationship to the historical world; it is a system with its own logic and rigour while also being an organic part of every society. In this sense he moves towards a Lacanian position in thinking of ideology as structures which impose on people. The preconceived, thinking, rational subject characteristic of most sociology disappears. The appearance of the subject is achieved by the process of interpolation wherein the individual is treated as an autonomous agent. The individual is thereby led to believe that s/he controls the situation, that reality exists for him/her. Conversely, for Althusser the truth is that every individual is merely a support for the relations of production. It is here that we recognise causality. Ideology serves to obscure the reality which derives from the economic order and, in this respect, the function of ideology is to reproduce the economic order. In some respects what has taken place is that an answer has been found to the problem of conspiracy in Marxism. Yet the structuralist strain in Althusser seeks to remove the concept of ideology from a simplistic form of false consciousness. This is done by implying that ideology has a material existence which determines the subject, and by simultaneously divorcing the concept from its conspiratorial associations in which the preconceived subject is responsible for its creation. Ideology is no longer a false representation of reality since its source is no longer the subject but material reality itself. Ideology does not project reality but, rather, the relationship between humankind and its reality. Yet there is also the insistence on the role of the material order, and in this respect, as we shall see, there is a fundamental division with reference to those who express an interest in ideological discourse.

Althusser has been accused of failing to reconcile the two perspectives according to which, ideology is seen, on the one hand, as a feature of the reproduction of class relations within capitalism, and, on the other hand, as linked to a subjectivity which has a distinctively Lacanian orientation. Thus the functional conception of the former fails to relate to the subjectivity of the latter. It is implied that the functionalism of the reproduction argument fails to accommodate resistance and struggle, leading to a mechanical conception of order within capitalism. Furthermore, he also failed to release the understanding of society from the preoccupation with social class to the exclusion of other dimensions of inequality. This despite his attempt to redress the former complaint in his postscript to his essay on ideology (Althusser, 1970).

Althusser's reference to subjectivity, on the other hand, does move away from the Marxist preoccupation with consciousness. He seeks to integrate psychoanalysis with Marxism, claiming that ideology represents the imaginary relationship of individuals to their real conditions of existence, implying that some form of 'real' existence does exist, and going on to claim that ideology always exists in material apparatuses, thereby making ideological practices material. That is, ideology is conceived of as embedded in the practices and rituals of apparatuses such as schools, religious institutions, the family, etc. The subject is the constitutive category of all ideology. As such, the function of ideology is to actualise the subject's recognition of itself as a subject, as a feature of common sense. Recognition is therefore vital where both the self and others construct the subject. The absence of an already constituted subject means that there is no point of origin, merely the constitution and the constant reconstitution. It is here that the concept of interpolation becomes crucial. It involves what he refers to as 'hailing': if I am walking down the street and someone shouts 'hey Taff', my turning round is the effect of both the confirmation of the subject in ideology and my own confirmation of my own self-recognition as 'Taff'. The signification process has its effect.

In a manner reminiscent of Gramsci, Althusser refers to ideology as the 'cement' of society, implying that it is an essential ingredient of all forms of society in that it ensures that certain social tasks are fulfilled. Ideology is a structural feature of any society. Since ideology is not an ideal existence but only a material existence, it 'exists in an apparatus and its practice or practices'. All individuals occupy ideology by involvement in certain practices within specific ideological apparatuses. Thus 'there is no practice except by and in an ideology', while 'there is no ideology except by the subject and for subjects' (Althusser, 1971:159). It appears that everything but the material is ideological. It was this insight, in his far-reaching article on ideological State apparatuses, which had such a profound influence upon the early stages of FDA.

None the less, the materialism of Marxism is retained and it is here that we recognise the appearance of agency. The usual criticism of Althusser in this respect is that he has reduced agency to structure, or agents to bearers of structures, a problem of all realist interpretations of Marxism (Urry, 1981). Yet the retention of Marxism demanded a materialist orientation. Lenin (1947:250) stated: 'it is this sole unconditional recognition of nature's existence outside the mind and perception of man that distinguishes dialectical materialism from relativist agnosticism and idealism'. This distinction between materialism and idealism is the crux of the division which has been at the core of FDA, one which we will encounter in the discussion of Pêcheux's work that follows.

In his early work, Althusser had distinguished between Hegel's tendency to see everything as a reflection of some basic principle, and Marxism's tendency to view the social formation as a series of contradictory relations which derived from specific determinations, each one with its own autonomy. Thus political and ideological institutions or national traditions were not to be seen as mere passive manifestations of the development of the economic order. He claimed that the economic operates on the social order within a process of interaction with the various instances which constitute the social whole, and is only determinant when there is an overlap of all of the effects of the various instances. Such an overdetermination, he claimed, was universal.

Such a stance allowed Althusser to deny the mechanical economism and reductionism of Stalin, which claimed that the relations of production and the superstructure were at the mercy of developments of productive forces. Indeed, such a position allowed him to explain Stalinism in that it allowed him to deny the economist argument that if the economy were the sole determining factor, then a revolution in the structure would result in the immediate modification of the existing superstructure and especially of the ideologies. Not only would they survive or re-create, but the new society created by the revolution could generate the reactivation of older elements through the new superstructure and specific circumstances. This argument became the source of considerable friction within the French Communist Party.

The idea of a reified consciousness which focuses upon the philosophy of the subject is rejected by Althusser on account of its assumption concerning the existence of some human essence which is somehow alienated from its true being. There is a distinct anti-humanism in Althusser's rejection of this essential humanity. Indeed his understanding of historical materialism rejects any sense of class consciousness. Rather he draws upon the concept of problematic discussed above in claiming that all thought occurs with reference to the unconscious problematic to which it relates. It is this problematic, including the silences, semi-silences and elisions, which limits what the human subject is able to conceive and express. Thus questions which can be presented within any problematic are already answered in their presentation.

There is an evident overlap between these views and those of Foucault, which we will discuss presently. However, there is also a link to the work of Nietzsche, from whom much of Foucault's work also derived, and also, of course, to that of Spinoza. As we shall see, Nietzsche argued that human action constituted a form of fiction in that it presumed the existence of a pre-formed, autonomous, rational human agent, capable of operating on firmly grounded beliefs and assumptions in a rational manner. The incompatibility of action and reflection which follows from this means that 'true' conditions of existence are inevitably excluded from consciousness at the point of action. The transforming of a human into a subject occurs only as a result of a repression of the forces which were responsible for making it. Similarly, for Althusser, all action occurs within ideology. Indeed, as should already be evident, it is ideology that is responsible for creating the practical social agent. Ideology now becomes clearly expressed as occupying the realm of social practice, rather than being some entity that determines practices. The problem of the absence of the autonomous subject is resolved by the claim that the subject is the project of a structure which is repressed in the moment of 'subjectification'. On the other hand, he would not go as far as Nietzsche in claiming that action involves a total ignorance of its enabling conditions, since that would deny the possibility of any theoretically informed practice. His position is that theoretical understanding is operationalised through the 'lived fictions' of the actor. The key feature of ideology is the misrecognition of the self as a result of the 'imaginary' dimensions of human existence, a clear return to Lacan's discussion of the mirror stage, where a child sees itself as both its image in a mirror and the body within the mirror, with the subject and object gliding in and out of each other. Thus ideology is understood as 'a representation of the imaginary relationships of individuals to their real conditions of existence'. In expressing how they live the relation between them and their conditions of existence, people presuppose the existence of both a real relation and an imaginary, 'lived' relation. However, in ideology the real relation is invested in the imaginary relation. It is through ideology that the subject views the world as natural, orientated to itself, as something that is there to be taken by the subject who feels part of a 'reality'. It is through ideology that the human subject is interpolated by society, creating the illusion that society cannot exist without it. As with the infant who believes that when s/he disappears, the world also disappears, so also society would disappear if the human subject disappeared. Thus the subject is hailed from among the masses of people, and is transformed into an individual subject.

As a consequence society is reduced to a collection of 'structures' and 'regions' of which the human subject is merely a bearer. More importantly perhaps, it is claimed (Eagleton, 1991:146) that Althusser shares with Foucault the metaphysical closure wherein subjectivity becomes a form of self-incarceration, thereby making the issue of political resistance obscure.

For Althusser, ideology is merely one of three instances, the other two being the political and the economic. Thus, not everything is ideological, and there is an extra-discursive materiality. The ideological State apparatuses of family, church, State, media, etc. function to equip subjects with the form of consciousness that is necessary in order to participate within material production. Thus there appears to be an inherent reflection thesis concerning the relationship between ideology and the economic order, a thesis which reduces the former to the latter. However, in claiming that each of these instances is autonomous, Althusser succeeds in veering between an economism of ideology which involves the reductionism alluded to above, and an idealism of ideology which seems to suggest that ideology is disconnected from social life.

The strength of Althusser's argument lies in the manner in which he referred to ideology as the medium for the production of the human subject. Ideology ceases to be a matter of 'ideas', becoming something which operates without the knowledge of any pre-existing author. In sociological terms it involves a series of material practices or rituals which are embedded in material institutions. Here it is the inspiration of Gramsci that is evident. This insistence on the relevance of concrete practices and institutions – the materiality of ideology – was influential in the early developments of FDA, but the focus on ideology as meaning, which was played down by Althusser, was also a central concern of FDA. Ideology becomes akin to lived experience and, as such, it is eternal, being a structure essential for all historical societies. The Hegelian evolutionist argument wherein ideology is a manifestation of the increased complexity of social life which prevents everyday consciousness from grasping its essence, leads to a claim for the need for an imaginary model of social life, and is the very basis of the claim for the dialectic reasoning of philosophy. It is also the basis of the claim that a 'myth' of society is necessary – Hegel's 'mythology of Reason'. Again we find Althusser conforming with this view in which ideology adapts individuals to their social functions through the provision of a model, albeit an imaginary model.

It is not that language and meaning were ignored by Althusser, but they did not become the focus of his work. In pursuing the relation between language, ideology and meaning, Althusser claimed that by reference to theoretical discourse:

> the meaning of words . . . is not fixed by their ordinary usage but by the relation between theoretical concepts within a conceptual system. It is these relations that assign to words, designating concepts, their theoretical meaning. The peculiar difficulty of theoretical

75

terminology pertains, then, to the fact that its conceptual meaning must always be discerned behind the usual meaning of the word, and is always different from the latter.

(Quoted in Norris, 1996:145)

This conception is not too far removed from the concept of discursive formation that Michel Pécheux develops within FDA, adopting a concept that is more familiar by reference to Foucault. I have already referred above to how Althusser also refers to the concept of reading and problematic and how these relate to knowledge. He refers to the application of the theoretical system of any work to 'certain terms of their discourse', etc. This operation reveals some '"blanks", "plays on words", lacunae, inadequacies which rectification can then reduce' (quoted in Norris, 1996:147). Clearly he saw knowledge in terms of the relationship between discourse and the construction of meaning. It is from this understanding that FDA commences.

Foucault and discourse

There is little doubt that the author who has adopted Saussureanism and transformed the Cartesian link between subject and object most radically is Michel Foucault. Yet Gadet (1989a:35) suggests that Foucault makes little attempt to acknowledge the role of Saussure in his work. None the less Foucault's influence on FDA has been greater than any other, to the extent that, even if it is not possible to think of FDA as the Foucaultian methodology, it is Foucault's work more than that of any other post-structuralist which has been of paramount importance for FDA. However, this methodology or 'instruments of analysis' has been employed to resolve diverse problems including those of Marxism, structuralism, phenomenology, existentialism and critical theory (Tavor Bannet,1989:95). Not of course that Foucault developed a coherent method of discourse analysis in the usual sense. Indeed Courtine (1981:40) explicitly claims that FDA represents an attempt to put 'Foucault's perspective to work'. What Foucault did do was to show that discourse analysis was much more than linguistic analysis pure and simple in the sense of trying to indicate which sentences might be grammatically possible. Rather, his focus was upon the systems of rules which make the appearance of certain statements rather than others possible in particular settings, at particular historical conjunctures.

It must be recognised that Foucault's work is by no means uniform and that there are different orientations to his work during his career. There is a distinction between his archaeological work and his genealogical work, while his final work involves a reflection upon the entire trajectory of his previous work. Some point out that his initial work lacked the radical thrust of his later work. However, it is accepted that even this early work fits into the tradition of Canguilhem and Bachelard involving a critical philosophy. After 1966 his work becomes much more political and focuses increasingly upon the issue of power. Throughout there was an attack on the centred subject, rationality and on Husserlian phenomenology. His focus upon 'man as subject' was his contribution to theoretical anti-humanism. Rorty also claims that there is a difference between the way in which North Americans have deployed Foucault's work and the way in which it has been interpreted in France. The former tend to define autonomy in purely human terms without recourse to human law. It is a Foucaultianism purged of its essential Nietzscheanism and is more in keeping with Dewey's liberalism. In contrast, French Foucaultianism focuses upon the Nietzscheanism of his work, wherein autonomy involves thinking the inhuman and where the political is an inherent anarchism. What does transcend his work is a rejection of the universal in favour of the local. Whereas society is universal, the universal explains nothing – it is there to be explained. It is this point and its relationship to the possibility of resorting to his work by reference to amethodological discourse which I return to in the final chapter.

Perhaps the best place to begin a discussion of the work of Foucault is by prefacing it with a discussion of Nietzsche. His influence is evident in what Foucault has referred to as a 'suspicion of language' that he claims is characteristic of Western civilisation. That is, there is a claim, most evident perhaps in the Marxist view of ideology, that somehow language does not 'say exactly what it says', that there are hidden meanings to be encountered and interpreted. This theme of a 'suspicion of language' is typical of that aspect of Nietzsche's work which Deleuze (1962:142) characterises as 'the dawn of a counter-culture.' However, having introduced Nietzsche into the discussion, it is necessary to state that Foucault's 'instruments of analysis' is divisible into two parts (Deleuze, 1972:41). The first method is essentially synchronic and revolves around the interrelationship of elements which are centred upon typological identities. This derives from the work of Bachelard, Canguilhem, Heidegger and Riemann. The second method, with which the first interlocks, derives from Nietzsche, and is essentially diachronic, beginning with the present in a search for historical continuities, what Foucault referred to as 'the history of systems of thought'.

For Nietzsche, humankind was trapped within language, there being no knowledge beyond language. There are no facts in the positivistic sense, merely interpretations, this perspectivism leading to what was an outrageous attack upon objectivity. It was this claim which lay behind his critique of Christianity, science and socialism, a position reminiscent of the post-modern refutation of the grand narrative. Here Nietzsche was denying the possibility of achieving a total and absolute view of the world. Not only is truth denied, but truth is equated with falsehood. This position was accompanied by an attack on philosophy in general, claiming that the history of philosophy was nothing more than the evolution of an error, an evolution which reached its pinnacle in the work of Kant. Referring to this evolution, Habermas notes (1990:243) that the end of the eighteenth century constitutes the 'threshold of modernity shaped by Kantian philosophy and the new human sciences'. The fundamental error involved the imposition of a real world, and the associated attempt to make that world increasingly accessible.

The Kantian position, according to which knowledge was possible under certain conditions, bore the brunt of Nietzsche's attack. For Kant knowledge relied on the combination of sensibility and understanding through linking intuitions and concepts. Nietzsche stated that in claiming that knowledge relied on concepts, Kant was employing the very tools that he was describing, while also emphasising that in begging the question of how knowledge is possible there is a built-in assumption that knowledge is possible! He proposes an alternative question: is knowledge a fact at all?, underlining his claim that the error of the history of philosophy involved the assumption of the possibility of knowledge. Added to this was the claim that the rise of nihilism led to its own disintegration.

Nihilism derives from the logic of prevailing values. The belief in truth obliges us to recognise that truth is value, thereby undermining the entire edifice. Since truthfulness was cultivated by morality it turned against morality, thereby discovering its teleology. There was an internal logic to absolute values which led to their demise. Thus nihilism was an inevitable future of evolution. It is evident in Foucault's reference to one of the fundamental problems of Western philosophy as the attachment to truth rather than its converse, how 'truth' has been allocated a positive value to the extent that we are subjected to it (Kritzman, 1988:107).

Glucksman (1989) has discussed the extent to which Foucault shares this nihilistic stance. Some have gone so far as to claim that the gloom of Nietzsche's nihilism is also to be found in Foucault's work, stating: 'there is no freedom in Foucault's world, because his language forms a seamless web, a cage far more airtight than anything Weber ever dreamed of, into which no life can break' (Berman, 1983:35). If nihilism is viewed as either the relativism of values, or as a refusal to believe in supreme values, there is no doubt about Foucault's nihilism. On the other hand, the conception of nihilism as the rule of absolute subjectivity opens some doubt about his nihilistic stance. At times it is possible to claim that 'Foucault is not disputing the existence of absolute or scientific truth, merely stating his interest in the processes by which effects of truth are secured – which is a different issue' (Barrett 1991:143). On the other hand, Norris reacts strongly to Foucault's position, claiming that it is the precursor of a fashionable trend that is damaging to any conception of human liberation. As we shall see, it is this concern with the effects of discourse which is the fulcrum on which FDA rests, and which unambiguously derives from the work of Nietzsche and Foucault. It is their shared influence that is important and not whether it constitutes a nihilism.

Kant had heralded an increasing role for language in philosophic discussion by linking concepts with intuitions, thereby implicating concepts by which experience is described in any discussion of experience. In his understanding of language Nietzsche takes the important step of eliminating the distinction between language and thought, with language not representing thought but, rather, generating concepts directly: 'every word immediately becomes a concept, in as much as it is not intended to serve as a reminder of the unique and wholly individualised experience to which it owes its birth' (Lawson, 1985:44). To speak of language was to speak of thought. He went further in claiming that reality, in its dependence upon concepts, was thereby also dependent on language:

> unspeakably more depends upon what things are called than on what they are. The reputation, the name and appearance, the importance, the usual measure and weights of things ... have gradually, by the belief therein and its continuous growth from generation to generation, grown, as it were, on and into things and become their very body; the appearance at the very beginning becomes almost always the essence in the end ... It suffices to create new names and valuations and probabilities, in order in the long run, to create new 'things'.
>
> (Lawson, 1985: 44)

This is a very strong position on the constraining force of language, even if it does not proceed to the point of claiming that the only reality is that which lies in language. Yet there was also a reaction against the linguistic claim that good reasoning relied upon good language, perfect reason being implicit in language – an argument that was very forceful in the evolutionary claim for the relationship between language, reason and progress (Calvet, 1974). He goes on to claim that: 'We cease to think when we refuse to do so under the constraint of language; we barely reach the doubt that sees this limitation. Rational thought is interpretation according to a scheme that we cannot throw off' (Lawson, 1985:45), which seems to imply that there is a prison house of language, to use Jameson's term (1972), with language being constitutive of reality. That is, he does not make a claim for different versions of some reality, but rather denies the existence of a reality beyond a particular perspective. This, in turn, is linked with a claim for the fluidity of meaning, there being nothing apart from the meaning generated in the moment of interpreting words. Every sentence is created out of nothing. It is by the denial of the fixity of meaning, and only thereby, that the creation of new meaning is possible. As if heralding the work of Saussure and his inheritors, he claims that truth is 'A mobile army of metaphors, metonyms, and anthropomorphisms ... truths are illusions which are worn out and without sensuous power ... to be truthful means to use the customary metaphors' (Lawson, 1985:46). The world is in a constant state of flux, always a world of becoming wherein nothing is eternal. It is, without doubt, this that constitutes the essence of

Foucault's anti-rationalist position, where rationality is presented as historically constructed while simultaneously being an effect of power.

It is here that we must pause to carefully consider two of Nietzsche's concepts: the Will to Power and Eternal Recurrence, both of which are linked to the metaphysics of a shifting, ungraspable reality. Such a world would appear to be devoid of order, and Nietzsche claims that it is through the Will to Power that such order is imposed on the world. In this sense, then, the Will to Power is what generates meaning. As Lawson implies, it is a knowledge which overcomes chaos: 'one should not understand this compulsion to construct concepts, species, forms, purposes, laws . . . as if they enabled us to fix the real world; but as a compulsion to arrange a world for ourselves in which our existence is made possible . . . The world seems logical to us because we have made it logical' (Lawson, 1985:50).

It is the Will to Power that creates individuals. This view of the Will to Power as knowledge is given a social dimension by the claim that the world is the consequence of conflicting wills to power, all of which struggle to influence and overcome that which is not itself. It is the means whereby truths are made possible: '"Truth" is therefore not something there, that might be found or discovered – but something that must be created and that gives a name to a process, or rather to a will to overcome that has in itself no end . . . It is a word for the "Will to Power"' (Lawson, 1985: 51). Yet the Will to Power cannot be granted any fixity even if it is responsible for fixity, and becomes a perpetual reflexive overturning of itself.

Clearly the Will to Power lends some fixity to the world of becoming, but there would then be a hint that there is some existence in order that creation becomes possible. Nietzsche's response to this is that in the metaphor of the Eternal Recurrence he combines being with becoming. While the world is a world of becoming, there is also the moment which is held eternally. Stability and change go hand in hand: 'the world exists; it is not something that becomes, not something that passes away. Or rather; it becomes, it passes away, but it has never begun to become and it has never ceased from passing away – it manifests itself in both' (Lawson, 1985:52). The world becomes the Will to Power and nothing more. Despite the various claims that Foucault's radicalism implies an adherence to Marxism (Smart, 1983), it is from this anarchist position of Nietzsche that Foucault derives his fundamental observations. Whereas modernism affirms the universal humanity that relates to moral obligation and the necessity for social institutions, Foucault infers the absence of all elements able to serve as a foundation that relates to some essential social institutions. Rather, society is seen as the effects of normative discourse, as a sort of common language between all kinds of institutions.

In Foucault's historical work there is one element that is very much reminiscent of Saussurean work, and that involves the manner in which he presents a synchronic analysis of a historical discourse at one moment in time without any attempt to account for the existence of that particular discourse.

On the other hand he does not refute the diachronic, and yet there is no attempt to see discourse as process. My own view on this is that the removal of the subject as causal creates profound problems for any discussion of the production of discourse, and therefore for any discussion of a historical analysis of discourse as process. It is in *L'archéologie du savoir*, *L'ordre du discours* and *Les mots et les choses* that the more theoretical side of his work is to be found. On the other hand his early work did serve to show how discourse constitutes society through the constitution of objects of knowledge and social subjects.

A fundamental goal of Foucault's work was, in his words, the writing of a 'history of the present' by focusing on what he claimed was a 'fundamental duality of Western consciousness' (Bouchard, 1977:230). This claim is shared with Nietzsche, being the central theme of his *The Genealogy of Morals*. In developing this theme, Nietzsche focused on three issues. First, what conditions led to the creation of value judgments concerning good and evil. Foucault adds to this, that in contemporary society this dichotomy is often replaced by normal and abnormal or deviant (Bouchard, 1977:230), this becoming the focus of much of his historical work. Indeed in the concluding chapter I will indicate how the main thrust of Foucault's work has been in the area normativity. Second, Nietzsche emphasised the existence of an 'inner split' of the subject into body and soul, a theme which Foucault developed, not in terms of the religious demand for the sacrifice of the body, but of the sacrifice of the subject to knowledge (Bouchard, 1977:263), with the subject being made an object to itself. Third, Nietzsche questioned the role of what he called the 'ascetic priest' in elaborating and promoting those divisions which dominate our minds. Foucault pursues this theme in asking about the role of those who have the right to speak in promoting the division between normality and abnormality, and the social divisions that it outlined. His focus upon the role of the intellectual in establishing and maintaining these divisions calls into question the entire intellectual endeavour.

In pursuing these objectives, Foucault is at pains to emphasise that he follows Nietzsche's practice of genealogy, where the energy of the strong meets the reactions of the weak – the point of division of dualities, where opposites mutually define and determine each other, yet retaining their distinctiveness. This he does by talking of limits and their transgression, absences and limits. By occupying the line of division between the normal and the deviant, and moving with it, he sought to demonstrate how it worked within a dynamic context.

In seeking to write a 'history of the present' Foucault follows Nietzsche's attack on the present by placing a question mark besides the self-evident truths and accepted modes of understanding and mode of analysis. In so doing he creates a counter-history. He shares with Nietzsche the claim that all knowledge and perception is a matter of perspective, a perspective which can be changed, thereby changing the conception and knowledge. This was his goal in employing what he called a *renversement*, or an inversion of existing values, modes of analysis and historical continuities (Foucault, 1971:72). He thereby follows Nietzsche in employing this *renversement* not merely in terms of a particular intra-historical period but also by contrasting historical periods, even if it is always done within the dualities. *The Genealogy of Morals* is a very good example of such a process in which Nietzsche argues that what Christianity has preached as the good are no more than domains for the poor and the weak, while Christianity simultaneously hides malice and selfishness. In *The Gay Science* he strives to reveal the complex modalities of the operation of the good/evil opposition. Similarly, Foucault denies the accepted modes of historical analysis, with its assumptions about the nature of society in an ordered process of change, and treats history as a series of specific, concrete events in change which occur by chance, but exist in their own right, according to their own regularities, and with their own interrelationships. The event he saw as a discontinuous moment in which a transformation is evident, and in this respect it bears some relationship to Canguilhem's conception of an epistemological break. His tendency, referred to above, to retain the distinctiveness and separateness and concrete specificity of the things he relates to one another, he draws from Heidegger, and is the basis of what he means when he refers to descriptive systems in their dispersion, differentiation and multiplicity. One feature the two share within this process of *renversement* is that of highlighting the present through comparison with the past: 'To diagnose the present is to say what the present is, to say how the present differs from all that it is not, that is from our past' (Foucault, 1969:21), with Foucault drawing mainly on the Renaissance, and Nietzsche on the Ancient Greeks and the Aristocratic Teutons.

In seeking to write his 'history of the present', Foucault was involved in collapsing into their component elements the fundamental abstractions of which the 'fundamental dualities of Western consciousness' are composed and in demonstrating the nascence of these components in history. Again he was following Nietzsche, who claimed that 'all terms which somatically condense a whole process elude definition . . . however, at an earlier stage that synthesis of "meanings" must have been more easily soluble, its components more easily dissociated' (Nietzsche, 1969:212). He emphasised the relationship between interpretation and power 'The lordly right of bestowing names is such that one could almost be justified in seeing the origin of language itself as an expression of the rulers' power. They say: "this is that or that"; they seal off each thing or action with a sound and thereby take symbolic possession of it' (Nietzsche, 1969:160). This, of course, involves what Foucault called the right to speak and the place of discourse. Nietzsche went further: 'everything that exists, no matter what its origin, is periodically reinterpreted by those in power in terms of fresh intentions . . . all outstripping and overcoming means, reinterpretation, and rearrangement in the course of which earlier meanings and purposes are necessarily either obscured or lost' (Nietzsche, 1969:209).

Evidently there is considerable overlap between the work of the two authors. However, Foucault took his work beyond that of Nietzsche in his development of archaeology as: 'the law of what can be said, the system which regulates the appearance of statements (enonces) as singular events . . . which differentiates the multiple forms of existence of specific discourses and specifies the duration proper to each' (Nietzsche, 1969:68). That is, he sought to discover the concrete mode of operation of each system of interpretation or discursive formation. Within history the interpretative systems existed in succession, and he sought to describe their laws by discussing regularities which govern different discourses, disciplines and practices, as well as the various modifications and transformations within them, without abandoning their differences and without unifying them.

Foucault prioritises discourse or forms of language without dissociating discourse and practice. In putting the accent on this discourse/practice couple he rejects the totalitising nature of langage as found in structuralism and, as a consequence, avoided the problem of formalism. None the less, he does accept the paradigmatic displacement of language without posing the question of social factors which make such a displacement necessary. Furthermore, the doing or the practice is internal to the discursive.

Foucault's concept of 'archive' is seen as that which regroups a collection of 'inscriptions' referring to the same positioning. He refers to it as that which in any given society defines: 'The general system of the formation and the transformation of enonces' (Foucault, 1969:223), that which, between tradition and the forgotten, makes the rules of a practice appear which permits enonces to be substitutable and to be modified regularly. It involves existing practice, past practices, the totality of discursive practices. Thus his archaeology derives from the Greek *arechion* or the Latin *archivum*, the etymon of archive; linked to *arche* as the source or 'principal' is power, the *archeion* giving the status of authority. Thus discourse analysis is interested in the authorisation of discourses which, beyond their immediate function, implies a relationship to fundamentals (origins) and rules. The function of memory, as one source in the form of the archive, wherein discourse analysis itself participates in manipulating the enonces already expressed, is thereby systematically related to the determination of an *enceinte*, of a power which is the power of stating, to the affirming of the legitimacy of a body of consecrated enonciateurs. The imaginary which constitutes the archive supposes a relationship to a source of meaning, to the delimitation of a founding, authenticating space. Above all, discourse analysis is, in effect, interested in authorising discourses which presuppose a relationship to fundamentals and to values.

Considered as an 'archive', a collection of texts is not defined merely as the response to practical constraints; it also allows the legitimisation of a certain exercise of *parole* for a given group – a certain organisation of the universe of a collectivity is implicated. It is concerned with a consideration of enonciative positions which link a textual functioning to the identity of a group. Thus, the archive is not the virtually infinite collection of grammatical phrases, it is radically linked to the exemplarity, to the repetition. Thus a discursive formation consists of rules which are responsible for forming a particular set of statements which belong to that discursive formation, rules which relate to the formation of objects in discourse, of subject positions, of concepts, and enonciative modalities.

In his work on morality, Nietzsche claimed that it had to be studied 'as it has actually existed and actually been lived' (Nietzsche,1969:156). This involved an awareness of interrelationships and changes in which there existed various processes of approbation which included resistance in the form of transformations. While Nietzsche failed to pursue this objective, it was a major focus of Foucault's work, and involved the relationship between both discursive and non-discursive practices without recourse to the orthodox features of thought and reality, infrastructure/superstructure, etc. In this respect he built on the work of Bachelard and Canguilhem.

It should be evident that Foucault was interested primarily in the conditions of knowledge within which organised knowledges are constructed. This was the topic investigated in *Les mots et les choses* and it is what he refers to as episteme. In that influential volume, episteme was discussed as the logical structure which conditions thinking and speech without the knowledge of the enonciateur. In this respect it was an aspect of the collective cultural consciousness which was capable of being revealed through what Foucault referred to as a mix of ethnology and psychoanalysis (1966:391). This of course merely creates a problem which we will encounter again, that of employing a discourse – psychoanalysis or ethnology – to analyse a discourse.

In his discussion of the modern episteme Foucault distinguishes between physics and sociology, the former being a science and the latter lacking the former's conditions and features. This is not to imply the science/error or ideology distinction. At the archaeological level their knowledges are equally structured and fully determined. Thus while physics and sociology are different, they share in the same modern episteme. The non-scientific character of sociology is an effect of the human sciences themselves, their form of knowledge and the fact that their conditions of existence lie in what is referred to as 'Man'.

Thus, for Foucault, episteme refers to the principles which govern a space of inclusion, or the conditions of knowledge within which organised knowledges are structured. As such it bears a clear relationship to his concept of power, which I will discuss below. In another sense it would appear that this concept of episteme is akin to the Kantian idea of an *a priori* of knowledges, but it refers not to knowledges in general, but, rather, to specific knowledges, for there can be no knowledge in general. The relevant epistemic principles determine which objects can be identified, how they are marked and ordered. They also determine the perceptions, statements and forms of knowledge that are possible or not possible. In some respects there is a clear overlap with

Bachelard's concept of problematic. It refers to how there may be a variation in which statements can count as knowledge over time. The implication is that knowledge is informed by definite rules, the 'relations that can be discovered, for a given period, between the sciences' (Foucault, 1969:249), together with the discoverable link between knowledges through the analysis of discursive regularities. Be that as it may, it is, however, the work of Nietzsche that is the driving force of Foucault's orientation.

Subject, object, concepts and enonciative modalities

In considering Foucault's position on the subject, it is perfectly clear that the subject is decentred, being constituted rather than pre-given. Indeed, a major part of his work focuses upon the practices whereby the subject is constituted. The subject is not something that exists prior to discourse; that is, the subject is created in and through discourse:

> discourse is not the majestically unfolding manifestation of a thinking, knowing, speaking subject, but, on the contrary, a totality, in which the dispersion of the subject and his discontinuity with himself may be determined . . . it is neither by recourse to a transcendental subject nor by recourse to a psychological subjectivity that the regulation of its enunciation should be defined.
>
> (Foucault, 1969:74)

The subjects fills positions and is thus a process within the network of signifiers. This is evident in the manner in which 'shifters' – personal pronouns, adverbs of time and place, tenses of the verb etc., forms in which the concepts of I and you, of here and now, are definable only in relation to the act of speaking. Similarly, for Benveniste subjectivity is premised on the linguistic category of 'person': 'It is in and through language that man is constituted as a subject; because it is only language in reality that establishes the concept of "ego", in its reality which is that of being' (Benveniste, 1966:259). However, Benveniste restricts the process of the subject to the constitutive operation of formal grammatical structures, which he distinguishes from discourse. For Foucault, on the other hand, discourse is a space 'in which the dispersion of the subject and his discontinuity with himself may be determined' (1969:74).

It should be evident that Foucault's decentring is tied to his rejection of humanism, much in the same sense as Nietzsche rejects humanism. Indeed, he describes humanism in terms of 'subjected sovereignties':

> By humanism I mean the totality of discourse through which Western man is told: 'Even though you don't exercise power you can still be a ruler. Better still, the more you deny yourself the exercise of power,

the more you submit to those in power, the more this increases your sovereignty.'

(Foucault, 1977:221–222)

There is a complex critique here, a critique of the transcendental subject of Cartesianism, of humanism and of the State in its all-pervading influence. They are intertwined in such a way that to unravel them defeats the object of the exercise. Part of Foucault's historical work involved demonstrating that humanism was institutionalised in Western society through Roman law, where any property owner submits to the very law which confirms property as the possession of the power holders. The sovereign subject of Western society is nothing more than a pseudo-sovereign.

The objects of discourse, on the other hand, are constituted and transformed in discourse in accordance with the rules of the discursive formation. Thus, objects cannot be treated as something external to discourse, as entities which are referred to and discussed by discourse, they are a feature of discourse. Objects, thus conceived, are objects of knowledge, things recognised by specific disciplines as lying within their scope of interest and which thereby become the focus of investigation and discussion. Thus, with reference to 'madness' he claimed that the entire concept of mental illness was constituted by the manner in which it was discussed (Foucault, 1972:32). Yet it was never stable as a concept or object, being transformed as it shifted from one discursive formation to another, and even within a specific discursive formation. That is, meanings change from one discursive formation to another, and it is the discursive formation that determines meaning. Thus the object cannot be the basis for the delimitation of a discursive formation. Rather, 'the unity of a discourse is based not so much on the permanence and uniqueness of an object as on the space in which various objects emerge and are continuously transformed' (Foucault, 1969:45). This also means that the driving force of change is not any force external to discourse, but discourse itself, it is that which shapes the objects of our social life. This is the basis of the objection to language as a reflection of society that is so customary in sociolinguistics (G. Williams, 1992). The determining agency in the above statement by Foucault is 'space', by which he means the relationship between 'institutions, economic and social processes, behavioural patterns, systems of norms, techniques, types of classification, modes of characterisation' (1969:62). Evidently, a discursive formation succeeds in limiting the form of objects, and, in his early work, he implies that this is a function of the interdiscursive relation between different discursive formations, and the relation between discursive and non-discursive practice, that constitute the discursive formation. There are two points here. First, that discursive formations have to be studied in association or articulation within orders of discourse, that is within that totality of discursive practices of society. Second, there is a suggestion in the above that the 'non-discursive practices' refer to forces external to discourse. I will turn to this second issue in a moment, but first of all I would like to consider what Foucault has to say about enonciative modalities, concepts and strategies.

We have already seen that the social subject does not exist independently or outside of discourse. Rather, that subject is the function of the statement. Thus any statement positions not merely the subject of the statement, in the sense of the source of origin of the statement, but also the subject that is addressed, and it positions them in particular ways. This is the basis for one of the most often quoted parts of Foucault's work:

> to describe a formulation qua statement does not consist in analysing the relations between the author and what he says (or wanted to say, or said without wanting to); but in determining what position can and must be occupied by any individual if he is to be the subject of it.
>
> (1969:126)

Discursive formations consist of specific configurations of enonciative modalities,[4] which are seen as types of discursive activity, each of which has its own subject positions. It relates to how statements referring to objects are made, and in this respect he is explicitly claiming that discourse is a practice rather than a monolithic theoretical architecture. In this respect his reference is to the form of stating as opposed to the content of statements. That is, statements position subjects in particular ways, both those who produce the statements, and those to whom they are addressed. Thus, in law, if seen as a discursive activity, the 'judge', 'prosecutor', 'defence' or 'charged' are all positioned. He viewed the normative as the modality of the object which afforded truth value to particular objects within particular configurations. Thus the normative was the effect of complex practices of normalisation.

The rules of formation of enonciative modalities within any particular discursive formation involve complex relationships which involve the idea of 'place', a concept which derives from the preceding statement concerning subject position in that it involves a social topography of speaking subjects. This concept of place, 'where the specificity lies on the essential trait from which each accedes to its identity and lying at the interior of a system of places which it surpasses' (Flahault, 1978:58), has a bearing on our understanding of subjective identity. If the subject is determined in and through discourse, then identities are also established in and through discourse, and do not involve the constructivist conception involving the separation of self and mind.

Thus discursive formations are made of configurations of enonciative modalities which are conceived of as types of discursive activity. The enonciative modalities have rules of formation which are constituted for any particular discursive formation by a complex group of relations. The manner in which enonciative modalities are articulated is not permanent, but is subject to constant modification, being a feature of social change. Thus, in the favoured example of medical discourse, the 'doctor' is a subject position which speaks from a specific place institutionalised by the existing rules of medical discourse – the doctor is constituted via a particular configuration of enonciative modalities and subject positions:

> If, in clinical discourse, the doctor is in turn the sovereign direct questioner, the observing eye, the touching finger, the organ that deciphers signs, the point at which previously formulated descriptions are integrated, the laboratory technician, it is because a whole group of relations is involved . . . between a number of distinct elements, some of which concerned the status of doctors, others the institutional and technical site (hospital, laboratory, private practice etc.) from which they spoke, others their position as subjects perceiving, observing, describing, teaching etc.
>
> (Foucault, 1969:72)

Science, and indeed social science, tends to treat concepts as the essential prerequisites of its discussion, and views them as stable entities which have a fixed relationship with one another. Once again Foucault denies this position, arguing instead in terms of a shifting configuration of changing concepts. Concepts are formed not by the pre-existing subject as scientist or sociologist, but as a consequence of the organisation of the field of statements associated with them. It is in the context of this discussion that Foucault comes closest to discussing the linguistic intricacies which are familiar to FDA. It is also the point where the main thrust of the work of Canguilhem and Bachelard, concerning the discursive nature of disciplines and the need to treat them as discourses, appears. Thus sociology becomes a particular order of discourse with a subject in the sense that all discourses have a subject which carries the enonce which is inscribed in its structure.

Referring to 'fields of statements', Foucault identifies different relationships. One such relationship involves the statements of a single text which are combined in ways that depend upon the discursive formation: 'various rhetorical schemata according to which groups of statements may be combined (how descriptions, deductions, definitions, whose succession characterises the architecture of a text, are linked together)' (1969:77). This is the intra-textual dimension that involves the relationships between statements of a single text. There are also interdiscursive relations involving different discursive formations which are distinguished according to whether they belong to fields of 'presence', 'concomitance' or 'memory'. A field of presence involves statements 'formed elsewhere' but taken up in discourse which may be judged as truthful, reasonable, etc. A field of concomitance, on the other hand, consists of statements from different discursive formations and pertains to the relationships between different discursive formations; while a field of memory relates to statements as traces being 'no longer accepted or discussed', but which lead to establishing 'relations of filiation, genesis, transformation, continuity and historical discontinuity' (1969:180). This link to the past involves the claim that 'there can be no statement that does not reactualize others' (1969:180), leading to an understanding of how prior discourse helps constitute the present.

Evidently Foucault sees a discursive formation as a specific kind of unity. It involves a dispersion of statements at different levels which is conceived of as a unity on account of the common conditions and rules which govern dispersion. The different levels involving objects, modes of enonciation, concepts and strategies, all entail restrictions on each other. The rules of discourse are constituted by the interrelation of these elements, together with their own conditions of existence. As I have noted in the introduction, for Foucault, enonciative modalities did not refer to propositional content but, rather, to the status and institutional setting of that statement. This clarification should indicate that Foucault did not refer to enonciation in terms of the relationship between a proposition and a sentence as the orthodox speech-act or performative perspective of linguistics would suggest. Indeed, his objective was to clarify that the enonce involved far more than this restricted sense. It is the link between the linguistic and the conditions of enonciation which was to become the focus of FDA.

The production of discourse

Here I would like to consider the extent to which Foucault's work suggests the existence of some reality beyond the confines of discourse. In his early work there does seem to be an extra-discursive dimension. It is in the relationship between the discursive and the non-discursive that we witness an attempt to come to terms with the issue of the production of discourse. However, the error here is to confuse non-discursive for extra-discursive.

It should already be evident that in discussing discourse, Foucault is not striving to demarcate the background of shared practices that make linguistic practices intelligible. He is not interested in the intentions of the speech-act participants. Such intentions could only be of relevance if there were a subject which existed prior to, and outside of, discourse. The extent to which there is a performative or pragmatic sense to enonciation involves the manner in which each enonce conveys an understanding. There is a doing that is internal to the discursive and, as such, the discursive constitutes a practice. Thus his relationship to 'tradition' was not a relationship of identification but was always an open question, a question of practice. Neither is he interested in treating knowledge as ideas in any other sense. Thus, when he refers to statements, they should not be understood within such epistemological contexts. The discursive formation consists of statements which refer to one and the same object within a dispersion of statements:

> Whenever one can describe, between a number of statements, such a
> system of dispersion, whenever, between objects, types of statements,

concepts, or thematic choices, one can define a regularity . . . we will
say . . . that we are dealing with a discursive formation . . .

(Foucault, 1969:53)

But within such statements language is not a system of referents and words, nor
something that points to objects, but rather statements contribute to discourse
as the practices that systematically form the object of which they speak. Yet
there is a non-discursive formation which bears relevance to the discursive
formation. This consists of the 'enonciative modalities' which clarify how the
statements of a discursive formation are made. As we have seen, they involve
who has the right to make statements, the place, in terms of power, from which
these statements emanate and what position the subject of the discourse
occupies, and must occupy, in order to be the subject. Also of relevance are
non-discursive social practices which become relevant in how an object is
enabled to appear or 'to be placed in a field of exteriority' (Foucault, 1969:61).
They consist of:

institutions, economic and social processes, behavioural patterns,
systems of norms, techniques, types of classification, modes of
characterisation.

(Foucault, 1969:61)

His task was to discover a means of discussing the interplay between discursive
and non-discursive practices without resort to the conventional relationships between thought and reality, theory and practice, or superstructure
and infrastructure. Although influenced by Bachelard and Canguilhem, he
departed from their work on science and chose 'objects of study which themselves were located between thought and reality, theory and practice,
knowledge and the political, social and economic structures of society, and to
show how, in these particular objects of study, apparent opposites intermeshed'
(Tavor Bannet, 1989:108). Within these objects of study he tried to study how
the discursive practice – be it psychiatric, medical or penal – institutions, and
the economic constraints and political policies which were associated with
them, determined the production of new knowledge, new theory and new
thought. This does have some similarity to the work of Bachelard on the
problematic, a similarity most evident in his concept of event. Similarly,
he would reverse the relationship by exploring how new knowledge and
technology governed the discursive practices by focusing on what happened in
the institutional setting of prisons, hospitals or asylums, without ignoring the
production of political and economic policies about them. He may have been
unable to consider social policy in the orthodox context of planning for the
future, but he was able to place existing and past policy formations in context.
However, he did not consider the link between knowledge, policy and practice
within a causal framework, but in terms of a question which asked how

conditions in one part of the system limited and allowed something in another part of the system (Foucault, 1969:211).

Relations are established between discursive formations, and such discursive relations are 'at the limits of discourse' and 'determine the group of relations that discourse must establish in order to speak of this or that object' (Foucault, 1969:63). The importance of these relations lies not in the various individual elements but, rather, in the manner in which they are organised by discursive practice. What we are not told is how discursive practice relates to these relations, and this may be why there is a shift of direction from a discussion of the production of discourse to the production of meaning. The emphasis is upon the rules which are involved in discursive practice, as a form of structure of discursive practice. While he implies that the non-discursive is important in forming objects, he emphasises that they are not as important as discursive relations. While institutions, political events, economic practices and processes (Foucault, 1969:212) affect what can be seriously said, it is discursive practice, and the way in which it organises relations, which is the most important element:

> When one speaks of a system of formation, one does not mean the juxtaposition, coexistence, or interaction of heterogeneous elements (institutions, techniques, social groups, perceptual organisations, relations between various discourses), but also the relation that is established between them – and in a well determined form – by discursive practice.
>
> (Foucault, 1969:95)

The situation is paraphrased by Dreyfus and Rabinow (1982:64):

> Then Foucault could be understood as holding that although what gets said is obviously causally dependent on many non discursive factors, one does not need to bring in these outside factors in order to systematise, and thus make intelligible, why certain types of speech-acts are performed and others not.

It would appear that in discussing 'rules' Foucault is stating that discourse employs the non-discursive factors which in a sense determine practice by seizing them and giving them unity:

> It can be said that this relation between different elements (some of which are new, while others were already in existence) is effected by clinical discourse: it is this, as a practice, that establishes between them all a system of relations . . . and if there is a unity, if the modalities of enunciation that it uses, or to which it gives place, are not simply

juxtaposed by a series of historical contingencies, it is because [clinical discourse] makes constant use of this group of relations.

(Foucault 1969:71–72)

At times it would seem that Foucault is implying that the non-discursive determines which strategies are chosen and what is said within discourse in the sense that it is the non-discursive that makes the choice of discursive strategy comprehensible:

> Archaeological analysis individualises and describes discursive forma-tions. That is, it must . . . relate them, on the basis of their specificity, to the non-discursive practices that surround them and serve as a general element for them.
>
> (1969:205)

It is as if they sustain and enclose the discursive formation. Clearly this is not correct since Foucault retains the autonomy of the discursive, which means that the converse is the case; it is the discursive which gives form to the non-discursive, the latter being transformed by the former. The non-discursive does not have productive powers in relation to discourse.

While this may sound like a circular relationship, this also is incorrect. While the discursive formation does constitute a unity in the sense that its constituent statements integrate in a dispersed way, it is the interrelationship of these statements, and the conditions associated with their existence, which, between them, constitute the rules of formation of discourse. But this is quite different than any reference to the rules of production of discourse. It is in discussing the issue of statements that meaning is clarified.

Foucault refers to enonciative modalities by outlining how discourse is a practice, and subsequently how statements are made. In *The Order of Things* Foucault states that in all societies discourse is produced in relation to a form which reduces to a limited number of procedures. Foucault's main concern with reference to enonciative modalities involves the place from which a dis-course emanates. Most observers have concentrated upon the medical example quoted above, and how the institutional setting generates status for a specific discourse, but in reality place refers to the site of power and the manner in which this generates privilege and preference within any interdiscursive context. It is this interdiscursive which sets limits upon what can be said, partly because any discourse which relates to the privileged discourse must encompass that discourse. Furthermore, in determining who has the right to speak, a discourse simultaneously denies that right.

Clearly, it is the discursive formations which regulate the production of discourse. However, they are defined neither ontologically nor formally, that is, as linguistic unities, but functionally, through their differential capacity to pro-duce particular forms of knowledge, and subjects appropriate to those forms.

The discursive formations themselves can overlap with, and even contradict, other formations. They may display internally contradictory codifications and in this respect they are neither self-contained nor coherent.

Discursive formations are the corpus of statements in relation to the existence of objects, mode of statement, concepts and thematic choices, the dispersion of such statements being governed by 'rules of formation'. The statements of a discursive formation condition what can be said, and even what must be said, from a given place. As we have seen, this is because they are responsible for organising the objects of the discourse. A discourse creates a space for a particular type of self to occupy, but they are spaces which have very definite constraints in so far as they are conditioned by what exists around them. That is, such statements never exist in isolation, since the discursive formation exists as the totality of its statements. Thus, it would seem that there is an internal organising force in all discursive formations, a force which conditions the production of meaning. In a sense, even though a discursive formation retains its internal integrity, it also conditions the production of discourse, since it limits what can and cannot be said:

> The analysis of statements and discursive formations . . . wishes to determine the principle according to which only the 'signifying' groups that were enunciated could appear.
>
> (Foucault, 1969:153)

This is the basis for confronting the issue of meaning. Discourses do not merely delineate what can be said, but also provide the spaces for making new statements within any specific discourse. Thus, metaphors and analogies are always available from within the discourse, as well as from other discourses, in a limitless way.

What is clear from the preceding discussion is that various forms of relationships involving 'fields of statements' exist within a discursive formation. Thus, it is the discursive formation that determines intra-textual relationships. Similarly, different discursive formations or texts can be linked to give interdiscursive relations which take different forms.

These relationships within fields of statements involve both the social context and the verbal context, that is, the relationship of a statement to other statements and the relationship of statements to the social context within which they occur. This is the basis for determining the form of any statement, albeit that the manner in which such contexts affect what is said will be subservient to the discursive formation within which it takes place. It does not involve the rational subject, but the articulation of relevant discursive formations.

These rules of formation merely constitute the possible and may not be actually realised. Which of the various possibilities are realised depends upon the rules for the formation of strategies, and, as we have already seen, in his early work they are constituted by both interdiscursive and non-discursive constraints. Again we refer to the right to speak and the associated status within specific contexts.

Power and resistance

There is a distinctive shift between the archaeological emphasis of Foucault's early work and the genealogical thrust of his later work. The archaeological work was to uncover the layers of knowledge which pertained to different orders of representation which have existed as Western metaphysics since the Renaissance. This work was characterised by the concept of episteme, which characterised different regimes of knowledge, involving different conceptions of language and its use. It relates to what, within any particular historical conjuncture, counts as knowledge. He claimed that knowledge is informed by definite rules, and leads to continuities across disciplines seen as discursive regularities. This focus of his work gives way to a more explicitly Nietzschean perspective that focuses upon genealogy and power/knowledge. His concern is with undermining the received account of 'truth' or reality by undermining the ground on which they are constructed.

It would appear that it is Foucault's conception and understanding of power which has received the most attention. This is hardly surprising when we consider the relationship between decentred subjectivity and power. This relationship would appear to imply that domination through subjugation is impossible. It leads to what Ewald (1989) refers to as *un pouvoir sans dehor*. Thus Foucault claimed that there is no power which is exercised by one person over the other as a form of rational, conscious action, and that power does not exist except as an act. Thus he conceived of power as something inscribed in a field of dispersed possibility supported by permanent structures. This becomes important in that, as we shall see, the linguistics of FDA claims that the relevance of language pertains to its existence as an infinite possibility of meaning and that meaning itself is socially constructed.

The impetus for Foucault's work on power appears to have been the publication of Deleuze's work on Nietzsche in 1967, since he does not speak of power until 1971. What Deleuze did was to interpret Nietzsche's *Genealogy of Morals* in light of the work in *Will to Power*, thereby demonstrating that the Will to Power was central to every aspect of Nietzsche's genealogical and critical philosophy. What is interesting is that Deleuze began from Foucault's understanding of critical philosophy and proceeded to show that Nietzsche saw meaning or interpretation as 'a force which appropriates the thing, which exploits it, which takes possession of it, and expresses itself in it' (Deleuze, 1967:3). Furthermore, since every word, phenomenon or event was subject to a multiplicity of meanings and interpretations, they were associated with a multiplicity of forces which were in competition for possession of it. Here again we encounter the claim that reality disappears on the grounds that non-phenomena cannot exist prior to or separate from interpretation.

The Will to Power enters the debate, according to Deleuze, as a feature of the relation between domination and submission, since relations of force always involve some forces ruling over others. Furthermore, domination and submission also exist in terms of the 'history of a thing', involving a 'history of the forces which take possession of it, and the coexistence of the forces struggling to take possession of it' (Deleuze, 1967:97). Within such a history the domination of the forces which possess it are over the forces which they have replaced or displaced. It is also the Will to Power, according to Deleuze, which is the force that interprets, being 'that which gives meaning and value' (Deleuze, 1967:88). He draws attention to what precisely is willed within truth. Nietzsche treats concepts, sentiments, beliefs, ethical systems and science as 'symptoms of a will which wills something' (Deleuze, 1967:97), this being the fundamental essence of his conception. Power is inherent in this will, but not as a fundamental goal, it is not something that is sought by the will. Rather, it is a force that gives meaning while appropriating. That is, power becomes that which makes interpretations what they are, and affirms them in their difference. This Will to Power, or the will which wills, is a feature of all meaning and interpretation. The link between knowledge and power is established.

Since all truth, knowledge and interpretation implies a will which wills something, thereby being a positive signification, the dualisms of power and truth, power and knowledge, and power and meaning or interpretation, could all be interlinked. More importantly perhaps, it could be achieved without recourse to analysis in terms of dominance and submission. The relevance of this for Foucault's work becomes most evident in his discussion of history, which he saw as a series of interpretations and reinterpretations. History became a series of competing and coexisting forces which implicated the Will to Power while seeping throughout social life and all histories.

For Foucault, knowledge does not exist separately from power. On the other hand there is no knowledge outside of discourse, which means that discourse does not exist separately from power, that is, power lies in discourse. There is no exercise of power without an associated discursive feature (Foucault, 1980:93) which confers power relations with an immanent rationality. Such a beginning to Foucault's discussion of power is necessary since he does not tell us directly what power is, but rather refers to how power is exercised. The reason should be obvious. The decentring of the subject means that the conventional approach to power must be abandoned and, with it, not only the conventional definitions of power, but also the customary approach to the discussion of power. To claim that a discourse has power is not to attribute agency to a system, but simply to acknowledge forces of constraints and production. It relates to the manner in which meaning is made possible. The emphasis in Foucault's work is upon the techniques by which power becomes operable. Power is made intelligible by a consideration of the pronouncements accompanying its exercise, such exercise being evident at the level of action rather than consciousness. This has confused some analysts (Taylor, 1986) who react to his claim that power is simultaneously intentional and non-subjective:

> there is no power that is exercised without a series of aims and objectives. But this does not mean that it results from the choice or decision of an individual subject; let us not look for the headquarters that presides over its rationality; neither the case which governs, nor the groups which control the state apparatus, nor those who make the most important decisions direct the entire network of power that functions in a society . . . the logic is perfectly clear, the aims decipherable, and yet it is often the case that no one is there to have invented them, and few who can be said to have formulated them.
>
> (Foucault, 1976: 124)

Of course, such a linking of non-subjectivity and intentionality is not strange to sociology, where the tendency is to separate behaviour from interests associated with socio-structural location. Clearly, such modern rationalism is not part of Foucault's bag of tricks.

The linking of Deleuze's emphasis on power as involving political relations of domination and subjection, and as inherent to the act of interpretation, is clear in *Surveiller et punir*. Power becomes a technological politic which generates productive and subjective bodies, being a 'network of relations, always in tension, always in movement' (Foucault, 1975:31) which permeates throughout the body politic. It is everywhere. Furthermore, in linking power and knowledge, Foucault draws attention to the various interpretative systems which are responsible for creating the knowing subject as well as the objects which that subject can know, and the modalities of knowledge. Thereby humankind becomes an object of knowledge to him/herself: 'a specific mode of subjection gave birth to man as an object of knowledge for a discourse with scientific status' (Foucault, 1975:28–29). Psychology and sociology seek to study the way humankind represent their lives as individuals, their world of work and everyday life, and the possibilities and potential of language to themselves. As such, the correct object of human sciences is representation. By linking the humanities and social science in language and discourse Foucault was capable of suggesting a more integrated analysis of culture and society while retaining the subject's position within them.

Foucault conceived of the space of language, culture and society as an open, dynamic set of interrelationships wherein power is everywhere. It is a feature not merely of interrelationships but of knowledge and practice, whether they be local or universal in nature. Power organises all discourses and can even be serving a number of functions simultaneously.

The relationship between power and knowledge is now treated in terms of how the relations of power define fields of knowledge and produce objects of knowledge. The shift from the question of the production of discourse to the production of meaning is complete, since the objects of knowledge are themselves constructed. This production of meaning is rooted in struggle, since truth is a contentious issue rather than an absolute, and, as such, it is the site of permanent struggle. It involves:

> the ensemble of rules according to which true and false are separated and specific effects of power attached to true.
>
> (Foucault, 1980:131–133)

In any struggle, where there is power, there must be resistance. Power needs resistance as one of its final conditions of operation, and it is through the articulation of resistance that power spreads through the social field. Indeed, the space within which the subject and the object occur is cleared and defined by the struggle and its power/resistance constituents. The object of Foucault's work is to outline the process whereby subjects are constituted within this particular sense of power and struggle (Foucault, 1980:73–74). This must mean that what has been produced in discourse can be overthrown and replaced, or at least that what is dominant becomes subservient. This, in turn, means that no one is as powerless as is generally suggested, even if the 'one' is no longer the rational, human subject. Each subject is a power-point where multiple power relations intersect – power, ethnic, gender, economic, etc. Even in subjugation there is a local power of resistance. Indeed, the potential of multiple local powers of resistance is evident within the field of discourse and power relations: 'as soon as there is a power relation, there is a possibility of resistance. We can never be ensnared by power: we can modify its grip in determinate conditions and according to precise strategies' (Foucault, 1977). Discourse is not merely an instrument or effect of power but also 'a point of resistance, a starting point for an opposite strategy' (Foucault, 1976:133). As such, discourse is a form of action, even if that action involves the social practice that is implicit in a refusal to accept dominant meanings.

From this outline we can begin to see the relevance of power for the analysis of discourse. The essence involves which statements can and cannot be made from a specific place within a complexity of discourses. The condition of possibility of statements depends upon the prevailing graph of power knowledge which is immanent in statements without being reducible to them. The constraints upon the sort of statements which can be produced within a particular discursive formation is an index of the power relations to which that discursive formation owes its identity. However, these statements need not be verbal, they can involve any form of social practice. Thus, in claiming that the relations of domination are fixed through rituals, we are not restricted to language, even if the focus of analysis is linguistic. Also, it would seem that if power demands resistance there must be the sites of the production of statements of resistance. However, these statements are restricted by the nature of the relationship to that which they resist, with the content of the discourse being conditioned by the need to respond to the dominant discourse. In a sense this is no more than a statement of discourses existing in terms of relationships, albeit specific forms of relationships.

Conclusion

In this chapter I have sought to draw together the work of Althusser and Foucault, the two intellectuals who have had the greatest influence on the emergence and development of FDA. Given the manner in which French intellectualism is organised, it is inevitable that there are points of convergence between the works of the two. On the other hand, there are also points of divergence, and it is there that some of the contradictions and tensions in FDA have concentrated.

The convergence involves the rejection of any sense of reified consciousness and it is this theme which draws the work of the two theorists together in FDA. They also share a refutation of the scientific understanding of ideology, but there are also differences here. Althusser alludes to a form of materialism in which the economic infrastructure functions 'in the last instance', whereas, for Foucault, such a suggestion was anathema in that his emphasis on the politics of truth was clearly different from Althusser's Marxist emphasis on the economic basis of untruth. In a fascinating paper, Etienne Balibar (1989), one of Althusser's closest collaborators, has discussed Foucault's relationship to Marxism. He suggests that Foucault's entire work represents a combat with that of Marx. In that paper Balibar refers to Macheray's comment that it is in Foucault's rejection of his initial Marxist position, conceived as a concrete critique of alienation, that one discovers the reasons for his mistrust of everything that derives from historical materialism. Given that Althusser's goal was to establish historical materialism as the true science, the tension between their respective approaches should be evident. This tension is evident throughout the history of FDA during the period 1966 to 1983.

Whereas the initial impetus for FDA derived directly from the work of Althusser, it is Foucault's perspective that for most, but not all, practitioners has become the theoretical basis for FDA. The emphasis of the early work on systems of knowledge as autonomous systems was supplemented in the later work by a shift of emphasis to the production of meaning, a shift which results in discourse and language becoming the source of any understanding of social practice and social process. Discursive practices, in Foucault's work, are restricted and inhibited by the procedures involved in the production of discourse, these procedures having the function of achieving mastery over the materiality of discourse. These discursive practices are defined by their relationship with others through interdiscursivity and intertextuality. Yet they are also dynamic, with discursive practices being a feature of social changes, with the rules of formation of discursive formations defining the field of their possible transformation.

The task for FDA was to transform the general rubric offered by Foucault into a basis for textual analysis, to develop the method of discourse analysis by integrating discourse as language into textual analysis, without reducing discourse analysis to a mere linguistic analysis of texts. As we shall see, this was taken up within the context of ideology, seen not in the terms which Foucault resisted, as a hermeneutic which conceals some 'truth', but as the production of a variety of possible meanings. This leads to semantics being considered in terms of the ambiguities of language. On the other hand, enonciative modalities and the formation of the subject are considered in terms of the linguistics of enonciation. It is these issues which become the focus of the following chapters.

4

MATERIALISM AND DISCOURSE

Introduction

Without doubt it is Michel Pécheux who should be regarded as the driving force in the emergence and development of FDA (Achard, 1993). His initial work derives primarily from the influence of Althusser, and involves adopting the Althusserian development of the concept of ideology while resorting to a linguistic analysis in order to pursue the incidence of a material ideological effect. An interest in language and linguistics led him to recognise that an interest in ideology alone was insufficient for an analysis of it. Evidently, such a line of enquiry persists with the economic materialism of Marxism, and many of the problems which the early work encountered derived from this insistence on the economic materiality of discourse. In this respect, even though an attempt at a synthesis was eventually made, the approach of Pécheux's early work differs from the Foucaltian form of FDA, which, to a great extent, was a later development. However, this is not to imply that Foucault's work was not influential with reference to Pécheux's own work.

In a reflection on FDA that was written in 1983, Pécheux referred to three stages in the work:

- The initial period he described as 'structuralist', when discourse was conceived of as an autodetermining and closed machine which fixed its enonciateurs and developed them on the base of a supposedly stable and homogeneous language. Closed corpora of sequences were constituted and analysed linguistically by privileging paraphrastic identities.
- The second phase made the relations between discursive formations the essential object of discourse analysis. Discourse was conceived of as the space where 'preconstructed' elements elaborated in other discourses are linked. But the idea that the homogeneous and fixed subject is an illusion of the surface is maintained from the earlier phase.
- The third phase was marked by the appearance of the problematic of enonciative heterogeneity and the intervention of linguistic analysis in the definition of corpus.

There are other differences, and we will strive to identify them in the following account of FDA.

The spate of political and intellectual activity in Paris during the early 1960s provided the background for the developments which promoted FDA. A number of research groups focusing upon different areas of activity were established. One such group focused upon political research within an Althusserian context and it included, among others, Jacques Rancier and Etienne Balibar. Another group, of which Pécheux was a member, worked on Marxism and epistemological problems and included Jean-Claude Milner and Jacques-Alain Miller. Similarly, another group with the same radical agenda worked on discourse analysis at the University of Nanterre under the direction of Jean Dubois. We should also not lose sight of the work on lexicology being undertaken at the Centre for Political Lexicometry of the Ecole Normale Supérieure, Saint-Cloud. The unifying force for this activity was a concern with the relevance of Marxism as the basis for a deeper understanding of society. Certainly this institutional background served as a tremendously invigorating context for the development of FDA, and it is no coincidence, for example, that the issue of *Langages* on 'Analyse du discours' edited by the Nanterre group appeared at the same time as the publication of Pécheux's initial attempt at developing a methodological framework in his *Analyse automatique du discours* (AAD69) (Pécheux, 1969).[1] It was this thrust which gave FDA the linguistic core around which the epistemological issues associated with neighbouring disciplines were focused.

The linguistic input of Pécheux's work, as we shall see, involved a listing of various integrable properties in a formalised model, while the other disciplines, most notably Marxism and psychology, by and large, tended to focus upon issues associated with how language makes sense for the subjects which were inscribed in various positions. There was a concern with how discourse involves both the subjective and social stakes of enonciation. It involves a focus on texts or enonciation in order to reveal how enonciation is constrained by its institutional constitution, how it is inscribed in an interdiscourse which fixes the social, historical and intellectual conditions of the production of discourse. It involves how the complex and relatively stable structuration of enonces have a value for a collectivity, how texts are associated with a divided conviction which they create and reinforce. That is, the concern is with how texts implicate a positioning in a discursive field. Thus the overlap with the work of Foucault (1969:201) involves the link between the corpus of material to be analysed and an institutional context which is defined by 'a social, economic, geographic or linguistic area giving the conditions of the exercise of enonciative function'. However, the object of discourse analysis is not the discursive formation itself, but its constitutive frontiers; that is, it is essential to consider not merely what can be stated, but also what cannot be stated from a given position at a given historical conjuncture. Thus, meaning is no longer a matter of semantic unity involving the concentration of a stable and homogeneous projection of what one wants to say, since such a stability is never achieved.

Again we shall see that the early work of FDA focused on the manner in which a discursive formation defines fields and enonciative 'points of origin', not as a form of subjectivity, but as a place for which the enonciateurs are substitutable, again leading to Foucault's (1969) dictum concerning the position which has to be occupied in order to be the subject of that discourse. To say that the enonciateur of a discursive formation does not speak in his/her name as a centred, rational subject is to claim that s/he assumes the status of enonciateur that defines that discursive formation in which s/he is placed. This is not to claim that there is simply one place of enonciative legitimacy within any discursive formation, but that there is a collection of enonces which return to the same positioning that can be distributed across a multiplicity of genres of discourse. The ritualised/non-ritualised character of the enonce is closely linked to the problematic of genres of discourse. Thus, a highly ritualised discourse implies a constraining institutional framing, a strong thematic restriction, a distinct stabilisation of formulae. Perhaps it is the highly ritualised discourse that has been the focus of interest for discourse analysis, and it is this focus that leads to the emphasis on the issue of repetition, where discursive objects are inscribed. This inscription is crossed by the imperceptible displacement of a constitutive repetition, involving a *parole* that re-actualises others, and which, of necessity, involves an earlier re-actualisation. *Parole* can be thought of as how subjects and objects are positioned in relation to each other. Within the discursive formation there are limitations on what can be said from certain subject positions. Clearly enonciation is never original, but is presented as a copy of the exemplary. The enonces treated within discourse analysis retain an essential relation to divergence and to memory, and in that respect they are inserted into a continual process of conservation and re-use.

Clearly it is incorrect to think of FDA in terms of the work of a single author. While it is correct that Pécheux worked on the theme of discursive materiality throughout his career, and that he was the main driving force for FDA throughout that time, he did not work alone. He had many collaborators who had a profound influence not merely upon his ideas but also on those of one another. This work continued over a period of almost twenty years and was subject to many variations, innovations and reflections throughout. It is a mistake to think of it as static. Indeed, as we have noted, Pécheux himself has referred to the achievements of the group in terms of 'three periods of discourse analysis' (Pécheux, 1990).

Having summarised the main thrust of Pécheux's work in this brief introduction, what must be done in the remainder of this chapter is to trace the developments of the ideas associated with this particular group, underlining the theoretical input and its link to a theory of society. What should become evident is the dilemma produced by the insistence upon the economic materialism of discourse when considered in relation to the broader concept of discourse as it developed within post-structuralism.

The Althusserian influence

Having graduated in philosophy in 1963, Pécheux entered the Ecole Normale Supérieure with the intention of working on the ideas of Sartre. It was here that he encountered two forces which had a profound influence on his subsequent work – Althusser and Lacan, both of whom taught at the Ecole Normale Supérieure. In 1964 Althusser wrote his paper on Freud and Lacan, a paper which was important in drawing together Marxism and psychoanalysis, a link which the orthodox position of the French Communist Party (PCF) had staunchly rejected. It was this paper which led to Pécheux's interest in psychoanalytical theory. This he drew together with linguistics and historical materialism and, despite frequent modifications, he retained this triple interest throughout his career. It is also important to note in passing that during the 1960s two highly important research groups were in place at the Ecole Normale Supérieure – the Cercle Marxiste-Léniniste and the Cercle d'Epistémologie. The latter published *Les cahiers pour l'analyse*. It was clearly an exciting intellectual environment.

There is no doubt that the most influential figure in Pécheux's work was that of Althusser, whose search for a Marxism devoid of a vulgar materialism gave Pécheux's theoretical work its direction. We have already seen that Althusser did not found his Marxism on the consciousness of the subject, and how he replaced the post Hegelain philosophy of 'praxis' with a form of anti-humanism. For him ideology came to occupy the place held in psychoanalysis by the illusion of the consciousness of the subject:

> It is customary to claim that ideology pertains to the consciousness in religion . . . In truth, ideology has very little to do with 'conscious-ness', and assumes that this term has an unequivocal meaning. It is profoundly unconscious as when presented (as in pre marxist philosophy) in a reflected form.
>
> (Althusser, 1969)

> Since Marx, we have known that the human subject, the economic, political or philosophical ego is not the 'centre' of history – and even, in opposition to the Enlightenment philosophers, and in contrast to Hegel, that history does not have a 'centre', but possesses a structure which does not have any necessary centre other than that in ideological misrecognition. In turn, Freud has discovered for us that the real subject, the individual in his unique essence, does not have the form of an ego, centred on the 'ego', on 'consciousness'

or on 'existence' – whether it is the existence of the for–itself, of body-proper, or of 'behaviour' – that the human subject is decentred, constituted by a structure which also does not have a 'centre', other than in the imaginary misrecognition of the 'ego', that is in the ideological formations in which it 'recognises' itself.

(Althusser, 1971:201)

Althusser's paper (1964/65) on Freud and Lacan, quoted above in the English translation, signalled a reversal of the orthodox Marxist disquiet with psychoanalysis, which was treated as a reactionary ideology. In his last published paper, Pécheux (1988) acknowledges this in quoting the following passage from Althusser's *Lire le Capital*:

Only since Freud have we begun to suspect what listening, and hence what speaking (and keeping silent), means; that this 'meaning' of speaking and listening reveals beneath the innocence of speech and hearing the culpable death of a second, quite different, discourse, the discourse of the unconscious.

(Althusser, 1968:16)

Althusser's paper also recalls Irigaray's (1969:111) reference to psychoanalysis as the 'technique of the subversion of the enonce, . . . psychoanalysis insists in turn on the breaking up of the text and on its intrication to a system, to a system of enonces, of enoncer, where it is not isolable. Always contesting that unity, the enonce is once more found, and always returns to its polyvalence, its ambiguity and its plurality'. Certainly for Pécheux it was this insight which, in his quest for the relevance of language for consciousness, inspired the emphasis on key terms and on the Harrisian method.

Surprisingly Pécheux makes no reference to the work of Lacan in his first important work – *Analyse automatique du discours* (AAD69). Similarly the references to Freudian and Lacanian concepts are very tentative and limited. This has been explained in terms of a hostility to psychoanalysis on the part of the head of his research unit who was a Piagetan (Gadet and Hak, 1990:49). On the other hand it probably also reflects a hesitation with reference to his personal involvement with the PCF. It has also been claimed (Gadet and Hak, 1990:51) that psychoanalysis does not intervene in a schema destined to give account of scientific practice as a level which accounts for the transformation of ideological elements in a conceptual system. None the less, psychoanalysis does appear in the work which Pécheux published under the pseudonym of Thomas Herbert (1966, 1968), where psychoanalytic concepts are used as 'instruments' related to the relationship between the analytic unconscious and the social unconscious linked to ideology. In this body of work he argued that Freud did not avoid the question of humankind as a feature of the reproduction of the labour force. That is, Pécheux was reacting to the Marxist excommunication of psychoanalysis on the grounds of it being nothing more than a petit-bourgeois ideology, and it is not inconceivable, since neither the papers which he published under his real name nor his *Analyse automatique du discours* make reference to psychoanalysis, that the use of the pseudonym was a way of avoiding the political implications of his interests. In this respect it is important to recall that the publication of Althusser's essay on Freud and Lacan in *La Nouvelle Critique* led to the journal being ostracised by the PCF. On the other hand, the Cercle d'Espistémologie of the Ecole Normale Supérieure consisted of a mixture of Marxist members of the PCF and philosophers who were profoundly influenced by Lacan (Henry, 1990).

None the less, Pécheux's early work can be seen as the systematisation of the theoretical position sustained in Althusser's work (Henry, 1990:30). In a sense, Althusser did for Marx what Lacan had done for Freud. This was achieved through his method of 'symptomatic reading', a reading which focused upon discontinuities, and in this sense it resembled the structuralist method of Vladimir Propp and Lévi-Strauss, where content was linked to myth. Pécheux's objective was to systematise this method in a way which Althusser had never attempted. It is interesting that Althusser himself rejected the link between his work and structuralism by claiming descent from the ideas of Spinoza, which led him to recognise how subversion was possible. Althusser claimed that Spinoza was the first to break with the idea that the subject was the origin, essence, or cause by questioning the origin and conception of the subject. In contrast to Derrida, Foucault and Lacan, who emphasised the impossibility of escaping 'the play of the order of the sign', Althusser insisted on the impossibility of escaping ideology, emphasising that ideology had no exterior, a claim which is distinct from claiming that 'ideologies have no exterior'. Certainly Pécheux's early work follows Althusser very closely in this respect.

Also important in the early work of Pécheux was the work of Althusser and of Canguilhem (1977) concerning the history of science and ideology, both in turn drawing on the work of Bachelard (Henry, 1990:15; Lecourt, 1978). It is here that we encounter Althusser's attempt to unravel the ideological nature of science by reference to the subject as the producer of scientific discourse, and to establish historical materialism as the only true science. This theme is very much to the fore in Pécheux's early work, where historical materialism and psychoanalysis are openly discussed. As early as 1966 he wrote 'Réflexions sur la situation théorique des sciences sociales et, spécialement, de la psychologie sociale' and this led towards his 1968 paper, 'Remarques pour une théorie générale des idéologies'. About the same time, a third article appeared in *La Pensée*, under the title of 'Les sciences humaines et le moment actuel'. It was this criticism of how epistemology serves to guarantee that scientific discourse is 'true', and of the specific role of the social and human sciences in invoking such a guarantee, that was the background for his doctoral thesis, which was published in 1969 as *Analyse automatique du discours* (AAD69), a work which will be considered in detail below. Pécheux maintained that all scientific production involved a conceptual mutation within an ideological field in relation to its recognition through earlier work which served as the guarantee of its proper scientificity. Thus, all science was a science of ideology which had two moments – first, the moment of transformation, producing its objects, which is dominated by a theoretical-conceptual elaboration which subverts the ideological discourse; and, second, the moment of methodological repro-duction of this object. The concept of production was extended to encompass intellectual activity, following the lead given by Althusser (1970). Evidently, in this phase of his work Pécheux was preoccupied with the explosion of the human sciences, and with the role of social psychology in that development. Of specific interest was the manner in which social psychology was christened as an objective science devoid of any political involvement. Pécheux saw the social sciences as pre-scientific, and in need of the instrumentation which would give them a firm basis. This involvement with the unconscious, and with ideology as the production of the effects of meaning, becomes central to his subsequent work. Indeed in 1966, under the pseudonym of Thomas Herbert, he wrote about linguistics and psychoanalysis as the science of the unconscious, and of history as the science of social formations.

In addition to the concern with historical materialism, social psychology and ideology, there is the inevitable link to linguistics. This is hardly surprising given his understanding of ideology as involving the production of the effects of meaning. Saussure achieves a position of prominence in Pécheux's work. Indeed his link to Saussure has been described as the basis of an original problematic (Maldidier, 1990:14). Maldidier states that his reformulation of the Saussurean *parole* constituted a distinctive development on Althusser's work (Guilhaumou *et al.*, 1994:176). For Pécheux, Saussure's work was the origin of linguistic science, the affirmation of the Saussurean break being of fundamental theoretical importance. The essential ingredient of the Saussurean break – the linguistic equivalent to the Marxist epistemological break referred to by Althusser – involved viewing language as a system. The emergence of the metaphoric effect had a profound impact with reference to meaning. However, he also claimed that the symmetry of the Saussurean distinction between what he called the creative subjectivity of *parole* and the systematic objectivity of *langue* was illusory: 'All is past, it writes, as if scientific linguistics (assigned by the object *langue*) liberates a residue which is the philosophic concept of the free subject, thought of as the indispensable reverse, the necessary correlate of system' (quoted in Maldidier, 1990:14). His fundamental objection was that the subject was conceived of as involved in the 'extra-linguistic systematicity of thought as a reflection or vision of "reality"' (Pécheux, 1975a:37–38). He simultaneously objected to the reflection thesis of sociolinguistics, and also to the concept of the centred subject. He was thus able to avoid the Marxist problem of ideology as conspiratorial. In place of *parole* he insisted upon the concept of discourse, *parole* being divested of its subjective implications. This leads to the fundamental premise of his work – the linking of *langue* with the Saussurean concept of system, and the manner in which the psychological subject is constrained by the linguistic order.

It is perhaps opportune momentarily to distinguish Pécheux's conception of the subject from that associated with Derrida, Lacan and Foucault. Foucault's (1969:126) famous dictum concerning how the subject involves a position which must be assumed in order to be the subject of a discourse clearly involves enonciative positions, since discourses are enonced. This was consistent with his objective of defining a new field hitherto occupied by the history of ideas. The subject for Foucault was the subject of the 'order of discourse' (Foucault, 1971). For Derrida, on the other hand, the subject related to the play of the order of the sign, while for Lacan it involved the unconscious being structured as a language. All of their conceptions of subject were linked to language or the sign. For Althusser the main focus was ideology, and he was never particularly interested in language. Thus, for Pécheux, the focus of the subject involved the link between ideology and language. Herein lies his originality. He adopted Althusser's reference concerning a parallel between the transparency of language and the 'elementary ideological effect'. This led to Althusser establishing a connection between them, and in turn it led to Pécheux's focus upon the concept of discourse. Despite the apparent similarity, and the claim that Pécheux derived the concept from Foucault (Maingueneau, 1991:14), Pécheux's understanding of discourse was distinct from that of Foucault. It can be claimed, of course, that in working with Marxism and Foucaultianism he was operating with conceptions which were difficult to integrate. Indeed, there is a sense in which his failure to make a greater impact upon French intellectualism than he did derives from the failure of his audience to understand how he was seeking to integrate the two directions. Furthermore, many of his students, while being to the left of centre, were not orthodox Marxists and this, together with his attempts to grapple with both Althusserianism and Foucault led to him being seen as someone who was enmeshed in an inescapable contradiction. Certainly until the mid 1970s his Marxism was very orthodox and his subsequent move away from this position left him carrying a heavy burden.

This link between 'the subject of language' and the 'subject of ideology' is to the fore in AAD69, where Pécheux seeks to establish the relationship between 'subjective evidence' and 'evidence of meaning – or of signification', and the link between linguistics and ideology. In so doing he renounced the possibility of developing a general theory of ideology or of ideologies. Rather, he focused attention on the links between the object of analysis, a theory of discourse, and the object of linguistics. This coincided with Foucault's emphasis on the articulation between discourse, knowledge and power. This orientation sought to link theory with method in a very concrete manner, and touched upon an issue which was to become crucial, that of the limit of analysis and linguistic theory when confronted with issues of meaning, signification and semantics.

It is in AAD69 that we encounter the concept 'discursive process', and it is clear that a fundamental influence on the emergence of the concept was the work of Etienne Balibar concerning the extent to which language can be thought to be 'indifferent' to social class struggle. In this respect he was also echoing Althusser in referring to 'the relative autonomy of the linguistic system' (Pêcheux, 1975a:59), and to the claim that '. . . every discursive process is inscribed in an ideological class relationship' (Pêcheux, 1975a:59). The retention of the materialist position is important, and becomes problematic in his later work. However, it is also relevant to note that he did not treat language as a simple superstructure, nor as a simple reflection of class structure wherein each class language has its own grammar. This allowed language, whether it be conceived of as a feature of superstructure or infrastructure, as something beyond the functional reductionism of the vulgar Marxism which Althusser objected to. More importantly perhaps, his materialist position avoided the structuralist position vis-à-vis universalism, this being particularly important with reference to semantics. Yet his main objective is, without doubt, to produce a materialist theory of discourse. This involved a claim that meaning was not determined by language; the fixing of meanings wherein the real has primacy over thought 'has nothing at all to do with purely linguistic properties, but concerns a completely different "exterior" . . . the class struggle in its various economic, political and ideological forms' (Pêcheux, 1975a:185). No clearer expression of the existence of an externality beyond discourse could be desired. Maldidier (1990:14) suggests that at the end of the 1960s this development, deriving from the contemporaneous philosophic concerns of the human sciences, together with the work of the linguist Dubois, led to the founding of a new discipline – the analysis of discourse.

Maldidier (Guilhaumou *et al.*, 1994) explicates the difference between the work of Pêcheux and Dubois, arguing that their contemporaneous concern with discourse analysis was the consequence of a particular conjuncture in the history of French intellectualism. Whereas Dubois saw discourse analysis as a mode of reading, removing the subjectivity of reading, leaving the grill of 'grammar' as the basis of literary criticism; for Pêcheux, at least in the beginning, discourse analysis was a substitute for content analysis. These two approaches were also different in other respects. For Dubois, discourse analysis, with its focus upon enonciation, was a natural extension of his concern with lexicology or the study of the word. He theorised the relationship between linguistics and an externality by drawing two models into relationship, one involving linguistics and the other that which relates to another discipline. In this respect Dubois lacked the critique of science that was central to Pêcheux's work.

'Discursive process' may well be inferred to mean 'process of the production of discourse', and the term 'conditions of production' is a formulation of the descriptive notion of 'circumstances'. Again one is drawn back to the work of Althusser and the manner in which he referred to the relationship between science and ideology. Maldidier (1990:15) suggests that it involves the equivalent in social theory of Jakobson's elements of a scheme of communication. In referring to the conditions of production, Pécheux was alluding to the central conception of discourse as 'determined by an externality, involving everything other than language that makes discourse what it is – the socio-historic tissue that it constitutes' (Maldidier, 1990:15).

In AAD69 Pécheux was pursuing the line of reasoning established by Canguilhem and Bachelard which saw the relevant instruments, prior to becoming scientific, as consisting of simple techniques. They cite the example of scales as instruments of commercial transactions which, through Galileo, became the object of the theory of balance, an integral feature of physics (Maldidier, 1990:12). That is, there is no instrument other than in relation to a theory. The scientific instruments of AAD69 could not be conceived independently of a theory which was inclusive, or which could lead to a theory in relation to this same instrument. The instrument could appropriate the theory. This was particularly relevant with reference to linguistics, and it was not possible to derive an instrument via any 'applied' linguistic analysis. For this reason he began his work with a critique of the method of textual analysis. He was seeking a transformation of social-scientific practice in order to discover a truly scientific practice. At the same time he insisted that social science was ideological, and emphasised that a critique of the philosophy of the social sciences was necessary. His goal was to develop a science of ideology. In this respect he rejected all objectivity. This is highly reminiscent of Canguilhem's (1977) claim that scientific ideologies were characterised as discourses which, in the absence of the possibility of experimental verification in their own field, founded their credibility on a calculus of a maximum of analogies with data established in other fields (Henry, 1990:37, fn 10). The use of instruments is seen as scientific, and scientific practices are linked to a continuity of non-scientific practices. Little reference is made to the relation of instruments or methods to epistemology and the philosophy of empirical knowledge.

At first sight this use of scientific instruments seems unrelated to common social demand. On the other hand instruments do seem to be linked to social order, where they are employed to guarantee ideological positions. Consequently, it is impossible to disassociate the use of scientific methods and instruments from political and ideological positions. Thus the issues of empirical and linguistic tools were not only technical problems, they were also theoretical problems. This is an issue which we will return to in Chapter 6, when we consider linguistic issues, since Pécheux was concerned with the type of linguistic analysis required by an operational system, and with the associated problems of the limits of analysis of a linguistic theory faced with questions of meaning, signification and semantics (Henry, 1990:23).

In discussing AAD69 it is as well to separate theory and method before proceeding to show the relationship between them (Achard, 1993). Maldidier (1990:16–17) admits to a naïveté in the work, but simultaneously claims that it served to lay the ground for subsequent work. On reflection, Pécheux himself saw AAD as the product of a 'theoretical urgency' related to the debates and politics of the sixties. His objective was to integrate historical materialism, linguistics in the form of syntactic mechanisms, the process of enonciation, and a theory of discourse which involved the theory of the historic determination of semantic processes. Within this conjunction there was a further ingredient, that of the psychoanalytic theory of the subject. This involved a rejection of the conception of the human subject as the source of all meaning which merely repeated a pre-existing universal meaning, even if the illusion is created that the subject is the source of all meaning. Evidently, this relates to the Althusserian claim for the material nature of ideology. However, discourse was not identified as ideology, this conception being described as an idealist deviation. Rather, he saw 'the discursive as one of the material aspects of ideological materiality' (Pécheux and Fuchs, 1975:11). Thus the objective was to develop a theory of discourse which was not founded on the subject, a theory premised on the idea that the subject is not the source of meaning even if s/he is involved in the illusion that s/he is at the very source of meaning.

A sequence or an enonce does not have 'meaning' for a subject other than in relation to a given discursive formation, which Pécheux understood as the components of a determinate ideological formation which articulates with the specifics of the conditions of production. The concept of ideological formation, in turn, derives directly from Althusser, and involves a body of attitudes, representations, etc. which are related to class positions, being capable of intervention as a force, while being confronted by other ideological formations within the ideological conjuncture characteristic of a social formation at any given moment. Clearly there is a link between the idea of social formation as the sum of various modes of production (Althusser, 1968:207), and that of ideological formation which consists of a series of discursive formations. This view of social formation has been highly influential in much Marxist theory, particularly with reference to economic development and the sexual division of labour, and is instrumental in refuting the claim that the solution of 'revolution' is an effect of contradictions in a single mode of production (Benton, 1984:75). There are, of course, other overlaps between the work of Althusser and Pécheux which should be considered here.

The analysis which Althusser provides of the base/superstructure relationship is a functionalist one – the persistence of a social formation depends upon the reproduction of the conditions of production. This involves the replacement of instruments of production, the replacement of labour power and the reproduction of these relationships within which production takes place. It is these concepts which are considered by Pécheux in his development of the concepts of ideology and discourse. Of course, as Althusser acknowledges, many of these ideas derive directly from the work of Gramsci. Thus, drawing upon Gramsci's distinction between the State and civil society, Althusser (1970) developed the distinction between Repressive State Apparatus (RSA) and Ideological State Apparatus (ISA), the latter being the means whereby the consent of the proletariat to the dominance of the ruling class is achieved. Drawing in turn upon the work of Lacan, he proceeded to discuss the manner in which the mechanisms whereby the reproductive requirements of the social formation are inscribed in the subjective world of individual social actors. The ISA prepares and distributes agents to different positions in the relations of production while retaining the illusion that it is done through free choice and consent. Humankind was seen as an ideological animal which 'lived' its struggles as a subject in the 'medium' of ideology through the transformation of its consciousness. Benton (1984:105) has implied that this position in Althusser's early work lacks a clear elaboration of resistance and opposition, an ingredient which, as we shall see, Pécheux does introduce. Althusser's modification appeared in the same year as AAD69, and involved the claim that material ideological apparatuses govern material practices and rituals into which material actions are inserted, these being the beliefs and ideas of the subject.

When Lacan (1978:16) expressed his famous axiom concerning the way 'signifying represents another subject for another signifier', it marked the incompatibility between the subject of the unconscious and whatever other localised form that could be identified as subject. It was this which prompted Pécheux to suggest that signification attributes places and identification to subjects from a specific point of view, a mechanism of differential identification which transmits the social effect (Pécheux, 1975a:108). Drawing on Lacan's conception of the mirror-phase of his psychoanalysis, he developed Althusser's concept of interpolation which sought to explain how humans are constituted as conscious subjects who voluntarily submit to the requirements of the social system. He argued that the constitution of individuals as subjects involves a recognition of other subjects, this occurring in the imaginary. This was then related to Lacan's discussion of the Oedipal phase in terms of submission to the prevailing symbolic order. It is as an elaboration of this position that Pécheux's work must be seen.

Pécheux argued that words, phrases, etc. change their meaning according to the position held by them – they are given a conjuncture determined by a state of class struggle, and an ideological and political 'position', in that conjuncture. Thus a discursive formation determines what can and must be said from that position. Evidently this is close to the concept of place as discussed above with reference to the work of Foucault. The crux of the argument is that meaning does not have anything to do with purely linguistic properties, but rather they are part of the ideological sphere. As such they involve a struggle over meaning, a struggle which relates to class struggle. Again drawing on Althusser's work Pécheux indicates that this class struggle involves economic, political and ideological dimensions, which operate to set up discursive meanings. Drawing on the concept of interpolation, he argues that individuals are constituted as subjects by the discursive formation, and the subject is thought to be the source of meaning so that it is carried, without rendering account, to identify with the discursive formation. Words change their meaning in passing from one discursive formation to another, and words, propositions, etc. which belong to the same discursive formation will have the same meaning in being subject to the same conditions that endow them with meaning within that discursive formation. That is, words change their meanings according to the positions from which they are employed.

He referred to discursive process, or the process through which words assume meaning, as the relations of substitution, synonyms, paraphrases between the linguistic elements of the same discursive formation. The effect of discursive meaning is constituted from the internal relation to that family of substitutes. Thus a word does not have a fixed meaning, meaning being indissolubly tied to metaphorisation – the meaning 'slides' in an unforeseeable way in the ensembles of paraphrases, substitutions, etc. proper to each discursive formation. As we shall see, this claim is fundamental to the methodological approach.

The methodology of AAD69

Let us now turn to briefly consider the methodological aspect of AAD69. It will not be surprising that Pécheux's understanding of the novelty of this approach simultaneously obliged him to interrogate the instrument of his analysis. It was inevitable that he would focus upon the conditions of production of discourse and the processes of the production of discourse (Guilhaumou et al., 1994:177). Given this perspective, the purely internal analysis of a single discursive formation is meaningless, and AAD69 emphasises that the creation of a corpus must involve an ensemble of concrete discourses dominated by the same conditions of production, there being a correspondence between a determined state of conditions of production of discourse and a definite structure of process of the production of discourse. 'It is impossible to analyse discourse as a text . . . it is necessary to refer to the ensemble of possible discourses, beginning from a definite state of conditions of production' (Pécheux, quoted in Maldidier, 1990:15–16). In referring to possible discourses, Pécheux seems to be returning to the idea of problematic which Althusser employed in his concept of reading, wherein one does not merely read what the text says, but also what it cannot say. The discursive corpus is defined as 'the ensemble of texts of variable language (or discursive sequences) returning to the conditions of production which are viewed as stable' (Pécheux, 1969:17). Despite the inevitable link between theory and method, there is a sense in which the criteria for the creation of a corpus lie outside of the analysis, being linked to the theory in the form of the conditions of production, and with the discursive not being capable of reduction, either to the linguistic, or to the ideological.

What becomes apparent in a consideration of this first phase of analysis is that while the theoretical work of AAD69 draws heavily upon the work of Althusser, and, from linguistics, that of Benveniste and Culioli, the methodological approach relies very much on the work of Zelig Harris. At first glance this reference to Harris seems misplaced, given the reputation which distributionalism has for being either behaviourist, empiricist or idealist. Certainly it is far removed from the economic materialism from which Pêcheux's work derived. On the other hand, Harris' work is firmly rooted in the ideas of Saussure, and it is in a consideration of how the claim is made that the linguist is not armed to discuss meaning, but can only 'define the occurrence of a linguistic element as a function of the occurrence of other linguistic elements' (Harris, 1969:10), that leads to his relevance for a consideration of the effects of meaning. Furthermore, the students of the linguist Culioli were very much involved in the contribution of Harris after the translation of his 1952 paper on discourse analysis into French in 1969 (Harris, 1969). In some respects, given the impact which the work of Harris and Chomsky had upon French linguistics at this time, it is unlikely that Pêcheux could have ignored it. Maldidier (Guilhaumou *et al.*, 1994:178) suggests that at this time both Dubois and Pêcheux resorted to relating the idea of a deep structure to the discursive structure.

Harris' contribution did not generate a systematic, operational method, nor did it serve as the basis for dealing with the referential aspects of discourse analysis. It was, basically, an empirical method of category construction, deriving from the earlier work of Troubetskoy and Bloomfield. Troubetskoy worked within phonology in trying to show how sounds, despite having an infinite variety of possibilities, bind together to affect meaning, thereby being free from the concrete object referred to. Harris' basic proposition was that if one has a sufficient corpus, the use of the speaker's intuition can lead to considering the distribution of recurring sequences, and to establishing the classification of categories at the different levels of phonology, morphology and syntax. Subsequent developments, associated with a thorough critique by Chomsky, and Harris' introduction of transformations, made this approach redundant. None the less, as we shall see in Chapter 7, distributionalism remains a concern, and while it is not of particular importance in linguistics, it is central to discourse analysis, being an empirical means of referencing repetition in the corpus, of organising the vocabulary of referential notions, of objectifying the 'semantic' fields by reference to formal analysis rather than intuition. Achard (1986) claims that it dovetails neatly with Foucault's description of discourse as a 'regular series of distinctive events'.

What is involved in AAD69 is an attempt to discover the principles of regulation associated with the formation of classes of equivalence. New enonciations derive from the saturation of such classes. It involves enclosing syntax by reducing the corpus to its elementary statements from a number of fixed places. This leads to establishing distributional classes which are comparable to Harris' classes of equivalence from which the semantic domains specific to a discursive process are registered. It does strive to go beyond orthodox distributional linguistics, which would merely claim to 'define the occurrence of a linguistic element as a function of the occurrence of other linguistic elements' (Harris, 1969:10). This is achieved by trying to establish the effects of meaning through looking at meaning as something distinct from that which is associated with the subject. Rather, meaning derives from the combination of units of language which are endowed with stable and clear signification.

The Mansholt Report (Pécheux *et al.*, 1979) is usually cited as an example of the potential of this form of analysis. However, the publication of this analysis was delayed for several years, and when it did emerge it included a potent critique of the method of AAD69 by the authors themselves. The source of the work was a single page from a report by Sicco Mansholt which advocated a radical solution to the crises of capitalism in a highly ambiguous manner. It was the 'ideological ambiguity of reformism' (Pécheux *et al.*, 1979:252) that was the focus of the work. This text was given to fifty students. With the first group of twenty-five, the work was ascribed to left-wing economists, whereas with the other group of twenty-five, it was ascribed to right-wing government officials. Each person was asked to summarise the text in a dozen lines from which a 'left corpus' and a 'right corpus' was developed. Three ambiguities were referenced: those inherent in the text, that involved in the ascription of the text, and that of the class position of the respondents, all of whom derived from the petit bourgeoisie, and who thereby occupied an ambiguous class position. It was discovered that similar lexical items changed their meaning from one corpus to the other, this serving to demonstrate the impossibility of a 'universal semantics'. The ambiguities of a reformist text such as the Mansholt Report generated a struggle over meaning associated with conflicting discourses and positions. Again we are reminded of Althusser's work on the problematic.

Given the innovative nature of the programme of AAD69, and the breadth and nature of its objectives, it was inevitable that it would be subject to extensive criticisms (c.f. Maingueneau, 1976:93–96). Many of these were self-criticisms which aimed at sophisticating the entire project. Thus Maldidier referred to the absence of enonciation, a weak conceptualisation of language which retains the very structuralism that the project was seeking to escape from, with the 'invariant base' replacing the selection/combination or syntactic/lexical distinction. Similarly, Fuchs referred to the problems thrown up by the morpho-syntactic analysis which was employed merely to delineate the text without reference to the semantic problem that was at the heart of the project. More importantly perhaps, she suggested, again consistent with the ideas of the problematics which were in circulation, that the traditional grammatical categories that were employed, deriving as they did from a functional theory, betrayed a philosophical heritage which was at odds with that of AAD69. The implication here is that linguistics itself is a discourse.

The team itself took on board the criticisms that the construction of domains was too arbitrary a procedure, that the criteria of comparisons induced certain consequences, and that the entire procedure lacked a system of balance (Maingueneau 1976:95). Similarly Pécheux, in addressing the issue of the signification of domains, asked whether there was an underlying orientation which had been forgotten and was affected by the manner in which metonymy and synonymy effaced syntagmatisation. Certainly in the 1975 issue of *Langages* edited by Pécheux, Fuchs, Gresillion and Henry there is a developed self-criticism. They present a global conception of discourse as involving language and ideology, the central notion of which is the paraphrase.

The co-text refers to the linguistic units which precede or follow the deictic referent, while intertextuality refers to the type of citation which an archive defines as legitimate for its practice. Given the theoretical perspective adopted by Pécheux, both co-textuality and intertextuality is weak if restricted to the corpus. The removal of the centred subject leads to a consideration of the enonciative act in a different light, and involves a discussion of the paraphrase where there is a paraphrastic relationship between speaker A and speaker B such that there is a derivation rule of A to B or B to A, where there is an effect of possible meaning for A which bears reference to the effect of meaning for B. That is, the subject is no longer in charge of the speech-act in the sense that the centred subject states what s/he wants to state as a conscious, rational subject, but is subject to constraints that are linked to the discursive position.

One issue emerges as problematic, not merely in relation to AAD69, but also with reference to subsequent work. This concerns the theoretical status of linguistics in discourse analysis. It is one thing merely to relegate linguistics to a methodological role, but this simply ignores the problem. What makes the issue obvious is first, that the same method appears to be acceptable for different theoretical propositions; and, second, that there may also be the inevitability of refusing to address the problem of the philosophical nature of linguistic theory by relegating it to the place of method. However, if we are to claim that Harris' distributionalism carries an implicit behaviourism, it means that linguistic theory does carry a relevant theoretical input which, in turn, must lead to a consideration of the relationship between the sociological and the linguistic theories. Perhaps this is merely to obscure the problem by creating a false dichotomy, and that it is essential to think of language as social, and linguistics as a discourse relating to the social. Of course this is not difficult with reference to sociolinguistics, where the political tends to be explicit. The problem lies with a linguistics which claims to be an objective science which merely considers internal structures devoid of the social, either internal or external to language. This position was useful for AAD69 in that it allowed such a linguistics to be employed in an abstract manner in order to avoid the problem of conspiracy in a discussion of ideology, while also allowing Pécheux to treat causality in the form of materiality as something that lies somehow beyond this linguistics. However, that would merely raise the further problem – if linguistics is merely a discourse, then what is its status in its methodological role in analysing discourse? Perhaps it is this issue, more than any other, that is highlighted in AAD69.[2] It is an issue which was central at the beginning of the 1980s, and will be considered in detail in Chapter 6.

Maingueneau (1976:95) claims that Pécheux's objective was, in part, to make linguists sensitive to theoretical issues in their linking of language and society, and to be critical of the implicit theory of their particular position. This he certainly achieved. The theoretical programme, deriving as it did from Althusserianism, was extremely elaborate, but it was also a project which sought to integrate this theoretical rigour with a methodological rigour. The difficulties of integrating historical materialism with both discourse theory and linguistic theory were hardly easy ones. Perhaps the central question concerned the nature of the relationship between the discursive and the linguistic, which leads to the question of the nature of the linguistics that is addressed. The emphasis on the syntactic, and a fairly traditional grammatical analysis in the methodology of AAD69, resulted in a functionalist orientation wherein the occurrence of a linguistic element is a function of the occurrence of other linguistic elements. This was later to be redressed by shifting the emphasis to enonciative process. There is little doubt that this intellectual enterprise did lay the ground for the subsequent study of the theory and practice of discourse analysis. Whereas Pécheux sought to deploy the Harrisian method in order to seize the traces of discursive processes, as Maldidier (Guilhaumou *et al.*, 1994:179) notes, he did so at a time when the shadow of structuralism remained cast upon French linguistics.

New directions

I have already underlined that Pécheux's training prior to AAD69 was in the fields of philosophy and sociology. His involvement with the rigorous link between theory and practice led him in the direction of linguistics. From 1968 two important influences – Culioli and Fuchs – guided his involvement in this field. At that time Culioli led a team which was engaged in the study of automatic translation, and this interest was particularly influential in the development of the computer aspect of AAD69. In 1970, following the appearance of AAD69, a new Centre National de Recherche Scientifique (CNRS) group was formed dedicated to furthering the venture. It included both a linguistic and a mathematical component. Throughout this period of Pécheux's work, the emphasis is clearly on the issue of enonciation that was missing in AAD69. In this respect he is turning towards the earliest work of Jakobson and Benveniste, but this issue was also central to the theoretical linguistics of Culioli. Pécheux's work focused upon the question of the production of a statement by a speaking subject, enonciation being the key to discourse and semantics.

In 1970 a collaborative work involving Culioli, Fuchs and Pécheux was published (1970). Its content was very much in the Culioli mould. The importance of this work for subsequent developments lay in the claim that discursive formations submit to their non-linguistic determinants, and it involved a comparison of rhetoric and stylistic modulations. More importantly, there was reference to the difference between the effects of meaning which reveals the conscious strategy of the speaker, and that which derives from the existence of interdiscourse – leading to the claim that interdiscourse has a theoretical and practical primacy over the intra-discourse. That is, the object of discourse analysis was not the discursive formation *per se* but its constitutive frontier, and its identity was linked to the stabilisation of a certain enonciative configuration. Interdiscourse was seen as a modality of a relationship which served to highlight such a configuration.

At the same time there emerged a complex of ideas which involved a number of themes. The first was an objection to the extension of linguistic structuralism to all human sciences. In this respect Pécheux was denying the possibility of a universal method for the 'general analysis of the human spirit', of a science of sciences which ignores the essential, social relationships. The second theme concerned a reflection on the theoretical basis of linguistics in a work which heralded a significant entry into linguistics, at a time when generative grammar and the impact of linguistics on the human sciences was profound. It involved the development of a case against the orthodox understanding of semantics, which relied on the centred human subject as the basis of meaning. Drawing on the work of Saussure, Pécheux sought to develop an argument reminiscent of Althusser's argument about the epistemo-logical break in Marx's work. Inevitably, this also involved a polemic against the scientific nature of linguistics, and an associated plea for the status of historic materialism as the only true science. In this respect a passionate political philosophy of science lay at the core of this intervention. There emerges what appears to be a plea to treat linguistics as a discourse which functions in terms of itself. This is a theme which was to become a preoccupation, involving a search for that which makes linguistics work. It is, of course, a continuation of the theme of problematic and the construction of scientific theory.

Pécheux's 1971 paper in *Langages* reworked the Saussurean break (Haroch, Henry and Pécheux, 1971). He argued in terms of subordinating signification to the idea of value as developed by Saussure. Following Normand (1970), he develops the idea of value, asking why Saussure persisted in linking *parole* to the rational speaking subject. He claimed that Saussure, despite placing the emphasis on the structural basis of *langue*, could not develop a break between *parole* and the subject. In refuting that link, Pécheux was laying a different emphasis on semantics, claiming that it had to escape from the grasp of a linguistics, which could not deal adequately with meaning. While Saussure had worked in terms of different levels – phonological level, morphological level and the level of syntax – Pécheux claimed that there was no semantic level homologous to the others. He claimed that 'the link which relates the "signification" of a text to the socio-historic conditions of that text is by no means secondary, but, rather, it constitutes signification itself'. The development was important – it sought to designate linguistic semantics as the site of recovery of the Saussurean break. It is at precisely this point that the problematic of discourse intervenes, involving the 'shift of ground' which such a development presupposes.

This stage of his work established discourse analysis as a specific field. In refuting the structuralist perspective he was denying the Jakobsonian conception of language as a global code, and the idea of language that he had employed in AAD69 was enriched. It linked to historical materialism and the theory of ideology. This emphasis on historical materialism involves a refutation of empiricism, which he described as 'the subjectivist problematic centred on the individual', as well as formalism, which confuses 'the language of objects with the field of language'. This phase of his work concludes with the following statement: 'As one of their components, the ideological formations necessarily carry one or more interrelated discursive formations, which determine that which can and must be said from a given position in a given conjuncture' (Haroche et al., 1971:106). As Maldidier (1990:24) comments, a reference to Althusser is missing. More significant perhaps is the absence of any reference to the work of Foucault, who lay outside of the Marxist endeavour of French politics and intellectualism! The difference between Foucault's discussion of a discursive formation and Pécheux's reference to ideological formations revolves not merely around a Marxist concern with ideology, but also around Althusser's discussion of Freud, where decentring involves the constitution of the human subject within an ideological formation which 'centres' that subject as the imaginary 'me' (Althusser, 1964:33–34). Once it is recognised that ideology is not conceived of as a conspiratorial process, the difference between Pécheux and Foucault is reduced to the relevance of the class structure as the dominant feature of society.

In 1970, Althusser's paper on ISA appeared, a paper which had a profound influence on the social sciences. Not least among its achievements was a reference to the subject of ideology in association with the concept of interpolation. As a committed Althusserian, it is no surprise that the influence of the La Pensée paper also appears in Pécheux's work. It takes the form of discourse being implicitly assimilated into a specific practice that is required for the relations of social forces, this always being realised within the context of an institution or apparatus. Certainly, in the work of Pécheux during the early 70s it is the Althusserian influence that is most evident.

The most significant development is the idea that 'ideology interpolates the individual as subject'. Given the relationship between discourse and ideology, it focuses on the claim that the subject does not appear outside of discourse, but is made to appear in and through discourse, and interpolation is a crucial concept in this respect. Evidently the work of Althusser had led to the key question of the nature of the relationship between meaning and the subject, this being the basis of the quest for a materialist theory of discourse.

On the linguistic side, the concept of the preconstituted was decisive, being fundamental in furnishing a linguistic anchorage for the understanding of interdiscourse. In this respect his work was closely associated with that of Paul Henry. There was something of a beginning in AAD69, which noted the work of the pragmatist Ducrot on presuppositions, wherein discourse intervenes in the link between understanding and the taken-for-granted, or that which was already understood. Culioli had employed the term preconstructed in relation to a theory of lexis, and it was this that was linked with the concept of pre-supposition. This development involved a materialist reading of Frege, as well as a critical reading of Ducrot. Evidently there was a fundamental opposition between the pragmatism of Ducrot and Frege on the one hand, and Pécheux and Henry on the other, particularly with reference to the question of subject and meaning. For Ducrot and Frege, from the point of view of logic, the discussion of the presupposition involved an imperfection in the relation between natural language and the referent. Certain constructions authorised by syntax 'presupposed' the existence of a referent, independently of the assertion of a subject. Ducrot sought to interpret this phenomenon in terms of a rational-pragmatics which derived from a specific reading of Frege – the presupposition defines the frame on which dialogue unwinds. This occurs within speech-acts for all subjects of enonciation, involving a play of forces instituted by the play of language. This process trapped the addressees in their discourse. It involved a modernist attempt to incorporate Bakhtin's dialogism by reference to rational human subjects.

For Pécheux and Henry, on the other hand, this issue touched directly on the relationship between syntax and semantics, being located at the same point as discourse articulates with language. In contrast to the pragmatic interpretation, they claimed that the syntactic structures which authorise the presentation of certain elements outside of the assertion of a subject as 'the traces of earlier constructions', involve combinations of elements of language which had been ossified in prior discourse, but which continue to have an effect. The concept of presupposition was replaced by that of preconstructed, which was rooted in the problematic of discourse. It was this development that allowed Pécheux to think in terms of the interdiscourse.

In 1975 an issue of *Langages* appeared under the editorship of Pécheux, that is, almost at the same time as the publication of his *Las vérités de La Palice*. However, the former work was put together some time earlier, and reflected the work of the early 1970s. In that work the emphasis is very clearly upon the linguistic, and in many respects it is transitionary, and should be understood as such. In this issue he works closely with Fuchs, with whom he and Culioli had written a paper in 1970, and with whom he continued to work on a 'grammar of recognition'.

The main thrust of the paper written with Fuchs (Pécheux and Fuchs, 1975) was the integration of a theory of discourse with a method of its analysis. Inevitably it constituted a response to the criticisms generated by AAD69, and, in a sense, it is a reworking of Pécheux's previous work. It involves three aspects of scientific knowledge: historical materialism as the theory of social formations and their transformations, including the theory of ideology; linguistics as the theory of both syntactic mechanisms and the process of enonciation; and the theory of discourse as a theory of the determination of semantic processes. The thread that links these themes is that of the theory of subjectivity, which carries a strong psychoanalytic intonation. Throughout there is an echo of the work of Althusser. By now the issue of discourse involves the questions of the subject and of meaning, while fully integrating that which hitherto had been missing – enonciation.

Guilhaumou and Maldidier (Guilhaumou et al., 1994) have referred to the emergence of enonciation in FDA. Beginning with an elaboration of Benveniste's differentiation of enonce and enonciation, it linked with Harrisian distributionalism in extending the analysis beyond a preoccupation with the phrase. The problematic of enonciation is what permitted the uncovering of the relationships between subjects by reference to situations and conjunctures within the enonce. This established two heterogeneous problematics which reproduced the base/form relationship. It recognised the marks of the speaking subjects in the text that was reduced to the paraphrastic totality. It contributed to reformulating the question of the subject in the theory of enonciation. The issue of the subject revolved around the question of the subject in extracting a psychologistic view on the one hand, and the empiricism of communication on the other. In this respect it related to the notion of discursive strategies which involve attention to the decentred subject. It involved empirical subjects confronting legitimate and acceptable discursive practices. At this time an allegiance to the link between ideology and enonciation meant that the formal aparatus of enonciation could not be thought of as the unique means of positioning subjects in a particular conjuncture, since subjects were determined by an exterior ideology.

The Althusserian intrusion is perhaps most evident in the manner in which the linguistic is constantly led towards the idea of how ideology interpolates the subject, and to the associated apparatus where politico-ideological positions are confronted. It focuses on an integration of the subject and meaning. Central in this argument is the theory of two forgottens, which briefly appears during this period, only to be heavily criticised and jettisoned. I will return to the issue of memory later.

Having created the concept of discursive formation, not in a Foucaultian sense, but on the model of the Marxist conceptions of social and ideological formations, Pécheux needed to develop this focus. The development of a theory of discourse based upon a theory of ideology derived directly from Althusser's ISA paper, where he makes direct reference to discursive formations. In the issue of *Langages* (Pécheux, 1975b:37), Pécheux classifies 'discursive space' within the 'ideological genre', seemingly presenting the existence of a new space in the form of 'discourse' side by side with previously recognised ideological practices while ignoring the 'relations of inequality-subordination' between the discursive and the ideological. This is acknowledged in *Les vérités de La Palice* (Pécheux, 1975a:145). At the interior of the discursive were displacements which reflected the 'relative externality' of the ideological formation. Here he refers to the preconstructed as the trace, in the same discourse, of prior discourses, which furnishes the primary objects of the discursive formation to which the evidence for the subject is attached. This position shifted the relationship between the subjective effect associated with language and the production of meaning to the interior of the discursive formation. Furthermore, what had been referred to in AAD69 as the semantic domains, by now become the 'paraphrastic families' which constitute the matrix of meaning. The Harrisian concept of paraphrase has been divorced from its orthodox linguistic and logistic context, and is related to the subjective illusion in which the subject thinks itself to be at the source of meaning itself.

Pécheux envisages a base on which discursive processes are developed, once again returning to the theme of language conditioning the possibility or potential of discourse, but also asking the fundamental question: 'if language is the material link which realises the effect of meaning, what is that materiality made of?' In his early work the answer was simply that the phonological, morphological and syntactic systems represented the functioning of the language in relation to itself insofar as the semantic exceeds the value of the linguistic. The work with Henry on the preconstructed focused primarily upon the relative proposition. It seemed that the relative propositions had started to assume a place of prominence in the reflection on discourse. Certain relatives had the power to be the object of a determinant or appositive interpretation. This observation revealed a linguistic phenomenon which straddled syntax and semantics, begging the question of the existence of an autonomous syntactic level. He claimed that the frontier separating the linguistic and the discursive was such that it was not possible to conceive of syntax in terms of a homogeneous block of rules organised on a logical basis. As a consequence it was claimed that it was essential to turn to the question of enonciation, which hitherto had received little attention. To a considerable extent enonciative linguistics was viewed as an alternative to an orthodox linguistics dominated by a concern with syntax.

However, as should be evident, it was necessary to divorce the earlier work of those such as Bally, Jakobson and Benveniste from a subjectivist stance in which the conscious speaking subject is the source which gives meaning to that which it has stated. Simultaneously, confronted by idealist theories, he sought 'to sketch a non subjective theory of enonciation', involving a reflection on the materiality of language and the subject effect. As such it refuted the 'formalist illusion which makes enonciation a simple system of operations'. Given that the enonciative mechanisms are considered as an integral part of materiality, there is a link to syntactic mechanisms. However, it emerges within the conceptual space associated with the theory of two forgottens.

This theory draws heavily on psychoanalysis, and particularly on the work of Lacan. It involves the illusion of the subject effect wherein the subject believes that it is the source of meaning. In what is referred to as 'forgetting No. 1', the subject suppresses the idea that meaning is formed in a process which is itself external, so that the zone of this forgetting is inaccessible to the subject. 'Forgetting No. 2' relates to the Althusserian concept of reading, and involves the zone where the enonciatory subject puts itself where it constitutes its statement, establishing the frontier between the 'said' and the 'not said'. While this second forgetting involves enonciative mechanisms that are analysable at the surface of discourse, the first forgetting occurs in relation to the para-phrastic families constitutive of the effects of meaning. The dominance of the first forgetting takes account of the (non-subjective) conditions of existence of the subjective illusion, while the second forgetting lies directly on the subjective forms of that illusion. This led to a new conceptualisation of a discursive formation as that which is constituted by that which is itself external, given by that which is strictly unformable, since it is determined externally, and that externality is not to be confused with the subjective space of the enonciative, an imaginary space which assures the speaking subject is displaced to the interior of that unformable. That is, a discursive formation incorporates the idea of the subject illusion by claiming that such an illusion is itself part of that formation.

'Imaginary' is to be read in its Lacanian sense, which emphasises the psycho-analytic nature of the 'two forgottens'. The opposition of the two forgottens operates in different zones – the preconscious for forgotten No. 2, and the unconscious for the forgotten No. 1. This suggests an analogy with the Lacanian opposition of the other and the Other, where the imaginary identifi-cation of the 'other' lies side by side with the processes of subjugated interpolation of the subject, Lacan's 'Other'. This is the kernel of a search for a link between ideology and the unconscious that was to be central to further developments. It also opened up a discussion about enonciation and the imaginary, and about enonciative mechanisms.

The Munchausen effect

This leads us to a discussion of *Les vérités de La Palice*, the translation of which caused a considerable impact in Anglo-Saxon social science. It is a very dense book, full of reflections, developments and criticisms. It covers a large span in both temporal and intellectual-philosophic terms. More than anything it is a summary of Pécheux's entire work during the preceding years, while also establishing the current position of that work. It was published as part of a series on theory edited by Althusser, and its main thrust is theoretical, based on a materialist theory of discourse while simultaneously vigorously protesting any idealist alternative. In summarising his prior works, the book also includes a concern with semantics in which it is made clear that any discussion of that field must also involve both philosophy and politics. He traces historically the emergence of the orthodox approach to semantics and rhetoric, with its focus on the centred, rational, human subject as the source of meaning, before proceeding to decentre the subject, thereby laying the ground for his main concern – the relationship between the subject and meaning within discourse in a theory of enonciation.

Once again the Althusserian influence is prominent. In refuting the scientific status of linguistics, Pécheux seeks to elaborate an argument within which the science of social formations, the only true science, is central. Drawing upon Althusser's ISA essay, he focuses firmly on the concept of interpolation, which, for him, was the key element in a materialist theory of discursive processes, linked to the problematic of the ideological conditions of reproduction/transformation of the relations of production. In taking this route he sought to avoid the functionalism of Althusser's work by introducing the concept of transformation.

Transformation relates to intertextuality in the sense that intertextual chains are linked with particular practices associated with institutions, these chains being series of types of texts that are related to each other transformationally. That is, each member of the series is transformed into one or more of the others in regular and predictable ways. Thus observations of behaviour may be transformed into ranks on scales, ethnographic notes may be transformed into elaborate accounts. Since social institutions and practices are associated in specific ways they restrict the emergence of intertextual chains. This does not mean that such chains are not complex, nor that the sorts of transformations are not numerous.

Another prominent figure in the book is Frege. It is through a materialist reading of Frege that he tackles the question of relatives. From this Pécheux proceeds to develop the concept of preconstructed, as we have already seen, and also the idea of 'articulation of enonces'. These two concepts allow him to shift the discussion of relatives from the rational-linguistic domain to the domain of discourse. It is the re-reading of Frege that also allows the political to emerge when Frege's interpretation of the 'will of the people', expressed in terms of rational subjects, is transformed through its link to ideology and the subject. In many respects Frege constitutes a whipping horse for modernism in general.

The preconstructed or the pre-formed elements that circulate between discursive formations as 'givens' derive from the determinative functioning of the relative, being at the source of what Henry (1975) referred to as the 'articulation of enonces'. The effect of the preconstructed lies in the syntactic, involving the displacement between 'that which is thought before, elsewhere or independently, and that which is contained in the global affirmation of the phrase'. The articulation of enonces, on the other hand, is realised by the relative 'explicative', and links two assertions, where one is the 'lateral relationship of that which one seizes for somewhere else'. The effect is that of a 'kind of return of knowledge on the thought'. The two concepts serve to designate the discursive processes of the development on the linguistic base, while also being crucial for the development of the theory of discourse. These involve the traces of relationships of displacement between the present and the prior discourses. The present discourse is not what it seems, for the subject is constantly involved in the unthinking of its thought. While the subject may believe that it is rationally the producer of discourse, it knows nothing of the traces which determine that discourse. This would appear to be close to Foucault's claim that power relations are both intentional and non-subjective.

This question of the subject believing that it is the creator of discourse is discussed under the title of 'Munchausen effect', or the subjective illusion where the subject believes itself to be the source of discourse. Once again it is Althusser that peeps through the text in that it is concerned with the relationship between the evidence of meaning and the evidence of subject, or with how both meaning and the subject are constituted, since the subject can no longer be envisaged as the source of meaning. At the heart of this concern are ideology and the unconscious, which share the capacity to conceal their real existence at the core of their operation by producing a veneer of 'subjective' statements. They are evident in the analogy between the evidence of the spontaneous existence of the subject (as origin or cause of itself), and interpolation or identification. The interpolation of the subject articulates on the preconstructed, defined as 'the discursive modality of displacement for which the individual is interpolated as subject', in creating the always already subject. In order to overcome the Munchausen effect of 'the subject of discourse being the subject of discourse', the intellectual must remain aloof by 'avoiding the repetition, through a theoretical analysis, of the Munchausen effect'. Clearly, as in other aspects of Marxism, the intellectual occupies a privileged position. By now Pécheux's argument is clear. The subject of meaning is no longer given, both meaning and subject are produced in history, that is, they are determined.

We have already referred to how the concept of preconstructed refers to the manner in which the prior discourse is 'forgotten' by the speaker. Discourse is created from the discursive that is already there. The concept of interdiscourse, which refers to the complexes of different discursive formations, is more than simply the designation of prior discourse, and is also more than the idea of that which is common to all discourses. Rather, it involves the Althusserian idea of the 'complex whole in dominance' of discursive formations which is subject to the law of unevenness-contradiction-subordination. That is, the interdiscourse designates the discursive and ideological space which deploys the discursive formations, in functions of relationships of domination-subordination-contradiction.

A word is in order about the concept of discursive formation. There is a strange silence concerning the work of Foucault, who is undeniably the source of this concept, largely, one suspects, because of Foucault's idealist position, and his not being involved in the Marxist venture. Yet, despite being the source of the concept of discursive formation as employed by Pécheux, there is a distinctive difference in the two uses. As I have already remarked, for Pécheux and his colleagues the concept of formation was very closely integrated with the Marxist concepts of ideological formation and social formation. As such, discursive formation becomes far more than discursive practice in that it is articulated on ideology and totally immersed in history, involving a relationship of forces which appear at a given conjuncture. This is expressed in terms of what can and should be said from a given position in a given conjuncture, a conceptualisation very similar to that of Foucault, except that Pécheux adds the claim that the conjuncture is determined by the state of the class struggle. This conceptualisation resulted in the development of various taxonomies, something which Pécheux wished to avoid. The development of the work on interpolation, and the manner in which it clarified the thesis according to which meaning is constituted in the discursive formation, together with the concept of interdiscourse, corrected this taxonomic drift. Henceforth, Pécheux was to refer to the intrication of the discursive formation in the ideological formations.

With reference to the subject, the notion of interdiscourse was important. The interdiscourse, in its relationship with the complex of ideological formations, furnishes each subject with its 'reality' as 'a system of evident truths and significations perceived-accepted-suffered' (Pécheux, 1982a:113). The individual is unable to recognise its subordination because of the manner in which the subordination-subjugation is realised in the form of the autonomous subject. Here Pécheux is focusing upon the relationship between the ideological subject and the subject of the unconscious, directly acknowledging his debt to Lacan.

One last concept appears, that of intradiscourse. It cannot be understood except in relation to interdiscourse. It involves the manner in which discourse works on itself – the link between what I am saying now and what I have said before and what I will say afterwards; that is, it answers the need for some form of coreference.

Taking stock

The second half of the 1970s, following the publication of *Les vérités de La Palice*, was a period of taking stock, leading to the emergence of a new direction. In many respects they were exciting years, involving contrasting orientations between different groups of Marxists working on language. Among the forces which were responsible for the forging of a new direction was the work of Marandin, who joined the group in 1978, and Gadet, whose work with Pécheux culminated in the publication of the forceful *La langue introuvable* in 1981 (Gadet and Pecheux, 1981a).

In 1976 a seminar group was formed by Pécheux, Henry and Plon (HPP) whose work was to extend over a period of three and a half years. Again, as if following Foucault, whose paper on the political function of the intellectual had appeared in 1972, this group had a strong anti-intellectualism attached to it. This also related to treating the university as one of the aparatuses of the State à la Althusser. Indeed the work of Althusser and Lacan continued to be of a fundamental guiding importance, the debate seeking to continue work on the integration of language, psychoanalysis and politics.

At the same time another group, the linguistic sector of the Centre d'Etudes et de Recherches Marxiste (CERM), was also active. The crux of an opposition between the two groups was to be found in the role of logic and sociology in the study of language. Gadet and Pécheux (1981) wrote a forceful piece which sought to establish discourse as an alternative to logicism and sociologism. Clearly the logicism referred to the emergence of generative grammar and the sociologism to that of sociolinguistics. It led to Gadet's (1977) claim that 'La sociolinguistique n'existe pas; je l'ai recontrée', the title of a paper which argued for a distinctive approach towards language in society. This perspective was in contrast to that of many associated with CERM. Particularly prominent in this respect were Guespin, and Marcellesi and Gardin, whose book *Introduction à la sociolinguistique* had appeared in 1974, at the end of the life of structuralism, but also at a time when sociolinguistics was flourishing. They claimed that French discourse analysis was a domain of sociolinguistics. They also emphasised, in contrast to virtually everything that Pécheux had emphasised over the years, that Marxism could enter into sociolinguistics with the idea of the centred subject involved in intersubjective interaction firmly intact.

At the end of 1977 CERM was the focus of an intense debate that was indicative of the distinctive approaches to discourse analysis in France. It revolved around the work of Voloshinov, whose book *Marxism and the Philosophy of Language* had recently been translated into French. This work had been known earlier thanks to the English translation of 1972, and the early work of Kristeva (1969), and it had been discussed in Marcellesi and Gardin's book. At CERM Gardin suggested that a new reading of Voloshinov, one that would integrate with the work of Saussure, could be responsible for generating another epistemological break.

Even though space is devoted to a discussion of the work of Voloshinov and Bakhtin in Chapter 6, it is necessary to discuss the impact of Voloshinov's *Marxism and the Philosophy of Language* here, since it had such an impact when it first appeared in French in 1977. Voloshinov's work enriched the discussion of the relationship between language and ideology through the discussion of the manner in which the sign is assimilated into an ideological object. He sought to think of the unity of language within the context of the class struggle, and assigned the task of understanding ideological phenomena through the study of forms of language and discourse to Marxist theory. Gadet and Pécheux (1981) noted the theoretical similarity between the work of Voloshinov and Plekhanov's social psychology, while Pécheux later claimed that Voloshinov, far from opening a new perspective for Marxist linguists concerned with the relationship between language and society, represented a return to a pre-theoretic state. Furthermore, Saussure and the question of language was not Voloshinov's principal concern. In his criticism of Saussure's 'abstract objectivism', Voloshinov tended to annul the proper dimension of language in opposing the 'social phenomenon of verbal interaction, realised through enonciation and the enonciations' to the 'abstract system of formal linguistics'. Thus he contributed to transforming linguistics into a vast semiology.

For Pécheux the true break was that of Saussure. For him the stakes of formalism and the subject, the possibility of thinking of the singularity of the subject in language, involved the articulation between language and the unconscious. Maldidier (1990:52) maintains that this conflict over the work of Voloshinov reflected a conflict that would always exist within discourse analysis in France. It was evident in Pécheux's antagonism to having FDA classified as a feature of the sociology of language. In 1976 Boutet, Fiala and Simonin-Grumbach published a paper entitled 'Sociolinguistique ou sociologie du langage?' which discussed Marcellesi's and Gardin's book, together with Robin's *Histoire et linguistique*, which provided a discussion of historiography from the perspective of discourse/ideology. The three authors rejected the sociology of language, citing Voloshinov in the process, and claiming that a break between the social and the linguistic was necessary in order to reach a global account of the phenomenon of language in their production, their circulation and their effects on the social formation. Clearly this sociology of language was far removed from the work of Pécheux and his colleagues. Many Marxist linguists sought to follow the route opened by Voloshinov in 1929 which began from a position quite different from the Anglo-Saxon philosophy and pragmatism of the early 1970s. This internal struggle was, of course, that of orthodox Marxism against the reformism of Althusserianism.

Pécheux's position was very clear: the question of meaning cannot be resolved within the sphere of interpersonal relationships, no more than it can be resolved in terms of social relations thought of in terms of interaction between human groups. He outlined the fundamental points of historical materialism: the question of the State, of political practice and of psycho-analysis. The turning point in this theoretical preoccupation came in 1978, when there was an evident shift to a concern with the dominated ideologies or, in effect, with the ideologies of resistance. Here again we seem to be drawn to the conclusion that it was a reaction to Foucault's claim that power could not exist separately from resistance. Not that this was a new venture – as early as 1970, in collaboration with Henry, it was already an issue of debate when the collaborative work focused upon Lenin's work on the 'national culture' and his reference to the dissymmetry between dominant ideology and dominated ideologies (Maldidier, 1990:54 fn 1).

Pécheux's link to the work of Foucault is made explicit in a paper delivered in Mexico during 1977 (Pécheux, 1980), but Maldidier maintains that Foucault's influence was evident from the outset of Pécheux's work (Guilhaumou et al., 1994:173). However, in the Mexico paper Pécheux was also again following Althusser in drawing on his materialist reading of Spinoza. Althusser identified the rationalist philosopher Spinoza as the only philosopher who had anticipated the conception of structural causality, and this led to the claim that 'the structure' has as its effects, the provision of its own conditions of existence. This 'being' does not derive from any external causality, but is the self-subsistent cause of its own continuation. This work was the basis for the theorisation of the Munchausen effect, identifying the subject as an effect of the process without a Subject (Pécheux, 1982a:198), so that it becomes Spinoza's 'cause of himself'. In many respects it would appear that Spinoza assumed for Pécheux the same role that Nietzsche did for Foucault. Whereas it always appeared that Pécheux was working in parallel with Foucault, at this point he launches an attack on his work, claiming that he possesses a 'parallel discourse', parallel, that is, to historical materialism. Again it is the defence of materialism in the face of the idealist threat. Yet, despite this attack, what stands out in this paper is the claim that the discursive formation, a concept borrowed from Foucault and modified, is not to be seen as a homogeneous block, but rather it is divisible, and non-identical to itself. It is this that lays the ground for the discussion of dominated ideologies. In reply to the orthodox approach of placing the dominant ideologies and the dominated ideologies in confrontation, associated with a relation of exteriority, Pécheux placed the emphasis upon the 'internal domination' of the dominant ideology with reference to the dominated ideology. In an abstract manner he was making a statement reminiscent of Spinoza, to the effect that the domination of the dominated ideology lies, in the way that it is organised, at the same interior of the discourse of the dominant ideology. It is this insight that gives rise to the concept of heterogeneity.

Evidently, despite the retrenchment of the Mexico paper, by the end of the 1970s a crucial shift in orientation was taking place. It reflected a willingness to move away from the strict Althusserian position towards a position which was closer to idealism. Although the concern with enonciation had been present in Pécheux's work for some time, it now took a new direction, allowing for a development that linked closely with Foucault's observations. This should hardly be surprising since there is a direct link between Foucault's *Les mots et le choses* and enonciative linguistics. The result was that it heralded a closer focus upon the issue of decentring by reference to linguistic form, heralding the emergence of a linguistics of discourse (Guilhaumou *et al.*, 1994:194). Clearly, the various reflections which had occurred as a consequence of the criticism of the early work, a criticism that was both internal and external, were taking Pécheux's work in a new direction, a direction which drew upon new insights and a far greater degree of openness to parallel ideas within French intellectual circles.

5

THE STRUGGLE WITH
IDEALISM

Theoretical anti-humanism

In the economic materialist perspective discussed in the preceding chapter,
there is a suspicion that, in many respects, the work involves the reworking of
much of Foucault's thesis within a distinctively Althusserian context. While
concepts such as 'discursive formation' have clearly derived initially from the
work of Foucault, they have, to an extent, been modified as a consequence
of their employment within a Marxist problematic. I say to an extent because at
times there is a tendency in the work of Pêcheux and his colleagues, as well as
in Althusser's own work, to treat the social formation in segments rather than
as an integrated whole. Thus, for example, even though the overall framework
is in the background, there is a tendency to treat the ideological instant *as if* it
were autonomous, and to that extent the individual concepts may not be so
firmly integrated into the overall problematic. Indeed, there are times when it
would appear that the economic materialist dimension is superimposed on the
ideological preoccupation as an afterthought. In this respect it allows a variety
of problematics to be dealt with simultaneously, and perhaps it is no surprise
that a certain eclecticism appears in the work. On the other hand, the explicit
Marxist nature of the endeavour initially served as a barrier to alternative
developments, and it is not until the end of the 1970s that we begin to see a
loosening of this orientation. It is this shift of direction during the early 1980s
that I would like to consider in this chapter.

By the end of the 1970s much of what had been written in *Les vérités de La
Palice* had been rethought. Some of the modifications appeared in the postscript
to the English translation, where Pêcheux refers to 'the French political
winter'. This is a reference to the rupture of the common programme of the
French left and the associated debate within the PCF which led to a general
despair among the left. At this time one theme preoccupied Pêcheux: if
humankind makes its history, how does one avoid the anthropologism and
subjectivism of that claim? Again we witness the relationship between Marx,
Lacan and Saussure. Hitherto the Althusserian approach of *Les vérités de La
Palice* had placed excessive emphasis on the issue of domination, failing to raise

the question of resistance that the work of both Foucault and Gramsci insisted upon. In this respect the issue of resistance was one of hope in the depth of despair. Maldidier (1990:59–60) refers to this process as one of correction or deconstruction, which she opposes to the process of incineration. In this respect Pécheux was drawing upon the work of numerous colleagues and contemporaries, as well as responding to the critical reviews of *Les vérités de La Palice*. Particularly relevant among such reviews was that of the Maoist Houdebine, whose book *Langage et marxisme* had appeared in 1977, and who had published a scathing article in *Tel Quel* in which he focused upon the concept of interpolation, accusing Pécheux of developing the theme of a 'process without subject' (Houdebine, 1976).[1] At issue was the question of the relationship between ideology and the unconscious, or that between historical materialism and psychoanalysis, and the danger in Lacan's work of 'reducing the subject to the me'. Once again it was the confrontation of the 'communist' and the 'leftist'.

Pécheux's 'corrections' involved a reflection on political history and on his own theory. For Althusser, ideological interpolation meant that 'subjects march all alone', this raising the question which traditional Marxists could not evade – the role of humankind in the creation of history. For Pécheux it was this concept above all else which allowed him to link Marxism with psychoanalytic concepts, as well as with political concepts: it allowed him to make explicit the process which tended to be explained in terms of the dominant ideology thesis. Furthermore, the ISA article, and particularly the 'transformation-reproduction' theme of the relations of production, was steeped in functionalism. It made reproduction appear to be a mechanical process which would work for ever. By 1978 Pécheux had rejected much of this. He looked to psychoanalysis for an opening to the question of 'forgetting', which he was wrongly accused of confusing with the psychoanalytic concept of suppression. Also, the adoption of a perspective devoid of the necessity of a subjective illusion meant that enonciation took on new possibilities. The domination of the dominant ideology, a notion adjacent to that of the interpretation of the interdiscourse, was questioned, and the theme of heterogeneity explored. J.B. Thompson (1990:86–88) has emphasised the consensual nature of the Althusserian work on ideology and social reproduction, and it would appear that this new direction taken by Pécheux was breaking with that earlier Althusserian orientation.

At the beginning of the 1980s Pécheux referred, within his Althusserian context of 'theoretical anti-humanism', to 'political structuralism'. Maldidier (1990:88) suggests that he was referring to a space wherein Foucault, Lacan and Derrida lay side by side with Althusser, this being a space that is associated with language. Indeed, in a paper written in 1982, Pécheux (1983) explicitly refers to how the work of Foucault, Deleuze and Derrida had contributed to a shift from the tendency to consider discourse analysis as a mater of reconstructing the homogeneous invariants of a structure of ideology, by considering the play of mobile discursive heterogeneities. Not, of course, that any of these authors, any more than Pécheux himself, would describe themselves as 'structuralists' (Henry, 1990:27). Yet structuralism did include a focus on language which is evident in their work, certainly with reference to Lacan and Foucault. Thus, for example, structuralism identified culture and language in such a way that any cultural fact could take a form of linguistic, semiotic or semiological analysis. This is not to imply, for example, that Lacan reduced psychoanalysis to a species of linguistic analysis. On the contrary, it was treated as a 'talking cure'. He referred to both Saussure and Jakobson in interpreting Freud's *Verdichtung* and *Versicherung* in terms of metaphor and metonymy, while also thinking of the unconscious as being structured like a language. Indeed it can be argued that it was structuralism that led to the rethinking of philosophy in France (Henry, 1990:28).

Henry (1990:38 fn 16) has recently pointed to the overlap between the work of Foucault and Pécheux, while emphasising that there were considerable differences during the early period. None the less, the interest which Foucault held for Pécheux is clear, and is evident in the notes which he wrote in the margins of what he had read of Foucault's work. The point of overlap between them is also evident in Henry's (1990:38 fn 18) reference to the importance of Nietzsche for Pécheux. Perhaps it is the theoretical anti-humanism which they shared which is reflected in any discussion of the overlap in their respective works, an emphasis which had a common reference to language as sign or as discourse. In that company, Pécheux's unique contribution was that of his involvement in the specific materiality of language. Rather than being the servant of thought, as in the orthodox Enlightenment conception, for Pécheux, language was its mistress. He sought to discover the process of material subjugation in language. In refuting the orthodox position, especially with reference to the subject and meaning, he was involved in a form of intellectual resistance to the pragmatic temptation. He had moved from a position where he sought to discover what determined discourse, to an understanding of discourse as something which was virtually impossible to capture other than as an understanding of construction.

It should already be evident that during the 1970s, on the other hand, the work undertaken by Pécheux and his colleagues was based upon debates within the French Communist Party (PCF). In this respect it was a closed debate, inaccessible to alternative ideas. I do not wish to imply that 'outsiders' were not welcome. On the contrary, a number of individuals who were not members of the PCF did work closely with the group. However, they did so with one foot in and one foot out of the group. The break with the PCF in 1981 opened the debate and allowed some of those hitherto on the periphery to be more directly involved. It is essential to consider the work of such individuals, not merely because of the importance of their own contribution but because, as we shall see, their work was unfettered by the institutional politics of the PCF. On the other hand, we must recognise that while the impact of such individuals, working alone, was significant, it was quite different from that of Pécheux's multi-disciplinary 'school' of scholars working together.

New voices

At the end of the decade a conference entitled Matérialités Discursives dedicated to the 'theory of discourse' was organised with the goal of addressing linguistics, history, discourse analysis and psychoanalysis in the context of the 'triple reality of language, history and the unconscious'. A new voice on Pécheux's team was that of Marandin, on whose thesis committee at Vincennes Pécheux sat. His entry brought in the explicit thrust of the work of Deleuze and Foucault. In his thesis Marandin had scrutinised Pécheux's early work, noting that the method of AAD69 was orientated towards 'delinearisation', and that the constitution of semantic domains neglected the intra-discourse. It was the relation between the intra-discourse and interdiscourse which he chose to explore. He rethought their relationship and facilitated the opening of the question of sequentiality or discursivity, as it was to be known. Distanced from Marxism, he delved into an unashamed Foucaultianism that allowed a reorientation of analysis towards the singularity of the discursive event. At times Pécheux felt that Marandin's arguments took him too far from his own conception of FDA, but by then the break with the PCF had opened up the debate. This is important in that Marandin represented a generation of social scientists without the same commitment to Marxism as their predecessors. It was he, as much as anyone, who facilitated a theoretic reorientation of discourse analysis among this group. Yet in the paper in *Matérialités Discursive*', which he wrote with Courtine (Courtine and Marandin, 1981), there was explicit reference to the Marxist problematic, and specifically to the conception of ideology as a superstructural form, alongside the emphasis upon the work of Foucault and Deleuze.

Another member of the team who diverged from Marxist orthodoxy was Conein. A former student of Poulantzas, he inherited the latter's willingness to develop an eclectic socialism.[2] He joined Pécheux's team to work with Guilhaumou on historical texts, and both were willing to deviate from the orthodoxies of the 1970s. In some respects the work of both Conein and Guilhaumou built on the early work of Robin and Maldidier, but in many respects it was also very different. It was open to the work of Foucault while also building on a view of the discursive analysis of texts in emphasising the Foucaultian concept of event. Their work was not only important but innovatory in this respect.

Yet another source of inspiration at this time was the linguistic work of Milner, which appeared in the form of *L'amour de langue* (Milner, 1978). His work was at the limits of language and discourse, at the point where language encounters the subject. It was this work which informed the work on enonciation. In this respect Authier's work, which focused upon the manner in which streams of discourse emerge, that is, how another discourse will emerge from the same discourse, was also of considerable importance. This was an important contribution to the issue of discursive heterogeneity. That concept encompassed what hitherto had been discussed under the Marxist concept of contradiction or ideological interpolation. However, it is also important to recognise the relationship between Marandin's contribution and enonciation. Whereas much of the earlier work derived from the modernist linguistics of Harris and Chomsky, with its conception of the centred subject and a focus upon the 'correctness' of the normativity in the grammatical approach, it was very much at odds with the decentred nature of the subject of the associated theoretical input. As will be outlined below, the shift towards the Saussurean emphasis of Benveniste's conception of discourse, and, subsequently, towards Culioli's enonciative linguistics, opened new doors in this respect. Marandin's introduction of Foucault's reference to language in *The Archaeology of Knowledge* was the crucial link to a decentred approach to linguistic form. It led to investigating how enonciative linguistics uncovers the marks whereby it is possible to describe the displacement of subjects from one enonciative place to another, thus contributing to the description of discursive events. However, it also allowed the uncovering of the social topology involving the relationship between subjects, objects and place. The novelty of the approach was in its exclusion of the meta-discourse on enonciation that was so evident in Foucault's work (Gilhaumou *et al.*, 1994:188).

All of this activity surrounded the Matérialités Discursives conference, which was devoted to the theme of deconstruction-reconstruction. It involved a shift which gave pride of place to textuality, bringing the work closer to the Foucaultian sense of archive. The work of both Conein and Guilhaumou was important in this respect, especially with reference to the relationship between the Foucaultian concepts of archive and history. Pécheux (1975a:25–30) had deployed the concept of archive at an earlier stage of his work in opposing the 'corpus of the archive', which consisted of pre-existing enonces, to 'experimental corpus', which is created under experimental conditions (Pécheux, 1975:25–30). This understanding of archive differed somewhat from that of Foucault, who emphasised the link to the orthodox use of the word as the conservation and memorisation of texts. From this he defined archive as that which, within any given society, involves 'the general system of the formation and transformation of enonces . . . entering the field of tradition and the forgotten, it reveals the rules of a practice which permits enonces to be regularly substituted and modified' (Foucault, 1969:171). The enthusiasm generated by this new insight led to the establishment of a new institutional setting, the Recherche Coopérative Programmée (RCP), and the Analyse de Discours et Lecture d'Archive (ADELA).

More significantly, perhaps, these developments signalled a significant change of direction. In a preface to Courtine's work in *Langages*, Pécheux (1981) developed the idea of a micro-relationship between the method of discourse analysis which centred on the paraphrase and repetition, and the privileged object that political discourse gives to discourse analysis. He was referring to the role of the Communist discourse, and suggesting that there existed a constitutive relationship between the analysis of discourse and its object. It was an indication that the political climate was quite distinct from that which had initiated the work during the 1960s. It heralded the abandoning of the study of doctrinaire discourse in favour of ordinary discourse, the conversational. Here the influence of both Gadet and Conein must have been of relevance. The former wrote, among other things, a book on 'ordinary French' (Gadet, 1989a), and the latter became deeply embroiled in the conversational analysis of ethnomethodology. However, it was Courtine and Marandin who developed the self-criticism which focused primarily on the homogeneous nature of discourse analysis most evident in the Harrisian concept of paraphrase. This led them to a discussion of corpus, a theme much in evidence among historian discourse analysts. The conception of corpus was modified, no longer being linked to a corpus restrained by the conditions of its production (Guilhaumou et al., 1994:6).

It was Courtine who was most influential in developing the Foucaultian emphasis, an emphasis which led to the reworking of the concept of discursive formation and its closure. He argued that any discursive formation was inherently unstable, not being of a once and for all nature, separating an interior and an exterior, but rather constituting a frontier which is constantly subject to displacement. The interdiscourse was thereby involved in a constant reconfiguration of the discursive formation as a function of the ideological position occupied by that discursive formation in a specific conjuncture. It thus incorporates preconstructed elements produced outside of itself, it generates redefinitions, it organises its repetitions while also provoking an eventual obliteration – the forgetting or the denegation (Courtine and Marandin, 1981:24). The interdiscourse of a discursive formation thereby becomes 'that which rules the displacement of its frontiers' (Courtine and Marandin, 1981:25). Part of the importance of this development was not merely that it conceived of discourse as a process, but that concepts which hitherto had been fixed by their Marxist problematic were now set free. The concept of 'discursive memory' – relating to the link between tense and repetition – was an important development, but it was also of significance for forgetting, for the defacing and the denial.

The issue of memory surfaced in the 1983 Round Table organised by *Langage et Société* on the relationship between history and linguistics (Achard et al., 1985). Achard claimed that the role of memory related to the implicits in discourse, while also recognising that a psychologistic interpretation had to be avoided. He emphasised that the structuration of a discourse constitutes the materiality of a certain social memory, which does not mean that there is some materiality external to discourse, as some kind of rhetorical mask which would be of the order of a collective unconscious. Materiality here involved the formal properties of an enonciation, the point where language meets the social. He argued that one will never discover the implicit in a stable form, but rather it exists in repetition and in the formation of an effect of regularisation within which the implicits exist in the form of returning, of recovery and of effects of paraphrase. This discursive regularisation tends to form the law of the series of what can be read, and always tends to break through under the weight of the new discursive event, becoming integrated in memory. Thus memory tends to absorb the event, but the discursive event responsible for the interruption can thwart the 'regularisation', producing, retrospectively, another series, under the first. The event delocalises and deregulates the implicits associated with the system of earlier regularisation.

Pécheux's contribution to that conference also revolved around the issue of memory in a discussion of how the historic event is susceptible to becoming inscribed in the internal continuity and the potential space of coherence of memory. He used the term memory to refer to the way meaning crosses mythic meaning as well as the constructed meaning of the historian. Memory is conceptualised as the structuration of a complex discursive materiality, set in a dialectic of the repetition and the regularisation. In relation to a text that is read, it involves that which re-establishes the 'implicits' – in technical terms, the preconstructed, previously cited and related elements, transverse discourse, etc. – all of which facilitate that reading. It sets the condition of what can be read in relation to, and in addition to, what is there to be read. It involves a consideration of the implicits which are 'absent by their presence' in the reading of the sequence. Repetition involves access to a material effect constructed out of commutations and variations, and assuring the space of stability of forms of paraphrase produced by recurrence, by the literal repetition of that material identity. But this recurrence of the item, or of the enonce, can also characterise a division of the material identity of the item, where the 'same' of the materiality of the word opens the play of the metaphor, as another possibility of discursive articulation. This opaque effect, which corresponds to the point of division of the same, and of the metaphor, marks the moment where the 'implicits' are not reconstructible, leading to discourse analysis focusing on the proposition, the phrase and the paraphrastic stability, and to investigating the material effects of how sequences are established without seeking to address and advance all their signification, nor their implicit conditions of interpretation. Pécheux also makes a curious reference to a tactical, provisional retreat from the question of meaning by focusing on interpretation, a position which would seem to imply a pragmatic stance.

Evidently, memory was not to be seen as some reservoir of knowledge involving a homogeneous meaning bounded by the historic transcendental. Rather, it is to be seen as a mobile space of divisions, of disjunctions, of displacements and of recovery, of conflicts and regularisation. It is the space of polemic and counter-discourse. It is the site of resistance. Pécheux returned to the point of entry made by Maldidier at the beginning of this conference, where he emphasised that the critique of the homogeneity of the discursive formation touched upon the question of dominated ideologies, on the importance of the paraphrase in discourse analysis, and on the privileged position of repetition of the interdiscourse. It was also a critique of the manner in which the PCF had expropriated the 'truth' of historical interpretation.

Similarly, Marandin worked on the concept of repetition from a Deleuzean perspective (Deleuze, 1968), leading to a questioning of interdiscourse, thereby leading to a conception of the heterogeneity of ruptures. Discourse is repetitive, synchronically as a feature of its unwinding, and diachronically as a consequence of time. The same themes, the same formulations, the same figures appear and reappear. It is the place where discourse is seized, the place on which its descriptive practices are authorised, and that which is constituted as its objects. In their speech, individuals talk and reassimilate that which is ignored in already having been said. Hitherto the work had taken the subject either as a mask, where the undefined individual finds its voice, or as the rules of syntax involving a 'collective speaker', which reduced the social reality of discourse to an apparently homogeneous existence as the plain subjects of their discourse. For Foucault, on the other hand, it all depended upon a play of words, the small passage between the rule and the regular. However, if discourse is repetitive, it is not repetitive word for word. Given the infinite nature of speech, statements are neither literal reformulations nor hazardous re-creations. It is not the identity of a discourse, or of a discursive formation, that inscribes the capturing of individual speech in an anonymous fashion. Discourse is based upon repetitions; it is the point where the problematic of the ideological efficacy is tied to heterogeneity. Thus Deleuze (1968:371) states: 'When the obsessed repeat a ceremonial, once, twice; when they repeat a numeration – 1, 2, 3 – they proceed to a repetition of elements in extension, but which conjure and translate another repetition, vertical . . . that of a past which is displaced to each time or to each number, and is disguised in the ensemble of numbers and of times'. This involved a double modality of repetition: the extensions which are used as reference points in considering a fragment of discursive sequence as determined by statements from a given place; and the vertical which does not pertain to a series of formed formulated statements, but to that which is repeated, such that there is an unrecognised displacement in the statement. This second repetition was taken to be that of the interdiscourse, as externally determined at the interior of the discursive formation and involving reformulation.

This line of enquiry generated a substantial amount of work within the group, much of it highly technical, leading to an awareness that the method, far from being a neutral tool, became an integral part of the research itself. It was necessary to reconsider the old concepts in their articulation with the method. This was the context of the reference to deconstruction, since in deconstruction it was necessary to consider the fragments of the new construction or the reconstruction.

137

Together, Marandin and Courtine (1981) maintained that ideological efficacy derived not from a process of interpolation–identification which metamorphosed the subject as 'person' but, rather, from a more or less ruled process of repetition, in the manner of 'knowing' its enonces and in the manner of the non-recognition of the interdiscourse. Their discussion of interpolation involved the recasting of Althusser's (1970) proposition whereby 'ideology interpolates the individual as subject' in terms of 'the ideology interpolates the subjects of enonciation as slave-subjects of a particular discourse and as imaginary masters of discourse in general' (Marandin and Courtine, 1981:31). Their emphasis lay on how the individual is constituted as subject by language, by the act of speaking and thereby is prior to all interpolation. In conceiving of discourse as one of the material instances of ideology, they sought to retrieve the tendency for ideological effects to be related to a process of identification. They objected to how that approach led to the subjects of enonciation being metamorphosed as 'person' through interpolation, by reference to a more or less ruled process of repetition, being polymorphic in the newspaper discourse and ritualised or institutionalised in the apparatus (in the Althusserian sense) discourse. The thrust of their argument was that if one accepts that discourse is one of the material instances of ideology, then ideological efficacy is not defined in terms of an interpolation–identification process; rather, it pertains to the complexity of reformulations involving conscious recognition of enonces, and also the non-recognition of the interdiscourse. That is, there is a degree of pragmatic effect, but it can never be complete. This was a significant contribution in that it placed the emphasis centrally on enonciative places and how they installed the subject in the continuous thread of discourse. Equally important was the significance of this conception for the awareness that interdiscourse was not of the 'order of discourse', involving an articulation of the discursive formation; rather, it involved the reconfiguration of the discursive formation where the enonces were constructed. It was a manifestation of a further distancing from the Althusserian input.

The other theme that emerged in this conference was that of resistance. Guilhaumou and Maldidier (1981) claimed that resistance was related to the presupposition that existed in discourse and the manner in which it involved the forgetting of voices which emerged through such presuppositions. They show how, buried within a text, there is a voice which corresponds to what they call the 'critic subject', or the 'accuser subject', which exist as points of resistance which are fully relevant to the text, even if they are buried.

The linguistic work presented at the Matérialités Discursives conference underlined how, for Pécheux, the fundamental anchorage of discourse analysis lay in the linguistic. Hitherto the question of the relationship between language and discourse had focused on the abstract terms of a base that was akin to Saussure's *structure* or *langue*; and a process seen in terms of *parole*, but with the latter modified to represent discourse, becoming a concept that was freed from the thinking subject. A concern with syntax was retained. Only the question of relatives, the privileged object of the reflection on discourse, was the object of particular study. The emphasis now shifts to a concern with the theme of discursivity. This is evident in Pêcheux's paper at that conference. In addition to relatives, co-ordination emerges to test the limits of grammar, the point of departure for a consideration of 'the order of discourse'.

More than anything this conference showed the directions in which FDA could be taken. Three such directions can be identified:

- Making the link between linguistics and discourse more explicit while also developing the work in this field by examining new ways of relating linguistics and discourse. The main protagonists here were Authier and Milner.
- Developing the use of computers for analysis. This had been the goal from the outset but by the beginning of the 1980s the technology was much more powerful and was capable of developing a formal analysis of the relationship between language and discourse. The main input here was from Marandin.
- Elaborating the relationship between archive and history through a textual analysis which would link with the work of Foucault. The main actors in this respect were Conein and Guilhaumou.

These three directions did not operate together but in parallel. Their respective importance and potential is amply demonstrated in the Matérialtés Discursives conference but nowhere are they coherently linked. Pêcheux was fascinated by formalisation, as was Milner. Their shared logistic bent led them in the direction of formalism and the signifier. It was the same interest as that which made Lacan's work so appealing in that Lacan's claim that the sign had no connection with meaning led to the search for the formal structure of discourse by developing a logic of the signifier. In this way it was possible to demonstrate that the subject was decentred. Some aspect of formalism was necessary once the subject was decentred. It was this that was responsible for his emphasis on the first two directions outlined above and his relatively low-key interest in the third.

In 1982 the Recherche Coopérative Programmée (RCP) was founded. This was a massive project involving twenty-six psychophysiologists and psychologists, and thirty-six linguists, literary scholars and musicologists. The programme was divided into three parts associated respectively with a socio-historic archive, linguistics research on discursivity and the method of discourse analysis. What is interesting here is the emphasis on the Foucaultian understanding of 'archive', or the relationship of practices to regularising rules or 'the law of what can be said, the system that governs the appearance of statements as unique events' (Foucault, 1969:129). The archive, for Foucault, was a form of hidden rule which 'delimits us' (1969:130). Its link to history was that it had to be perceived from afar, with history being a form of a critical social theory which, through an investigation of the past, threw a critical light on the present. The New History treated a document as text, as a dissociated trace in a history (Pécheux, 1984a:10). It was argued that the issue of the construction of intertextuality and the general concept of interdiscourse had to be rethought in order to discover how the official written discourse always assumes the status of 'legitimacy'. This concern opened the discussion to the topic of corpus and its selection, and to how preceding texts contributed to the interdiscourse.

The clearest expression of this development is found in the paper prepared by Conein *et al.* (1984) for the *Mots* collection. Pécheux (1982a) had addressed the social division of labour of reading, again recalling Althusser's work on the problematic. In distinguishing between literal reading, document collection and the privilege of interpretation, the materiality of language was played against a model of logical languages and the evidence of referential reading. It was concerned with the issue of the hold which power has over collective memory. This led to considering how historians and social scientists use textual materials, and how a heuristic status involving interpretative sociology, the social history of mentalities, textual pragmatics, etc. relates to textual description. It led to the Histoire et Linguistique conference which I will return to below.

Adopting the Foucaultian concept of archive related to the formulation of socio-historic hypotheses from textual characterisations. Foucault's distinction between the document and the moment raised the issue of intermediary concepts. Another interest concerned the way documentary analysis is traversed by descriptive agencies which serve as the props of historical interpretation. Discourse analysis is no longer concerned with articulating formal descriptions with interpretations, but with how the intermediary notions explaining the text from its interior are made to appear: 'to locate the points where a subject position and the possibility of an interpretative act appears' (Conein *et al.*, 1984:27). The meta-discourse no longer dominates the text, which is no longer invested with notions external to discourse. The analysis highlights the places, the subjects, and the intermediary objects between the experience of reality and the arguments concerning that reality.

Discursivity represented a novel theme of the work and involved working on chains of phrases. This was the theme of Ducrot's book *Les mots du discourse* which was published in 1980, a work which adopted a pragmatic stance, thereby raising the problem of meaning and the subject once again. The main objective was to study the effects of intra-discursive sequentiality in both a written and an oral context. In some respects it linked with the ethno-methodological interests of Conein, but this seems strangely out of place among work where the subject is entirely decentred. Indeed this was one of the themes of the work: the imaginary space of the displacement of the subject of enonciation. An immense amount of energy was devoted to studying the contribution made by the combined functioning of linguistic, syntactic, lexical and enonciative marks in producing the effect of sequentiality. Where hitherto the emphasis was on the abstract claim for the manner in which interdiscourse 'worked' on the interior of intra-discourse, by now this had been developed into a discussion of enonciative marks. Authier's work on constitutive hetero-geneity, and Pécheux's work on interdiscourse, led to the introduction of the concept of the double heterogeneity, thereby elaborating on the relation-ship between interdiscourse and intra-discourse. Simultaneously this subgroup worked on the question of modalities, especially with reference to intertextuality and interdiscourse.

On the methodological side, the team collaborated with colleagues at the University of Quebec in an attempt once more to develop a computer-based methodology. Once again the shadow of AAD69 came into view and is evident in the work of Bonnafous (1983). However, again it is the name of Foucault that appears in the form of Courtine's reference to the vertical axis of the historical dimension, and the horizontal axis of the putting in sequence.

There is a strong suggestion that a theoretical eclecticism was replacing the Marxist problematic during the early 1980s. It is evident in the work of Marandin and Courtine on Foucault and Deleuze, respectively, and in Conein's interest in ethnomethodology. Yet Pécheux's last paper was delivered in a conference entitled 'Marxism and the Interpretation of Culture: Limits, Frontiers, Boundaries'. Despite the Althusserian focus on epistemological purity in the work on problematics, this does not appear to have caused any undue concern.

Maldidier (1990) claims that the central theme of the entire work was that of 'reading', or the practice of recognising / misrecognising / failing to recognise the significance of a social phenomenon. It involves an attempt to determine the signified meanings of a series of signifying units in returning to the Saussurean source of the work. In his paper 'Lire l'archive aujourd'hui', Pécheux (1982c) discusses the 'traditional social division of labour of reading' which opposes the literal reading to the privileged status of interpretation, where the former accedes to the latter, while the second accedes to meaning. These are akin to two cultures, usually designated as 'science' and 'literature'. This dichotomy was reflected in the difference between, on the one hand, the 'logically stabilised discursive universe' of mathematics, and the science of nature, of industrial and bio-medical technologies, and – with reference to the social sphere – of the method of administrative management; and, on the other hand, the 'logically unstabilised discursive universe' of the socio-historic space of ideological ritual, of philosophical discourses, of political statements, of cultural and aesthetic expression. It is the latter that constitutes the proper domain of discourse analysis. This is a theme which appeared at the very beginning of Pécheux's work in AAD69 in the distinction between docu-mentary analysis and non-institutional analysis. At the end of the 1960s the objective was to develop a method of non-subjective reading. The concepts of the theory of discourse that emerged, and which were employed to justify this discovery, had retained their initial position. The subject was doubly foreclosed. In the corpus studied, the positions of subjects and of the subject-effect were analysed. In so far as the subject-reader was the discourse analyst him/herself, s/he became anonymous behind the 'scientific'. Indeed, the developing of the procedure seemed to guarantee that effacement. The initial phase, that of selecting the corpus on the basis of stable and homogeneous conditions of production, pertained to its theoretical responsibility. It was the moment of the problematic. In the terms of that procedure, the interpretation of the results seemed to 'support' the responses to the questions asked.

The critique of the 'prosthesis of reading' is tied to the critique of the foreclosure of the subject of reading and therefore of the reading itself. Any reintroduction of the subject would drastically alter the nature of the discipline. Focusing as it did on the question of meaning, under the sign of science, it sought to take on board the question of the materiality of meaning. As such it lay very much on the side of the interpretative disciplines.

Despite the link between history and language in discourse analysis, and despite the persistent reformulation of the historical, there was a much more evident continuity in the approach to linguistics. It rejected any conception of a universal metalanguage inscribed in the innate nature of the human spirit. It did not function as some metalanguage of intra- or interdiscursive descriptions, and the objects of description were not of that order. However, it is also clear that the linguistic was highly developed over the years, leading to what Milner (1978) refers to as the 'real of language'. By the 1980s language was claimed to be indiscoverable: 'internally resisting the evidence of logic . . . the materiality of syntax is the possible object of a calculus . . . but simultaneously it escapes to the extent that the sliding, the failure and the ambiguity are constitutive of language' (Pécheux, 1982c:38). If syntax is that which 'comes closest to the real of language as a symbolic order' (Pécheux, 1982d), the discursive description can no longer rest enclosed in the base/processes duality, or in the idea that more or less partitioned levels exist. There is an intrication of three orders – syntax, lexicon and enonciation.

From the historical perspective there is a fundamental rejection of the dominance of a theory preoccupied with its objects. The discourse historians were working on a discipline which was condemned by the structure of its method to confirm or deny a hypothesis while being devoid of all heuristic capacity. They had sought to break this vicious circle by widening the corpus. The RCP/ADELA involvement brought new ideas into the discipline, introducing the possibility of a relationship between the social history of mentalities and a discourse analysis characterised by new ways of reading. Again the influence of Foucault is evident.

Some of the directions which the work was now taking are exemplified in Pécheux's paper 'Analyse de discours: trois epoques'. He refers to the question of how to catch the interlacing, collection and disassociation of textual sequences; how to describe the channels of the signifying systems from which the interpretations of the subject derive; how to tackle 'the open space of repair, forming the trajectories in the system of texts with their points of unstable accumulation, organising the systems of provisionally regularised memory, exposed at the clash of events' (Maldidier 1990:85).

The debate concerning corpus had made it clear that the initial concern with Foucault's stable and fixed conditions of production of discourse which determine that which can and must be said was no longer valid. Guilhaumou's suggestion concerning the thematic trajectory and the co-text, nursed things in the same direction as the group working on methods. Rather than determining the choice of corpus from an external historical knowledge, as was originally the case, it was claimed that the question of corpus was henceforth to be considered in terms of the interior of a discursive field containing an immense circulation of statements. In the broad sense, the corpus allowed singular discursive sequences to be placed in relation to their system of 'memory', thereby opening onto an interdiscursive space. On the other hand, in its narrow sense, the corpora never return to some initial or inaugural condition, to a definitive expression. One speaks of the 'displacement of the corpus', of the displacement of the periphery by the centre of the corpus. This position contrasted with the conception of a fixed order that existed in the early years of discourse analysis. In this respect Pécheux referred to the cumulative interaction of moments of linguistic analysis, and of discourse analysis in terms of the 'spiralling' production of a reconfiguration of the corpus.

By the end, the concept of discourse appears to have displaced that of discursive formation, which is by now absent (Gadet and Marandin, 1984). The focus of the work is on 'the incidences of interdiscourse in the linguistic-discursive analysis of the sequence'. Also retained is the concept of memory, which is now discussed in terms of 'the socio-historic body of discursive traces that constitute the space of memory' (Maldidier, 1990:87), and is clearly assimilated to the concept of interdiscourse. The point had been reached where the object of discursivity as a theoretic object involved relating linguistic research with socio-historic research in order to create a new discipline which focuses upon discourse analysis. This is the clear thrust of the collection presented in *Mots* which was prepared by members of ADELA (Pécheux, 1984a:8). What such an approach had to reject was made very clear. It was argued that the linguistic input involved a new approach to 'text' which derived from the emphasis on the discursive sequence, an approach which was virtually inaccessible to orthodox linguistics. The tendency to focus on language acts within a pragmatic context was singled out as being devoid of relevance. Rather, discourse analysis involved the enonciative analysis associated with sequentiality in order to formally study the textual processes or oral conversation. Similarly, the reluctance of historians and sociologists to come to terms with Milner's 'real of the language' left the majority of workers in this field remote from such developments. The micro-sociological interest in interactional research which focused on different 'strategies' of power on the part of rational speaking subjects was summarily dismissed. Discourse analysis was not to be regarded as the kind of interpretative discipline that discovers **the** meaning of a particular text, as some kind of hermeneutic, but, rather, as a reading, where the subject is simultaneously dispossessed from, and responsible for, the meaning which it bids (Marandin, 1983). This twist of orientation with reference to linguistics and enonciation will be the subject of the next chapter.

Linguistics and the subject

Having established the multi-faceted nature of identity in relation to language, giving the locuteur, enonciateur, time and location specific functions which are not necessarily coincidental with the production of the enonce, perhaps involving a locuteur which the text will not reveal, the analysis of linguistic turns takes a new turn. Being concerned with the issue of ideology and how meaning is structured, not in terms of a hermeneutic which seeks some form of truth or reality, but rather in terms of possibilities of meaning, it is evident that much of the focus will be on those aspects of syntactic process and lexicality which relate to ambiguity. For Pécheux ambiguity was a central notion for discourse analysis, being a feature of the title of the important paper on the Mansholt Report (Pécheux *et al.*, 1979). He refused to consider ambiguity merely as a question of language: 'the forms of compromise, where the discursive traces are retrievable, do not have their origin in language as system, or as the act of a subject, but in the relationships of force as non-subjective elements' (quoted in Bonnafous, 1991:275 fn 17). If ambiguity is revealed, it is related to the multiple possibilities of interpolation to meaning, this in turn being related to the multiplicity of subject forms in discourse. In this respect it opposes the formalist tendency to make enonciation 'a simple system of operations'. On the other hand, there is also the need to return to the theoretical issues of, for example, the Foucaultian emphasis upon the procedures, external delineators and internal organisation of discourse that limits what can be said and indicates the impossible (Milner, 1978), or to Foucault's insistence on the importance of intertextuality: 'there can be no statement that in one way or another does not reactualise others' (1969:130). It was this development which was the focus of the work which sought to employ enonciative theory in studying ambiguity, polysemy, the paraphrase and synonymy (Fuchs, 1992:221). Thus the focus was upon the mode of correspondence between the forms (lexical, syntactic, grammatical . . .) and meaning, with reference to a system of language within which the enonciative mechanisms are inscribed. That is, ambiguity, polysemy, paraphrase and synonymy were considered with reference to enonciation. The objective was to establish a dialectic of the stable and the unstable constitutive of these phenomena, in order to explain how an expression deploys a variety of values and infinite effects of meaning in context; how ambiguity, seen as alternatives between two mutually exclusive values, does not constitute a case of an interpolative figure among other possibilities (Fuchs, 1992). It was held that syntax and enonciation are related, and that it is not possible to treat syntax without an awareness of enonciation. This orientation towards orthodox linguistics was an inevitable development of FDA.

As has been emphasised at the beginning of this chapter, orthodox linguistics operates on the principle of the rational subject. This is evident in the manner in which this assumption concerning the rational human subject has been integrated into the very construction of orthodox linguistics in terms of the subject in relation to grammatical forms. Not that there was not a tendency for historical and positivist linguistics to be asemantic and even anti-semantic. This was based on the belief that the semantic content of linguistic expressions was scientifically unfathomable, thereby leading to a concentration on other topics, most notably syntax. This scepticism, in turn, led to the claim that words and phrases do not have a stable signification, making literary originality inaccessible. It meant that semantics fails on account of the impossibility of determining the identity of significations and their communication (Parret, 1991:16).

Such points were taken on board by Gadet, Leon and Pécheux (1984), who began a systematic consideration of orthodox linguistics, or Standard Understood Theory as they referred to it, as discourse. They recognised that an analysis of the play of language cannot be reduced to orthodox grammar. They emphasised how the distinctive nature of enonciative linguistics involved the difference between the subject of enonciation and the grammatical subject. In so doing they criticised the manner in which Ducrot related polyphony to the difference between enonciateur and locuteur while rationalising the 'conception of the responsibility of the speaking subject' (Gadet *et al.*, 1984:48 fn 2). This was a reference to the relatively late entry of pragmatics into the field of enonciative linguistics, and the feeling that this was shifting the ground away from the focus on the decentred subject and the manner in which FDA wished to pursue the study of ideology. In this respect they proceeded to refer to how orthodox linguistics treats the completive as establishing the independence of the object of thought, which constitutes the linguistic mark of an externality/independence anteriority. In contrast, they argued that the status of the object of thought is linked to the enonciative positions. Thus a grammatical perspective had, at least, to be associated with a discourse perspective, since the regularities of language which grammar addressed were capable of being destabilised or displaced through discourse.

In this respect the three authors were building on the work of Gadet and Pécheux (1981a), which, among other things, offered a hefty critique of Chomskyan linguistics. Indeed *Les vérités de La Palice* can be read as an extended critique of orthodox linguistics. One of the central points of that book was that the opposition between explicative and determinative, between situational and permanent properties, betrays a focus upon logic and rhetoric, objectivity and subjectivity, necessity and contingency, the emotion and the rational, etc., the very cornerstone of modernist philosophy. That is, Pécheux was underlining that 'linguistic' issues are inscribed in a philosophical problematic. Linguistics is seen as a political enterprise. This was the reason for focusing upon semantics and for, simultaneously, seeking to dispel the idea that syntax constitutes a homogeneous block of rules which serve as a kind of logical machine (Pécheux, 1982a:209). In contrast, his objective was to link semantics and the subject within a specifically non-modernist context.

The difficulty which Gadet, Leon and Pécheux expressed involved how to relate syntactic arguments and discourse in any analysis. They argued that neither grammar nor dictionaries cover all of the constructions of meaning possible, obliging them to focus on what they called 'the impossible in the language'. They then proceeded to indicate how deviation from an ideal situation in which a stable, logical form exists for each verb within a stable discursive universe, where each verb offers a closed and constant list of arguments, leads to possible displacements, which they refer to as *forcage*. This 'forcing' involves the grammatical manipulation necessary to make a verb accept a construction which would be complementary to its precise construction. Thus a completive is introduced where only the infinitive is in principal possible, or the co-reference, or a subjunctive in place of an indicative. It leads to the question of the relationship between that type of operation and its acceptability – is it possible to force a construction that is not acceptable? They reply that it is conceivable that such a forcing can be seen as an operation rather than merely as an extension of acceptability. This involves the heterogeneous nature of the relationship between grammar and the discursive. Such forcing reveals the importance of enonciation and dialogue associated with the destabilisation of properties. However, they note that this is easier for the passage from the completive to the infinitive than vice versa, and refer to this resistance in terms of dissymmetry and saturation. Clearly, they are stretching the limits of orthodox linguistics in seeking to demonstrate the relevance of enonciation. In this respect their work recalls that of Wittgenstein with reference to how speaking reveals the limits, and how playing with the rules is also to speak, and, thereby, to practise and construct the contours of a silent horizon (Borutti, 1991:283). The normative nature of orthodox linguistics was highlighted and questioned and its political nature brought into focus.

To the difference of effects and the similitude of effects they add the principle whereby a unique form can be ambivalent. This was done in an innovative manner, by developing an experimental method. In establishing that a unique form can be ambiguous they sought to force the ambivalence against the forcing of the difference (the paraphrase), the strict distinction between two stable points (ambiguity), in order to oblige a process of distinguishing, where language merely offers the indistinct. The conditions of acceptability of the indistinct are of the order of discourse. In this respect they were forcing language to its limits.

It is perhaps Gadet more than anyone who contributed to the reassessment of the epistemological status of orthodox linguistics. In the paper she wrote for the Matérialités Discursives conference, she built on the book she wrote with Pécheux (Gadet and Pécheux, 1981a) in considering the relationship between writing and language. She drew together the binary opposites word/phrase and liberty/constraint in arguing that the word constitutes the point of application of creativity, while syntax is treated as a factor of rigidity and constraint as a consequence of the manner in which it has been constructed as a system of rules. Tamine (1979) expresses the point clearly when he refers to metaphor as one word standing for another, but adding that placing the words within a syntactic frame makes it a feature of a language rooted in syntax. It also links with Milner's systematic exploration of this point in his consideration of pleasantries on the one hand, and the 'errors' of interpretation on the other: 'I insist on that the fact that in general many pleasantries that return to a lexical ambiguity, in fact, rely on that syntactic analysability' (Milner, 1979:80). Gadet concludes that making the opposition word/phrase a real opposition, as two modes of being of language, merely leads to what she calls a lexical phantasm or to a 'phantasm of imaginary syntax' (Gadet, 1981:119). If creativity rests in the ambiguity of the word, it is impossible to have an imaginary syntax which can be violated.

This work, and other works circulating at the time, emphasised the importance of language both as play, and also as the focus of social order, recalling the relationship between Saussure and Durkheim. It refers to what Barthes (1976) regards as the 'great subversion', where literature constitutes a social intervention. In establishing this point, Gadet was not merely reflecting upon syntax, but also on how orthodox sociolinguistics sees language as a means of communication. This communication, established through a norm or a social consensus, creates the impression that it is communication which facilitates the social bond, since the possibility of meaning is linked to the creation of its meaning. This is achieved, not necessarily and not only, as a voluntary and conscious act, by the possibility of intervention in the language, by the systematisation of a rupture in the rules which can only be conceived of as deviance (Gadet, 1981:121). It was an explicit reference to how sociolinguistics conceives of both language and society as normative entities. It is a theme which Achard (1993) developed in depth some time later.

Gadet claimed that literature could be revolutionary, and that tricking the language could involve changing life. If the violation of rules is impossible, but the rule carries the possibility of a subversion which is a component of meaning, then linguistic rules themselves are subversive. Such rules have to accommodate a space of play which lies between the mirage of a language without rules, and the phantasm of language ruled in a stable manner. This space of play, rather than being the product of a rule, is a dimension of each rule operating in the general functioning of language. The relationship between liberty and constraint must accommodate the system of language and the play which it permits. Her paper which criticised sociolinguistics (Gadet, 1977) had a clear message in this respect, and yet her work also supported a sociolinguistics in its opposition to a rule-bound understanding of linguistics. Thus, that paper should be understood not as the rejection of sociolinguistics *per se* but as a claim for a particular form of sociolinguistics. In this respect it should also be seen as part of the political debate that was put in place within French academic circles.

Gadet's reference to literature was a direct reference to writing as a representational system, a point which Derrida (1967b) commented upon with reference to the *Cours de linguistique générale*. Both he and Foucault (1966) referred to the problem of the autonomy of writing with reference to Saussure. In so doing they revealed the importance of the philosophy of the sign, and of the analysis of representation in any discussion of writing (Chiss and Puech, 1990:49). Foucault (1966:81) insisted that after the eighteenth century the general science of the sign was linked with a general theory of representation, and that the classical theory of the sign was associated with an ideology. What Saussure rediscovered was the classic condition associated with the binary nature of the sign. In a sense it is here that both Derrida and Foucault were involved in their most explicit critique of orthodox linguistics. The issue of representation was a rich vein for such criticism.

This issue was taken on board by Milner (1978) in asking how do you write the real of language in the discourse of linguistics? In pursuing this question Milner made a succinct critique of orthodox linguistics in noting that making semiology the object and goal of Saussureanism led to Chomsky's formalism which was integrable to a theory of systems (Milner 1978:33). Chiss and Puech (1990:54) make the point, which should not surprise us, that Derrida, Foucault and Milner converge in their discussion of writing in developing the problematic of the relationship between natural language and formal language. The two authors conclude that any consideration of the theorisation of language by linguists should not be independent of the writing of linguistic science itself!

Achard (1990) claims that the difference between the oral and the written rests on the functional division of language use. He treats the written not as a genre but as a register, since it is the functional division that creates the specificity of which the enonciative correlates are a consequence. In so doing he emphasises that the linguist is obliged to take account of social delimitations which predetermine their object. Thus the existence of a written register lends itself to an intensification of those practices, and to a displacement of the epilinguistic to the metalinguistic; that is, from the practice of correction, to the explication of theoretical elements characteristic of the language. This claim for the discursive status of writing was, simultaneously, a critique of a linguistics based on the idea of the oral practice of language studied on the model of natural sciences, separate from a normative practice that was internal and was revealed by speech. The separation of linguistics and the discursive is merely conceptual. Again this was a stab against orthodox linguistics, and especially Chomskyan linguistics, for being merely a linguistics of writing.

Gadet also had an important contribution to make in this respect in the issue of *Mots* compiled by members of ADELA. Writing with Marandin (Gadet and Marandin, 1984), he claimed that the linguistic problematic had been transformed as a consequence of the activities of discourse analysis. Given the limited interplay between discourse analysis and orthodox linguistics, the evolution of linguistics has not played the role of catalyst in discourse analysis. However, there does exist a conjuncture involving two points of view on language – the linguistic point of view and the discourse analyst point of view. As early as 1971 (Haroche *et al.*, 1971) it was recognised that 'to speak was something other than the production of grammatical examples', this partly being a reaction to the tendency for linguistics to operate on the enonce as already enonced. The emergence of new directions in linguistics during the seventies opened new possibilities of linking grammar, logic and textual perspectives. These new directions involved, among other things, a focus on anaphora and co-reference, the link between the functioning of connectors and the dependence/autonomy of sequences, and the problematic of textual connections involving tense, systems of determinants, and chains operated by the 'words of discourse'. Simultaneously, the development of enonciative linguistics involved the study of traces in the act of enonciation, and led to raising the problem of the effects of that which is put to work on language, a key problem for the issue of grammatical representation. Where orthodox linguistics does not require a symmetrically neutral subject, the introduction of the work of grammar in enonciation insists on the necessity of a producer or receptor subject, thereby fixing the points of language in a way that a grammar of neutral subject cannot explain. At the same time, modifying the place of the subject in this way, by passing from a single pole to two poles, leads to the suspicion that a consideration of each pole in isolation is no simple matter. While this does not involve imposing discourse on the linguistic, it does generate a new reflection on the linguistic/discursive relationship. It was a manifestation of Pêcheux's claim that the linguist could no longer impose his/her models on the 'materiality of language in the discursivity of the archive' (Pêcheux, 1984c:29). It involved a rejection of the hermeneutic subject of history, of the scientific subject of positivism as well as a rejection of the classic philosophic subject.

The work on local functioning means that the relationship between grammatical rules and language regularities, and the link between the syntactic and the lexical, had to be reviewed. Fiala (1984:86) claimed that envisaging syntax as a collection of enonciative operators involved transgressing the traditional linguistic frame. For anyone wishing to combine the linguistic and the discursive, a form is not a meaning, a text is not a phrase, a phonological interpretation has little to do with a semantic interpretation. There are no syntactic schemes to be filled by the lexical, merely local regularities which invite applying a Saussurean concept of value to things other than lexical terms. It also leads, inevitably, to a consideration of the Saussurean concept of the arbitrary. Thus, in considering the relationship between linguistics and discourse analysis, it is evident that linguistics is neither a tool nor a model for discourse analysis, and it is not concerned with two complex disciplines moving in the same direction. It was at this time that Milner (1984b:188) referred to how linguistics implies a homogeneity between cause and effect that was incompatible for the historian, while adding that 'fact' is essentially a fragment of theory.

As should already be evident, Gadet and Marandin describe how the evolution of the problematic of discourse involves the emergence of a theory of relationships between interdiscourse and discursive sequence, leading to the description of interdiscourse as a space where the regularities which escape to the phrase or the proposition are deployed (Gadet and Marandin, 1984). The principal object of discourse analysis is seen as the problematic of the relationship between a discourse delivered by a locuteur and a given moment of a socio-historic conjuncture, and a pre-discursive in the Foucaultian sense, and the manner in which this makes possible or determines that discourse. The practice of analysis becomes a reduction of discursive sequences, and a socio-historic reconstruction of a system of constraints performed by those sequences. Whether that system consists of families of paraphrases, consistent systems of enonces, or as systems of contradictory formulations does not change things one iota. Discourse analysis has abandoned the idea of the discursive formation as a point of identity within the interdiscourse. This is a consequence of recognising the problems associated with the selection and closure of corpus, and how this relates to the idea of discursive formation. It was a consequence of Pécheux's claim: 'In borrowing the concept of discursive formation from Foucaultian archaeology, AD derives three rapid (too rapid) facts from that notion, concerning the idea of a semiotic machinery coinciding with the "conditions of production" determining "that which can and must be said", this leading to the idea of an origin-structure of enonciations, without the position of the enonciateur' (Pécheux, 1984b:28–29). This is a valid criticism of Foucault, who operated on the margins of the developed conception of enonciative linguistics; that is, it should not be seen as involving, in any way, the idea of an extra-discursive rational thinking subject. Instead the emphasis shifts to a consideration of the relationship between discursive sequences, and the exterior which dominates them – the exterior here being seen in terms of the preconstructed – in such a way that the sequences are linked to other sequences in their textuality or in their interpretation, Pécheux's 'traces in a residue of memory'. Thus, repetition allows the corpus to be seen as a co-textual reassembling, while the concept of transformation allows all sequences to be viewed as a singular event in history. To describe intra-discourse is to open a field of description of regularities which one can establish in a domain other than those of the phrase or of the proposition. These regularities are placed between two orders, those of language understood as enonciative references, and those of a Foucaultian sense of discourse:

The tense and the place of the enonciation, the material support which it uses becoming indifferent at least to a great extent: and that which detaches, it is a form which is indefinitely repeatable and which can give place to very diverse enonciations. Or the enonce itself can not be reduced to that pure event of the enonciation but in spite of its materiality it can be repeated . . .

(Foucault, 1969:106)

Clearly, discourse analysis is concerned both with the unique features that are capable of being described in language, and with the regular elements which return to forms repeated in singular enonciations. Describing effects of meaning associated with the displacements that affect the temporal benchmarks in any textual sequence cannot be undertaken in the same way as in describing the effect of meaning involving the emergence of themes associated with anaphoric chains and patterns of lexico-syntactic repetition. In neither case is there a global relationship to the linguistic, but rather to the local regularities, where there is a continuum between what can be related to language, and what can be related to discourse. The role of linguistics had clearly been redefined.

This theme was taken up by a special issue of *Linx* devoted to syntax and discourse which appeared in 1984. The introduction consisted of a posthumous paper by Pécheux (1984c) in which he sought to place the 'subject of enonciation' at the interior of the grammatical space associated with syntactic theory. He objected to the manner in which grammatical 'facts' were hierarchically structured in relation to 'natural' criteria, such that all description of facts of language relied on an already existing grammatical position which developed a normative conception of enonces. Again the theme is that of the production of knowledge and the manner in which linguistics is a social process structured by philosophical references. Interestingly he pursues this theme via a critique of Frege, with reference to the related issues of truth, thought and knowledge; a critique which also served as an indirect reference to the work of the French pragmatists Ducrot and Anscrombe, who had wandered into enonciative linguistics without abandoning their pragmatist stance.

In support of his position Pécheux invokes the work of Wittgenstein on the declarative proposition and the play of language. This is not merely because of Wittgenstein's position vis-à-vis Frege's work, but because of a genuine interest in Wittgensteinian work on language play among the French discourse analysts. We have already seen this with reference to Gadet; it is also evident in Henry's paper for the Matérialités Discursives conference (Henry, 1981). Pécheux demonstrates that the grammatical question of the completive-infinitife-infinitive is associated with distinctive philosophical positions which are entangled with two registers which one associates with propositional logic and modal logic. The entanglement of linguistic functions involving the constructions of 'propositional attitudes', and the constructions

151

of the 'modalisation of enonciations' leads to questioning the grammatical distribution of these functions, since it does not seem that one can place the difference of grammatical constructions and the differences in the construction of signification in parallel. In conclusion Pécheux draws on Wittgenstein to suggest that the distribution of grammatical functions and the constructions of meaning are arbitrary:

> Why does one not say that culinary rules are arbitrary; and why am I tempted to say that the rules of grammar are? Because I think that the concept of 'cuisine' is defined by the finality of the cuisine; whereas, I do not think that the concept of 'language' would be defined by the finality of language . . . when one follows grammatical rules other than the rules of use, one does not say anything false, one speaks of another thing.
>
> (Wittgenstein, 1978:133, quoted in Pécheux, 1984b)

Marandin contributed two papers to the issue of *Linx* (Marandin 1984a, 1984b), both of which were concerned with Wittgenstein. One of the papers (1984a) referred to the Wittgensteinian concept of displacement. Marandin refers to how Pécheux distinguished between a 'terminal stage of discourse' and 'a pre-discursive', the latter referring to the collection of conditions of possibilities. In contrast to Foucault's definitions, the pre-discursive is conceived of as families of paraphrastic invariants; that is, as a collection of arguments and predicates or of modes of arguments and of predicates. Thus discourse analysis involves recognising that the pre-discursive derives from the texts of corpora, and that they submit to ruled manipulations, as a consequence of the presuppositions involving the textual organisation (Bonnafous, 1983; Courtine, 1981; Marandin, 1979). Marandin went on to analyse how the relationship between arguments and predicates is determined by the socio-historic order of discourse and its relationship to the speaking subject. To question the relationship between arguments and predicates in a given enonce involves not merely presenting them as (socio-historically) necessary, involving 'what can and must be said from a given position in a conjuncture' (Haroche, 1971:102), but also it needs to reference the social relationships of an epoch via the traces of prior discourse. The procedure by which this is achieved has involved a shift from the early stages of FDA where the word is taken to be an element of a language or ideological system, to a semantic problematic where it is marked by its occurrences in other texts. This observation Marandin related to Wittgenstein's questioning of the circumstances in which a phrase which contains a specific word already contains the shadow of other uses of that word (Wittgenstein, 1978:54). The overlap between FDA and the work of Wittgenstein is evident.

In the second paper Marandin's work focused on the lexical, involving Wittgenstein's (1978) description of the meaning of a word. This was an attempt to contest the nature of semantics in orthodox linguistics, involving a semantic interpretation of a collection of items or expressions. It involved shifting away from conceiving of meaning in terms of the intuition of the centred subject. Marandin concludes with Wittgenstein's assertion that a concept-word does not involve a kinship between objects based on the common sharing of a property or constituent, but rather on how it establishes linkages between objects. Evidently the work of FDA on repetition and linkaging had established a common ground with the work of Wittgenstein. Indeed these two papers, perhaps more than any others, indicate the manner in which enonciative linguistics, discourse and Wittgenstein's work on language play come together. In this respect it confirms Achard's observation concerning how disciplines are defined by their horizons of closure and the relationship established with other disciplines based on the definition of their object. Thus the focus of linguistics on form, where language is a signifying form, differs from philosophy, which he sees as bordering on the social sciences and the interpretative orientation. It emphasises that FDA was orientated towards language in a distinctive manner, a manner which emphasised the importance of interpretation devoid of the rationalism of modernity, this being what served to define its closure.

A voice at the periphery

Perhaps the most obvious place to begin is with the work of Achard, partly because as early as 1967 (Achard, 1967) he gave notice of an interest in what was to become FDA, and partly because of his influence as editor of *Langage et société*. It is also Achard, perhaps more than anyone else, who has sought to give a sociological focus to FDA. His recent work assumes a position of significance in the subsequent chapters. In his early papers he shared with Pécheux the development of a break with the structuralist emphasis in the study of language in society. He also shared with Pécheux the experience of not having been trained as a linguist nor as a sociologist. Rather, he was initially trained as an engineer, but the climate of the 1960s took him in the direction of economics. This must have involved the same suspicion of the alleged 'objectivity' of science and the social sciences which Pécheux expressed with reference to social psychology, since his early work claimed that while there was no contradiction between science and ideology, it insisted that science was constructed within an ideology which permitted it to exist. In so doing he drew an analogy with the anthropological concept of magic, claiming that it was essentially effective insofar as the natural sciences were concerned, but that other phenomena affected the position of the social sciences. Once again we witness the same kind of preoccupations as those found in the work of Lévis-Strauss and Althusser.

Much of the impetus for this early work derived from anthropology, most particularly from the work of Lévis-Strauss, as well as from a rejection of the way in which Marxism presented a superstructural role for language and culture. However, for a number of French social scientists the experience of those Frenchmen who had fought side by side with the FNL (Front de Libération National) against French colonialism in Algeria, but who were subsequently not accepted as 'Algerians', also served to highlight the importance of ideology for social practice. However, it was the French translation of Chomsky's *Syntactic Structure and Issues in the Theory of Language* which led Achard away from structuralism. While being adequate for the study of phonology, structuralism made little contribution to syntax. This search for a syntactic basis was also evident in his flirtation with Troubetskoy, the precision of whose work appealed to Achard's mathematical training. Particularly revealing was Troubetskoy's application of distributionalism to phonology in order to show how the designation of sounds, taken analytically as discrete units, bind together to the effects of meaning, thereby freeing the object from the variety of its realisation.

Also influential at this time was the work of Martinet, a one-time colleague of Troubetskoy's, who had a profound impact on French linguistics following his return from Columbia University to teach at the Sorbonne in 1955. As for many French linguists, he was the source of Achard's early contact with the Prague Circle, and most notably with Saussure. Of course, Martinet's work focused upon the possibilities associated with *langue*. Working initially from a syntagmatic approach, he delineated the inventory of possibilities prior to proceeding to a paradigmatic analysis. Martinet's work opened linguistics to the social by his consideration of communication. His distinction between 'movemes' as units of first articulation, and 'phonemes' as the second level of articulation was the basis of his *Eléments de linguistique générale* which was so influential during the 1960s.

Yet there is little doubt that it was Chomsky who was the main influence on Achard's early work. More specifically it was Chomsky's work on transformations that was of primary appeal. To an extent, the idea of distributionalism was supplemented by competence, the objective being to discover some form of model which would assist in generating articulated propositions. Chomsky's deep structure was seen to generate a structure of pre-significance of meaning, this in turn being determined by a logical structure. The emphasis was very much on a closed theoretical system rather than on the epistemological. None the less, the objective of developing an understanding of ideology through an analysis of the production of meaning was firmly in place. Indeed, as early as 1966 Achard referred to ideology as a kind of condition of truth, wherein the truth of a statement can only be considered through assuming formulations which are themselves grounded in ideology. This was the basis of his objective of seeking to discover the existence of disciplinary discourses on the one hand, and a meta-disciplinary level involving the active use of 'created' theory on the other.

It was at the end of the 1960s that Achard first established contact with Michel Pécheux and Paul Henry, and it was this contact which introduced him to Culioli's linguistics of enonciation. It is here that the early emphasis upon meta-discourse yields to a focus on enonciation. The Foucaultian emphasis in Achard's work had been evident from the beginning, and the use of Chomsky's work was an attempt to ground Foucault's perspective in a linguistic method. Particularly influential was the publication of Foucault's *Les mots et les choses*, which gave him the idea that sociology should be autonomous vis-à-vis social psychology, this position being supported by Lacan's refusal to allocate psychoanalysis the status of social science on the grounds that its concerns lay with the outward manifestations of the functioning of the human mind, this precluding it from being a positive science.

Clearly, the Chomskyan model was at odds with any subjective pre-occupation, and Achard's adoption of enonciative linguistics was no surprise when it came. This development also had an impact upon his conception of ideology. Whereas his earlier ideas involved conceptualising ideology as a global entity, not necessarily tied to any specific group, but rather as the manner in which dominated society partakes in ways of thinking which appear natural to all members of society, and which approved the legitimisation of that domination, he now focused not upon domination itself, but rather on its consequences, and on how the human actor enters understanding armed with pre-existing organisational concepts. It was the discovery of enonciative linguistics which led to an awareness that the problem of ideology lay not so much in representation as in the active part of discourse, that is, in enonciation. This was to be the basis of the non socio-psychological conception of representation which he was seeking.

The awareness of the empirical importance of meta-disciplinary discourse contributed to an awareness of the need to proceed beyond the mere structure of the disciplinary enonciation. The structure of the enonce took second place to the study of how the discourse register connects with action and other discourse registers through enonciation. Meaning becomes located within ideology since, without an unmarked social consensus on meaning, there is no possibility of the production of meaning. Even though it is historically grounded, this unmarked situation is lived by the individual as something natural.

The critique of content analysis by Henry and Moscovici (1968) brought Achard into contact with Henry, who invited Achard to participate in their seminar programme. One consequence of this participation was the assump-tion of Pécheux's emphasis on competence not being reducible to corpora, and that distributionalism was more relevant for discourse than for language. However, rather than following Pécheux's path of treating the production of corpus by statistical and distributional means, Achard focused upon the competence of the open domain, this leading to the selection of what he called a restrained corpus which was the empirical basis for investigating the enonciative possibilities of a discipline. Thus, when he adopted enonciative linguistics, it was not with reference to distributionalism, which was linked to the *enonce disciplinaire*, but rather to the *meta-disciplinaire*. At the level of representation, distribution can be operationalised as concrete distribution in concrete corpora, whereas for Achard the focus was on the distributional rules which made enonciation possible at the level of representation.

As noted above, it was also through Henry and Pêcheux that Achard was introduced to Culioli's work. This was a crucial development which led to his abandoning Chomsky on the grounds that Culioli's use of a model of enonciation was much closer to the speech-act than Chomsky's work ever could be. Whereas Chomsky's systematisation had the advantage of giving the formal dimension which Benveniste and Culioli lacked, this is not really seen as a step forward. Clearly, modalities are directly relevant to Culioli's enonciative linguistics, and, for Achard, modalities became operations on the basis of the enonciative framework. The importance of Foucault's position in *L'ordre du discours*, where he put forward the corpus effect of the accumulation of discourses in the same place, in the same locality, and of the importance of this for the constitution of meaning of the substantive vocabularies, was recognised. However, it was not the same as Culioli's position in that it ignored the internal enonciation, and how things are repeated in the same place. This leads to an awareness that specific genres have specific linguistic forms, which, in turn, have specific effects, and create the meaning of the words which are used through distributional effects in that situation or context.

This input, during the early 1970s, led Achard to adopt the idea of the implicit and how it can be reconstituted. This in turn led him to seek a way of integrating the two levels of discourse and meta-discourse, since in the discourse of economics he encountered many texts where the separation between them was not respected. The enonciation was not only meta-discursive, but it was also an enonciation which ensured the separateness or non-separateness between discourse and meta-discourse. This is the focus of his contribution to a collection of papers on biological discourse (Achard *et al.*, 1977). This was, in some respects, the precursor of his later work. It involved an attempt to bring together discourse analysts and social scientists interested in a particular theme with the practitioners of that theme. In several respects, this work of Achard's was taken by many – erroneously – to be merely a variant on Pêcheux's Althusserianism, whereas it was very much a product of the attempt to apply Foucaultian ideas to the investigation of disciplinary discourse.

In 1975 Achard called a meeting which was to be the prelude to establishing the journal *Langage et société*. The journal was never meant to be simply a forum for discourse analysis, but instead was to be based on a much broader interest in sociolinguistics and the sociology of language. It thus filled a gap that the various linguistic journals such as *Mots, Langage* and *Langage française* did not fill. None the less, since its inception it has been the forum for a number of stimulating papers on discourse analysis. It has appeared quarterly and has also sponsored bi-annual conferences and one important colloquium on discourse analysis. More important, perhaps, with reference to Achard's work, it opened a broader perspective on the epistemology of discourse analysis. Furthermore, the work around *Langage et société* included a number of working groups, one of which was devoted to discourse analysis.

At this time Achard's published works reflected his work on the discourse of economics. Among them was a paper on the sociology of development (Achard, 1982), which emphasised the manner in which the whole problem of economic development was constructed within the context of colonisation and the creation of the nation-state which existed within a plurality of nation-states, and that the concept of under-development was merely a specific form of 'progress' which involved a comparison of nation-states within which national unity was taken for granted. Thus 'development' was not a scientific concept, but a political operation deriving from a sociological critique of international relations. His goal was to establish the manner in which this sub-discipline was constructed in such a way that the forces associated with the historical development were displaced and forgotten.

In developing his argument he showed how there were three nominalisation values for the verb 'to develop' which served to establish an ambiguity of the position of the enonciateur with reference to her/his object. First, there is the relationship to the established value of the term, where the enonciateur is fixed as subject of knowledge of the world. Second, there is the term 'development', which assumes an unestablished value when it is used with the value of a middle route, where the agent is also the beneficiary and the enonciateur is congruent with that agent. Third, there is the case where the agent-beneficiary is the implied totality – the nation-state, with the economist occupying the place of the 'expert'. This led him to reconceive ideology. Rather than being ideal-type representations of knowledge or encyclopaedic beliefs of the world that rules discourse, the emphasis was placed on the manner in which discourses constitute social acts in assigning social places to interlocuteurs by the use of enonciation. Some of these social acts do not possess a guaranteed efficacy since they derive from the taking in charge of the oral or written text by the 'receptors', who exercise an act of interpretation.

This paper was characteristic of the way in which Achard retained the sociological input while deploying the FDA perspective to cast doubt upon the taken for granted in sociology. This kind of textual politics contrasted with his more technical work on enonciation and discourse. It was also at this time that he wrote on the ideology of *langue*, through an application of the discourse problematic to the problem of variation and the differentiation of languages. These papers clearly indicate that by the mid-1970s, not only was the focus of his work firmly on the linguistics of enonciation, but that his work on the disciplinary discourse had reached a level of sophisticated coherence. In contrast to others within FDA, he was concerned with employing FDA as a method, as a means for the analysis of concrete texts.

One of those involved with *Langage et société* from the outset was Josien Boutet, a linguist whose work involved a distinctive economic materialist position on discourse analysis at odds with Achard's position in that it assumed that there is an economic material causality external to discourse. It was through Boutet that Achard was introduced to the work of Bakhtin at the end of the 1970s. Bakhtin's work had a profound influence in France after its translation into French in 1977.[3] It was through the introduction of the Bakhtinian concept of dialogism that Achard was able to expand on the sociological significance of the manner in which enonciative communication is operationalised.

Achard's position on the materiality of discourse is clear. He makes an argument for the existence of an *ordre de grandeur* involving the individual speech-act and the fact that it does not derive its meaning from production but, rather, from its circulation, that circulation being linked to a prior existence which is of a higher order of magnitude. This does not relate to the issue of heterogeneity, as it might appear at first glance, since it is homogeneous, but rather to how a word assumes a new meaning when it is employed in an enonce, that is, it is new for the order of magnitude vis-à-vis the weight of the statement in terms of the horizon of intertextuality. In this respect he clearly differs from Pécheux's early tendency to divide external determination and discourse, as well as from his tendency, after the publication of *Les vérités de La Palice*, to claim that this was paradoxical, the paradox being the constituting of the discourse. For Achard, prior discourse is beyond the control of the individual, even though s/he submits to its discursive materiality. However, this feature of intertextuality is not important since the social construction of meaning does not depend on the subject's control of the act. Evidently there is no reference in his work to any transcendental force, nor to any extra-discursive materiality beyond intertextuality.

By 1980, as is evident from the appendix to the English translation of *Les vérités de La Palice*, Pécheux and his colleagues were adapting a far less dogmatic stance. When they left the PCF, the preoccupation with PCF's internal disputes, which, to an extent, had structured their work in such a way that it almost became an internal debate, disappeared, and this led to a new climate which was much more congenial to collaboration with those outside of the PCF who were working on discourse analysis. This is not to suggest in any way that they had hitherto operated as a closed shop. On the contrary, they were always open to debate and yet the terms of the debate were at least partly dictated by their activities as members of the PCF. This was also a period when Pécheux and his colleagues were increasingly developing a more public posture, both in terms of international collaboration and conference participation.

At the 1982 World Congress of Sociology in Mexico, Achard organised a section on discourse analysis which included contributions by Pécheux and his colleagues. This followed the Matérialités Discursives conference at Nanterre in 1980. However, it was the Histoire et Linguistique conference (Achard *et al.*, 1984) organised by *Langage et société* in April 1983 which opened up the prospect of more direct co-operation. Once again the focus of this conference was Achard's preoccupation with disciplinary discourse on the one hand, and the relationship between language and its external determination towards the sentence on the other. Thus the conference centred on the relationship between history and linguistics. Each discipline was considered as an open discourse field whose closed complementary discourse fields are other disciplines, with the consequence that there is a tendency for those working as linguists, for example, to accept that social facts are studied by sociologists, thereby relying on a form of reported discourse of the other discipline's discourse. Thus the conference was organised into workshops which consisted of a historian, a linguist and a discourse analyst. Among the participants were several members of Pécheux's group, including Pécheux himself, Maldidier, Conein, Courtine, Guilhaumou and Marandin.[4] In some respects the conference built on the earlier work of another of Pécheux's early collaborators, Regina Robin, whose book *Histoire et linguistique* (1973) had served to clarify the relationship not only between these two disciplines but also between sociology and linguistics. Similarly it reflected the interests of the special issue of *Mots* edited by Pécheux which was also published in 1984 (Pécheux, 1984b).

This conference was quickly followed by another in the following year which was organised in Paris as part of the sociolinguistic activities of the International Sociological Association. The theme of this conference was Orwellian Linguistics. Clearly the theme derives from the work of Fowler, Hodge, Kress and Trew (1977). Useful though this confrontation of perspectives on ideology and language was, it does not appear to have been very fruitful in linking Hallidayan and Benvenistean or Culiolian linguistics, again partly because of the tendency for the Norwich school of critical linguistics to insist on the importance of the extra-discursive and on orthodox syntactic analysis, orientations which Pécheux and his colleagues were abandoning, and which to a great extent had only been partly accepted by Achard.

This period of intense collaborative activity during the first half of the 1980s culminated in the publication of two position papers on theory and method of discourse analysis respectively in *Langage et société* (Achard, 1986, 1987). These two papers represent not only a summary of Achard's position on discourse at that particular time, but they were also a developed critique of preceding work, while also being a very useful statement of the epistemological place of discourse analysis within sociolinguistics and the sociology of language. In many respects it is this familiarity with both sociology and linguistics which stands out as the force of these contributions.

Achard prefaces his theoretical paper (Achard, 1986) with the claim that sociologists cannot hope to come to terms with their attempt to study society without taking language into account in all social processes. Indeed, this essential point, which is at the core of discourse analysis, has something in common with what ethnomethodologists have been saying through the concepts of accountability and indexicality. It is implicitly assumed by most sociologists that the social can be studied directly by observation, question-naires and empiricism. Achard also makes a second point with reference to sociolinguistics which emphasises the tendency to resort to a reflection thesis wherein a model of social structure is taken for granted, and the assumption is made that language 'reflects' this model. Sociolinguistics is reduced to a process of establishing correlations between the social and the linguistic. Now these two points are related, the second helping to explain the sociologists' indifference to language. Among the most prominent of those sociologists who bear the brunt of this critique is Bourdieu (Achard, 1984) whose work systematically ignores the fact that sociology is caught in language, rather than language merely being a tool for analysis. The same point is forcefully made by Authier-Revuz (1995:51), where she objects to the *sociologisation* of language and discourse.

This paper of Achard's (1986) also makes the link between Foucault's conception of discourse and that of Benveniste which fuelled the linguistics of enonciation. In this respect the theoretical orientation of the work is never in doubt, and is reflected in the author's insistence that there cannot be an extra-discursive reality. He ascribes to this Foucaultian position the label of French Discourse Analysis, identifying the current of future developments while simultaneously distinguishing this enterprise from other forms of dis-course analysis. In so doing he incorporates much of the work of Pécheux and his colleagues, to whom he ascribes the origin of this field, despite their earlier economic materialist stance. This theoretical orientation involves 'discourse and its conditions of possibility', which Achard sees as a project of an enon-ciative theory of semantics with 'the sense of an enonce being conceived of as the effects of meaning which is supported on its literality, are socially constructed from itself' (Achard, 1986:16). This is accompanied by a series of sophisticated reflections on the linguistics of enonciation, orthodox linguistics and discourse analysis, which, to a great extent, draw on the various topics which he has analysed through discourse analysis. He concludes that French Discourse Analysis stands out in taking the linguistic component of society seriously, and, as a consequence, it assumes a unique position in linguistics, either in terms of distributionalism, enonciation, or in terms of the semantic. In so doing it rejects both the notion of 'content' and the communication model. One could add that, as a consequence, it assumes a specifically political role in its focus on the importance of discourse for the understanding of ideology.

In a small but important introductory text (Achard, 1993), has recently sought to demonstrate how he was seeking to develop a sociology of language which assumed the thesis of the decentred subject, language as discourse, and enonciation and dialogic relationships. I will draw on this piece of work in the next chapter. For the moment I would merely emphasise that this reorientation of the sociology of language does not proceed so far as to deny the relevance of sociology *per se* and yet, implicitly, it does lay the ground for treating modernist sociology merely as a discourse, albeit that its academic institutionalisation does serve to make it a privileged discourse in terms of its effect.

Translation and meaning

Another who worked on the margin of the Pécheux group was Patrick Sériot. In many respects he represents a later generation of discourse analysts who were the students of those such as Pécheux, Henry, Authier-Revuz, Maldidier, Fuchs and Robin who pioneered the field during the 1960s and early 1970s. In this respect he stands alongside Conein, Marandin, Guilhaumou, Bonnafous, Courtine, Gadet and Maingueneau. It was a generation which was somewhat more sceptical about the relevance of Marxism and which was, perhaps, more open to ideas drawn from outside of that frame of reference.

Sériot's first contact with FDA was at the end of the 1970s when he attended a seminar by Robin and Maldidier at Nanterre. A fascination with the potential of FDA led him to apply some of its principles to Russian, soon appreciating that, in some respects, working on discourse analysis in a language other than one's native tongue means that separating the purely linguistic from the discursive is easier. This separation often depends upon the analyst's interpretation of how the text is constructed if the grammar does not reveal it. It was this awareness that lay behind his claim that discourse analysis on translated texts is impossible (Sériot, 1985). In this work he notes that political texts in Russian are strongly nominalised, giving them a style in which the preconstructed has a considerable importance. It retains, after nominalisation, a series of diverse complements where French or English would link the noun complements introduced by the unique prepositions 'de'/'of'. Furthermore, this is often the case outside of political discourse, Russian resorting to nominalisation where related languages such as Bulgarian resort to the 'completive'. It is in this context that Sériot, recognising that nominalisations cannot carry the same status across languages, sought to analyse contemporary political discourse on the basis of linguistic operators and other discursive constructions relevant to Russian. He sought to discover how enonciative space was stratified in the Soviet political discourse (Guilhaumou, Robin and Maldidier, 1994:188). He concluded that it is not possible to conduct discourse analysis on translated texts, since all translations imply a double difference: that of the marks present in the original language and without any equivalent in the target language, and that of the obligatory marks in the target language which are incapable of being the object of any indication in the source language. Whereas it might be possible to partially control the first problem by subjecting the translation to an exhaustive gloss, there are numerous locii that reclaim the obligatory precision but do not figure in the original text.

Achard (1986:37), on the other hand, suggests that translation can be treated as a paraphrase: the obligatory marks of the target language revealing the potential ambiguities of the source language, suggesting the implicits whose status is questioned, not in any absolute sense, nor with any reference to any 'universal' semantics, but as carrier of a question in the original discursive formation. These paraphrases make those paraphrases which are in the original language 'natural', as well as certain ones which would be discursively non-pertinent. This non-pertinence in itself constitutes a result, since it integrates them in a description of a linguistic-discursive structure in relation to the function of the studied discourse. He proceeds to suggest that theoretically it is conceivable that different languages could systematically be employed in order to analyse certain aspects of discourse. Thus, for example, French could be employed for narrative on account of the past dualism – *passé simple / passé composé*; Russian for the aspective dimension; Spanish for copula status, etc. Benveniste (1966) appears to have considered this orientation with reference to his 'category of thought and category of language', as also have the pragmatists Anscombe and Ducrot (1977).

This observation in turn led Achard in another interesting direction when he sought to ensure that Sériot's work was not taken as an extension of the Sapir–Whorf hypothesis. He referred to how that hypothesis links linguistic structures and discursive organisation, while also discussing social organisation. Appearing to agree that the categories of thought are the categories of language, he adds that they are formal categories whose effect of meaning is restricted to use in the discursive formation. It is the essentially mobile and conflictive character of these categories that justifies Pécheux's (1975b) claim that semantics is essentially a science of discourse, or Voloshinov's (1973) claim that the formal step on its own is incapable of creating a meaning that negates any conflict of meaning. Achard proceeds to emphasise that sexism, for example, in any society, does not derive from that society's language vis-à-vis its grammatical genre, but rather relates to a discursive formation, and to how stable and regular discursive assignations are determined. In a sense this is merely a restatement of the position which he adopts in emphasising his position on materiality and causality, when he claims that social class does not lie outside of language (Achard, n.d.).

Such reflections on translation offer the advantage of furnishing a neat distinction between discursive formations, while also leading to a more challenging orientation towards linguistics and discourse analysis. It leads to questions concerning the possibility of effects in different formal universes. Pragmatists would answer in the affirmative, whereas discourse analysts would reject the proposition, claiming that a good or bad translation is not possible, whereas the choices proposed by the translator in order to preserve certain effects of meaning in preference to alternative choices can lead to arbitrary choices whose effects of meaning are not necessarily recognised. The intentions of the translator may be linked to reason or intuition, whereas the destinataire, be it as reader or listener, is the true master of meaning. However, the destinataire is subjected to the same text and submits to the materiality of the furnished translation. Only an explicit work of criticism, based on the source text, can permit reading the effect of meaning as relevant to an effect of translation.

Clearly this intervention on the part of Sériot has introduced a new dimension to discourse analysis. He was convinced that differences of language constituted the field of linguistics and discourse, to the extent that discourse analysis on one's own language alone is not possible. Working on one's own language involves a transparency to the extent that it is only the 'proof' of other languages that consolidates the claim that there is something in the linguistic that resists the reduction to meaning. While the linguist is aware that language is not transparent, the 'linguist as ordinary citizen' must operate as if it is. Working with another language produces an almost permanent opaque materiality of language. It is only through the comparison of languages that Saussure's sense of the arbitrariness of the sign becomes obvious.

This insistence on working in a plurality of languages, together with the claim for the impossibility of working on translation, distanced Sériot somewhat from mainstream FDA, but there were other reasons for this distancing. Not being a member of the PCF, while having a first-hand know-ledge of the Soviet Union over many years, led him to treat the dogmatism of the PCF with disdain. Furthermore, he was in the privileged position of being able to work on the political discourse of the Soviet Union. In a sense, of course, Pécheux was reacting to the dogmatism of Marcellesi and Houdebine, among others, in a similar way, but from a different place, from within the PCF. Pécheux sat on Sériot's dissertation committee, but it took the break with the PCF to open the debate between the two. Certainly Sériot's work on the Soviet Union opened new considerations at an opportune time.

Sériot's theoretical position, like that of Achard, was unequivocally Foucaultian, and the two of them have worked closely following Sériot's parti-cipation in the Histoire et Linguistique conference in 1983. Foucault's position on how discourse generates categorisation without having to resort to an extra-discursive materiality was a central theme in Sériot's work. Superimposed on the Foucaultianism is a concern with the epistemology of language. At times he asks very simple but probing questions such as how do linguists allocate names to objects that are supposed to exist, that is, how do they construct a discourse object? Clearly this leads to treating linguistics as a discourse, thereby overlapping with Achard's interest in disciplinary discourse. In this respect Sériot's focus is on how Soviet linguists construct linguistics, and how this construction ultimately leads to an understanding of the political nature of linguistics.

This focus on the work of Sériot and Achard, two of those currently working on FDA, is, admittedly, highly selective. Another person who, despite being a member of ADELA, had a marginal involvement in Pécheux's group and has made a considerable contribution to FDA is Jacqueline Authier. Her work on reported discourse began in 1978, leading to a focus upon the theme of the presence of the Other in the discourse of the speaking subject. Her contribution to the Matérialités Discursives conference in 1980 made a profound impact. In one respect her position is quite different from that of Achard and Sériot in that she was a convinced Marxist and a member of the PCF. Yet her relationship to Pécheux's team was also peripheral, despite the profound influence which her work had on their ideas. Her important contributions will be considered in detail in Chapter 6.

Conclusion

The 1980s saw a shift in orientation within FDA, a shift towards a more explicit adoption of the work which, within a philosophical context, was to the forefront of post-structuralist thinking in France. Of course the traces of this work had always existed in FDA. It was the disquiet with the totalitarian tendencies of Communist regimes, and the unwillingness of Communist parties in the West to criticise these tendencies that was the catalyst for this change. The anarchism of Foucault was expressed in terms of a disquiet with State systems which was difficult to ignore. The concern reverberated within the PCF, where different orientations towards Marxism, language and ideology were the subject of dispute. In many respects this disquiet can be seen as a disquiet with modernism, and with how the entire premise of the modern State had explicitly political underpinnings, sustained by academic discourses which claimed to be objective. It was as if the understanding of ideology which the earlier work had stimulated was now applied as a critique of the ideological nature of the work itself.

In a sense the development that ensued was a criticism of the manner in which linguistics, Marxism and psychoanalysis were integrated. This criticism was coupled with a faith that it would lead to a new, and more exciting, development (Pécheux, 1982a:212). What is interesting is that Pécheux himself undertook this critique without abandoning the Marxist position, while at the same time opening up that position to what would appear, in philosophical terms, to be alternatives. It is as if the critique of the State that was implicit in Althusser's work had proceeded to the point where Marxism had discovered the same anarchist ground as Stirner, thereby allowing that terrain to be shared with Foucault through the common suspicion of the modern State. What was retained was the decentred subject, although Houdebine accused Pécheux of developing a history devoid of a political subject (Houdebine, 1976). It is as if he was heralding the recent debate in Anglo-American sociology over post-modernism and rationality. Yet in acknowledging the role of Foucaultianism he still felt obliged to defend Marxism against the implications of the accommodation of Foucaultianism. Not so some of his co-workers and colleagues, some of whom embraced the idealism of the alternative. Pécheux's Marxism persisted to the end, whereas the politics of many of his collaborators was becoming very confused.

One feature of this rethinking was a consideration of the nature of linguistics, what Pécheux (1988) referred to in terms of Milner's (1978) *le propre de la langue*. This derived from an awareness of the importance of signification, enonciation and language play. It involved a rethinking of the epistemological role of linguistics. This is the topic of the next chapter.

6

FORM AND DISCOURSE

Having undertaken an overview of the main developments in FDA, I would now like to devote this chapter to a deeper consideration of some of the linguistic issues which were touched upon in the two preceding chapters. This, in turn, obliges us to consider the relation between form (linguistic) and meaning (social), in developing a distinctive approach to language in society. Two issues stand out in this survey. On the one hand, the manner in which orthodox linguistics is premised on the idea of the centred subject, which FDA was seeking to reject; and, on the other hand, how the structuralist approach was interpreted as having an imperialist orientation which denied the relevance of local knowledge. Addressing these issues generated an exciting breadth of work on the status of linguistics, work which has largely by-passed the Anglo-American social science fraternity. This much is evident in Frow's recent claim (Frow, 1986:67) in discussing the relevance of Bakhtin's work that:

> Recent linguistic analysis, however, has largely failed to move beyond the *langue/parole* opposition. It has been dominated on the one hand by a formalism which treats the text as an extension of the syntactic and logical structuring of the sentence, and on the other hand by an embarrassed empiricism which, in attempting to take into account the role of context and enunciation in the shaping of text, finds itself unable to formalise the infinity of possible speech situations. In both cases the result is a renewal of the traditional dichotomy between text and context or between *énonce* and *énonciation*, in which only the former is seen as properly linguistic, and the situation of utterance is conceived of as contingent, circumstantial, 'subjective', nonsystematic.

Indeed, much of the work discussed below involves an overlap between the achievements of enonciative linguistics and the work of Bakhtin.

The chapter begins with an overview of the orthodox linguistic context of the early work in FDA. This leads to a discussion of how a concern with the subject led to an evaluation of phenomenology, and to a critique of the work of Husserl. This critique derived partly from the developments in enonciative linguistics which threw light on the need to match what was claimed about the Munchausen effect and the decentred subject with an approach which permitted an analysis from an orientation on language that also involved the concept of the decentred subject. This leads us to a discussion of enonciative linguistics, how it met that need and the manner in which it linked with developments in the analysis of discourse and a deeper understanding of the nature of discourse. This, in turn, leads us to a consideration of how these developments inevitably led the work towards the writings of Bakhtin and Wittgenstein. The chapter concludes with a discussion of the extent to which those working in FDA have recognised the limitations of orthodox linguistics and have established a thorough critique of the field.

Orthodox beginnings

It should already be perfectly evident that the orientation of the early work in FDA derived primarily from the social and philosophical critiques of both structuralism and the orthodox social science approaches in vogue during the 1960s. The concern with linguistics was grafted onto this base as a consequence of a desire to develop the ideas which emerged from this critique. Thus, with reference to the work of Althusser, it was evident that his reflections on ideology led to a concern with both a psychological and a linguistic orientation which could be very fruitful, but which he himself either did not recognise, or chose not to pursue. Furthermore, the ideas of Lacan and Foucault were, similarly, leading the work in a specific direction, towards enonciation and away from any psychological orientation involving the centred, rational subject. As is clear from the early flirtation of the pioneers of FDA with the work of Harris and Chomsky, it took some time for the critical edge associated with reorientating the understanding of the social to work through in the same way with reference to the interest in language.

Orthodox linguistics was steeped in the modernism of the eighteenth century. It was constructed out of the claim that Greek and Latin were languages of reason par excellence. The objective of the Port Royal school was to construct a 'general and rational' grammar, as the basis for 'good' language. As in subsequent linguistics, an attempt is made to assign a linguistic base to normative rules – a political act within an 'objective' science. A tension between orthodox linguistics and the ideas which developed around FDA was inevitable. Despite the tendency for the early work to turn to linguistics in order to develop a methodological tool, we have already seen how the anti-modernist reference of the work, together with the gradual emergence of linguistics as a central feature of discourse, would lead to an inevitable re-evaluation of the status of linguistics. The establishment of linguistics on the explicit assumption concerning the separation of language and mind, which allowed rationalism to be an associated ingredient, had to be challenged and displaced. We are fortunate in being able to turn to recent accounts of these developments in FDA (Henry, 1990; Gadet *et al.*, 1990).

Despite the breadth of Pécheux's reading, six names stand out as being of primary importance in his linguistic interests: Saussure, Harris, Chomsky, Jakobson, Benveniste and Culioli (Gadet *et al.*, 1990). Much of the French work in linguistics has tended to focus upon grammatical and logical analysis, and the principles of rhetoric. The more orthodox orientation of Pécheux's early work, which contrasted with the self-critical nature of his later work, was a promotion of this orientation. Thus the work of the structuralist Martinet, who was highly influential in France during the 1960s and whose text *Eléments de linguistique générale* had reached its sixth edition by 1966, was an obvious influence. In what now appears to be an orthodox approach, he claimed that 'Linguistics is the scientific study of human language. A study is said to be scientific because it is founded on the observation of facts and abstains from making a choice from among these facts in the name of certain aesthetic or moral principles. "Scientific" is thus opposed to "prescriptive"' (Martinet, 1960:9). Such was the nature of linguistics in France when Pécheux began his work.

Following the completion of AAD69, Pécheux's work began to pay closer attention to the writings of Saussure (Haroche *et al.*, 1971; Gadet and Pécheux, 1981). Certainly, after 1969, Pécheux demonstrated an increasing familiarity with Saussurean texts. Not that Saussure was missing from AAD69. Indeed, his influence is clear in Pécheux's general understanding of language as a system, and in the manner in which the *langue/parole* distinction is deployed in developing an emphasis on *parole*. It is also evident, in an indirect way, in his reference to Jakobson's work on the 'metaphoric effect'. It also goes without saying that anyone in France who was interested in Saussure at this time could not ignore the work of Benveniste.

Yet it is perhaps inevitable that it would be the work of Harris and Chomsky which was to be the focus in his early work. The influence of the North American academics on French social sciences was particularly strong during the 1960s, at a time when these disciplines were expanding in Europe. As a manifestation of this influence, much of the work of Harris and Chomsky was translated into French during the second half of the 1960s. There is reference to generative grammar in AAD69, not as an object of formalism, but as an innovative theoretical orientation. It was the contrast between the work of Jakobson and Chomsky's insistence on 'linguistic science' which led Pécheux towards what might be termed a neo-subjectivist critique of language. Given the strength of the Marxist critique of science which we have encountered in preceding chapters, this development is not surprising.

Pécheux's initial line of thinking involved an attempt to employ the model of generative grammar, and the opposition between deep and surface structures, in order to develop a method for the study of the production of discourse. However, it is evident, even at this early stage, that the tension between some of the aspects of the work of Saussure and Chomsky was causing him concern. This emerges in his emphasis on what he referred to as 'the science that deals with the sign' (Pécheux, 1969:8), or on the relationship between the theory of the sign and linguistics, a position which was in direct contradiction to Chomsky's conception of language.

On the other hand, it was Zelig Harris who served as the inspiration for Pécheux's methodological orientation. It is interesting that Harris' work was, simultaneously, an inspiration for another French Marxist, the linguist Dubois (Guilhaumou *et al.*, 1994: 173–178). This is perhaps less surprising than it now appears, since, at that time, the critical awareness of the relationship between epistemology and methodological systems was unfocused. Furthermore, the tendency for discourse analysis to link to a structuralism within which semantics was essentially a lexicology is also of relevance. What is surprising is Pécheux's use of Harris' work for the development of a methodology, given the absence of any developed methodological procedures in Harris' work. What appealed to Pécheux was the manner in which Harris reduced enonciations to their elementary form in serving as the basis of transformations, which, of course, was the essential grammatical technique of his method. Clearly this methodological orientation was viewed very much as a process, rather than being seen as a manifestation of any involvement in any 'theory of language'. There is no doubt that it was this interest in Harris' work that led Pécheux in the direction of issues surrounding synonymity/substitutability, semantic variability/invariability and, in turn, to the emphasis on the paraphrase. Despite a profound shift in general orientation, such issues remained central to the work of FDA throughout the 1970s.

I have already made reference to the link between the works of Saussure and Jakobson. The latter's *Essays in General Linguistics* was translated into French and published in 1963. It was an important development, in terms of both theoretical reflections and methodological suggestions. Jakobson's rejection of anti-subjectivist linguistics appealed to Pécheux, and it was also Jakobson's work which gave Pécheux the insight to extend the limits of linguistics as he then understood them. Thus the scheme of communication which Jakobson presented in terms of a 'system of sub-codes in reciprocal communication' led Pécheux to search for a theoretical orientation based on the contact between discursive variation and the invariant of language. The discursive surface was analysed by using the notation of pronouns, of elements of verbal syntagma involving enonciated/enonciation (tense, voice, mode, person) opposition. It was this insight which led Pécheux in the direction which involved a concern with the consistency of the 'forms of enonciation'.

The other overarching influence on Pécheux's work, and indeed on the entire orientation of FDA, was the linguist Antoine Culioli. Milner (1992) has recently maintained that structuralism took a minimalist stance while simultaneously refusing to give language any 'natural' reference. That is, there was a tendency to refer to language as a system whereas, for Milner, language involves much more. Thus, he claims that neither Lévi-Strauss nor Jakobson produced anything more than a general theory of systems. It was Culioli who elaborated this tendency in a systematic manner, by emphasising a theory of enonciation rather than a theory of language, while also emphasising the importance of 'natural' language. In so doing he discovered a phenomenon not recognised by syntactic theory. Indeed he suggests that his work overturns the traditional syntactic/lexical relationship. On the other hand, Fuchs (1981) maintains that enonciation does have a strong pre-modern historical context to it, and that Culioli's work is a rediscovery of that history in renewing an approach which focused upon the activity of subjects in a discourse situation (Fuchs, 1994:v). In some respects he departed from the Kantian tendency to discover the most general form possible of that which can be stated. Indeed, in philosophical terms, he makes explicit reference to Fichte's doctrine of thetic judgment.

Culioli treated the lexis as the minimal unit, claiming that it was indissolubly linked to the activity of enonciation. This degree of precision was taken further in his suggestion that a lexis relies not merely on the question of the statement in general but also on the existence of languages with different characteristics. That is, he was emphasising that the lexis permits the most refined description of empirical properties. From a strictly descriptive point of view the relationship between lexis, enonce and the quasi-paraphrase is evident, with the lexis being that which allows access to the common properties of a quasi-paraphrastic paradigm, and the enonce permitting the seizing of the differential properties. Materials that are lexico-morphologically similar assume a relationship of quasi-paraphrase when all of the enonces are organised in relation to the calculable combinations of enonciative operation with reference to the same lexis. Evidently, Culioli's work carries two dimensions: the transcendental, where he reflects upon the essence of all languages as a kind of philosophy of the spirit of the mind; and the empirical, involving a series of propositions concerning the contingent substance of 'natural' language.

Predication and positioning

From the outset Pécheux's interest was firmly rooted in the construction of meaning and this was echoed in Culioli's (1992:5) consideration of the relationship between syntax and semantics. Culioli argued that there was a tendency to confuse two problems – on the one hand, form, without which textual structure was impossible, and, on the other hand, those issues which derive from a confusion of the essence of syntax and semantics. Here he refers to the intention of the signifier, and how the reference to the intentionality in Husserlianism is devoid of theorisation. These problems associated with phenomenology reflect the tendency to simultaneously establish relations which furnish a family of objects, a family of terms, a family of schema, etc. That is, things are not related to the object, but, rather, they are understood as a collection of operations which can be applied to the object. Here he is objecting to the dictum that translates into a static lekton, where the content of that which is signified is seen as the representation of thought, and has, on the one hand, a content, and, on the other, a form. In this respect his critique of Husserl's phenomenology is of particular significance.

What is interesting about the critique of structuralism is that it focused upon a consideration of phenomenology, and, more specifically, on the work of Husserl. In this respect, Culioli's recent observations build on what both Pêcheux and Kristeva (1969) were saying during the 1960s. With reference to Pêcheux, such criticisms involved a desire to move away from a conception of language premised on the centred, rational subject, and the way the alternative to this position tended to lead to a confusion with the phenomenological denial of an objective material externality. It also related to the tendency for structuralism to ignore what Kristeva (1975, 1980:127–128) referred to as the implication of the constraining force of language. Pêcheux's critique of Husserl related first to the link between logico-philosophical reflection, and to pre-occupations with the nature of language, and second, to the manner in which the subjectivism of phenomenology led to a preoccupation with pragmatics. This focus upon pragmatics represents a preoccupation with a desire to refute the pragmatism associated with the work of Austin and Frege, an orientation which was assumed in discourse analysis in France by, among others, Ducrot and Anscrombe. Pêcheux was seeking to distance himself from this orientation, while emphasising his focus upon discourse and enonciation. He sought to demonstrate that Husserl had inherited the thesis of Port Royal humanism, while at the same time developing the subjective/objective opposition. In this respect he referred to the rhetoric wherein situation, enonciation and determination implicated intersubjective communication.

Pêcheux and his colleagues (Haroche *et al.*, 1971) went on to link what they called the Saussurean break to the emergence of a formalist empiricism in relation to semantics. For Saussure, the idea could only be subjective and individual, leading to *parole* becoming a form of creative subjectivity, and to *langue* becoming a systematic objectivity. In contrast, Pêcheux argued that this led to an ideological opposition, with *parole* reacting to language, while an extra-linguistic systematicity of thought existed as a reflection of truth or reality. Similarly, Kristeva (1969) referred to how Husserl touched upon the fundamental logic of signification. She proceeded to claim that, providing the theory of an immanent meaning outside of language is denied, it becomes possible to draw upon Husserl's work when it is linked with the Lacanian idea of a necessary positionality in language, in order to develop a materialist theory of language. In so doing, she was also highly critical of Husserl's idealism, in which grammatical order, together with a configuration of signs, are accounted for in terms of 'generalities' and the logical.

The interesting feature of Husserl's work was his attempt to account for the manner in which objects are constructed through mental relations and acts. Similarly, his concern with the distinction between epistemological foundations of knowledge and its logical aspects was of obvious relevance during the early years of FDA. Thus, for example, his desire to show that logical concepts are the products of categorical activity, which, in turn, leads to a theory of object-constituting subjectivity, has obvious parallels in Achard's work. Yet the tension between phenomenology and FDA, based on the metaphysics of meaning, remained.

Husserl distinguished between two types of signs, one with meaning and the other without meaning. The first is an expression while the second is merely a 'mark' that is established through relations of convention and association. The sign involves a judgment about something which is an expression of meaning. The 'intentionality' of the sign that is implied in this claim is a mental relation that involves the pre-existing subject, and describes the experience in which this pre-existing subject stands in relation to pre-formed objects. This matter/ form dichotomy is presented in terms of the intentional act grasping material multiplicity, in a sensory non-intentional context, that material multiplicity being activated through the intentional form-giving acts. The intentional, non-material aspects of human experience Husserl called 'noesis', which related to 'noema', the objective meaning-content that is essential in order to complete the act of understanding. This is the basis of his phenomenological reduction to essences and generalities, a phenomenological reductionism from which Husserl's idea of transcendental consciousness derives.

What was of particular relevance for Pécheux and his colleagues at this time was how Husserl argued that consciousness develops into judgment, this denying the existence of any 'natural attitude' related to an external 'real' world. Thus consciousness is no longer the logical expression of a 'real' world but, rather, it is the consequence of the act of predication, which positions the signified 'being' and the operating consciousness itself. The transcendental ego is constituted only in the act of predication, and the subject is the subject only of predication, of judgment, of the sentence. Thus a relationship is developed between the signified object and the transcendental ego, the operating consciousness, which is constituted in the act of predication – Husserl's 'thetic'. Object-constituting subjectivity produces positioned consciousness in the act of predication. Logical acts, concepts, propositions and so on involve the mental acts of the judging subjects. It was this thetic constraining factor of language which Kristeva claimed was missing in structuralism's consideration of subjectivity. This is also the basis for Benveniste's emphasis upon a constitutive subjectivity in language.

What is evident in this critique of Husserl is that the attempt to deny objective reality, while simultaneously addressing the problem of subjectivity in the construction of meaning, reflected the interests which were emerging in FDA. It would have been difficult to develop the themes raised in Althusser's insights concerning the nature of ideology without making reference to the work of Husserl. On the other hand, the denial of the centred, rational subject led the work in a direction that was antithetical to Husserl's ideas, a direction which came to focus upon the enonciative linguistics of Benveniste and Culioli. As will be evident, this orientation had the added advantage that the separation of language and mind that was implicit in Husserlianism was no longer paramount. It allowed the focus of the work to shift more directly onto linguistic issues. Yet it is difficult to avoid the similarity between the way in which Husserl developed an understanding of the relationship between predication and positioning, and the work that developed on enonciation. Of course, the key point in the critique of Husserl was that the notion of subjectivity which sees logical acts, propositions, concepts, etc. as involving mental acts of judging subjects, was the very basis of structuralism, which, as a consequence, was incapable of considering the thetic constraining factor of language. By ignoring the social and linguistic constraining factor, it remained locked in a blatant idealism. It is this problem that was confronted by Benveniste.

Enonciation

Enonciation is understood as the individual act of language use that differs from the enonce, which is the linguistic object that derives from that use. On the other hand, Saussure presented *parole* as pertaining to the domain of the individual which would suggest that enonciation overlaps with *parole* as the second feature of the *langue/parole* distinction. However, enonciation is what makes the enonce possible, as an indispensable but unrecognised activity, with the enonce being the object of linguistic study. The main thrust of enonciative linguistics has been to show that there is a need to reassess the *langue/parole* relationship, claiming that enonciation cannot be dismissed to the unsystematic world of individual behaviour, but that it is capable of being described as a system or a form, that behind the multiplicity of acts of enonciation there exists a general schema of enonciation. This leads to the awareness that, as an abstract system, *langue* is set in operation within discourse through a set of intervening mechanisms. Thus, any description of the operationalisation of *langue* implies the operationalisation of a system that makes the production of enonces possible, a process that involves the conversion of *langue* into discourse by the enonciateur. Therefore, whenever the term discourse is encountered within the context of enonciative linguistics, it does not refer to some unit that is larger than the phrase, nor to the socio-historic conditions of the production of enonces; rather, it refers to the relationship between the enonce and the act of enonciation that supports it.

Any enonciation as the act of making a statement, for example, 'mothers feed their children', is an event that is constituted by reference to time and space, and in this respect it conveys a sense of stability beyond the multiplicity of possible events. This implies that there are types of enonces but that different possibilities of occurrence are external to this stability. However, an enonce does not have an existence independent of its enonciation, and any individual case can be described by reference to specific occurrence in terms of it being emitted by a specific person in a specific place at a specific time. That is, beyond the general it is impossible to understand the meaning of an enonce except by reference to the circumstances of its enonciation. There is no external domain that can be drawn upon. None the less there are certain classes of linguistic elements – shifters – which 'reflect' the enonciation, serving to integrate certain aspects of its enonciative context. Such elements are an integral part of the meaning of an enonce. These morphemes cannot be interpreted except in relation to the specific act of enonciation that has produced the enonce. Thus in the example 'Rhodri is here', the adverb 'here' conveys a stable linguistic signification, but in order to know its reference one is obliged to link it to the individual act of enonciation. It is not that shifters are devoid of meaning, but that their interpretation insists upon knowing the situation of their enonciation (Jakobson, 1963:178). Clearly, shifters are simultaneously both linguistic signs and things or concrete facts inscribed by their occurrence within a determined list of spatial and temporal co-ordinates. They facilitate the converting of *langue* as a system of potential signs into discourse, whereby the enonciateur and her/his allocutaire confront what they say in the world.

However, there are other linguistic phenomena that are included in enonciative linguistics. In refusing to reduce language to a mechanical, 'neutral', instrument merely involved in transmitting information, it insists upon focusing on language as an activity involving two protagonists – the enonciateur and the allocutaire – an activity within which the enonciateur is situated in relation to the allocutaire, to the enonciation itself, to its enonce, to the world, to earlier and to future enonces. This activity leaves its trace in the enonce and it is these traces that the researcher seeks to systematise. This means that language is not a simple intermediary between a thing and its 'representation', with a focus upon 'that which is said', but also involves 'the fact of stating', the enonciation that is reflected in the structure of the enonce.

This is of central importance in relation to decentring since it allows the recovery of relationships between subjects, and between subjects and objects, by reference to place and time without resorting to the rational subject. Thus enonciative linguistics denies the illusion that leads to the meaning of all linguistic signs and enonces being reduced to their representative content and to the claim that they can be considered independently of their exercise, use and discursive positioning. This, in turn, leads to the recognition that linguistic signs possess what is referred to as a pragmatic value, a value that does not relate to the arbitrary nature of the linguistics system but leads, ultimately, to a reconsideration of the *langue/parole* relationship. This choice of the term 'pragmatic' can be confusing in that it clearly does not necessarily involve the centred, rational subject of pragmatic linguistics, and the distinction between the two meanings is essential. While it is true that the work of Austin and his followers focused upon the relationship between enonces and acts by reference to the centred subject, this is not the case with FDA and its involvement in the linguistics of enonciation, in that the emphasis is upon the formal marks of the relationship between enonce and situation.

Benveniste's contribution to post-structuralism has not been widely recognised. In the early work of Barthes, for instance when he analysed Soller's novel *Drame* (Barthes, 1964), Benveniste was the seminal influence in the reference to the subject. It was also Benveniste's work, together with that of Lacan, that lay behind the decentring of the subject, deriving as it did from the French linguist's analysis of the subject in language in terms of the subject of enonciation. His insight concerned the search for an alternative to the metaphysical affirmation of 'being', with its associative claim to be the origin of meaning. This is the crux of his contribution to FDA. It focused upon the distinction between enonciation as the individual act of using language, and enonce, which is the linguistic object that derives from that use. It revolves around the study of the functioning of language involving putting the system into practice in the production of enonces – the conversion of *langue* into discourse by the enonciateur. This insight clarifies the way in which linking discourse with the theory of enonciation does not involve a consideration of the conditions of the socio-historic production of enonces but, rather, involves relating the enonce to the act of enonciation that it supports (Maingueneau, 1991:8).

For Benveniste the phrase is the final level attained by linguistic analysis, regarding it as the site of creativity where there is a correspondence with what he called 'language in action':

> with the phrase one leaves the domain of language as a system of signs, and one enters another universe, that of the language as an instrument of communication, called discourse.
>
> (Benveniste, 1966:259)

The focus is clearly on language use rather than on language as an abstract form. It brings into play the words that organise the phrases – the various logical connectors, anaphoric pronouns that functionally span the frontiers of the phrase, adverbs, etc. Emphasising the distinction made above between type and occurrence, Achard (1993:11) makes the point that the difference between language and discourse rests on a point of view wherein an enonce is a phrase as a consequence of its internal structuration, whereas it is a discourse as a consequence of it being stated or written by specific persons under specific circumstances. Discourse is the effective use of a phrase. It was Benveniste's awareness of this difference that made discourse analysis an interpretative process rather than merely a linguistic discipline. For him, the problematic of enonciation facilitated the identification of the relationship between subjects, situation and conjunctures at the interior of the enonce (Guilhaumou *et al.*,

1994:185). This allowed the establishment of a complementarity of two heterogeneous problematics which reproduced the base/form duality. The notion of discourse rests on the fact that speech use is a social act, the linguistic system being the form that permits that act to be significant.

For Benveniste, discourse derives from an awareness that there is an apparent paradox in French wherein the past tense takes two forms: the 'simple past', which is supposedly reserved for the written, and the 'composed past' which is supposedly restricted to speech. Evidently the evolutionist assumptions of historical linguistics would predict the disappearance of the 'simple past'. Benveniste showed that what was assumed to be the 'simple past' was, in effect, not a past at all; rather, it was the present of *recit*, what he referred to as *d'aropiste*, the character of historical enonciation. In opposition to *recit* Benveniste used the term discourse, stating:

> The historian never says 'I' nor 'you', nor 'here', nor 'now', because he never borrows the formal display of discourse, which consists of the reference to the personal relation I/you.
>
> (Benveniste, 1966:257)

Clearly Benveniste is expressing his claim that predication is that within which the social identity of 'I' and 'you' becomes the basis of meaningful communication, and that this is the central point of linguistics. This leads to a consideration of discourse, which he sees as the opposite of 'account':

> it is necessary to understand discourse in terms of a very broad extension: all enonciation implies a speaker (locuteur) and an audience (audiateur), and that the former has the intention of influencing the latter in whatever way. It is in the nature of the diversity of oral discourse, in turn taking and in the ending of correspondence, memoirs, theatre, didactic work, in short, in all of the genres where whoever is addressed by anyone, is spoken as a locuteur and organises that which he says on the category of person. The distinction which we make between historic account and discourse does not coincide at all well with the distinction between written and spoken language. But discourse is written as much as it is spoken. In practice one employs the one and the other simultaneously. Each time that we confront a historical account there appears a discourse, when the historian for example reproduces the speech of a person or when he himself intervenes to pass judgment on reports, one passes into another temporal system, that of discourse.
>
> (Benveniste, 1966:259)

Clearly this conception of discourse presupposes an intervention by the speaker within the narrative, as well as an orientation towards the other.

The focus on enonciation developed by Benveniste served to challenge the notion of the relation of arbitrariness and the equilibrium of the sign which is so central to the notion on which formal linguistics justifies neglecting the extra-linguistic. In this respect it was precisely the basis which was necessary in order to create the gulf between the interests of FDA and the work of Chomsky. Gadet (1989a:133) expresses his importance in the following terms:

> Benveniste taught linguists to examine the relationship between the notion of the speaking subject, previously regarded as unproblematic, and the explicitly problematic notion of the subject of the enonciation.

This was the base upon which Culioli's enonciative linguistics was constructed.

Before proceeding to a consideration of the work of Culioli, one further point needs to be made. The metaphysical tendency of linguistic science gave Saussure the capacity to separate the signifier and the signified by insisting that the signified is conceived of in terms of the signifier that produced it and vice versa. The focus on the production of the subject and meaning in discourse leads to a theory of the primacy of the signifier over the signified such that the subject and the signified no longer exist – they are produced by discursive work. It leads to an awareness of the manner in which signification interpolates an enonciateur. Benveniste and Lacan were crucial in this development and it is, evidently, from this that Pécheux reversed the role of primacy in Saussure's work.

Culioli's work, together with that of Benveniste, has been of paramount importance in enonciative linguistics (Culioli, 1990). There is a tendency to link the work of the two, but it can also be argued that Culioli sought to depart from the traditional representationalist thrust of Benveniste's work (Auroux, 1992:47). It was not until after the publication of AAD69 that enonciative linguistics made a forceful entry into Pécheux's work, and he acknowledges that up to that point his work failed to take full account of its importance (Pécheux, 1975a).

In contrast to Jakobson, and as a consequence of his introduction to Benveniste's work, Pécheux placed an increasing emphasis upon the phrase in relation to the unity of discourse at the frontier of a domain that was not reducible to the order of grammar. This was the cornerstone of his sensitivity to the infinite creativity of speech and its link to ideology. Pécheux saw Benveniste, above all, as a linguist of subjectivity in whose work he identified the possibility of a return to the question of psychological subjectivity, which structuralism and the work of Saussure had banished from linguistic theory. Despite this rather late familiarity with the broader range of Benveniste's work, it did stimulate an enthusiasm concerning its relevance for what he referred to as 'the necessary illusion constitutive of subjectivity' (Pécheux, 1975a:16).

Pécheux was introduced to the importance of Benveniste's work by Culioli, whose seminars he attended during 1967, and with whom he published a joint paper three years later (Culioli *et al.*, 1970). The influence of Culioli himself was already evident in AAD69, which includes a discussion of how a focus on lexis leads to an awareness of the potential associated with applying a form which carries determinative status and modal value to morphosyntactic structure; and also in Pécheux's discussion of the relationship between noun, verb and enonciation. However, at this time, the importance of Culioli's work relates to the manner in which his work offered an alternative to the Chomskyan perspective (Fuchs, 1992).

Whereas Chomsky's approach was essentially that of the syntactician, Culioli's theory of enonciative operations conceived of syntactic phenomena in a transverse manner, and certainly did not give them a central role in his work. Furthermore, for Culioli there existed an interdependence between syntactic and semantic phenomena. The privileged domain was not the combinatory syntagmatic of constituents of the phrase, but the syntagmatic and paradigmatic functioning of the marks constitutive of the enonce. This was an important departure, underlining the essential difference between the two approaches. Whereas transformational generative grammar (TGG) operated on the phrase, Culioli's enonciative linguistics focused on the enonce. The former sought to engender well-formed expressions in the form of grammatical phrases within the context of an autonomous syntax in constructing an interpretative and pragmatic semantics involving the centred, rational subject. In contrast, enonciative linguistics had the objective of outlining the conditions of enonciability in explicit contexts. That is, it sought to define the mechanisms of constructors of referential value associated with situational variation. Whereas TGG sought to establish what was possible and what was not possible by reference to grammar, enonciative linguistics focused on the conditions which allowed the unenonciable to become enonciable, by focusing upon the play of markers, by clarifying the margins of tolerance and deformability of enonces, by retrieving various enonciative operators.

Fuchs (1981) expressed the difference between enonciative linguistics and orthodox linguistics by reference to the anti-enonciative orientation of classical logic. She characterises the latter in terms of extensional privilege – for example, the primacy of the assertion over other modalities, or the emphasis placed on the transparency of language; the tendency to refer to syntax in terms of relationships of signs, semantics in terms of the relationship between signs and objects, and pragmatics in terms of the relationship between signs and their users. These are placed in a hierarchical but independent relationship on three levels: syntax → semantics → pragmatics. It is this that is rejected by enonciative linguistics, which focuses upon the analysis of subsystems of units of the language, progressively extending to the analysis of other units, and eventually to the entire enonce.

The process of analysis proceeds from the strictly deictic involving the 'me' of the enonciateur to the category of person, then to the various naming terms (appelatifs), terms of address, etc., from the 'here' of the enonicateur to the category of space, from the 'now' of the enonciateur to the temporal category, and, in a very general way, from the strict aspects of temporality involving both tense and aspect. From there, the analysis proceeds to the indicating ('indicielle') and 'anaphoric' deixis; one perceives in effect that the 'same' marks are employed in each case, and one is then led to suggest that context plays the role of situation in the discourse – each enonce, once produced, creates a series of what Culioli calls 'references' for the following enonce.

With reference to modalities, one proceeds to a consideration of enonciative registers, and to a typology of discourse established on the basis of the registers, as we have already seen in Benveniste's distinction between history and discourse. This, in turn, is followed by a study of the diverse modes of intervention of the subject in the discourse by reference to phenomena such as the reporting discourse, relayed assertion, etc., introducing notions such as the taking in charge, degree of implication and the engagement of the subject in its enonce – that is, to what are usually referred to as language acts. Thus one refers to the more or less defined formal and notional categories, where the link to linguistic marks is increasingly blurred.

Similarly one pays increasing attention to the collection of operations constitutive of the enonce, thereby integrating the analysis with the enonciative field. Thus, in relation to the lexical, the objective is that of seeing how meaning is formed in words by reference to signification; while in relation to syntax, the focus is on the processes whereby the linguistic forms of enonciation are diversified, while also being creative.

This double process of expansion, from the formal categories to the notional categories, and from strictly enonciative operations to the collection of operations constitutive of the enonce, leads to the construction of 'enonciative models' of language. Evidently what Fuchs describes subordinates everything to enonciation, in the sense that all the units, and all the relations intervening in the enonce, tend to be analysed by reference to the enonciative parameters. In this respect it rejects all perspectives related to the syntactic semantic interpretations.

Fuchs summarises the essential characteristics of the enonciative approach as follows:

1   The fundamental enonciative categories, e.g. person, aspect, determination, are presumed to be universal in the sense that one discovers a system of person, an aspectual system, and a modal system in all languages.
2   The enonciative categories are conceived of as systems of correspondence between collections of operations and collections of linguistic marks which will vary from language to language.
3   The enonciative categories are conceived of in terms of 'operation' dynamics rather than as fixed taxonomic classes.

A small number of basic operators, such as Culioli's 'referencing', may assume an equally limited number of values, for example, 'identification', 'differentiation', 'rupture', and it is the combination of these operators and their values that gives a considerably larger number of possible configurations. Within this concept of enonciative category it is the idea of the inscription of the subject in the same system of language that one tends to make operational, the intuition of the 'non-transparence' of language which is not held to have a purely instrumental role.

In a collection of papers dedicated to Benveniste, Simonin-Grumbach drew upon Culioli's insight in order to elaborate on Benveniste's work (Simonin-Grumbach, 1975). She sought to demonstrate how the principal of categorisation can be refined by taking the entire range of the formal marks of discourse into consideration. Her goal was to characterise types of discourse – scientific discourse, political discourse, etc. – by resorting to these formal marks. She was able to demonstrate that the term 'discourse', as employed by Benveniste, did not merely designate that which Benveniste intended, but was capable of extension to outline genres of discourse which can be studied by reference to the kind of stabilised constraints of enonciation that they display. The historic discourse which Benveniste referred to is thereby characterised as an extreme case, where all of the anchorage functions in enonciation are suspended. Thus, in linguistic terms, discourse becomes the use of speech that is characterised by the specific enonciative marks that are employed. As a consequence, the multiple analyses of discourse which are pursued in the field of linguistics vary as a function of the discipline that supports them, as a function of the tendencies at the interior of these disciplines, and also as a function of the type of discursive phenomenon in which it is interested. However, it clearly goes further, in that there is a concern with the relationship between the specific genre and the social conditions of its application. The relevance of this insight for the study of ideology, and also for Achard's interest in disciplinary discourse, should be evident.

Simonin-Grumbach employed a series of operators of enonciation far larger than that proposed by Benveniste, this being the basis of what she termed 'the inventory'. In the resultant work on categories of discourse, the theory of enonciation assumes a specifically sociological connotation, albeit with reference to the appearance of discourse in enonciation, without the speaker being the source of that discourse. The reported discourse constitutes a series of social relations which are enriched by the articulation of the referential functions with the enonciative functions. Achard (1986:13) makes the point that the concrete analysis of the discourse must involve the implicit in discourse, rather than merely an interpretation in terms of operation. Again we are drawn to the topic of intertextuality and registers. Intertextuality refers to the type of citation that a discursive formation defines as legitimate for its practice. Conditions of possibility must exist in relation to intertextuality, linking respective texts in a coherent context. In contrast to genres, registers are defined in terms of social function. They represent the relatively stable relationships between syntactic, lexical and enonciative forms and social practices. In this respect they involve a link to discursive tradition in terms of Foucault's (1969) archive effect, involving discourses which are repeated within a given socio-institutional environment.

What is evident in the emergence of enonciative linguistics is that the linguistic subject, the generic subject and the subject of a discursive formation are not to be confused. In enonciative linguistics the subject is the correlate of a destinataire, or a co-enonciataire to use Culioli's term, and of a collection of retrievals in time and space. The linguistic subject is presupposed rather than being the object of study. The generic subject, on the other hand, is distinct, since 'the individual is not interpolated in the discourse as subject, under the universal form of the subject of enonciation, but in a certain number of enonciative places, which determine that a discursive sequence is a harangue, a sermon' (Marandin, 1983:41). Statements are not seen simply as fragments of natural language of some discursive formation, but are also seen as samples of a certain genre of discourse. These 'genres' are akin to a series of speech-acts involving constrained enonciateurs.

Evidently, enonciative linguistics represents quite a different orientation towards language than does orthodox linguistics. One of the major differences relates to the presence of the subject within the processes of orthodox linguistics and the absence of such a performative subject in enonciative linguistics. Thus, themes such as argumentation, referential function and intersubjective functions are interpreted in quite different ways. As a consequence of this difference, the separation of the functioning of language and the subject of language is displaced, and with it the *langue/parole* distinction. This, of course, is why Pécheux replaced this couplet with the *langue/discours* relationship. This serves to reject the contrast between linguistic analysis and the extra-linguistic, but also between the analysis of isolated units and the combinatory – this is essentially the distinction Benveniste's makes between the semiotic analysis of the sign 'in language' as pertaining to structural linguistics and the analysis of the phrase 'in discourse' as a feature of the semantic, the core feature of enonciative linguistics. Whereas the former points to language as signifier, the latter is the basis of communication. In contrast to Saussure's *parole*, discourse is given a positive position, and is viewed as an object of analysis. Even this is taken a step further in enonciative linguistics, which seeks to integrate the subject of enonciation in the analysis of the enonce.

Perhaps the most evident distinction between enonciative and orthodox linguistics relates to their differing conceptions of semantics. To place the semantic within the frame of verbal exchanges challenges the models which place the rational subject as central to production/recognition. The enonciative position admits the possibility of a play involving emission and reception, with a focus on phenomena such as lapsus, ambiguity, the sliding of meaning, paraphrase, etc. I shall turn to this point in a moment. For now I would like to consider how these developments stimulated a lively criticism of orthodox linguistics within FDA.

Enonciative linguistics

Having considered the context within which enonciative linguistics entered into FDA, it is appropriate to give a more detailed consideration of the nature of enonciative linguistics and the specific context in which it was integrated into FDA.

Enonciative linguistics does not focus upon discourse in itself but on the regular properties of formal processes that facilitate their 'shifting' in real situations. It is in this sense that there is a link between 'form' and 'linguistics'. In terms of French linguistics, Achard (1986:11) has argued that there have been two strains of development pertaining to enonciation, and it is important to distinguish between them at the outset. The first involves the work of those such as Ducrot, Anscrombe, Farmancier and Rescanti who have pursued what is essentially a pragmatic stance, with its focus on the centred, rational subject. It leads to concrete studies based on a psychologistic and communicational orientation in which the centred subject operates by reference to what are referred to as discursive strategies (Guilhaumou *et al.*, 1994:186). The second, involving linguists such as Culioli, Fuchs, Desclées and Simonin-Grumbach, has taken its lead from the work of Benveniste and Guillaume, and is, as a consequence, the basis of the linguistic input into FDA. It shifts the focus away from the enonce *per se* to the situation, viewing *langue* as a system of repairable forms that are linked directly to social action. This important distinction is sometimes overlooked in discussion of FDA (Fairclough, 1992).

Subject, person and enonciation

What Benveniste achieved was the introduction of the idea of a stratum into the formal theory of language, an idea which hitherto only existed in semantics or pragmatics. This involves the subject of enonciation where the modal relations between speakers exist. The role of Culioli was partly in removing the transcendental ego from Benveniste's proposition by developing the issue of decentring the subject. In a sense this move derived from Lacan's theory of the unconscious, which gave evident support to the idea of positionality that is necessary in order to achieve meaningful communication between two speaking subjects. Its importance for FDA is that it contributed a decentred entrée into the form of linguistics that matched the decentred emphasis of the theoretical orientation. The problematic of enonciation allowed the relationships between subjects, situations and conjunctures to be encountered at the interior of the enonce. It is as if the speaking subjects have left an imprint of their mark on a text. In this respect it was a highly appropriate approach for developing a method which would allow the investigation of the subject without falling into the trap of the rational subject directing signification via her/his rational intentions.

It allowed an investigation of how the subject was created across the conditions imposed on her/his enonciation by the archive, and how the text reveals the traces of enonciative processes related to the enonciative positions that they render possible. There is an important point to be made here. Reference to the archive produces a subtle turn that differs from the ordinary verbal exchange of a conversation where two interlocutors are in contact, the co-enonciateur being able to intercede at any moment, thereby menacing the conversation. In contrast, the texts of archives imply a different conversation, one where the moment and the place of enonciation mediate. The *parole* is not threatened but is protected by the enonciative ritual in which the enonciateur and the co-enonociateur, rather than being singular individuals, occupy positions assigned by the archive.

The fundamental point of Benveniste's work is that it is only through language that humankind is constituted as a subject, since it is only through language that the concept of ego can be established in reality:

> the subjectivity we are discussing here is the capacity of the speaker to posit himself as 'subject'. It is not defined by the feeling which everybody experiences of being himself, but as the psychic unity that transcends the totality of the actual experiences it assembles and that makes the permanence of consciousness.
>
> (Benveniste, 1966:223)

The establishment of the coherent social identity of 'I', 'you', 'she', etc. makes meaningful communication between two subjects a central concern of linguistics:

> Language is possible only because each speaker sets himself up as a subject by referring to himself as 'I' in his discourse. Because of this, 'I' posits another person, the one who, being as he is completely exterior to 'me', becomes my echo to whom I say 'you' and who says 'you' to me. This polarity of persons is the fundamental condition of language, of which the process of communication in which we share, is only a mere pragmatic consequence.
>
> (Benveniste, 1966:225)

This is because it is through language that humankind constitutes itself as subject, since it is only language that establishes the concept of ego in reality. Thus all linguistic acts, in so far as they constitute a signified or a meaning that can be communicated in a phrase or a sentence, are supported by a transcendental ego. Without it, communication would be impossible. Importantly, it is also the source of social identity.

The study of 'I' and 'you' involves the customary grammatical category of 'person'. However, it is not possible to interpret an enonce containing 'I' and/or 'you' without taking into account the individual act of enonciation that they support. It is the act of stating 'I' that gives the reference of 'I', in the same way as it is the act of stating 'you' to anyone that establishes that person as the interlocuteur. It is not possible to know the referent of 'I' and 'you' independently of their use in individual acts of enonciation. 'I' and 'you' are not simply linguistic signs of a particular type, they are the operators that convert language into discourse. In every exchange every 'I' is a 'you', and every 'you' is an 'I', the roles inverting in the play of dialogue. Enonciation is supported not by the isolated feature of the enonciateur but by the 'I-you' couple which Culioli termed the co-enonciateur of an activity. It is not merely the roles of the locuteur and the allocutaire that change in the course of a dialogue, but they are both linked as protagonists of the act. There is no 'I' that can be established as enonciateur and a 'you' that can be constituted as allocutaire. These roles are taken by 'we' and 'you' (plural). It is customary to think of these two words as the 'plural' of 'I-you', but they are not plural in the sense that 'horses' is the plural of 'horse', and are best thought of as 'an extension of person' which gives the opposition 'specific person' and 'extension of person'. In many respects 'we' and 'you' are ambiguous, with 'we' capable of being 'I and I' or 'I and you' or 'I and him', and 'you' capable of being 'you and you' or 'you and him' and so on. Structurally 'we' can designate several groups of people: locuteur + locuteur; single locuteur; locteur + allocutaire; locuteur + third person(s); locuteur + allocutaire + third person(s).[1]

'I-you' and 'we-you' are not the only constituents referred to in an enonce since the interlocutors also have a discourse on the world.[2] If these persons constitute the 'sphere of locution', that locution returns to an external universe, that of the non-person or 'suspended position', by opposition to the persons of the linguistic exchange. This non-person corresponds to the nominal groups and to their pronominal substitutes, mainly those elements with the syntactic status of nominal groups. They are all of those objects about which the 'I' and 'you' speak, but the non-person should not be seen as the 'they' which is thought of as the third person of grammar. 'They' is distinguished from 'I-you' as a pronoun or an anaphoric element that replaces a nominal group from which it takes its reference, and has been previously introduced in discourse, whereas 'I' and 'you' are not pronominal substitutes.

The 'I' and the 'you' are opposed to the non-person in significant ways. First, as with shifters, the persons are defined by the situation of enonciation whether the non-person is defined or not, as in the examples 'Paul's brother' or 'certain friends'. Second, the persons are necessarily present and in contact – on the other hand, for the non-person it makes little difference whether the referents are visible, present or absent. Third, the persons are not the only possible substitutes. Each enonciateur reiterates 'I' and 'you' throughout the time that they assume the discourse. In contrast, the nominal groups use a large range of pronominal substitutes. Finally, the persons cannot be, *a priori*, other than the speaking subjects, whereas there are examples in literature where the enonciateur addresses inanimate objects.

The functioning of linguistic persons involves a continuous process of exchange between two indissociable roles, that of the enonciateur and that of the allocutaire. It involves an indefinite reciprocal relationship within which every 'I' is a virtual 'you' and vice versa. The structurally equal nature of this reciprocal relationship also involves an inequality that modulates the reciprocity. It is only the enonciative context that makes it possible to determine whether or not the use is 'normal'. Thus the term 'Madame is served' may be a token of respect or it may be an enonce that speaks of an absent being, as is the case with the non-person. The use of the non-person in place of the second person, together with the elimination of 'I', is held to be a mark of extreme respect in that in not using 'you', whether or not there is a respectful or formal form as in Welsh, German or French, the locuteur is excluding him/herself from the reciprocal linguistic exchange. It is as if s/he addresses anyone who is not constituted as the allocutaire. Involved here is what is referred to as a 'sphere of locution' which separates the co-enonciateurs and the universe of the non-person as a kind of invisible circle that delimits a shared space.

Deictics

In addition to persons there are the 'deictic' shifters which define the spatio-temporal co-ordinates that are implicit in the speech-act, that is, in the collection of references that are articulated in the triangle: (I ↔ you) – here – now. These inscribe the enonces in space and time in relation to the enonciateur, who is constituted as a reference point. Thus it is impossible to disassociate person from deictics. Every text has a zero point of origin or reference for its enonciation, the 'I-here-now', and two kinds of operations, one designating an alternative enonciative position – 'you' or 'there' or 'then' – and the other a kind of operation designating points outside the field of present enonciation – 'he'/'it' or 'elsewhere' or 'once upon a time'. This constitutes the apparatus of enonciation which is made up of three coordinates – the category of person, the category of localisation or place, and the category of tense. Evidently, these are relevant at the level of grammar. Modalities constitute other dimensions which are relevant in discourses – to say something is also to situate what is said, in the sense that every text is inhabited by the presence of a subject who situates what s/he says in relation to the certain, the possible, the probable, etc, or in relation to judgments of value. Each act of enonciation is made visible through a series of marks which are capable of analysis.

In describing semantic operations in discourse it is necessary to consider how the basic positions generated by this model are either neutralised or involve oppositions. Thus when 'we' is encountered in discourse with a meaning that includes both 'I' and 'you', it marks a reference that neutralises the opposition between 'I' and 'you'. In treating the zero position as origin it follows that if there are no marks, then the enonciating position includes at least all the zero values of person, location, tense and modalities. To return to Achard's example used in the introduction, the statement 'It is raining' includes the I-here-now and a non-determinate space. It will normally include 'you' and presupposes that 'raining' is not fixed in terms of time and space. On the other hand the statement 'It is raining' made over the phone activates the opposition 'I-you', the face-to-face neutralisation not operating. The statement 'You see, it is raining' involves 'I' being aware that it is raining, but that 'you' is not aware of it raining. That is, the presence of the word 'you' prevents the position of 'you' being the same as that of 'I'. In these examples the point is made that, within a speech event, both the locuteur and the allocutaire must use the marks in the text, and must also use their knowledge to operate on the 'free' part of the interpretation. Thus there is a distinction between enonciative places defined by the abstract enonciative space on which the discourse is operating, and the practical places in the social and psychological space of the speaker and the hearer. The problem of mapping these two spaces – enonciateur with speaker, co-enonciateur with addressee, etc. – involves what is referred to as 'taking in charge' (for the participants) and of interpretation (for the analyst). Pécheux (1982a:156) refers to taking in charge in terms of how the subject of enonciation is 'supposed to take responsibility for the contents posed' or becomes 'the subject who takes up a position'.

The issue of taking in charge can be exemplified by reference to a text from Joseph Heller's *Catch 22* (Heller, 1962:17):

> 'They're trying to kill me', Yossarian told him calmly.
> 'Who's they?' he wanted to know. 'Who, specifically, do you think is trying to murder you?'
> 'Every one of them', Yossarian told him.
> 'Every one of whom?'
> 'Every one of whom do you think?'
> 'I haven't any idea.'
> 'Then how do you know they aren't?'
> 'Because . . .' Clevinger spluttered, and turned speechless with frustration.

In this example 'how do you know' takes the role of 'why' and constitutes an excellent gloss of its operation demanding the renewal of the taking in charge. What is at stake here is the validation of the taking in charge by the enonciateur. Through his various questions, Clevinger seeks implicitly to demonstrate to Yossarian that what he is seeking to establish is false. This taking in charge is queried by Yossarian's question 'how do you know they aren't?'

Replying with a simple 'Because . . .' presents a new taking in charge linked to the predicative 'they are not', and revalidates the taking in charge by reference to the enonciateur (himself) without specifying the new conditions of validation. It is also evident that 'Because' allows the enonciateur to reimpose the necessity of the validation of predicative link and in this respect, as a connector, it appeals to a trace of an enonciative operation of referencing and of modalisation. That is, in enonces of the type 'p because q', the operator 'because' allows the enonciateur to present q as containing the conditions of validation of the predicative relation in p, and to reimpose the taking in charge.

There is a need to conceive of a discursive deixis in terms of a similar function, but in relation to the universe of meaning which creates a discursive formation by its enonciation. Generally the three instances of the discursive deixis tend not to reveal a close correspondence with designations within the text, but recover each one of a series of expressions in relations of substitution. It is conceivable that more than one of the discursive locuteur, destinataire, the chronography and the topography can be occupied simultaneously by the same object. Thus, for example, in a school text on the British Empire, 'the Empire' is the locuteur in the sense that it addresses the children, the topography, in the sense of delineating a specific territory, and the chronography, in being a phase in the history of the relationship between Britain and the territorial space outside of its immediate confines. It is only the schoolchild as destinataire that avoids the term. On the other hand, even the schoolchild is implicated in its integration into 'the British Empire' as a British 'citizen'.

If there is such a thing as a discursive deixis it is because a discursive formation is not stated by a rational subject, in a particular historical conjuncture, and in an exterior assignable, objective space. As we have already seen, for the archive, the instance of the situation of enonciation is different from that of verbal exchanges with empirical points of anchorage that derive from the speaking subject, her/his effective destinataire, the material context, or the precise moment of interlocution. Of course, as in all enonciation, the enonce of the archive constitute occurrences and events inscribed in space and time, but the essence of the enonciative rituals of the archive involves the parameters of the situation of the enonciation being constructed by the archive itself, which, thereby, establishes the legitimacy of its *parole*. For this reason the term scenography is employed in preference to 'situation of enonciation'. This scenography consists of two components – the instituted deixis and the founding deixis, both defining the enonciateur and the co-enonciateur, the topography and the chronography. It is from the founding deixis that the existing deixis derives much of its legitimation, since the founding deixis draws upon earlier enonciations. Thus one recognises the original locution, the chronography and the original topography. A discursive formation is unable to speak in a valid manner without drawing on the traces of an earlier deixis where it is institutionalised and which captures its essence. I shall return to this issue when heterogeneity and interdiscursivity are discussed below.

From these principles it is possible to assemble a typology that derives from the function that different elements have in terms of the relation between enonciateur and allocutaire. Thus it is possible to focus upon the spatial and temporal deictics in turn before subdividing each of them. Thus the spatial deictics can be divided into the presentatives and the demonstratives, the latter comprising determinatives and pronouns. The relevant morphemes can function either as a situational deictic, as in 'look at *that*', or as an anaphoric deictic, as in 'I have read *Das Kapital*; *that* book made a great impression on me'. The distinction between anaphoric and situational use derives from two different spatio-temporal environments that allow the referent of these deictics to be identified. On the one hand there is the discursive environment or the linguistic units that immediately precede or follow – the co-text; on the other hand there is the extra-linguistic environment – the context. Clearly there is a problem here in that both the idea of an extra-linguistic context and a pre-judged relation between enonciateur and allocutaire implies the existence of an extra-discursive which is anathema to FDA. This is the basis for the distinction between FDA and the pragmatic use of enonciative linguistics.

Modalities

The second aspect of enonciation involves the modalities. They are specific operators of enonciation, being the grammar of the clause which corresponds to the interpersonal function of language. The enonciative study of modalities focuses upon issues which include the typology of modalities, systematic links between modalities, opposition between modalities of the enonce and those of enonciation, and between those of enonciation and performative modalities (Fuchs, 1981). The subject enonciateur is the point of origin (zero point) of referential references – 'I' indicates that the subject of the enonce is identical with the enonciateur – and of modalisations. Modalities play a crucial role in the act of enonciation since all enonciations imply a certain 'attitude' of the enonciateur with reference to what is said. Thus for Culioli 'all acts of enonciation imply an attitude taken with reference to the relation which contains the lexis' (quoted in Grize, 1992:70). However, for FDA that attitude is not the expression of the thought of a rational subject, but an expression of the constant interaction involving the co-enonciateur. An enonce simultaneously plays on two linked registers – on the one hand it states something about something, and on the other hand this relationship is made the object of a taking in charge by the enonciateur. In any case we cannot separate that which is said from the manner in which it is posed.

Furthermore, nominalisation involves what Pécheux referred to as the preconstructed in the sense that the trace of taking in charge of verbs is missing. Modalities relate to assertions and these are important in FDA because the truth of an enonce does not have any independent stable property as in the modernist discourse, rather it is the product of an enonciation, of a process of validation constructing its guarantee by the enonciateur. The diverse types of enonces – declarative, imperative, interrogative – correspond to the multiple acts of language, to the multiple 'illocutionary forces' – to baptise, to greet, to demand, etc. Among these language acts, privilege tends to be accorded to assertion because it presents the enonce as true or false. Implicit in the act of assertion is a subject enonciateur who presents, and validates, his/her enonciation and whose presence is inscribed in the marks of person and of tense, of mode of attachment to the verb. For discourse analysis it is not the type of mark of assertion that is of interest, but the explicit marks which add to the verbal flexion. From the point of view of the modal, presuppositions have a specific relevance in that they constitute the given which recalls the 'truths' already established elsewhere, and which need not be validated by the enonciateur. Clearly modalities are crucial for the issues of memory and forgetting.

The tendency of orthodox linguistics to relate modalities to the modal auxiliary verbs, e.g. 'must', 'may', 'should', etc., and the extension of modalities to include a variety of modal features including tense, e.g. 'is', or adverbs, e.g. 'probably', 'possibly', etc., and associated adjectives is further expanded and, indeed, takes a new direction. The tendency for modalities to indicate affinity with others is placed within the enonciative framework in indicating the relationship between 'the signification of reality and the enactment of social relations' (Fairclough, 1992:160). Thus social practice is conceived of in terms of discourse relations, where the taking in charge of concrete verbal productions opens the way to revealing a textual, communicative and discursive exterior with the traces of the inscription of the enonciating subject in the enonces capable of being revealed, while analysing how the enonciative mode is operationalised in concrete language productions leads to revealing the determinate enonciateurs, situations, genres, etc.

In her recent book Authier-Revuz (1995:47–49) makes the point that modalities carry a heterogenous form that links the enonciateur with an exterior in the sense that a meta-enonciative 'position' of 'distance', 'externality', etc. by reference to words taken as objects reveals an attempt to intuitively represent a subjective mechanism related to a meta-enonciative reflexivity. She proceeds to express this heterogeneity in terms of a reflexivity that is a measure of how the enonciateur comments on his/her statement. That is, she emphasises how language is always a reflexive exercise involving the enonciateur in relationship to language, involving an intuitive representation of subjective mechanism adjacent to observable forms of meta-enonciative reflexivity. Such a conception leads to non-linguistic theoretical conceptions concerning the relationship between the subject and his/her language. This clearly has implications for the Munchausen effect. In moving beyond the describable linguistic forms of the enonciative configuration in terms of syntax and lexis to consider the relevance of discourse with a focus upon ambiguity, such a perspective inevitably leads to a consideration of the relationship between the subject and the production of meaning as something that is produced in interaction (Normand, 1985). It is a comment on what Milner (1978) called 'the real of language' and which Benveniste referred to as 'subjectivity in language' (1966:266).

It is evident that enonciative linguistics has an important significance for any consideration of the subject. The description of the enonciative subject across the places that it occupies in discourse, whatever the judgment on its legitimacy, is of crucial importance. It bears witness to the dynamic nature of the subject, how it assumes different positions by reference to its constitution, and how it serves as the basis for a social understanding of the relevance of discourse. It focuses upon the idea of the subject in process within the un-winding thread of discourse. In this respect it pertains to what Pécheux referred to as the 'tendential delocalisation of the subject enonciateur' (quoted in Gillhaumou *et al.*, 1994:189). More importantly it locates the subject at the point where meaning is achieved, without that subject being at the centre of the process of legitimation.

Meaning, heterogeneity and interdiscourse

Intertextuality involves how texts contain elements of other texts. Such an organisation involves a chain of textual elements which can be added to, the new elements responding to prior texts, while also having the capacity to modify prior texts, that is, to transform the past. Interdiscourse, or the con-figuration of discursive formations, on the other hand, assigns priority to the concept of discourse, but does not conceive of discourse in terms of homogeneity, but rather, as a reality that is 'heterogeneous to itself' (Courtine and Marandin, 1981:24). Thus Courtine's (1981:35) reference to the relation between the 'interior' and the 'exterior' of a discourse involves heterogeneity as a feature of intertextuality. That is, the interdiscourse involves the complex interdependent configuration of discursive formations, giving it primacy over its constituent parts, and revealing properties which are not predictable from a consideration of its parts. Furthermore, as has already been implied in our reference to intertextuality, the interdiscourse consists of a process of incessant reconfiguration in which a discursive formation is led to incorporate the preconstructed elements produced outside of itself. It was this awareness of the dynamic nature of the interdiscourse that lay behind Courtine's insistence on the diachronic construction of a corpus (1981:29).

Interdiscourse also has a relationship to the issue of ambiguity of meaning. Courtine claimed that ambiguity derives from, among other things, the combi-nation of discursive formations. This relates to the above claim concerning the manner in which the interdiscourse involves the fusion of prior and present discourses, and the reconstitution of meaning associated with the relationship. It is this that makes FDA an essentially interpretative discipline, and in this respect it is important to realise that within FDA there is never a reference to the 'real' effects of an enonce without reference to all of the potential effects.

Yet, despite the implicit claim that intertextuality shapes the interpretation of contemporary text, it is also necessary to recognise that intertextuality incorporates relationships with the orders of discourse.

We have already noted how the archive is conceived of as working on an interdiscourse, the archive being thought of as a divided unity within a heterogeneity in relationship to itself (Courtine 1981:35). Thus the interdiscourse is the space where the objects which link to their intra-discourse, with the illusion of expressing 'thoughts' and of expressing things of an external world, are constituted and articulated – and, in so doing, forgetting that this involves the 'preconstructed' character of these elements. Thus the interdiscourse is not merely a collection of 'circumstances' surrounding the discourse, but, rather, it is a modality of that discourse that traverses the enonciation of the subject. Furthermore, in a general way, all discursive formations are associated with a discursive memory, constituted of formulations involving repetition, refusal and transformation. This is not a psychological 'memory', but one associated with the idea that the enonce is inscribed in the past. We have already referred to this in outlining how scenography involves both the instituted deixis and the founding deixis. Courtine referred to a list of formulations corresponding to the possible reformulations of the enonce within the interdiscourse. The collection of such lists represents the discursive process inherent in the discursive formation. Since it is in this list of formulations that the reference of objects of discourse are stabilised under the form of the preconstructed, it is also at this level that the instance of the universal subject intervenes, referring to the 'place from where one can enonce' (Courtine 1981:50). That is, each interdiscourse dominates each particular formulation, fixing that of which it speaks and the subject which it guarantees.

Thus all formulations are found in an intersection involving two axes, the vertical of the preconstructed, involving the domain of memory; and the horizontal, involving the linearity of discourse, which occults the first axis since the subject enonciateur, in an illusory manner, is produced as interiorised in the preconstructed that imposes its discursive formation on all formations. Memory represents the interdiscourse as the instance of construction of a transverse discourse which prevails for a subject enonciateur, the means of constructing the objects which the discourse refers to, and thereby the mode of articulation of the objects themselves. Deriving from this formulation, the intervention of that interdiscourse is particularly evident in nominalisations, where it exists as the preconstructed. In reaching this conclusion, Courtine revealed a chain effect in which the objects which take charge of the enonciations acquire a referential stability across the domains of memory. Thus, for example, a nominal syntagm pertains to the domain of memory, together with the predications that it authorises, and the terms for which it is substitutable. To this domain of memory Courtine associated two other instances – the domain of actuality, involving sequences around an event which refuses, supports, etc. in a definitive conjuncture, and the domain of anticipation, involving earlier enonciations which the discourse anticipates. This last domain is necessary, because if there is an 'always already' in the discourse, there is also an 'always once more', which the discursive formations must take into account.

This is the background to the importance of Authier's seminal work on enonciative heterogeneity.[3] Enonciative heterogeneity refers to the manner in which any statement is populated by the statement of others, either in an explicit or in an implicit form. Such statements carry their own particularities, which have been assimilated into those of the speaking subject. As we shall see in a moment, this is often made explicit by specific and explicit marks within the text, marks involving conventions such as quotation marks and a reporting verb. In a sense the distinction between, on the one hand, the manner in which the marks within a text are employed in evaluating the enonciative places, knowledge, and, on the other, social practice, is drawn upon in order to work on the 'free' part of the interpretation. With reference to heterogeneity, or the integration of prior discourse with the present, the 'free' part of the discourse is employed in linking the speech event to prior discourse. Thus any interpretation associated with mapping the enonciative places and the practical places is constrained by the interdiscursive effect, this framing inducing pre-interpretation.

A good example of the concretisation of discourse organisation and its relationship to signification is to be found in what is called reporting discourse, or discourse representation, as Fairclough (1992:118) calls it. The space of signification – which interpolates the enonciataire – constructs a 'referential' of the situation from a point of departure, or zero point (not described) of the enonciation, and by the construction of an alternative value and a radical altered value for each one of its dimensions. That is, discourse reporting or representation permits the attaching of a new origin, thus constructed, out of which develops a combinatory grafting on the initial statement.

Discourse representation is a specific example of what is referred to as manifest textuality, and it is here that we are obliged to consider Authier's contribution in detail. She distinguished between manifest heterogeneity and constitutive heterogeneity. The latter is where the inherent properties of dialogism and intertextuality are discovered in discourse, whereas the former pertains to the explicit manifestation associated with a diversity of sources of enonciation. Manifest heterogeneity involves texts which include other texts, this textual difference being explicitly marked by, for example, reporting clauses such as 'he stated' or 'the Prime Minister claimed'. Constitutive heterogeneity, on the other hand, is not marked at the surface level, and has to be discovered through the development of hypotheses involving the constitution of a discursive formation through interdiscourse. Ambivalence relates to this constitutive heterogeneity. The emphasis on deixis in constitutive heterogeneity leads to a consideration of how a variety of subject places into which the individual can be interpolated are created in and through discourse.

Discourse representation involves the three forms of discourse: direct, indirect and indirect free. In terms of orthodox linguistics they are treated as follows:

- Direct discourse involves a reporting clause followed by a representation of discourse as in Fairclough's (1992:107) example: 'Mrs Thatcher warned Cabinet colleagues: "I will not stand for any backsliding now".' The words represented are specifically marked by quotation marks, and the tense and the deictics refer to the source. That is, there is a specific frontier between the words of the reporter and those of the reported. It is claimed that the direct discourse has a 'simple' function on the syntactic plane, while being 'faithful' and 'objective' on the semantic-enonciative plane.
- In indirect discourse, on the other hand, there are no explicit marks of reporting such as quotation marks, and the discourse that is reported becomes a clause that is grammatically subordinated to the reporting clause, this relationship being marked in English by the conjunction 'that'. Again Fairclough (1992:107) furnishes the example: 'Mrs Thatcher warned Cabinet colleagues that she would not stand for any backsliding then'. It is claimed to be subordinate to the direct discourse in the sense that it is a morpho-syntactic derivative created through the transformation of persons and tense.
- Indirect free discourse, on the other hand, tends to be treated as a literary form, consisting of a mixture of the direct and indirect discourse, that emerged during the nineteenth century (Frow, 1986:159). This amalgamation of the other two discourse types involves the mixing of the voices of the two prior discourses, but it also lacks the reporting clause: 'Mrs Thatcher has warned Cabinet colleagues. She will not stand for any backsliding'.

In the orthodox linguistic interpretation, the three types are presented as a progression. Evidently what is involved here is the variation in discourse types on account of their being different representations and functions of discourse in the representing or reporting text. Thus, for example, historical, academic or media texts will all be different in this respect. Also this orthodox approach treats voices in terms of points of view associated with the consciousness of the rational subject. Evidently it is removed from the orientation of FDA.

Authier (1978) developed a critical analysis of this interpretation of discourse representation, a critique that was based not only on the description, but also on the exercises of grammar which followed. It is this work that stimulated much of the work by Courtine referred to above. Authier claimed that direct discourse is far from simple, being more complex than indirect discourse; that it was neither 'objective' nor 'faithful'; and that its real character was that of autonomy rather than textuality. This second observation should not be surprising given that the dynamic, shifting quality of enonciation is established – to restore the exact materiality of an enonce is not akin to restoring the act of enonciation.

With reference to indirect discourse, Authier claimed that it was not a subordinated form of direct discourse, revealing some derivation of a morpho-syntactic order. Rather, it displayed two radically different operations – the display of citation of direct discourse, and the translation-reformulation of indirect discourse. Furthermore, she argued that the indirect free discourse constituted an entirely separate form – original and not subject to being treated in terms of the other two. Neither is it a specifically literary form, since it appears in oral discourse associated with politics and the media.

Clearly Authier has sought to demolish the evolutionary relationship between the three discourse types, which, within the orthodox schema, constitutes an incomplete, impoverished field of a discourse represented in another discourse. It is incomplete on account of the existence of other forms such as the direct free discourse, and in that it ignores the importance of the modalisation of a discourse in a second discourse. It is impoverished because it does not locate the inventory of forms of representation of another discourse within a discourse. To these forms she applies the term manifest heterogeneity (*hétérogénéité montrée*), which involves the explicit presence of a discourse in another discourse. It involves linguistically characterisable processes which attest to the intervention of enonciative sources distinct from the enonciateur or of different instances of that enonciateur. This referencing of marks of enonciative heterogeneity, where the multiform presence of interdiscourse in the discourse is stressed, rests on the thesis of the primacy of the interdiscourse. Authier contrasts manifest heterogeneity with constitutive heterogeneity (*hétérogénéité constitutive*) – the configuration of discourse conventions that enter into the production of a text, involving the permanent presence of the 'already said' of other discourses, which condition all the words and which resonate in them.

Onto this critique Authier (1982, 1984) grafted Bakhtin's dialogism, suggesting that all discourses exist within the milieu of the already said of other discourses. In this respect she alluded to Pécheux's (1975a) claim that, in all dis-courses, the 'I' of any given moment involves the speech of others, previously and independently expressed. This also involves Foucault's (1969:130) assertion concerning how a statement never exists without activating previous statements.

While defending the orthodox position according to which there is a correspondence between meaning and context that can be described and predicted by a linguistic analysis, Fuchs (1991) opposes the orthodox view on plurivocality and suggests that univocality be viewed as the result of a signifying construction at the interior of a constitutively plurivocal field. Furthermore, ambiguity is not a case of the subject not achieving constructed univocality. Thus she advocates a focus upon the issue of univocality rather than on ambiguity. Furthermore, she adds that context is of importance with reference to signification, claiming that context aids the subject in constructing one or more significations. Such a signification is difficult to fix by reference to a metalanguage, partly because it slides in the movement of interpretation and in the (re)formulation. The danger of this position is that it leads to the idea of incommunicability on account of each subject having his/her own signification, everything thus being ambiguous. She therefore advocates returning to the linguistic conditions of the construction of signification at the interior of the field of plurivocality.

A recent collection of papers – which admittedly includes papers which have a pragmatic orientation to the problem, but also includes a number of papers by those who were involved in FDA at the beginning of the 1980s (Fuchs, Authier, Gadet, and some who have remained within FDA such as Boutet and Fiala) – addresses the possibility of developing a grammar of heterogeneity (Parret, 1991). The remainder of this discussion derives from the debates found in this very important volume. It claims that orthodox grammar is incapable of absorbing heterogeneities of meaning because of epistemological constraints. While it is capable of recognising prescriptive and normative functions, these constitute limited objectives. Indeed, given its emphasis upon correctness, there is a tendency for orthodox linguistics to evaluate heterogeneity in terms of sense/non-sense. If one poses the question of constitutive heterogeneity radically – that is, where the problem of heterogeneity as constitutive of its subject and of its discourse is presented – it involves altering the orthodox theoretical approach, questions no longer being presented in the context of a theoretic description of linguistic phenomenon (Borutti, 1991:276). Rather, heterogeneity should not be evaluated in terms of such a dichotomy, since it relates to Wittgenstein's claim that 'The meaning of the phrase is such that the phrase does not have meaning' (Wittgenstein, 1958b:500). It was also Wittgenstein who referred to a 'profound grammar' which revolves around the meaning of non-homogeneous phrases – that is, meanings which are stabilised, returning in their transparency to their fundamental. Such a grammar pertains neither to linguistics, nor to philosophy, but rather it reassembles discourses, cultures and communities in a single domain associated with the meaning of its heterogeneities. It involves the imprisoned subject producing, with and for others, a field of ruptures, a constantly fleeting presence, the illusory realities and the inevitably fragile intersubjectivities. The various 'fabrications' of meanings are constantly escaping or disappearing, the 'devices' of meaning break up, obliging the work of the interpreter to focus upon the ruptures of meaning. As much as anything, it obliges a focus upon the prohibited or cancelled subjectivities.

This concern about the relevance of linguistic theory for the study of heterogeneity was taken up by Authier (Authier-Revuz, 1991). She expressed particular concern about the manner in which the subject was theorised. What her earlier work had achieved was to show that the forms of manifest heterogeneity represented in discourse are the forms of the illusion of the subject in relation to itself and the denegation of constitutive heterogeneity (Borutti, 1991). That is, they constitute the form of negotiation with the forces of the disaggregation and the dissemination of the subject. As such they are the discursive strategies which offer forms of compromise with that 'other' that constitutes our discourse. An enonciating subject offers its interlocuteur the 'ensigns' (Barthes and Flauhaut, 1980:425) which constitute the indirect demands of recognition of itself, or appeals to suture the rupture that is heterogeneity. They are the demands to participate in a local region of the achievement of meaning that are constructed at the same time as the enonciative space. They thus relate to the local strategies which employ ruptures and heterogeneities. It is hardly surprising that Authier objected to the manner in which the subject was theorised. If the speech–act influences the preconstructed/prior discourse, and the prior discourse affects the speech–act, then the interpolative base which creates the subject place is constantly shifting: 'what then is the subject, the discourse is made, constantly menaced by the unmaking; that in which it is constituted is also that which, heterogeneously, escapes itself' (Authier-Revuz, 1984:107). Clearly a particular orientation to the subject is involved. It focuses upon the ontological constitution of the subject as intersubject.

Despite this critical orientation towards orthodox linguistics, the focus remains upon the relationship between the statable and the unstatable. Whereas orthodox linguistics expresses this in terms of the relationship between the grammatical and the ungrammatical, involving allusion to the pre-formed normative and prescriptive linguistic forms, the approach linked to hetero-geneity takes quite a different orientation. This should not be surprising, given that one of the principal objectives of FDA from the outset revolved around Foucault's (1969) concern with the manner in which discourse sets limits on what can and what cannot be said.

Authier (Authier-Revuz, 1991) advocates the systematic study of meta-enonciative forms which can be formally described as ruptures in the enonciative threads or chains in order to establish types of ruptures. This involves the work of Gadet (1991) and Boutet and Fiala (1986, 1991), who refer to what they call 'syntactic telescoping', involving a syntactic rupture of a particular type within enonces. What these authours discuss involves an excess of material, rather than gaps which disturb the continuity or thread of discourse. In suggesting this focus, Authier rejects the need to resort to orthodox linguistics in order to articulate a structure and a thread or current. This stance was the consequence of refusing to see ruptures as performative failure, as in the orthodox approach, preferring rather to see them as an apparent irregularity that assigns a structural regularity of another order.

In contrast to the excesses are the silences. Here the focus shifts to a Heideggerian position which rejects viewing language ontologically as com-municating messages which can be objectified, thematised and are useful for a disposition, while allowing the linguist to assume analytical and theoretical distance. Rather, language is conceived of as an entirely original opening on the world – the limits of my language are the limits of my world. Thus the being of a language is not a linguistic fact but is ontological. That is, our relationship to language and to silence is not a metalinguistic description, but a relationship of hearing and of appertaining (Heidegger, 1959). In this respect, the debate shifts once again towards Wittgenstein's discussion of the limits of language, involving the constitutive link between stating and its limits, a line also developed in Derrida's (1967b) criticism of phenomenology.

The intersubjective constitution of a language involves the impossibility of assuming a metalinguistic distance of the subject from language. The relationship between language and subject is such that silences and opacities are revealed in a constitutive way, while this relationship is entirely unspeakable in that it cannot be represented in a metalanguage. The subjects are appropriated by language. It constitutes the absolute heterogeneity in that the origin of meaning is entirely undiscernible. Thus silence constitutes the fact that there are always subjects that we cannot see, but which are revealed in heterogeneity. As such, silence is the absolute heterogeneity of discourse. Thus Wittgenstein emphasised that the subject cannot leave language and that in speaking it reveals its limits.

Authier's own orientation identifies different forms of non-coincidence or heterogeneities involving (1) interlocutive non-coincidence between the enonicateur and the destinataire, (2) non-coincidence of the discourse to itself, highlighted by the marked presence of words from a different discourse, (3) the non-coincidence between words and things, and (4) the non-coincidence of words to themselves. These non-coincidences correspond respectively to:

- places involving subjects which cannot be symmetric (Milner, 1978);
- the production of all words in the already said of other discourses;
- the symbolic order of the system of language and of things; and to the play of Lacan's *Lalangue*.

The non-coincidence relates to the central operations of forms of representation which locally designate the non-coincidence in the statements. In the enonciative process, the forms of representation of facts of non-coincidence appear to fill out a positive function of misrecognition relative to the non-coincidence that they mark. That is, the function of these forms is to recognise, in the sense of knowing again, in a double plane – those where they represent operations that can be described in terms of 'communication' strategies, and those manifested in a way that is not relevant to intentionality. This involves a negotiation that denies authorship by reference to an accident, local failure, etc., thereby leading to what Authier (Authier-Revuz, 1991:149) calls 'the phantasm of coincidence associated with the speaking subject'. Thus the problem confronting the analyst is that of articulating the imaginary of coincidence to the real of non-coincidence or heterogeneity.

Dialogism

I have already referred to how enonciative linguistics conceives of the speech-act in terms of a constant dialogue within which there is a reciprocal relation between enonciateur and co-enonciateur, with every 'I' being a virtual 'you' and vice versa. It is in this context that we are obliged to consider dialogism and the contribution of Bakhtin. It is clear that some of the problems considered by Bakhtin during the 1920s were encountered independently by Benveniste and Culioli some time later. The fundamental issue revolves around the idea that meaning is not substantially attached to the enonce, but links to a social conflict over the interpretation of the sign. It must be said that Bakhtin's position was accepted in France and reworked in order to integrate formalism with the social world (Achard, 1986:50 fn 5). Within this reworking, we also encounter Foucault's thesis on the struggle over meaning.

The contribution of Russian formalism in general, and Bakhtin specifically, was to conceive of the 'literary word' as existing, not as a point, but at the intersection of textual surfaces, as a dialogue amongst several writings, including that of the writer, the addressee and the contemporary or earlier cultural context (Kristeva, 1980:65). Manifestations of what has already been discussed with reference to Benveniste and Culioli should already be evident, as also should what has been said about heterogeneity, interdiscourse and the preconstructed! Texts are viewed as located within history and society, which are themselves texts into which the writer inserts him/herself by rewriting them. The word carries status, which is discussed in terms of the writing subject, the addressee and the exterior texts. It can be defined horizontally, with the word in the text belonging to both the writing subject and the addressee; and vertically, with the word in the text being orientated towards a prior or synchronic literary corpus. The addressee is included within a text's discursive universe only as discourse itself, rather than being external to it. This allows the horizontal and the vertical to coincide, bringing subject–addressee and text–context together. Thus each word (text) is an intersection of word (texts), where at least one other word (text) can be read. That is, any text is constructed as a plethora of quotations, being an absorption and transformation of another. Intertextuality has replaced intersubjectivity. The word becomes that which links structural models to cultural or historical conditions, while also controlling the shift from diachrony to synchrony, that is, to literary structure. The word functions in three dimensions – subject/addressee/context as a set of dialogical elements or as a set of ambivalent elements. Texts carry a dialogical space.

Russian formalism extended this argument to claim that all linguistic communication involved a dialogical character which was prior to the mono-logue or the embryonic form of common language. Bakhtin, on the other hand, employed the dialogue/monologue pair in terms of a linguistic infra-structure which should be studied via a semiotics of literary texts. He insisted on the difference between dialogical relationships and specifically linguistic ones. Those which structure a narrative – writer/character and subject of enonciation/subject of utterance – are a manifestation of dialogism, being inherent in language itself. The link to Benveniste should now be clearer in that Bakhtin refers to Benveniste's view of discourse as 'language appropriated by the individual as a practice'.

Frow claims that despite its preoccupation with a psychologism that comprehends the dialogic in terms of a pre-given intentional consciousness (Frow, 1986:99), Bakhtin's influence was far-reaching in France at the end of the 1970s. Yet there is room to believe that it had less of an impact on the work of Pécheux than on others, most notably Kristeva. More importantly, it seems that Frow reaches his conclusion through a confusion of the work of Bakhtin, Voloshinov and Medvedev.

The issue of authorship creates considerable confusion with reference to Bakhtin's work. There is a body of 'disputed texts' written in the name of either Voloshinov or Medvedev which some claim were Bakhtin's work. Morson and Emerson (1990) argue that these texts were not by Bakhtin and that there is a fundamental difference between the Marxism of Voloshinov and Bakhtin's work. Indeed, they claim that Voloshinov disapproved of some of Bakhtin's work on dialogisation and double-voicing, regarding it as 'relativistic individualism', arguing, à la Habermas' universal pragmatism, that the triumph of the working class would erase such speech forms. Raymond Williams (1977:35–44) similarly argued that Bakhtin did not write the influential *Marxism and the Philosophy of Language*, a book which Williams claimed represented a sophisticated attempt to develop a Marxist perspective on language. Furthermore, Voloshinov reworked some of Bakhtin's theories in terms of historical materialism, arguing that the asystematic nature of language was to be explained in terms of Marxism as a system external to language. Bakhtin argued that even though dialectic relations were often mistaken for dialogic relations, they were essentially different, in that the latter were embodied in language through logic. Bakhtin is treated as a non-Marxist.

It is useful to consider Bakhtin's dialogism carefully since it constitutes the sociological component of FDA which relates to the deixis of enonciative linguistics. His work constitutes a criticism of orthodox linguistics which is not unlike that produced by some of the French discursivists at the beginning of the 1980s (Gadet *et al.*, 1984), and is essentially a critique of such linguistics as discourse or as ideologies of language – I shall return to this body of work below. Bakhtin extended this criticism to Saussure, claiming that the *langue/parole* distinction led to a complete misunderstanding of the enonce, giving rise to the claim that the enonce is merely an instantiation of the linguistic system. Again we are reminded of Pécheux's reworking of this dualism. While enonces may contain words and sentences, they also contain other elements which he regards as extralinguistic. The essence of the distinction lies in the claim that sentences are units of language whereas the enonce is a unit of 'speech communication'. Even where the two coincide, where an enonce is a sentence, for that sentence to become an enonce the idea of someone saying it to someone must be added to the sentence's linguistic composition. It becomes possible to respond to an enonce, but not to a sentence – this is the essential difference between the sociological and the linguistic. Enonces can be exchanged even if they are constructed out of units of language.

Furthermore, sentences are repeatable whereas enonces are not. Even when two enonces are verbally identical, they never mean the same thing, simply because the listener (locuteur) confronts them twice and will react differently each time, since context will never be identical. Each enonce is unique and cannot be repeated. As a consequence, Bakhtin felt obliged to distinguish between contextual meaning, which involves the sense of situation, and an abstract, dictionary meaning. There is a tendency for linguists simply to recognise the abstract meaning, and thereby to collapse contextual meaning into this abstract meaning. The abstract meaning is merely a potential, this being the essence of the focus upon ambiguity and ideology in FDA – the possibility of having a meaning within what was called a 'concrete theme' (Voloshinov, 1973:101).

In interaction, 'understanding' is anticipated by the enonciateur, while also being a response to prior enonces, and it thus enters into a dialogical relationship with the locuteur. The enonciateur/locuteur relationship is not one of interpreting an enonce after it has been made, but involves the enonce being shaped as it is made. Enonces thereby belong to at least two subjects – the enonciateur and the locuteur. This clearly refers to the orthodox position according to which the enonce is assigned to a pre-formed subject:

> The word cannot be assigned to a single speaker. The author (speaker) has her/his own inalienable right to the word, but the listener also has her/his rights, and those whose voices are heard in the word before the author comes upon it have their rights (after all there are no words that belong to no one). The word . . . is performed outside the author, and it cannot be interjected into the author.
>
> (Bakhtin, 1986:121–122).

This is a clear statement of decentring and of intertextuality.

Evidently Bakhtin's work involves a concerted attack on orthodox linguistics, involving as it does the claim that the orthodox problems of linguistics change their character when related to the dialogical nature of language. Thus the syntax of enonces are shaped by their dialogicality, with syntactic forms arising in response to changing dialogic situations. Every enonce is dialogic, with dialogue being possible among subjects and not between sentences. Furthermore, dialogue cannot be found by looking at linguistics since it is an extra-linguistic category. Thus Bakhtin, much like the French discourse analysts, was seeking to establish a new discipline which would draw upon orthodox linguistics, while simultaneously reflecting on its procedures. For him this was metalinguistics, a field which was not reducible to logical relations, since logical relationships are only realised through dialogue. This is reflected in the example of two enonces being enonciated by two subjects: 'Life is good' and 'Life is good'. From the linguistic standpoint there is a repetition of the same sentence. For the logician there is the logical relation of identity. On the other hand, a metalinguistic standpoint involves the dialogical relation of agreement.

Bakhtin's concept of voice and tone are important. Every response to an enonce posits an author, whether there is one or not. That is, it is endowed with a 'voice'. Furthermore, every act involves a new element, and tone is the witness to the unique quality of every act and its singular relation to its performer. Referring back to Saussure, he claimed that every generally signifying value is only truly signifying in an individual context. The unique quality of each subject's experience leads to tone being imbued with the 'imprint of individuality'. He held that the ambiguity of language permitted transcribing such individuality into a law of the act, but regarded this as a vacuous exercise. Thus every enonce must be involved in evaluation.

A further feature of the enonce is the way it is shaped by the locuteur's 'understanding' or reading. However, in addition to the locuteur as a second person, there is also a third person for every enonce, the superlocuteur. Total or complete understanding is not possible. Thus, to some extent, each enonce is constituted by some other kind of listener whose supreme understanding at a metaphysical or historical level is assumed. Such a superlocuteur would understand the enonicateur in 'just the right way'. This third party stands above all the participants in the dialogue. In some respects it is reminiscent of Habermas' conception of perfect communication, but on the other hand it refutes the idea of distortion of communication. The existence of this superlocuteur is the consequence of discourse, 'which always wants to be heard, always seeks responsive understanding, and does not stop at immediate understanding, but presses further and further on' (Bakhtin, 1986:127).

In addition to the shaping of enonces by this anticipated third person, Bakhtin also makes reference to the role of the 'already spoken' or, in FDA terms, the interdiscursive. Again he is critical of the tendency to draw upon the instantiation of the resources of abstract language. He claimed that every enonce is a response to some prior enonce, which shapes the content and style of the enonce. These earlier traces are embedded in the object itself. It was this awareness which led Bakhtin to reject the conception of dialogue as a sequential form of expressed dialogue, arguing that the complexities created by the already-spoken-about quality of the word, and by the listener's understanding, together generated an internal dialogism of the word. Indeed he claimed that words 'remember' earlier contexts, thereby achieving a 'stylistic aura' which is the effect of manifold voices.

There was a reaction in Bakhtin's work not only to the treatment of enonces as *parole*, but also to the treatment of language as a system of abstract norms. He regarded all order as incomplete, as being in need of constant work. Language was treated as an essence, in complete contradiction of the Cartesian tendency to treat it as an ideal. In this respect he has interesting observations upon how different professions might have distinctive ways of speaking. Such different 'languages' are not simply a mater of lexical variation, but are to be treated in terms of the extralinguistic phenomena of variation in conceptualisation, understanding and evaluation. A complex of experiences, shared evaluations, ideas and attitudes converge to generate a way of speaking. Again this creation of discourse types based on the relations of voices is reminiscent of the work on register/genre in FDA.

In order to conceptualise this variation, he resorts to the term heteroglossia, or, an amalgam of languages, each with its own way of 'accenting' and 'intoning' given words, sometimes referred to in terms of 'many voices at once'. More importantly, perhaps, each way of speaking resorts to distinctive principles of marking differences and for establishing units. As such, they constitute different forms of conceptualising the world, each with its own objects, meanings and values. Again we encounter the idea that words only carry potential, there being no 'neutral words', nor a dichotomy involving denotative and connotative meanings. Even the 'monoglot' speaks many languages!

Bakhtin went further, arguing that heteroglossia was always dialogised. He argued that languages are learnt through interaction rather than by access to dictionaries, grammars, etc., or through the conscious and meaningful application of rules. Thus the language is learnt already dialogised. That is, speech is always dialogical, being metalinguistic rather than being an entity that is reduced to linguistic categories. The various 'languages' of heteroglossia are, as we have seen, associated with tones and meanings, and these are already dialogised meanings.

In claiming that an enonciation does not have meaning in itself, Bakhtin was referring to how it is party to a variety of plays of language which he referred to in terms of polyphony. In this respect he was emphasising that meaning is the result of confrontation between social groups in the form of social practice related to the signification and language play. Polyphony has to do with the position of the author in a text, and thus with enonciation. Evidently it should not be confused with heteroglossia. For Bakhtin it was a crucial feature of 'form-shaping ideology' (Morson and Emerson, 1990:234) associated with a dialogical sense of truth, and with the special position of the author necessary for visualising and conveying that sense of truth. As such it was a rejection of modernism's monological conception of truth, which rests on the assumption of the separation of the world from its description. Truth is treated as separate from its enonciation. This, of course, is why a Marxist reading of Bakhtin appears so misplaced. In contrast, dialogical truth is inconclusive, being a manifestation of a plurality of unmerged voices. They are unmerged because they cannot be contained within the context of the dialogue. Even when they agree, they do so from different perspectives and from different senses of the world. Evidently it is immensely difficult for a single author to represent or to convey the associated plurality of consciousness.

In some respects this is not too far removed from the concept of problematic, and Althusser's concept of reading. Certainly the manner in which Althusser's work referred to alternative readings of the same text, appears, on the surface at least, to have much in common with Bakhtin's dialogical sense of truth. Thus monological works represent the author's truth, which permeates the work in conveying the author's position. Dialogical works, in contrast, imply the existence of alternative truths which require alternative readings. In polyphonic works, several consciousnesses meet as equals and engage in a dialogue. Thus, characters in a work of literature must be 'not only objects of authorial discourse but also subjects of their own directly signifying discourse' (quoted in Morson and Emerson, 1990:239). The direct power to involve meaning belongs to several voices.

Authier-Revuz (1995:94–97) has recently offered an appreciation and criticism of the relationship between dialogism and FDA in which she makes some telling remarks about the relationship between enonciative linguistics and sociology, something which we will encounter below in discussing the work of Achard. She makes the point that there is a distinct difference between how Bakhtin and Voloshinov treat what she calls the 'dialogical trans-linguistic' approach. Whereas the former offers a limited acknowledgement of language as an object for the linguist, this is systematically ignored in the work of the latter, leading to an integral sociologism that derives from underestimating Saussure's concept of value or 'differential'. However, this is no less a critique of these two authors than of the manner in which their work has been adopted by French orthodox Marxists, most explicitly by Houdebine. She claims that it leads to a closed approach which always escapes to a preconstructed social conception based upon the singular inscription of a subject in the signifieds of his/her language. As such, it is a direct attack on Houdebine's outright rejection of the post-structural position, ignoring the dimension of the 'other in the one' in any approach to meaning. She proceeds to claim that for Voloshinov the subject is formed in terms of social psychology, whereas for Bakhtin there is an explicit intentionality with reference to the subject. This reference to Bakhtin's work is echoed in a recent comment by Boutet (1994:41), who claims that a number of Bakhtin's formulations can be interpreted as the precursors of pragmatics (Todorov, 1981; Moeschler, 1985). However, she rejects such an interpretation, claiming that Bakhtin's emphasis on analysing grammatical and discursive forms in relation to concrete social situations of enonciation, and the way his semantic theory rests on dynamic tension between the theme and the signification of an enonciation, ultimately leads to a radical critique of the pragmatic thrust (Ebel, 1986; Fiala, 1986).

Boutet claims that neither social consensus nor negotiation play any part as principles of organisation of verbal exchanges in Bakhtin's work. Rather, organisation rests on an opposing principle involving the contradictory nature of language activity and interaction. Thus there is a dynamic contradiction between the immutable aspect of the linguistic sign and its changing aspect dependent upon the situation of enonciation; between the stable signification of an enonciation and its shifting and unique theme; between the different social 'accents' of the same linguistic sign.

Given the contribution which Authier-Revuz has made to heterogeneity (see above, pp. 192–197), it is hardly surprising that her evaluation of dialogism is in this context. She questions the value of conceiving of a dialogical relationship in discursive terms simply by developing a constitutive relationship of 'one' and 'another' when both are of the same nature. They may well be different but they are commensurable. Rather, she insists upon recognising the dialogue of the one with the Other. More radically, she claims that an approach to heterogeneity that implicates the two dimensions of the real of language – as a system that is fundamentally non-coincidental with things, and as an ambiguous space that affects all sequences of non-coincidence to itself – appears to be entirely the sphere of dialogism. That is, she underlines the need to recognise that discussing heterogeneity by reference to a structure in which interlocution and interdiscourse inscribe it in speech within the dialogical problematic of a constitutive relation between one and the other, is insufficient. In her view, it is the heterogeneities which language inscribes in speech, in terms of words to name things and the excess of ambiguous words, that is important, and yet it is this heterogeneity that appears incongruous with dialogism since the 'non-one' within speech cannot be understood in a dialogical relationship.

Dialogism and language play

In the preceding chapter the impact of the work of both Voloshinov and Wittgenstein on the work of FDA at the beginning of the 1980s was commented upon. A number of authors have recently drawn attention to the relationship between Bakhtin's dialogism and Wittgenstein's language play (*inter alia* Silverman and Torode, 1980:8; Frow, 1986:158–160). With reference to FDA, Achard (1993) has recently developed this relationship. In so doing he is referring to two heterogeneous elements: on the one hand, the linguistic, which involves constraints on forms; on the other, the social, which involves meaning. There is a constant necessity to move from one to the other, this being the essence of Wittgenstein's language games, and his insistence on how language games are a form of life. Achard begins by restricting enonciative linguistics to the relationship in living speech (Boutet 1989, 1994) between the enonce and the situation where person, tense, place and attitudes pertain to the taking in charge of the enonce. He specifically omits the pragmatic work on argumentation and performative effects undertaken by Ducrot and Anscrombe. Thus enonciation situates the concrete enonce within a specific space between two extreme points. He resorts to Milner's (1989) discussion of the difference between signification (linguistic) and meaning (the real effect and pragmatic understanding). Two different enonces have different significations, this being a feature of the linguistic composition of enonces. The notion of signification depends on the possibility of abstracting the effects of the possible meanings of different forms − Milner's 'variation'. The link between this and syntax does not involve enonciative changes which bring it in line with the syntactic, nor does it mean that syntax changes without the signification changing. In contrast to the pragmatists, Milner refuses to limit meaning to its pragmatic effect. He wanted to go beyond the position where lexical items referred to properties outside of their use as a lexical function, or the focus on indexical functioning, where signification lies in association with context. Rather he refers to the formal apparatus of enonciation. Achard explains this with reference to the following schema:

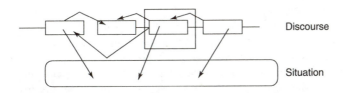

Source: Achard (1993:77)

Discourse is presented as a series of linked enonces which are also linked to the situation by a series of returning operators − the discursive chain. The arrows in the above diagram represent the thread of discourse. The arrows internal to discourse which return to context are the anaphors, while those pointing towards the situation are the deictics. In this respect one is 'in the meaning' which he refers to as 'the functions envisaged concerning the concrete discourse and the real situation' (Achard, 1993:77). He presents a second schema in explaining signification:

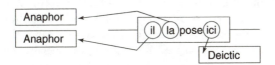

Source: Achard (1993:78)

Signification involves a systematic structure of places in relationship to the formal dimensions of person, tense, place or of diverse modalities, which, with the connection to effective situations, allows language to perform the role of

205

operator of interaction. This is achieved by situating the discourse in relation to a series of places of enonciateurs, where the taking in charge by the locuteur carries along the effects of the system. Social interaction occurs when the locuteurs, in taking charge of the enonces, establish relationships between the enonces which conform to those which the formal apparatus of enonciation implicates between the enonciateurs. Between the signification, which interpolates an enonciateur, and meaning, which constitutes the real of the allocutaire, lie the act and the event, which are constrained by the internal structure of enonces, of which the 'putting in discourse' is akin to setting the social process in action.

The linguistics of enonciation allows us to conceive of an articulation which the pragmatists reject in the name of a social determination based on an extra-discursive materiality. The understanding of the relationship between sociology and linguistics is here distinctive in that language is seen as social activity, rather than as a means of implementing some reality external to it. This follows from the influence of both Benveniste and Culioli, who viewed language as a system of reference forms which are directly linked to social acts, even if that link is not mechanical in nature (Achard, 1995:85).

This rejection of pragmatism does not mean that the individual is relegated to some kind of mechanical automaton. Accepting the localised effects of position, disposition and communication, the sociological idea of received knowledge can be viewed as a rational process, even if the considerations of truth are not treated directly by the actor (Boudon, 1986). Achard (1994) argues that rejecting a passive conception of scientific knowledge, with its preoccupation with truth and reality, in favour of an active conception, leads to rational behaviour or judgments of truth involving nothing more than the result of reflexive work on a prior base. In many respects this is similar to the ethnomethodological concept of accountability. For any enonce there is room to distinguish between what one calls an assertion, or the act of pro-nouncement, and its modalisation – the semantic operations that allocate a status to it, and the linguistic marks of these operations. Those assertions which can be defined as those enonces which could reveal the category of truth or false, or those which do not carry a modal mark, do not always function as such if one views them as acts. Our conversation is full of examples such as 'It's a nice day', which may function as much to sustain a conversation as to be a claim of truth, and, if it is pouring with rain, can be interpreted as ironic rather than as false. That is, truth is treated not as a property, but as a constructed modalisation which assumes that a discursive environment exists that can accept that such a 'truth' makes sense. There is no guarantee that the conditions which permit a proposition to function in terms of the modalities of truth or false for a locuteur are also in force for the interlocuteur. The rationality of a behaviour implies a reflexive activity. Clearly dialogism insists upon this kind of rational, conscious behaviour on the part of the interlocuteurs. However, this is quite different from assuming that the social actors are in control, and determine the thread of discourse in its entirety. It is impossible for any actor to be fully in control of any discourse, as a consequence of which rationality is not only limited, but is also reflexive. In taking in charge a preconstructed, the subjects who are interpolated as actors accept, either partially or totally, both the social places which relevant linguistic marks construct, and the point of departure which they presuppose (Achard, 1995:86). Any social actor can render account of her/his behaviour, and such accounts can be formulated by reference to presuppositions and implicits that delimit that which is thinkable, and thereby the space of choice. None the less, between the linguistic level and the reasoning of the rational individual, there are other levels of presuppositions which interject and which constitute the discursive organisation. That is, there exists a materiality that is imposed on the locuteur and on the interpretative apparatus that organises the effects of position and disposition.

Wittgenstein (1969) discusses such issues by reference to certainty. He also adopts a position wherein the author proclaims the irreducible singularity of the act of interpretation and the impossibility of understanding language in itself. His concept of 'language play' relates to a fictive situation which allows him to define the practical meaning given to enonces in a rule form. The play of language is seen as a practice of interpretation, being a practical relationship between the locuteur and the enonce. He succeeds in showing that the practices within which language is placed cannot be reconstituted from that which is said. Achard draws on the example of the surgeon, who, during an operation, calls for his tools, and how this involves a play of language around the objects which the surgeon requests from his assistants. The same words could be spoken by a professor in creating a book design. There is nothing in the external form of the enonce which allows us to know which play it pertains to – the play of language is a practice of interpretation. In this respect the focus is upon Wittgenstein's point that the signification of a word is its use in language (Wittgenstein, 1961:4,126).

For Wittgenstein, language play is an 'experience of the spirit', addressed to the universal subject of philosophy. Language play presupposes conventions of fact which cannot be explicit. From the sociological perspective, each sector of social life can be seen as a play of language, a point often made by Wittgenstein. If the structure of enonces does not indicate the play of language in which they are implicated, and if the social actors are engaged in numerous different activities which can be seen as plays of language, then the same enonce can be placed in different plays of language. It is here that Achard encounters the link to Bakhtin's dialogism. In his notion of polyphony, Bakhtin rejects what he calls the 'abstract idealism' whereby words mysteriously exist outside of use through a psychologistic positivism. In contrast, dialogism ascertains that an enonciation does not have meaning in itself, but that meaning is created out of a multitudinal (polyphony) plays of language. Not, of course, that the Wittgensteinian term is contained in Bakhtin's writings, but there is a clear overlap of philosophical orientations between the two authors.

Dialogism does allow a number of developments. First, the notion of language acts designates the pragmatic act linked to the individual enonciation, but confronting a supposedly homogeneous linguistic signification. Second, the play of language indicates that the language acts are structured in domains linked to the genres of life, of practices. Third, dialogism itself indicates that meaning is not a pre-given entity, always already there, within an already completed signification. Rather, meaning is the result of a practical meeting of social groups around signification, and language play is the product of open options at the heart of a discursive organisation, together organising points of view, practices and interests.

What Achard demonstrates is how language play involves viewing speech-acts as assuming a structured form associated with specific social practices. By drawing upon dialogism, he indicates that meaning derives from social confrontation associated with signification and language play. The possibilities deriving from the essentially ambiguous nature of meaning relate to a discursive organisation. This means that there can be no fixed boundaries, either to language or to society. Rather, they constitute a dynamic fluidity involving constant composition and recomposition.

While the idea of the decentred subject has always been the central feature of FDA, this does not mean that the conscious subject is entirely denied. The social aspect relies upon the effects of discourse and therefore there must be the conscious subject which exists to be affected. The transition from language (form) to meaning (social) involves an effect in terms of practice. Whereas the linguistic sets constraints on forms, it is meaning that sets constraints on the social, through the effect of meaning. This division of the form and the social is crucial with reference to pragmatics in that the work of Ducrot, which has focused on the topic of argumentation, has retained the centred subject by inserting the social context within linguistics. It is essential to recognise the difference between the reference to pragmatics in FDA, as the value that a discourse assumes in inducing an action, and that of rationalism, which rests on the separation of speech and action. In opposing 'discourse' and 'acts', it becomes impossible to recognise discourse as action (Achard, 1992:75).

On the other hand, it should be evident that the play of language is conceived of as an arbitrary and constraining external structure. The individual believes that s/he speaks, that speech crosses the individual, this being the central feature of Foucault's concept of episteme. That is, the knowledge on which the individual operates is extremely constrained, both in terms of the effects of prior knowledges which the individual cannot be aware of, and in terms of the constraints that are placed on what can be said from a given place. Furthermore, the constant shifting between form and meaning has its effect, such that meaning is never truly fixed. Thus social practice is constantly modifying the meaning of objects which are constructed and reconstructed. The Munchausen effect implies that the subject is held to be responsible for his/her acts in the practice in which s/he is inscribed as subject as a consequence of being the responsible subject, taking in charge the relevant discourse. Clearly the role of the conscious subject is extremely limited.

We are now in a position to consider how dialogism is implemented in discourse. The stabilization of a discourse is a feature of legitimising, where features of discourse are taken for granted, or assume a non-marked quality. Where this is not completely achieved, there will exist a dialogical tension over meaning and, for one group or another, the discourse, at some point, assumes a marked quality. This tension is a manifestation of contradictory places, and is evident in terms of enonciative relations. When a relatively stabilised relationship between forms and social practices is established, to the extent that discursive registers assume a non-marked quality, the implicit tension of dialogism is precluded. Since meaning is treated as the real effect, and as pragmatic understanding within a context of a total ambiguity of meaning, it is conceivable that the struggle over meaning has a dialogised context. The multiplicity of possible meanings associated with different forms is the basis of each enonce having the linguistic attribute of signification. This signification is the site of confrontation between social groups, the change in the individual identity of terms involving a change in signification. That is, signification assumes that the terms (lexemes) are not describable outside of use, since signification derives from the use of language and the link to pragmatic meaning. As a feature of discursive organisation, different enonciative dimensions assume a specific value and a radical value.

The relationship between form and meaning is dynamic, unstable and dialectical. It is unstable because, within the signification which puts forms and social meaning in operation, is inserted the indeterminacy of the act of interpretation, play of language or discursive formation. It is also unstable to the extent that the speech-act in the world modifies the world. To say 'we' is to express solidarity, to say 'they' is to break it; to express the norm is to exclude the deviant in the designation. It is also unstable because the space of forms can be designated, evaluated, modalised, being operationalised in the execution of meaning, and by the displacement of the formal universe by that meaning, without suppressing the former character, thereby affecting the intertextualities and values of the various markers. The significant value is not attributable unless it is relatively stable within the sociological space and the non-contiguous variations are eliminated.

Where the locuteur takes in charge, the place of the enonciateur is effectively legitimate, and thus lies outside of signification. That locuteur in enonciation has pretensions of legitimacy which may (non-marked) or may not (marked) be accepted. Where the taking in charge of an enonciation is unmarked, signification is the material feature of the language act. That is, signification supports the language act. It is the discursive register that is responsible for establishing correspondence between the enonciateur (formal) and the locuteur (real social place). With reference to this articulation, it is necessary to separate (1) the internal unwinding of the discourse from (2) the social action which that discourse supports. These actions can either be carried by the enonce or they can collapse.

Dialogism assumes a conflict between parties occupying the same ground when, for example, the same notion is spoken differently by different parties. Thus the notion 'Wales' might involve the Welsh nationalist treating it as the territorial space that expresses the will of the people, whereas the British nationalist treats 'Wales' as a geographical space that constitutes a region of Britain – the territorial space that expresses the will of the people. At the level of register, there is a unity, where both sets of nationalists are engaged in the same practice, where they occupy different places which are placed in discourse using the same word. The place from which they speak allocates different meanings to words in that they are inserted in the enonciation in different ways.

The integration of enonciative linguistics with a concern for meaning and discourse led to an opening onto other dimensions. It led to an awareness of parellels with the work of Bakhtin and Wittgenstein and, ultimately, to the possibility of investigating the process of the social construction of meaning. The relationship between signification and meaning relates to the constitution of the subject in an innovative way. By the same token the relevance of Authier-Revuz' work on heterogeneity pertains to how the discursive organ-isation is subject to specific operations within the intertextuality involving the co-existence of prior discourses within an existing discourse. It is this which allows the historical to be related to existing social practices, with signification playing a central role in the various plays of language.

Conclusion

What begins to emerge from this survey of the traverse across orthodox linguistics to enonciative linguistics, dialogism and language play is that orthodox linguistics is a product of modernism. That is, its concern is with a description of the normative, seeking to encounter an order that links with normative practice. Given the extent to which standardisation was such a central feature of the attempts to relate grammar, reason and the State at the beginning of the nineteenth century, this should be no surprise. This order is then presented as a series of laws. The resultant form is linked to the centred subject, albeit that this occurs without an *entrée* into the world of the social, but rather as the mechanism whereby the form of language is rationally transmitted as a mental process into linguistic practice. There is a match between the order of form and the reason of the speaking subject. It is tempting to suggest that this concern with normativity and order echoes the same concern that one finds in sociology and its preoccupation with normative consensus (Williams, 1998b). If this is indeed the case, it is hardly surprising that a post-structuralism that expresses a concern with the Marxist conflict perspective, even if it is a perspective that assumes many of the modernist concerns, would find itself at odds with orthodox linguistics.

On the other hand, the work discussed in this chapter is remarkably similar to that of Hobbes, who maintained that knowledge was the effects of what he called 'the consequences of motion' or meaning. This he linked to the geometry of the deictic through which humankind creates its world. This deictic consisted of the geometry of different places or positions from which the perspective of the world derived, leading to a deictic of perception and the space which he regarded as society (Hobbes, 1839–1845, vol. 3).[4]

From the outset, FDA was an attempt to develop the radical alternative. Despite its more orthodox beginnings in relation to linguistics, it has moved in a direction distinct from the normative and prescriptive orientation of orthodox linguistics. As we have seen, the theory of enonciation in linguistics is, to an extent, transformed into the study of enonciative operators, and syntax is taken out of its orthodox context and placed within enonciation. Much of the disquiet concerning orthodox linguistics revolves around the issue of the subject, and it is evident that the subject of enonciation is different from the grammatical subject. Benveniste's realisation that discourse did not pertain to the addition-combination of phrases, but involved a rupture with the grammatical of *langue* was the starting point. Discourse became the empirical object which the linguist encounters when s/he discovers the traces of a subject of enonciation as formal elements which denote the appropriation of *langue* by the speaking subject within any enonce (Guilhaumou *et al.*, 1994:193–194).

It is evident that within FDA, form assumes quite a different conception of language from that of orthodox linguistics. Building upon the foundations established by Benveniste, language and discourse are radically opposed. It proceeds beyond an interest in linguistics as the science of language, as a system of signs, to confront the manifestation of *langue* in active communication. It leads to the creation of a linguistics of discourse involving the description of marks and discursive function, how they relate to empirical subjects within situational and institutional frames. As we have seen, it also leads to an awareness that discourse lies at the limit of *langue* and linguistics. Uncovering subjects of enonciation, the traces of relations to context, and discursive functions, obliges an awareness of the limits of linguistic formalism associated with the formal approach to language. It touches on an awareness that discourse is not the 'other of language', to be considered as a consequence of theoretical difficulties. Indeed, it goes beyond a grammatical concern with the phrase and the transphrastic, focusing upon the analysis of potential discursive agencies and regularities that are manifested at the level of specific phenomenon such as the anaphor or the thread of discourse. In this respect it is proposed that it leads to a grammar of discourse that contrasts with the grammar of the phrase (Guilhaumou *et al.*, 1994:194). On the other hand, this perspective appears to persist with the disciplinary boundedness of linguistics, seeking to create a new linguistics or new branches of linguistics. Yet it is also clear that discourse analysis collapses the distinction between disciplinary boundaries which divide linguistics and the social sciences, obliging the linguistic to confront the social and the social to confront the linguistic. In this respect it is appropriate to recognise that disciplines are modernist constructions, involving distinctive discourses whose objective is the discovery of an already constituted, external truth and reality.

It is also evident that, despite the break up of ADELA, much of the initiative of that group has continued in a fragmented way. Additionally, there are those who are seeking to steer FDA in a direction that orientates with sociology by resorting to Bakhtin's dialogism. Having considered form and meaning, and its relationship to orthodox linguistics, I would now like to consider lexis, which held such a position of prominence within FDA. A concern with meaning inevitably leads us to consider the relationship between lexis and linguistics, and how this relationship pertains to meaning.

7

LEXICOLOGY AND DISTRIBUTIONALISM

Introduction

On the surface it would appear that the most important textual segment in the penetration of an archive is the lexical unit, which occupies a privileged role in the discursive positioning of subjects. However, in discourse analysis it should be recognised that there is an important distinction between the lexicon and vocabulary, between the possibilities of language and the specific value terms assume across the original relations which they occupy in relation to other units. Furthermore, the relationships between lexis and vocabulary are constrained by various factors. Bakhtin addresses this issue in terms of what he calls an immense dialogical rumour:

> Oriented on its object, it penetrates in that milieu of strange words deriving from dialogue and the bending of words, it links with the one, detaches from others, it crosses with a third . . . A living enonce, significantly rises at a historic moment and in a socially determined environment cannot manage to touch the thousands of living dialogical threads, tissues for the socio–ideological conscience around the object of such an enonce.
>
> (Bakhtin, 1981:100)

Orthodox linguistics measures meaning in terms of its pragmatic effect associated with the rational subject, thereby playing down the relevance of signification. In contrast, within FDA, signification plays a central role, being the site of maximum common meaning. Indeed, Milner (1989) refers to signification as 'the semantic'. It rests on the assumption that the lexicon can be described by reference to properties outside of use, since, if the signification of a term derives from its use, then it would be linked to a pragmatics of meaning, a position that is anathema to FDA. Achard (1993:76) notes that this leads to the division of words into two categories:

- Those with a lexical function, drawing together the substantives, adjectives, radical verbs and certain adverbs, where the signification derives from their use, constituting a sort of limit of themselves. Such words constitute an accumulator of references and properties.

- Those referred to in terms of indexical functioning, where signification relies on a relationship to 'context', involving the anaphorics including pronouns such as 'he', 'which', 'in', or those where signification relies on a relationship to 'situation'; the deictic, including personal pronouns such as 'I', 'you', 'one', tenses of verbs, passive and active, spatial terms such as 'here' and 'there', modal verbs such as 'to want', etc. The signification of these terms is not capable of representation by reference to the properties of the referent.

Again we should note that orthodox linguistics treats lexical functioning as normal, and the terms or shifters as deviant with reference to indexical function. That is, whereas lexical terms are numerous, the relatively small number of indexical marks are strongly structured and occur frequently. Evidently, FDA has quite a different orientation towards lexicality than does orthodox linguistics.

However, it is fair to note Maingueneau's (1987:97) point that discursive semantics has been obsessed with lexicology, whether with reference to statistical analysis or the Harrisian method of distributionalism. Its value as a statistical tool should not be surprising, given the emphasis upon a realist analytic perspective that prevailed during the early years of FDA. Certainly AAD69 was heavily involved in both of these trends and, despite the extensive self-criticism of this aspect of the work, they have persisted as key features of FDA. Not that the orientation has remained static, for while the early work tended to homogenise the object, this tendency was redressed by the introduction of theories of enonciation and textual grammar.

Given that FDA systematically rejects any understanding of semantics associated with the conferring of meaning by the centred, rational subject, the same reorientation of orthodox linguistics as was discussed in the preceding chapter is also relevant for lexicology. Benveniste's (1966) emphasis on the importance of the phrase in terms of rejecting the idea of language as a system of signs, in favour of language as an instrument of communication, is pertinent here. Phrases, in turn, are organised by lexical items – logical connectors such as 'but', 'in effect', 'then'; anaphora 'he', 'in', etc., which function linguistically in establishing the frontiers of the phrase; adverbs such as 'then', 'already', 'meanwhile', etc., which function to return to the text. However, an enonce is a phrase only in terms of its internal structure, whereas when it is effectively pronounced it becomes discourse. Evidently, discourse analysis relies on a specific role for the lexic, a role which emphasises its importance with reference to organising discourse. That is, a lexeme is not a simple unit, but the result of work, while also being the meeting point of a plurality of structuration processes. A discourse does not reveal its elements within a neutral space of semantic possibilities, but occupies a contradictory position within a field of discourse. We have already discussed the way in which the analysis of this organisation has focused upon the thread or chain of discourse and, in this respect, the lexicality plays a crucial role. Whereas orthodox linguistics assumes that a series of enonces reveals a system, discourse analysis relates a series of enonces to the same supposed use of language that is specific to a particular corpus.

Any consideration of the lexicality invariably relates to the orthodox idea that a word has its own meaning (Collinot and Mazière, 1997). In contrast, drawing upon the primacy of the signifier over the sign, Pécheux (1982a:188) argued that a word does not have a meaning of its own that is attached to its literality. Nor does it have several meanings that can be dervied from that literality through a logico-linguistic exercise whereby ambiguity is resolved via a consideration of all possibilities in the manner of generative semantics. The point he was seeking to establish was that 'meaning is always a word, expression or proposition *for* another word, another expression or another proposition', and that the bringing together of signifying elements in 'taking on a meaning' is not pre-determined by properties of *langue*. This breaks the relationship between syntax and the lexicon of orthodox linguistics, where it is assumed that the signifying elements are already endowed with meaning. Rather, words, expressions and propositions derive their meaning from the discursive formations to which they belong.

This leads to an awareness that, in considering lexical analysis, we are concerned with the formation of objects of discourse which are constituted and transformed according to the rules of a discursive formation. This simple observation clarifies the relationship between AAD69 and transformational grammar. More importantly, it also leads us to an awareness of the relationship between lexical analysis, enonciation and the archive. Whereas in the preceding chapter the focus was upon how enonciative linguistics was deployed in order to analyse the constitution of the subject, we are now able to shift to a consideration of the formation of objects. The Foucaultian reference to 'objects' involves reference to the objects of knowledge, or those elements which particular disciplines recognise as within their scope of interest – 'madness' as an object for psychopathology, or 'nation' as an object for political science. Clearly, such objects are not stable, but are subject to transformation within and across discursive formations. The point made by Pécheux above was that language signifies reality in the sense of constructing meanings for it, rather than merely referring to pre-given, 'real', objects which conform with the word that represents that reality. Each discursive formation pertains to a 'space', defined in terms of relationships involving 'institutions, economic and social processes, behavioural patterns, systems of norms, techniques, types of classification, modes of characterisation' (Foucault, 1969:45). Thus, developing a means of relating subjects, objects and such spaces is central to the analysis of discourse in that a discursive formation constitutes objects in highly constrained ways.

In considering the relationship between syntax and semantics, Culioli (1992:5) maintains that there is a tendency to confuse two problems: on the one hand, form, without which it would be impossible to have textual structure, and, on the other hand, the problems which derive from a confusion of the essence of syntax and semantics. This relates to what he calls the intention of the signifier, where the focus on intentionality in Husserlianism has no theoretical basis. These problems reflect a tendency to simultaneously establish relations which furnish a family of objects, a family of terms, a family of schema, etc. – that is, things which are not related to the object, but which are understood as a collection of operations which can be performed on the object. He objected to the dictum which translates into a Stoical lekton involving the problem of content as the representation of thought, of that which is signified, having on the one side a content, and on the other side a form. Within his concept of lexis, in making a functional space of the enonce, he sought to generate predicative relations which themselves wish to become the enonce. That is, that one constructs a being of representation which in fact is associated with a collection of ruled realisations, in the sense of regularities and rules for intersubjective activity. In other words, each time we have an enonce, of necessity it is put in a system of relations, in a system of possibilities, because it derives from the lexis. For Culioli, lexis is a sort of schema which furnishes the possible routes along which one is led, by diverse circumstances, both determinate and contingent, to make a choice.

Evidently the lexicon must be included within the field of enonciation since lexical terms have enonciative references. Thus, for example, a dog refers not merely to the qualities of a 'dog' but also whose dog, etc. The lexicon is not a purely informational, neutral element which exists in a language conceived of as a vast system of 'values'. Rather, a lexeme pertains to vocabulary which has a reference, and which already constitutes a particular use in a specific language. That is, the lexicon enters into a certain number of semantic micro-systems as codes in particular discourses. To study the 'meaning' of that lexeme is to study it in relation to the extremely constrained language which already pre-structures it, no matter what its function. Furthermore, for example, reference to 'nationalist' involves not merely contemporary nationalist language, but also the sub-language of prior discourse; it involves the manner in which 'nation' and 'nationalism' were stabilised in a particular way within eighteenth-century political discourse and the formation of the modern state. Interdiscourse assumes importance. In order to study the use of a lexeme, we must consider that to which it is opposed if we are to avoid naively believing that each discourse designates across the system of, say, a nationalist discourse. We must reject the idea of a static, self-contained system which ignores the dynamic aspect of meaning. In reality, within an interdiscourse, two discourses will construct their categories and will not 'choose' their lexemes from an undifferentiated stock of possibilities; rather, they will do so within a space of very constrained reciprocal delimitation, where coherence with the 'language', the political discourse, the nationalist discourse, etc. is simultaneousely established. A lexeme thus employed does not simply repeat the constructs which some 'earlier structuration' has imposed upon it. As a consequence, a lexeme is not a simple unity, but rather it is the result of work. It is also the point of inter-section between a plurality of processes of structuration. A discourse never takes a portion of its elements within a neutral space of possible semantics, but occupies a contradictory position within a field of discourse.

In this chapter I would like to consider how this issue of distributionalism, involving lexicality and the enonce, has been handled by FDA. Such work has placed substantial emphasis on computer analysis, much of it focusing upon key terms in the organisation of discourse. As we shall see, this was a primary concern from the inception of FDA. Second, there has been an attempt to deal with lexicology in terms of enonciation, and Achard's discussion of anaphora and deixis is a useful case in point. Third, attention should be given to the paraphrase, which has also been of central importance.

Of necessity, this survey of lexicology in FDA cannot hope to be exhaustive, but will serve as the basis for understanding the manner in which viewing language as discourse leads to a particular orientation towards lexicology. It is perhaps useful to begin this discussion by considering the importance of distributionalism and enonciation in FDA.

Distributionalism and enonciation

Harrisian limitations

In a recent paper, Gadet *et al.* (1990) have claimed that it was the work of Zelig Harris which inspired the establishment of the method of AAD69. That work sought to reduce texts to elementary or 'nuclear' phrases, which, when linked to transformationalism, was the basis of a search for discursive regularity and the constitution of semantic domains. It was employed by reference to an objectivty which claimed that any corpus could be described without any prejudgment concerning that corpus. Harris' objective was to discover recurring sequences as a basis for establishing a classification of categories at the different levels of phonology, morphology and syntax. This involved an empirical analysis of repetition, of the referential notions of vocabulary organisation, coupled with objectifying the 'semantic' fields on which they were based. That objective was to be achieved not via the intuition of the analyst, but by recourse to formalism. In operating in terms of discourse, he took account of the external constraints on language, but without developing a method which treated discourse as fundamentally different from a linguistic analysis.

Harris' use of syntax underlined generative grammar's reference to the possible, so that any corpus is restricted in terms of reference to the possibilities permitted by the rules. The situation is quite different with reference to

217

discourse, since what we observe is the organisation of effective production, and the local and provisional regularisations which allow the production of meaning from their literality. To be able to address the point where these regularisations carry meaning can be the objective of the hypotheses of the discourse analyst, but it is necessary to submit to a descriptive phrase of the repetition of form in order to outline the series. In this respect AAD69 was a tentative attempt to discover the principle of regularisation via the formation of classes of equivalence, where the saturation would be the moment where all new enonces of the postulated intertext would merely involve repeating the same sequence of classes linked by the same connectors. The distributional method lends itself to a consideration of repetition of the same, providing that it is accepted that the same form can be immediately stabilised, that is, that it regularly returns to the same notion. This distinction is clearly expressed in Pécheux's appendix to the English translation of Les vérités de La Palice (Pécheux, 1982a:208).

This Harrisian thrust was also taken up in France by Dubois, whose initial goal was to establish a structural dictionary. This work became the focus for a number of people who played a subsequent role, directly or indirectly, in FDA. Thus at the University of Rouen, Marcellesi and Guespin, with whom members of Pécheux's team struggled within the PCF during the 1970s, were closely involved with the work of Dubois, as was Maldidier. Similarly, the lexicologists at the Ecole Normale Supérieure, Saint-Cloud, began their work on the statistical study of vocabulary in discourse under similar influences. It was the manner in which the work of the Dubois–Marcellesi group developed along theoretical lines different from those of FDA, and the influences of 1968, which led to the polarisation of these two schools. In a sense, the focus of the opposition related to the manner in which discourse was conceived of in terms of the materiality of ideology. Despite our focus on the work of FDA, the importance of the Marcellesi group should not be dismissed. Its focus was very much upon classical Marxism and, to a very great extent, there emerged a resistance to the deviations from this orthodoxy, particularly after 1968. Furthermore, their work had a distinctive historical orientation which differed from the more sociological concerns of FDA (Achard, 1986:20), the analysis focusing upon politico-historical texts, and the discourse of organisation. Achard (1986:20) notes an exception to this in Gardin's work on the discourse of negotiations between trade unions and management. They were also important in recognising the relevance and importance of Voloshinov's work, and its relationship to enonciation in discourse, prior to the translation of his work into French. Yet their analysis involved a theory of reflection which the work of Pécheux sought to shy away from. This again is a manifestation of the manner in which the base–superstructure relationship was envisaged in orthodox Marxism. It is also interesting that their work did not focus merely upon discourse analysis, but extended to encompass a much more conventional Marxist analysis of the relationship between social structure and minority languages. Yet, during the early years, the two groups were close in the sense that they were both operating against the same positivist dominance in the social sciences, and in so doing were subject to the same intellectual influences.[1]

In a posthumous publication, Maldidier (Guilhaumou *et al.*, 1994) has written an interesting account of the differences between what Dubois and Pécheux were seeking to achieve when they first began their work on discourse analysis during the 1960s. She begins with the point that the coincidence of their work derived not from mutual contact but, rather, from the manner in which French intellectualism had developed at that point and the particular theoretical–political conjuncture that existed at the end of the 1960s. Whereas they shared a commitment to Marxism and were deeply involved in the PCF, their disciplinary backgrounds were different – Dubois was a linguist involved in literary studies, and Pécheux a philosopher working on epistemology who was eager to come to terms with language and linguistics. Interestingly, Maldidier also places considerable emphasis on the relevance of Foucault for Pécheux's early work. The militancy of the Marxism which they shared was linked with linguistic science. Unsurprisingly, given his literary bent, Dubois shared the emphasis upon reading which we have identified with Pécheux.

However, their conception of discourse analysis was different. Dubois conceived of discourse analysis in terms of a continuum with lexicology or the study of words, leading to the study of the enonce, which was akin to discourse analysis. For him this was a natural progression permitted by linguistic science. As we have seen, Pecehux saw discourse analysis in relation to the epistemological break with the ideology which dominated the social sciences. This difference largely conditioned the way in which the two conceived of the relationship between linguistics and the exterior. For Dubois it involved linking two models, one based upon linguistics and another based upon sociology, psychology or history. For Pécheux, on the other hand, at least at the end of the 60s, it involved articulating the question of discourse with that of the subject and ideology. The analysis of discourse only had relevance by reference to a theory of discourse. Their understanding of the relationship between language and linguistics also differed. Dubois was profoundly affected both by structuralism and by the deeply influential generative, transformational grammar. In a sense, he – and others – sought to elaborate on the relationship between lexical units and syntactic structures, the enonciative processes and communicational frames within which the lexical item is inscribed. The connections between vocabulary and the other dimensions of discursivity were elaborated. This contrasted with Pécheux's critique of the scientific status of linguistics. His work focused upon the lexical unit in the creation of particular texts, seeking to place the occurrence of the unit within the dynamics of enonciation. The development of a grammar of text and argumentation furnished new techniques for an analysis of the 'explication of a text' and it is in this technical sense of textual deconstruction that lexicometry assumes its importance.

In AAD69 Pécheux drew upon Saussure's emphasis upon the rules that facilitate the functioning of language, noting that linguistics fails to take account of the signification of texts and how one text differs from another. He regarded linguistic phenomena larger than the phrase as functional, claiming that this function was not merely a measure of the linguistic, but also had to encompass what he referred to as the 'conditions of the production of discourse', among which were the mechanisms which established the relationship between the protagonists and the object. Notwithstanding that the emphasis both on the supraphrastic and on the conditions of discursive production were subsequently rejected, it remained an important development. In this respect lexicometry assumes that a corpus is submitted to the constraints that relate to the positioning of the enonciateur rather than to a linguistic system *per se*. Such constraints are revealed through a reading that is capable of disarticulating the discursive surface. By reference to this discursive surface, or the sum of marks relevant to the same archive, the text was edited in order to establish the predicative enonces which were bound to the operators of dependence. This related to the work of Culioli, concerning how the lexis and the meta-lexis are implicitly mobilised, whereas the nominal and phrastic determinations are explicit (Culioli *et al.*, 1970). If an enonce is ambiguous, the different possible interpretations are coded and linked to the connectors. The next stage, which was computerised, involved applying classificatory procedures to the enonces in order to establish the similarity between them, and to construct classes of equivalent enonces. If these classes of enonces are regularly connected by the same series of operators, they are referred to as semantic domains. In turn, the connections between the semantic domains are established in the form of a graph, leading to the third step, which involved establishing the relationship between the domains. The link to the Harrisian method is evident, with lexicometry being deployed in order to refer to lexical positioning in terms of quantifying the significant relations between lexical units.

At this stage of his work, Pécheux focused upon what he called discursive process or the relationships of substitution, synonym and paraphrase between the linguistic elements of a specific discursive formation such that what was stated in relation to a specific position was determined by the specific discursive formation, with words changing their meaning from one discursive formation to another. In some respects it seems that his work involved adapting the concepts and methods of Harris to fit in with this framework. The analysis began with an attempt to construct a discursive corpus as a function of the dominant conditions of production. The criterion for the selection of corpora at this stage was external to the method. The 'discursive object' was the result of the transformation of the linguistic surface of a concrete discourse into an object of knowledge which is produced by linguistic science. Here he was resorting to Althusser's attempt to conceive of knowledge in terms of the

Marxist concept of production, where work is undertaken on raw material in order to transform it into a commodity. That is, it is a linguistic object given in a new context. This led to defining the discursive process as the consequence of a ruled relationship of the corresponding objects at the linguistic surface, which, in turn, are the result of stable and homogeneous conditions of production. Linguistics was reduced to a preliminary phrase, even if it was indispensable. The analysis of the phrase conformed with the orthodox 'logical analysis' which sought to uncover the nature of the relationships between the clauses in terms of coordination, subordination and complementation. In this respect he followed Harris in resorting to 'elementary enonces' which are not dissimilar to Harris' classes of equivalence. Once encountered, these 'elementary enonces' were decomposed by a process similar to Harris' 'nodal schema'. The corpus was subjected to computer analysis in order to compare the binary relation between each discourse uncovered and all of the other discourses of the corpus. When two binary relations had the same connector, they were submitted to further analysis in order to reveal the 'proximity' of these relations by reference to the content of their enonces. The goal was to determine which words and expressions occupied a relationship of 'substitution', occurring in the same positions within clauses which have a similar grammatical structure, and which are related in the same way to other clauses. This clarified the semantic relationship that existed between words and expressions, since semantic relationships between words derive from their substitution through synonymy, implication, etc., these relationships being specific to the discursive formation.

The articulation between the two parts of the work involved at least three problematic relationships. First, while the coding procedure served to resolve many of the problems involving the relationship between the text and its enonciative analysis, it also led to limiting the space of such solutions. Second, resorting to parpahrastic operations which were regarded as semantically neutral, permitted them to touch on the canonical enonces, but this involved reducing enonciation to the enonce. Third, the classificatory procedure relied on linking the structure of the enonce and the structure of enonciation within a homogeneous space via balanced relationships, which, once again, eliminated the relationship between enonce and enonciation (Achard, 1986:23). In reality, this involved a failure to give sufficient consideration to the relationship between the discursive and the linguistic, so that the relationship between form and meaning was limited to a positivist procedure.

While the influence of Harris' work is clear, in more general terms distributionalism derives from behaviourist psychology, and its structuralist orientation involving the idea that human behaviour is entirely explicable across all situations in which it occurs. Certainly the work of Harris involved a strict behaviourism in that he resorted to a study of non-observable meaning by seeking regularities in appealing to the environments which allow the definition of the 'distribution' of a unit rather than to function or signification.

Thus distributionalism is more classificatory than explanatory in nature. This procedure leads to deriving a theory of the homogeneous language from the phoneme to the phrase (Gadet, 1989a:14). Furthermore, within distributionalism the determination of units is not made the object of a test of commutation to the extent where they are held to relate to the speaking subject.

Textual grammar argues that the frame of the proposition is insufficient in order to characterise the context of the lexical unit, and that it is also necessary to consider the transphrastic relations if the complexity of discursive processes is to be recognised. This observation led to a call for an integrative approach that focused on the archive. It was forcefully argued that the Harrisian method was not really appropriate for a properly constituted linguistic approach since the traces of enonciative operations are eliminated. Furthermore, operating as if lexical content could be disassociated from both syntax and its enonciateurs results in the exclusion of the form/structure opposition. With reference to textual grammar, Harrisian distributionalism is insufficient since it fails to construct an appropriate definition of discursive context. It suggests a context for lexical unity that is inappropriate for discursive processes that develop on highly complex and vast linguistic units. This was the line of critique established by Marandin (1979b), Guilhaumou and Maldidier (1979) and Courtine (1981) in criticising a method that relies on an *a priori* knowledge vis-à-vis the selection of key terms by the analyst, this serving to define the themes of discourse. By referring to his/her presupposition, the analyst is imposing certain questions of a socio-historical order on the corpus: 'The analysis responds to the question presented by the analyst; but in presenting that reply as a structure at the base of a text, the analysis involves a shift to the limit where its interest confronts discourse' (Marandin, 1979b). This, in turn, leads to the delicate problem of the articulation between the two types of knowledge which are crucial for the discourse analyst – a linguistic knowledge and a non-linguistic knowledge.

It can be claimed that resorting to the Harrisian method that was employed in this early work implied a simple conception of language that was strongly influenced by structuralism. It involved conceiving of an invariant base which consisted of the syntactic element and which was opposed to combinatory selection, which consisted of the lexical component. Reference to enonciation was limited to the problem of coding related to the registering of the surface, and the conception of the subject suffered as a consequence.

Paraphrase

After AAD69, questions of synonyms and substitutability, semantic variability and invariability led to the focus on the paraphrase, which had been introduced by Harris. Such questions were essential for developments throughout the 1970s. This reference to the paraphrase begins from the principle that within an archive, meaning is discovered in the sliding from one formula to another at the interior of classes of equivalence: 'words, expressions and propositions which are literally different can "have the same meaning" at the interior of a given discursive formation' (Pécheux, 1975a:145). These types of paraphrastic relations are constructed by the analyst following a decontextualisation of propositions when the paraphrases that are of interest are produced by the enonciateur him/herself. It draws upon the metalinguistic capacity that Fuchs (1982) referred to as 'meta-predictions of identification', where there is an identification of two terms within discourse whose equivalence is not instituted by language. That is, it is not possible to rely simply on a classificatory analysis of distribution.

The notion of paraphrase relates to the linguistic notion of transformation. Within orthodox linguistics, transformation originally referred to a strict relation of paraphrase, in the narrow sense of a relationship of equivalence between phrases. Chomsky's modification involved an understanding of transformation as involving operations on structures. In both the original and subsequent work of orthodox linguistics, the transformation is considered to be semantically neutral. In contrast, enonciative linguistics gives no place to transformations. Thus, for example, the difference between the active and the passive consists of making a choice between two arguments of the predicate as a starting point, and even if the choice of one over the other is more neutral, it does not mean that they are different. Thus the relationship between the phrases is not one of a semantically neutral transformation, but rather one of paraphrase. Thus all paraphrases present the double problem of possibilities of equivalence, and of possibilities of distinction between an attested enonce and another which is not of necessity equivalent or which, if it is, does not relate to exactly the same place. In a sense, the paraphrase is employed in FDA in order to reveal what is of the order of the event within an enonciation, and to reveal that which uncovers the constraints of filtering pertaining to the discursive register that defines the intertextuality. That is, the transformation is allocated a quite different status, one in which the the form of the transformation is voluntarily given to the enonce by the subject of enonciation.

In a technical sense, the interest is not in the paraphrase as a collection of phrases equivalent to an attested enonce (A) in its conditions of enonciation, but rather it involves describing the ruled relationship that allows passing from (A) to enonce (B), attested or not. It is the collection of ruled relationships of passage between (A) and (B) that constitutes the paraphrastic relationship between (A) and (B). If a paraphrastic relationship exists between (B) and (C), the paraphrastic relationship between (A) and (C) includes the paraphrastic relationship composed between (A) and (B) and between (B) and (C) (Achard, 1986).

Once again we return to a comparison with generative grammar in considering nominalisation as a transformation (Milner, 1992:29–30). Generally two arguments are invoked, one which refers to the syntactic component, and the other to the relationship between lexemes in the semantic component of the grammar. The combinatory perspective of generative grammar does not accommodate the first option, and it is the lexical hypothesis that is generally invoked. Enonciative linguistics has a quite different orientation since the break between syntax and semantics is treated differently. Thus the nominalised form is thought of as an instantiation in a predicative scheme without ignoring the enonciative component. Culioli distinguishes between the predicative schema, its instantiation and its taking in charge. The taking in charge leads to the presence of a verb with its marks of diathesis, of tense and of person. However, if a predicative schema instantiates the place of another predicative schema, it appears under the nominalised form, and without marks of taking in charge. In a sense one refers to a predicative schema that is common to both the nominal form and the verbal form.

The notion of preconstructed leads to interpreting this situation discursively in that it is considered as constructing the notions that make the object of an enonciative reference complete, the others being taken to be preconstructed. This signifies that the preconstructed are susceptible of receiving the enonciative reference marks, but that they have not been received. Thus, when nominalisation occurs, so also does preconstruction, in the sense that there is no trace of the taking in charge that one has with verbs. Thus the example 'the development of steel production is important' claims that something is important without implying any responsibility for that development. The series of marks of person and modality is absent, leaving the taking in charge and agency within the context of the preconstructed. If, in the paraphrase operation, one modifies the enonciation into 'denominalisant', one is led to 'returning' the enonciative references that are necessary in order to make the enonce exist in an autonomous fashion. This makes it possible to explore the different possibilities that are tantamount to an inherent ambiguity of the nominalised enonce. To speak of a preconstructed is to postulate that all predicative enonces present in a discourse under the pre-assertive form are meant to have an implicit status in the associated register under one or more of the constructed forms. This reference to implicitation carries the double value of substantial implicit, and the reconstructed implicit, and their ambiguity.

Thus, resorting to the implicit and the preconstructed allows the paraphrase to be a useful methodological means of mixing the linguistic and the discursive. The paraphrastic space associated with a particular textual analysis constitutes the analysis of an effect of meaning in classifying the paraphrases following their pertinence, their situation in relation to the envisaged discursive universe, etc. (Gadet *et al.*, 1984). Achard (1986:36) demonstrates the way in which the eventual transfer of a verb from one category to another is linguistically describable; but the inventory of syntactic categories remains unchanged, it is only the inventory of lexemes relevant to this or that category that is modified. It underlines his point that it is erroneous to think that all lexicological problems pertain to discourse and not to the linguistic.

Distributionalism has not been rejected by those working in FDA. Rather it has been allocated a secondary analytical role in discourse analysis, being applied in a controlled manner. The problem of selecting key words on the basis of an *a priori* historical knowledge is resolved by seeking to ascertain the existence of key terms by analysis. Thus Boutet *et al.* (1982) emphasise that the analysis must exist within the context of an enonciative phenomenon, rather than in terms of content analysis. In this respect they emphasise the dialogical structure of the corpus:

> the homogeneous paraphrastic series are crossed by the relevant disparities of enonciative phenomenon, where the analysis necessitates not only the conceptual instrument of a syntactic–semantic analysis, but also the taking into consideration of the dialogical frame and its contextual givens.
>
> (Boutet *et al.*, 1982:73)

The importance of these contextual problems relates to the need to simultaneously consider in context, lexicals, syntax and enonce.

Key terms

We referred above to how a discursive formation constitutes objects in specific and constrained ways according to specific rules. It is this that leads to focusing upon key words in order to identify the specific value given to objects in relation to other units within any corpus.

Given the nature of the Harrisian method, it is difficult to apply it to texts which are feebly recurrent. As a consequence, in the early work of FDA many discourse analysts created a corpus that was strongly repetitive, starting from explicit hypotheses – one chooses one or more strongly correlated words, and one reveals all the phrases containing that word/these words in the corpus. Thus, obtaining a highly recurrent corpus, one proceeds to discover classes of equivalence, thereby facilitating the transformations by the regularisations of phrases. In general one aims for a decomposition of phrases into nodal phrases, and one expects to construct one or more fundamental or baseline phrases. Such baseline phrases imply a theoretical proposition that gives a sort of model of a determined collection of propositions. In the same corpus one can discover a number of baseline phrases around the same invariant, and between numerous invariants, which one needs in order to structure the one by the other.

One presents an explicit hypothesis in order to authorise considering such invariants as representative of the collection of discourse of a locuteur in a defined situation and at a defined time, since, without that 'homogenisation', the representativeness of propositions extracted from the corpus has little guarantee. Schematically one can define two main orientations to this type of analysis. First, a 'lexicological' orientation seeks to clarify the meaning of one or more invariants inscribed in a paradigmatic and syntagmatic system. Second, the 'baseline phrases' approach seeks to clarify the semantic functioning of invariants which, with the help of formal manipulations, give a kind of reduced model of the enonces of discourse.

Robin's early work (1971) adopted the first approach in seeking to study the terms 'peuple' and 'nation' in a text *Cahiers du doléances*, terms which a superficial scrutiny would suggest are synonymous. The work was divided in accordance with reference to rural and urban contexts. She found that in both cases the term 'peuple' was reserved for 'country folk', and was never employed as a synonym for 'nation'. 'Peuple' and 'habitants des campagnes' are combinatory invariants. The opposition between rural/urban involves the urban being presented as a place of luxury, laziness and corruption, but it also contains a certain ambiguity in being the place where the 'enlightened citizens' live. In the urban texts, the word 'peuple' is often also the combinatory variant of 'habitants des campagnes'; this is why the urban texts use 'nation' rather than 'peuple' in order to designate the 'national' community. The citizens, as equal individuals, are the nation. The functional identity of the lexeme 'peuple' in the two discourses is not apparent – the urban texts extend their ideology to other locations.

On the other hand, Maldidier and Robin's (1974) work on the Parliamentary Reports of 1776 relegated the lexicological perspective to a secondary role. They asked two simple questions of the text: 'What does one speak of?' and 'Of whom does one speak?'. From the analysis they discovered eight key words as a result of their recurrence, and a historical hypothesis – The Royal Decree could replace the ancient labour dues of corvée labour by a new tax, suppressing the former situation by instituting the freedom of labour. The formal or notional substitutes of the eight key words were added to them.

The operations of regularisation of the corpus were achieved by transformations constituting the collection of predicates of an invariant lexical unit into classes of equivalence. The enonces then regrouped into two main types of syntactic structures which, while not being realised in the text, occurred frequently – 'X is Y' and 'X means that Z'. Thus, for example, the phrase 'that freedom extends to the diverse branches of commerce' is transformed into 'that freedom leads to the different branches of commerce being understood'.

All of the lexical units treated as invariants belong to the same class of equivalence by the play of environments. However, this is of little consequence since the antithetical functioning words are found in the same class. Thus Robin and Maldidier created a distinction between pejorative and praise in accordance with which a group of lexical units is considered favourably or unfavourably by the locuteur. Another class called 'counter-class' allowed them to arrange the pejorative enonces in a discourse which always mixed them, these being treated as real or rhetorical concessions.

In contrast to the Harrisian analysis, this work contained 'semantic pictures'. Thus the enonces of each text are regrouped under four rubrics: in the pejorative series the enonces of the type 'X means that Z' and of the type 'X is Y' are grouped; this is repeated with the praise series in distinguishing the parliamentarian and adversary discourse. Finally, they sought to structure the baseline phrases and, in referring to the parliamentarian discourse, to relate them to an ordinance which is placed in relation to the destruction/production semantic axis:

1	Predicates praising the *ancien* institutions	X' was good
2	Effect of *ancien* institutions	X' produced good things
3	The *ancien* order attacked by that process	X led to the destruction of X'

Processes of destruction/production

4	New social order	X produced W
5	Pejorative predicates of the new social order	X or W is evil

Robin and Maldidier succeeded in showing that the adverse discourse is constructed by the same rules, but with one difference – the third phase of destruction is occulted and it does not mean that:

(R = the *ancien* order) R was bad, R produced bad things
(R' = the Edict) R' produced good things, R' is good.

It should be clear that FDA was moving away from the Harrisian emphasis upon a technique for the analysis of the regularisation of phrases. As we have seen above, during the 1970s this work developed around theories of enonciation and textual grammar. In some respects it involved discovering how the study of vocabulary articulates with syntactic and enonciative functions. The textual grammarians argued that the propositional frame was sufficient to characterise the context of a lexical unit and that the transphrastic relations had to be introduced in order to address the effective complexity of discursive processes. In this respect they sought an integrative approach to the archive. From the perspective of enonciation, on the other hand, the linguistic approach of key terms lacked any reference to the traces of enonciative operations. Transformations were no longer treated as simple techniques which maximised membership of classes of equivalence, but it was argued that the reduction of the complex phrase into simple propositions served to neutralise the relations of propositions at the interior of the phrase, and thereby neutralised the syntactic modulations and rhetoric. The transformation was rethought in terms of the subject of enonciation. Furthermore, the criticism referred to above – that the work involved returning to an *a priori* knowledge – was evidently relevant to the manner in which key terms were selected and how this served to define the themes of discourse. It was not the text that defined the themes, but the presupposition of the analyst in imposing specific socio-historical questions on the corpus.

Similarly, the lexis was no longer thought of as an atom of meaning but as the point of confrontation with other words, as a feature of relations inserted in the textual tissue. Thus the same term does not have the same value in its syntactic role as it does in its enonciative role. This was the main thrust of Courtine's (1981) work on thematisation, where he sought to relate specific syntactic structures, in this case 'it is the revolution that . . .', to an enociative process in the determination of a theme, that is, where an enonce displays that about which it speaks. In so doing, he emphasised the importance of phenomena of determination. The key-term method tended to unwind its data on any noun without reference to its determination. Given that the referential process plays a key role in the construction of the discursive universe, this could not be ignored. It led Courtine to claim a correlation between thematisation and nominal expansion.

One of the most common approaches to the study of key terms involves defining such 'themes' as a consequence of a knowledge that is external to the functioning of the discourse in question. Thus Courtine (1981) proposes reversing the problem of the delimitation of themes of discourse in presenting the following question: 'How, in and for the discourse itself, does an element determine if it can be characterised as a theme of discourse?' That is, how, given the existence of specific structures, and in relation to which linguistic forms, are the themes designated? As a consequence the analyst is obliged to look to linguistic structure rather than to historical knowledge for the information that fuels the answer. This led Courtine to focus his attention upon syntactic structures of the thematisation and most specifically those of the type:

'It is X that P'
'That which P is X'
'X is that which P'

These are formulae which refer to elements (X) which are made the object of a question and which can be localised within context. In employing them one produces two effects of meaning:

'I speak of that and not of any other thing'
'It is that which I would say when I employ that term'

What is at stake here is the dialogical switching which occurs with reference to emphasis and identification. These themes are once again ambiguous and can be interpreted as contrastives, deictics or constatives. The phrase 'It is democracy that we want for France' can thus receive three readings:

- contrastive: 'we want democracy and nothing else';
- deictic: 'that democracy is the democracy that we want';
- constative: 'there is a democracy, and eventually other things, that we want'.

The distinction between these three readings can rely on rigorous criteria. Considering the first of these with the additional information 'violence does not derive from the Communists, it derives from mass capitalism' – here the phrase challenges an adverse statement (violence derives from the Communists) while simultaneously constructing an opposition between 'Communists' and 'mass capitalism', an opposition which, together with others, allows us 'to materialise the frontier' between discursive formations, to 'designate that frontier, to show as a rule for all subjects, prior to expressing or interpreting such a formulation': 'one states that the violence derives from mass capitalism/ one does not state that the violence derives from the Communists'.

Courtine's example serves to illustrate the types of polemic refutation associated with that structure:

- The complete refutation: the statement makes explicit the elements which are opposed in the intra-discourse.
- The refutation by denegation: the elements of the interdiscourse are incorporated and dissimulated, the antagonistic statement is designed as such (the violence does not derive from the Communists) but it alone is preserved.
- As a result of reversing, the refutation works at the interior of an antagonistic discourse by subverting while assimilating: 'the collectivity which erases conscience, the regime wherein a small number think on behalf of everyone, exists in our country today'.

This evidently demonstrates how the lexical analysis undergoes a displacement. The syntactico-enonciative structures define the object of study and the analysis is constantly placed in the interdiscursive.

Lexicometry

Salem (Lebart and Salem, 1994:13) refers to lexicology as the 'study of the origin, history and relationship of words'. What lexicometry has achieved is to extend the analytic approach by elaborating the relationships within a text that are not accessible to consciousness, leading to an encounter with textual organisation. Having no recourse to context, it is reduced to a mere content analysis of a corpus of categories which are listed in terms of their conditions of production. With the introduction of the study of co-occurrences and repeated segments, the incorporation of syntactic analysis and a focus upon enonciative order, it has assumed a different status within which the mode of inscription of elements in the text is highlighted. In this respect, lexicometry is not a uniform method but a panoply of approaches which seek to capture the different properties of a corpus. It raises the question of interpretation and shifts the emphasis from a fixed method to one where a dialogue between the analyst and the corpus is revealed.

In broad terms, lexicometry is an approach which seeks to delinearise texts, implying that a corpus is submitted, not to constraints which are under the jurisdiction of a linguistic system, but to constraints which are related to the positioning of the enonciateurs, involving constraints that are not accessible at the level of consciousness and only appear across a reading that is capable of disarticulating the discursive surface. This positioning of the enonciateur is characterised by an elaboration of the significant and quantifiable relations between the units of that positioning. Rather than being a single coherent method, it involves a series of methods which are applied to appropriately chosen texts that relate to socio-historical hypotheses, while also being constrained by the research instruments. One of its values is its ability to confront large segments of text, thereby facilitating a comparison of discourse types or situations of enonciation. As such it does not privilege any particular element within discourse, being based upon the exhaustiveness of what is revealed by the analysis, and by the statistical patterns that it reveals.

Evidently, much of the early lexical work in discourse analysis was of an empirical nature, involving:

- the measure of frequencies of lexical forms in relation to items, thereby generating a coefficient of lexical repetition;
- measuring the number of functional items in relation to the number of functional forms, giving a coefficient of functional repetition;
- establishing the simple relationship between the number of items and forms to give a coefficient of general repetition.

An attempt was made to establish which lexical forms allow the characterisation of the originality of discourse of an *émetteur*, and which forms pertain to a common base. This emphasis on frequency related to the claim that a generality of terms could be associated with a particular historical conjuncture – state of language – or, with a situation of communication – state of language related to specific themes, genres or registers or, of course, to the idiolect. It is fair to claim that from its inception FDA's approach to lexicometry assumed that a corpus submitted to constraints associated with the positioning of its enonciateurs, seeking to uncover the nature of these constraints by employing a technical method. As such it always emphasised that the norm was established at the interior of the corpus and not by reference to *langue*, this being the link to the concept of discourse. Thus the goal of lexicometry was to characterise a positioning by the elaboration of a quantified system of significative relations between its units.

Much of the work of lexical statistics constituted the very content analysis which Pécheux (1969) criticised in AAD69. On the other hand, it did serve as a methodological basis for the further development of empirical research involving the computer programs DEREDEC and KWIC. Pécheux's (1969) criticism focused upon what he termed 'frequential deductions'. He claimed that statistical linguistics, such as it was, addressed a non-linguistic problematic relevant to a pre-Saussurean theoretical field, where the only concept relevant to the linguistic is 'that of the biunivocite of the relationship Sa/Se, which authorises noting the presence of the same content of thought each time the same sign appears' (1969:3), thereby fixing the irreducible polysemy of lexemes. Furthermore, that deduction does not take the organisation of text into consideration, how the text is organised in terms of relationships between its elements. That is, the effects of meaning which constitute the content of text are ignored. Evidently the lexicometric analysis, while revealing a particular type of relationship between elements, is a comparative method based on models rather than on isolated signs.

Similarly, Robin (1971) objected to what she called the 'isomorphism between socio-political and lexical groups'. She referred to the tendency for each political group to be referred to according to the specific use which it would make of certain words; that which is claimed of political groups is held to be valid for all *émetteurs*, thereby making the vocabulary a sort of labelling or ruled behaviour imposed on each type of producer of discourse. Marcellesi, following Prost, observed that 'one has to realise that in the circumscriptions of the right, a candidate of the left employs the words generally employed by the candidates of the right . . . the candidate is capable of holding different discourses' (1971:55). In his view, this form of statistical analysis was devoid of theoretical reflection and of the need to consider any lexical unit in terms of its context. Similarly, Pécheux sought to employ a statistical method as a feature of a methodology that destructured the formal surface by linking lexicals, syntax and the phenomena of enonciation within a statistical context.

The initial fascination with lexicometry which Pécheux revealed during the 1960s resurfaces at the beginning of the period of re-evaluation at the end of the 1970s and early 1980s, when a significant emphasis was placed on computer programming. Whereas in the early work of Pécheux and his colleagues, they did not resort to computer analysis of syntax, that being undertaken manually, the potential of resorting to computer analysis was evident by the 1980s (Lecomte et al., 1984). It was recognised that describing or reading texts constitutes material operations on words, enonces, sequences and any configuration which they compose. It was also recognised that the linear order of any series of enonces could be overturned in extracting constituent units and recomposing them according to other laws in a different space. This form of analysis was facilitated by the introduction of computer programming involving a morphological approach. This approach was employed to define a collection of 'manipulations' specified by the exigency of ruling these manipulations, operating on the base of formal references. Thus, one constructs the hypotheses which designate the lines of fracture and of cohesion which inform the intra-text and the reading. Certain of these manipulations were claimed to be sufficiently rule-based to justify the application of computer methods.

DEREDEC was the program chosen. It derived from the work of Plante (1981) written in LISP, which is particularly adept for symbolic treatment. The syntactic description constructs a series of hierarchical analyses of constituents of phrases of the text. That description facilitates a search for elements specified by certain categories of words in various positions. While the exploration of a text cannot precede its description, it is possible to integrate the two procedures, thereby leading to new descriptions.

The text is sorted into branches, which allows the coalescence of these branches to be joined, sorted and analysed and to be modified by earlier procedures. The objective is to describe in an exhaustive manner the lines which descend from general symbols (P, SN and SV in syntax) to lexical items. Plante's contribution was to consider an ascending approach in which he constructed the syntagmatic structures, step by step, starting from lexical items. This has the advantage of being less constraining. DEREDEC permitted the construction of descriptive grammars of texts and the simultaneous exploration of the systems of text via a homogeneous formalism – the two procedures involving the manipulated objects and the rules of manipulation are of the same syntax; these are the branches. The syntactic description constructs a set of hierarchical analyses of the constituents of the phrases of a text. That description permits an exploration of specific elements in relation to certain categories of words in any position. The descriptive grammars of texts and the procedures of exploration serve to put both descriptive function and exploratory functions in operation. While the exploration of a text cannot precede its description, it is possible to integrate the two procedures, thereby leading to new descriptions, as shown in the diagram.

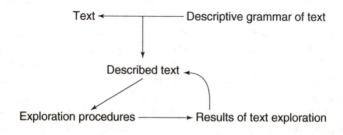

Source: Lecomte et al. (1984:148)

The text described can thereby enrich the information obtained in the course of the analysis. Reciprocally the enriched text can be submitted to further analysis by reference to descriptive grammar.

Lecomte *et al.* (1984) maintain that this program is particularly useful for the treatment of ambiguities. Recall that for Pécheux ambiguity was not the consequence of some imperfection of language, or something that related to the effect of a subject's intention. Rather, ambiguity was not only a question of language, but related to relations of power associated with non-subjective elements (Pécheux, 1979). Beginning with lexical items, the syntactic analyst proceeds, step by step, to build the structured syntagms by returning them to the nodal phrase that lies where the branches meet. If ambiguities are evident, the various analyses of the same series generates the various semantic possibilities.

Lexical items which exist at the nodes of the branches (the syntagmatic categories) are called EXFAD (expressions of forms that are admissible in being used for the description). EXFAL (expression of linked atomic forms), on the other hand, refers to information of a paradigmatic order, that is, those bits of information which do not depend upon any particular context in which they are found (e.g. the indication of genre or a substantive). Thus EXFAD gives a syntactic analysis of sequences, whereas EXFAL allows the introduction of information from the co-text in these sequences.

This leads to the possibility of relating various bits of information with any given item:

1   The lexical items with which it co-occurs in the textual proposition. This gives the item its discursive referent.
2   A sub-collection of these items, e.g. the syntagms which it determines. This gives the access to the discursive construction of the object that it denotes and the means of studying the impact of that determination on the construction of propositions.
3   The syntagms of which it is equivalent in the Harrisian sense. That is, those that appear in a lexically and syntactically identical context. This is very similar to what was undertaken in AAD69.

The information that derives from this analysis serves as the basis for textual exploration. This opens the practical possibility of considering a lexical item or an enonce in a text as a point in a list of formulations or of enonces. In confronting an element with what precedes or follows it in a text, one has access to the dynamic aspect of the intra-discourse. This may involve, for example, the manner in which a phrase is nominalised as in 'The Revolution has triumphed' becoming 'The triumph of the Revolution'. By sorting the limits of the phrase in this way, one can expect to obtain a better comprehension of the factors that concur in giving a discursive coherence. This may involve the condensation of earlier fragments, the stabilisation of co-references, etc.

The advantage of DEREDEC lies in its ability to integrate lexicality with certain enonciative processes outside of the syntactic dimension. Certain functional forms which are syntactically ambiguous are effected by a temporary category of the procedure of categorisation, prior to the application of syntactic analysis. The disambiguation of these categories – e.g. 'the' as an article, and 'the' as a pronoun – can be realised by the surface descriptive grammar (GDS) prior to syntagmatic regrouping. The GDS program binds the syntagmatic categories by the relation of contextual dependence. There are five relations of contextual dependence (RDC):

1   the *theme-propos* (TP), or relating theme, which binds all nominal non-propositional syntagms to the left of a conjugating verb in a proposition to the rest of that proposition;
2   the two relations of 'development of relations' (P1 and P2) corresponding to the complement of the verb;
3   the relation of 'determination' (DET), regrouping the nominal complex groups, or a relative and its antecedents;
4   the relation of 'coordination' (CO), which binds the enumerations or the coordinating propositions.

In the case of a structural possibility of ambiguity in the analysis of constituents, the GDS generates two relations of RDC. Thus in the phrase given as an example in Lecomte *et al.* (1984:149), 'J'ai voulu faire insérer un article dans un journal régional pour la continuation de la peine de mort' (see p. 236), GDS generates two relations from the syntagm 'pour le continuation de la peine de mort':

1   DET? binds that syntagm to 'dans un journal regional' (cf. 'un journal pour la continuation de la peine de mort');
2   P2? binds that syntagm to 'insérer' (cf. 'insérer un article pour la continuation'); 'pour la continuation' is then considered as a circumstantial complement.

In the same way, from the syntagm 'dans un journal regional', GDS generates the following relations of contextual dependence:

1   DET? binds that syntagm to 'un article' (cf. 'un article dans un journal');
2   P2? binds that syntagm to 'insérer' (cf. 'insérer dans un journal').

The presence of the question mark (DET?) is an indication that two relations coexist: one being the complement of the verb (P1?, P2? or P1 P2?, here P2?), the other being indeterminate (DET?). This possibility has the advantage of not presupposing the unity of syntactical analysis. In not reducing the ambiguity, it leaves a number of strategies of disambiguity open. In effect the

234

Source: Lecomte *et al.* (1984:149)

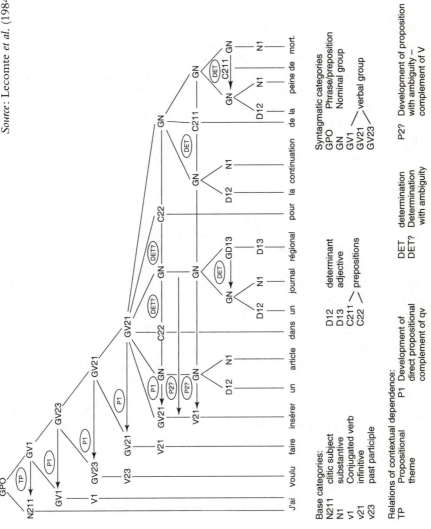

Base categories:
N211 clitic subject
N1   substantive
V1   Conjugated verb
v21   infinitive
v23   past participle

D12   determinant
D13   adjective
C211 ⟩ prepositions
C22   ⟩

Syntagmatic categories
GPO   Phrase/preposition
GN   Nominal group
GV1   ⟩
GV21 ⟩ verbal group
GV23 ⟩

Relations of contextual dependence:
TP   Propositional   P1 Development of
     theme   direct propositional
                          complement of qv

DET   determination
DET? Determination
      with ambiguity

P2? Development of proposition
     with ambiguity –
     complement of V

analysis is not stopped, and the terms of the ambiguity remain explicit and retrievable to a treatment introducing new parameters. Recalling that GDS operates in the same way in the case of atypical phrases, if the grammar does not succeed in constructing an analysis for a given phrase, it stores that phrase and continues to analyse the other sequences.

It is these properties of DEREDEC which make it very appropriate for the morphological description of discourse (Pécheux, 1982b; Marandin, 1983; Lecomte and Marandin, 1984). It was this method which permitted progress beyond what was achieved in AAD69 (Pécheux, 1969), while allowing a textual approach which did not reduce to a single level of structuration. Thus the problem that existed in AAD69, where the procedures did not relate to the syntagms of constituents of propositions (SN or SV, with a factual primacy given to SN) in generating the zones of lexical substitution and in approaching the phenomena of determination, is resolved. That reductive approach characterised the analysis of discourse which was rejected. Instead, DEREDEC permitted the planning of the descriptive montages informing the texts.

It is recognised that relying solely on the syntactic dimension is not sufficient for the study of the linguistic materiality of a text. The description of forms of enonciation, of forms of lexemes and of forms of sequentiality has to be constructed within the discourse-analysis perspective. Furthermore, a textual description should not be confused with an analysis which reduces in isolation, it must relate to a type of functioning which would be representative of discursive function (syntax, enonciation, lexis, etc.). The description of such a complex object involves a multiplication of descriptive perspectives, and DEREDEC leaves open the possibility of diverse approaches, and of serving to enrich the description. This multiplicity of descriptive viewpoints is not only induced by the complexity of the object, but similarly by the suggestions of textual description (Todorov, 1983). If all description involves interpretation – for example, if all morphology is already placed in a reading – then a description cannot be univocal. Recognising the irreducible heterogeneity of levels of structuration of language, and their destratifying nodes in discourse, means that the plurivocality of these descriptive points of view is essential.

In this respect the self-criticism of AAD69 was taken on board. It involved the claim that AD was little more than a detour which always returned to a concern with the discursive externality of conditions of production, situation of enonciation, or the history of ideas which were mobilised in order to close a corpus. This criticism is justified when one considers the effect of an interpretative discourse on a particular corpus, and it underlines the difficulty encountered by AD in disengaging its knowledges – *langue*, the history or the science – which it reassembles, 'articulates' and projects onto the texts.

It was the absence of a syntactic analysis side by side with enonciative analysis which frustrated the computer analysis of discourse, since it severely restricted the description of corpus and, indeed, limited description to a restrained corpus which was claimed to be representative of a larger corpus. It was argued that syntactic analysis should not be conceived of as a perfect isolated world which warranted priority, as was the case in AAD69 with reference to the work of Chomsky, but should be understood as a provisional phase where it was possible to change the terms in function of use in textual description, and to enrich the analyses by refinement.

The duality of structures associated with the EXFAD and EXFAL distinction between the syntactic analysis of sequences and the introduction of information about co-texts, coupled with the syntax of exploratory models, opens the possibility of considering a lexical item or an enonce in a given text as a point in a system of formulations of enonces. It allows the confrontation of a textual sequence at each one of its points in relation to what precedes and follows it, and within a strategy of constructed co-text, with the sequences pertaining to other texts. This is crucial for FDA. The description of texts or of sets of enonces invariably involves reference to more than the material that is available for analysis, with the consequence that the non-material must somehow be explained. Lecomte *et al.* (1984) dismissed Ducrot's argumentation, Bellert's inference, and the pragmatic reference to some semblance of 'truth' within a universe of belief as an acceptable basis for the reconstruction of that non-material because of the constant reference to the consciousness of the co-enonciateurs. That is, what they referred to as 'that omnipresence of the subject' (1984:158) is staunchly rejected. Rather they claim that DEREDEC offers the possibility of discovering the absent enonces in the interpretation or the reading of the co-enonciateurs because it is inscribed in the interdiscourse, it is to be found in establishing the traces.

In pursuing this objective they referred to exploratory models. This involved establishing the syntactic and discursive constraints on lexical items, and discovering the propositions where there is an explicit referencing of person in order to 'demagnify' the textual sequence under consideration in terms of its enonciation. The syntax of exploratory models allowed a combination of the syntactically relevant characterisitcs – lexic, co-occurrence and relevance to a paradigm. This corresponds to the morphological approach of discourse analysis in establishing the configuration of elements pertaining to the different levels of language. Such configurations were observable via DEREDEC and were referred to as 'forms', defined as the units that integrate the formal constituents of language which are distributed in a ruled form in the thread of discourse.

Recovering the phrastic domain via textual description (DDT) does not imply that this description is closed. Exfalisation introduces the co-text in the phrase, which is the first step towards opening the phrastic boundaries. The sequence was perceived of as a dynamic space where reformulation and transformation took place. Using DEREDEC Lecomte *et al.* (1984) sought to place all of the phenomena which they isolated in relation to their precedent and consequent, and to work on sequential units larger than the phrase, where the phrase boundaries are one element among others.

This play on the frontiers or boundaries of the phrastic domain corresponds to the questions 'What is it that makes a sequence?' and 'How is that effect whereby the formulations are grouped realised in a discursive surface?' In this respect they were focusing upon intra-discourse and how the homogenisation of a series of constituents is operated by various links between, for example, anaphorisation, co-reference and deixis. The anaphor and the cataphor lend coherence to a sequence which gives stability at the interior of the discourse; the deictics pertain to how a sequence is designated as relating to an object of discourse; and co-reference constructs a stratification of the sequence in terms of which certain matching expressions operate in abstracting or condensing a collection of earlier formulations and are put in position of reference to an object of discourse.

Again it was Courtine (1981) who employed the DEREDEC program in order to articulate thematisation and determination by distinguishing between different collections of lexemes in terms of syntactic, thematised and determinate categories. The corpus of this influential work consisted of a speech delivered by Georges Marchais at Lyon in 1976 on the subject of Christians. From Courtine's analysis the following groupings of frequency emerged:

L1: plain lexemes (nouns, verbs, adjectives), 3,251 entries;
L2: plain theoretised lexemes, 303 entries;
L3: plain propositional lexemes (21), 2,134 entries;
L4: nominal thematised lexemes, 248 entries;
L5: determinate nominal lexemes, 437 entries;
L6: plain form lexemes that determine the nominal, 1,236 entries.

This distribution allowed him to establish comparisons. Thus, for example, by selecting the elements of L4 with five or more occurrences he came up with eight nouns (Christian, Communists, crisis, French, France, party, country, people). He then considered the use of these eight nouns within L5 and discovered that some of the thematised lexemes were weakly determined: People, Christians, France, Communists. On the other hand, taking those nominals which were listed under L4 which appeared most often in the form of a determinate nominal, he discovered that some of them were weakly thematised: Class, Democracy, World, Union, Life. This analysis led Courtine to state, with reference to the complementary distribution of the nominals, that:

> Certain nominals, while often thematised, are infrequently determined; notions such as 'the people', 'the Christians', 'France', 'the Communists' which frequently occur in thematic positions, are not determined; 'one knows that which it is', one can in speaking, in making a theme of his/her discourse, because 'there he goes'. These notions . . . are saturated by the ideological consensus that stabilises their reference: within French political discourse they realise a

veritable lexical intersection between the forms of lexical organisation and the construction of the reference of words proper to different, and eventually, antagonistic discourses.

The highly determined and little-thematised nouns, the words which have to be explained, are opposed to these active notions:

- the words of party vocabulary: the class ('working', 'exploited'), democracy ('political', 'modern', 'socialist'), etc.;
- the words which the common language has reinterpreted: the world ('better', 'of tomorrow'), the life ('very fair', 'very free').

Thus he singles out different zones of vocabulary in terms of the function of their stability:

- that of discursive neutralisation where the words are placed in the form of a consensus which gives the same meaning for everyone;
- that of the closure of a knowledge, where the meaning of a word is strictly defined;
- that where contradiction appears, where meaning is at stake.

Evidently Courtine's study insisted on the importance of phenomena of determination. The analysis of key terms has tended to operate on nouns without reference to their determination, the emphasis being placed upon the definite/indefinite opposition. There is no doubt that this is of some relevance in that the process of referencing plays a not inconsiderable role in the construction of a discursive universe. None the less, Courtine's work clearly demonstrates that the relationship between thematisation and nominal expansion makes the consideration of determinants of central importance.

It is not easy to define the status of the nominal groups which are referentially 'saturated' (**'the** crisis', **'the** free countries'). They are presented as self-evident, being located in a vast interdiscourse which assures their pre-constructed form. None the less, they do touch upon the problematic of proper nouns. While it is possible to claim that the definite article conveys a presupposition of existence and unity which the destinataire knows, this is insufficient reason to ascribe a referential status to, for example, 'the communists' in a Communist text.

In AAD69, the syntactic analysis was undertaken manually. Resorting to computer analysis for this work served to transform the approach to discourse analysis. Clearly the strategy of description depends upon how the potential of the computer is exploited. Those working within FDA were able to blend that potential with the methodological requirements of their theoretical principal in a way that was of immense advantage. It allowed them to construct a particular descriptive grammar while analysing texts with a homogeneous formalism.

239

I would now like to shift from this emphasis on the empirical analysis which has been of so much value for distributionalism and lexicology, to a consideration of the logical connectors which organise this distribution. In so doing, I will draw on Achard's (1992) recent discussion of anaphora and how it can be treated in terms of deixis. This overview, selective though it may be, will help in demonstrating how FDA demands a fundamental reorientation in shifting the emphasis from the situation to the discursive and to a focus upon enonciation. It will help to demonstrate how the focus is on the importance of enonciation in relation to the recovery of prior discourse within heterogeneity.

Anaphora and deixis

In the preceding chapter we suggested that certain morphemes which were central to deictics were ambiguous out of context, and that they could function either as anaphoric or as situational decitics. In this section, I would like to focus specifically upon anaphora and deixis. In some respects there is a similarity between argumentation and anaphora in that both relate to clauses which are usually linked by connectors. Anaphorics are elements recovering another segment of discourse. Thus in 'Fred is nasty, he stole my book', 'he' is the substitute for 'Fred' to the extent that it replaces a second occurrence of 'Fred' which makes the same referent and would be the same morpheme as the first 'Fred'. One can state that 'he' has 'Fred' as a discursive referent, an earlier lexical unit appearing in the same text. One speaks of co-reference in designating the fact that, in the same discursive universe, several linguistic units have the same referent – the problems raised by anaphors bring a number of complex semantic and syntactic phenomena into play. It is possible to anaphorise one substantive with another, e.g. 'Eric Cantona is transferred . . . The footballer has left the club' where 'The footballer' is an anaphor of 'Eric Cantona'. A single substantive can recover a series of phrases. Anaphorisation also induces the possibility of making this or that affirmation acceptable. It would appear that there are discursive constraints which regulate that genre of phenomena. The possibility or the impossibility of a particular anaphorisation is determined by the type of discourse involved. Thus, for example, 'the Palestine commando' could be anaphorised as 'the terrorists' or 'the revolutionary fighters', or 'the group of extremists'. Thus the signification of the anaphor cannot be correctly disengaged without taking the discourse in which it is inserted into consideration. Evidently anaphorisations are numerous and omnipresent in interpretative relations, and to a great extent they furnish the coherent weave that assures the unity of texts. Pécheux (1982a:117–118) pays particular attention to the importance of co-reference, and specifically anaphora, for interdiscursivity.

Achard (1992) builds on this understanding of anaphora in offering an interesting discussion of the relationship between anaphora and deixis. He claims that it is customary to relate anaphora to context, and deixis to situation, but in so doing a number of exceptions are left to be explained. Thus the anaphoric use of deixis is interpreted as pointing towards the object already mentioned, such that it figures in the situation and not in the discourse. 'Textual deixis' is similarly explained – the discourse is not relevant beyond the world, an attempt is made to reveal that which was meant to be said, with reference not to context, but to the object in the situation. This discussion in turn relates to a confusion over whether anaphora and deixis are the same, or whether they are only the same in certain cases. As we shall see, Achard attempts to avoid the tendency to take the situation in question as a real situation, and the context as a real context, while also seeking to avoid the tendency to confuse situation and context.

The focus of Achard's discussion is the anaphoric return, where there is no recalculation of the referential value. Deixis, on the other hand, is taken to involve the anchoring of reference from the point of view of the origin of the enonciation. However, not all referential processes are deictic since they can be achieved through description. Deixis, as we have seen, involves a referential calculus. Thus, with reference to time, the series 'today', 'yesterday', 'tomorrow' speaks from a relatively general time while anchoring the reference. On the other hand, '23 April 1989 at 2.30 p.m.' is fixed in a much more absolute space. The anaphor in terms of time is possible, and one can ignore deictic markers such as 'at that moment'. Taking the context as not being external to the situation leads to an account in terms of time being obliged to relate to the unwinding of the enonciation. This creates relations between the time of the unfolding of the discourse and the referred time, albeit that this varies according to the discursive genre.

A further point is made concerning referencing and time. In accounts of events, there is a tendency to assume that the order of enonces relates to events; that is, there is a correspondence between the time period of the enonciation and the reference time, even if this can be presented in diverse ways. The continuing correspondence between the referred tense and the unfolding of the enonciation thus precludes the possibility of a temporal anaphor, as in the following example cited by Achard:

the 5th of June he rose early, but during the course of the following week one did not see him leaving his home before the beginning of the afternoon. That day there, he had a splendid time.

'That day there' is to be interpreted directly and not anaphorically (June 5th). Furthermore, the recourse to the temporal deixis has the effect of changing the relationship between context and situation. The account ensures the continuity of correspondence between the series of described processes and the succession of enonces, while the temporal deixis serves to attach one to the other at a precise point.

He then proceeds to a consideration of the connectors 'then' and 'now'. It is tempting to consider 'then' as a temporal anaphor where it refers to a reference constructed in an earlier context. On the other hand, the dictionary sense of 'at that moment there' leads to a deictic interpretation:

He has attended the arrival of a sailor, who then commanded the Saturn.

The effect of meaning is not restricted to the recovery of the temporal reference, that is, of the anaphoric effect, but serves to rupture the continuity of the enonciation.

This temporal use of 'then' reveals that the time duration of the enonciation is locked in a problematic relation with the time reference. The enonciation is punctual whereas the time reference can be extended. In the course of the unfolding of the discourse, the problem of the continuity of the enonciation constantly arises, and involves the extent to which a new enonce derives from the same formal origin of the enonciation, rather than from the preceding enonce. If we suppress the word 'then' in the above example, we have:

He had attended the arrival of a sailor, who commanded the Saturn.

While this has no bearing on the account in terms of sequence, it does serve to indicate how 'then' marks the existence of a deviation between the origin of a point of view and the real enonciation. In the case of the present tense, 'then' forces the narrative value of the enonce by signalling the splitting of the situation:

He attends the arrival of a sailor, who then commanded the Saturn.

Thus 'then' cannot be interpreted as an anaphor and yet its deictic interpretation is not entirely satisfactory.

It is at this point that Achard makes the innovative claim that the functioning of 'then'

rests on a very complex relationship: it is the trace of an operator assigned for the effect of closing the earlier temporal context while discussing within that situation.

This hypothesis has the advantage of easily unifying the two domains of the use of 'then', the temporal 'then' and the logical 'then'. The difference does not rely on the functioning of 'then', but rather on the discursive genre.

An account is a genre characterised by the provisional forgetting of the situation of the enonciative situation, giving way to a displaced vantage point. Thus the operator 'then' intervenes in simplifying the anaphor – it breaks the continuity of the discourse and integrates that earlier context as a description of the displaced situation. This corresponds to what has been referred to as 'point of view'.

The same applies to the logical 'then', but this time with reference to the 'argumentation' discursive genre. Here the origin of the point of view co-incides with the origin of the enonciation, while the opposition between the enonciateur and the enonciataire is neutralised with reference to responsibility, or taking charge. It serves to convince the returning interlocuteur, in linguistic terms, to construct the discourse in such a way as to induce the enonciataire to appear as the one in charge of the enonce.

Thus the intervention of 'then', which returns the earlier enonces to 'context' in the 'situation', has the consequence, in that genre, of not having much value in that discourse, but of asserting value in a prior discourse. The status passes from supposed to presupposed. Thus it acquires the status of fact, presupposing a common consensus among enonciateurs. It passes from the modality of assertion to that of proven. Clearly this unification of the two uses of 'then' demonstrates that its intervention relates not merely to the temporal element, but also to the collection of modal elements.

'Then' is often paraphrased as 'there at that moment' but it cannot be substituted for 'now' without altering the argumentation:

> He attended the arrival of a sailor, who commanded there at that moment the Saturn.
> He attended the arrival of a sailor, who now commands the Saturn.

In the first sentence, it is presupposed that at some future moment the sailor in question has ceased to command the Saturn, while in the second there is the presupposition that he did not always command the Saturn.

However, it is conceivable that 'then' and 'now' can be placed as opposites, as in:

> That man, who is now a hurdy gurdy player, was then a healthy young man.

or as substitutable, as in mathematical equations:

Given the equation $x^2 - 2x + 1 = 0$
Knowing that $x' = x - 1$ and $x = x' + 1$
One then has (now has) $x'^2 = 0$

Achard concludes with reference to 'then' and 'now' that the latter does not introduce a break in the enonciation, and does not return the context to the situation, this being valid for all uses of 'now'. It is conceivable that 'now' introduces a break without returning the context to the situation, in which case it leads to an argumentative orientation in which the reader is offered another term which is constructed by the text. 'Now' signals that the enonciation in process is to be judged in relationship to the existence of an alternative enonciation which is not yet realised.

If 'now' is opposed to 'then', it is as the future to the past rather than as the present to the past. 'Then' takes the action of an earlier context as acquired, whereas 'now' problematises the posterior context in relationship to an alternative possible position. This alternative possible position can be situated in relationship to the enonciation, or in relation to a point of view.

Much as the temporal and logical uses of 'then' can be interpretated by the structure of discourse rather than in terms of different functions, the preferential temporal interpretation of 'now' relates to the priority of time over aspect, and to the other modalities in the imaginary of the language. This priority is to be placed in relation to the fact that the 'spontaneous' representation of semantics privileges absolute referential process in relation to deictic referential processes. The tense can be taken as an adjacent collection that is useful for rendering an account of aspect, a deictic account phenomenon concerning the relationship between the process and the situation, involving sufficiently abstract terms of closure. Once again the modal dimensions appear as highly abstract, to the extent that they reveal the formalism rather than the aspect, while being unable to mobilise the adjacent dimension of tense.

'Now' is then the minimal operator signalling the virtual existence of an alternative enonciative situation. 'Then', on the other hand, gives an earlier context the value of an alternative situation, one which underlines the case where the two operators are discursively contrasted. To the extent that an occurrence of 'now' signals the existence of a possible alternative enonciation, a principle of discursive economy identifies the enonciation prior to the enonciation opened by 'now'.

In an earlier work, Achard (1980a) formulated the hypothesis which claimed that the situation can be formalised by reference to the notion of 'refraction of the enonciateur'. Thus all novel modalities introduced in the discourse return to the placing of displaced images of the formal apparatus of the enonciation in the description of the situation. These are maintained by the relationships which depend on the unfolding of the discourse and of operators which are assigned to put them in place.

This observation leads to interpreting modalities in terms of discourse relationships rather than in terms of rational actors associated with the interpersonal function of language. Thus in:

He attends the arrival of a sailor, who now commands the Saturn.

one would be led to consider the functioning of 'now' from the point of the refracted enonciateur who is at the point of origin of the point of view. Thus the formal apparatus of the enonciation plays the role of a reference, and the unfolding of discourse situates the referents in relationship to that reference, while engendering other references which are articulated on the first, or displacing the first reference in the discursive universe that is already in place.

Thus the lexical items can be divided in two – the terms which are traces of operators calculable from the point of the enonciative reference, and those which are carriers of more or less stable descriptions in terms of predication. The former constitute a closed class and a regular function which, according to Achard, principally characterise the linguistic dimensions of semantics.

Conclusion

It should be evident that, with reference to discourse, the dictionary plays a limited role in semantics. This is because the lexicon of a language cannot be considered independently of the ideologies that circulate at the interior of society. The value of a word in a discursive formation cannot be established through recourse to a dictionary.

This evidently involves the relationship between language and discourse. That which we call language crosses multiple discourses and cannot be reduced to the situation where locuteurs of different status have variable access to the lexicon. Discourse analysis is resigned to having to go beyond the dictionary, even though the existence of the dictionary as discourse cannot be denied. It also resigns itself to a space of relative semantic uniformity, which Marandin (1979a), as if referring to the normative effect of the discourse of language standardisation, refers to as a 'national discourse' where 'each entry constitutes a consistent collection of statements, a source of the discursive formation where they are produced and in some way "naturalised"'. This collection of statements consists of enonces 'defining' a term, constituting a particular type of preconstructed: 'a preconstructed assimilated to the same existence of the national language' (Marandin, 1979a:55). However, it involves far more than ascertaining how a given discursive formation constructs its proper space across the virtualities of language. It also relates to the pressure of the interdiscursive, which narrowly constrains the interaction between the linguistic and the discursive.

There is also the argument that the meaning of words is not entirely determined by ideological positions, but that the semantics of the language also intervene in a forceful way. Thus the use of substantives can signify that their associates are the dictionaries of language. Some words have certain virtualities in language, and their efficacy should be respected. Thus in an electoral discourse with very little interdiscursive penetration that is addressed to a specific audience, meanings tend to be fixed. The conventional term for this genre of production is 'programme'. Marandin came to a similar conclusion with reference to the use of 'paysan' in the opening chapter of a book on China by Peyrefitte, *Quand la Chine*:

The collection of statements within which these statements are constructed seem to be the same as the collection of statements on which the article 'paysan' is constructed in the *Grand Robert* and the *Grand Larousse de la Langue Française* . . . *Quand la Chine* is a form of system of expansion of that minimal system of phrases. One could say that the dictionary entry 'paysan' in the French national dictionary constitutes the 'situation' decreed by Peyrefitte's text (generated some distance from China!).

(Marandin, 1979:75)

Such a coincidence is not devoid of meaning. Peyrefitte's statement exists within the circle of a culture, of a preconstructed, crystallised in the dictionary. The reader retrieves that preconstructed via the illusion of an exotic detour, which confers a particular authority on the text.

None the less, it is difficult to accept such a conformity between language and discourse when one considers cases where meaning does not enjoy such a direct relationship with language. Thus, for words such as 'socialism', 'liberty', 'democracy', for example, the dictionary is of limited value, and recourse to the political interdiscourse is essential in order to circumscribe their value. Furthermore, these are the privileged words in any consideration of key terms since they open directly onto the doctrinal content. Key words which relate to certain discursive positions hold an antagonistic position in systematically avoiding any marking of the discursive position's alteration. Thus a key word may display a positive register, with each substantive with which it is associated *ipso facto* affecting a positive status. Clearly, in any competing discourse, this key word would have to pass into a negative register that would completely modify the value of the term. A linguistic analysis pure and simple would be unable to reveal this process.

Evidently the interdiscursive dimension plays an important role in the use of vocabulary. To enonce certain signifiers is to signify the place from which one speaks, it is also to signify the place from which one does not speak, that from which one could not under any circumstance speak. A word does not appear as a projection of that which a group 'would wish to say', or as the medium of expressing a doctrine, which, as the result of negotiation, always has to be understood as involving diverse constraints, across a space that is saturated with signs.

Vocabulary is situated at the crossroads of multiple instances, of the enonciative display of modes of textual cohesion associated with the inter-discourse. Discourse analysis aims to give access to that complexity. However, the 'tone' of the legitimate enonciateur, its 'character' and the genre of requisite enonciative stages are also relevant, thereby leading one from lexi-cology to a global semantics capable of integrating the diverse dimensions of discursivity. It is not necessarily the case that these assume the same dependence with reference to the same system of semantic constraints, but none of these elements lies outside of a pertinent analysis.

In a recent discussion of the importance of Culioli's work, Milner (1992) has emphasised that Culioli has discovered a phenomenon not recognised by syntactic theory. Syntactic theory does not take the 'incorrect' predicate into consideration, and refuses to consider the 'unacceptable' predicate. In contrast, enonciative linguistics claims that the discriminating predicate does not change, but rather it is the entity to which one applies the predicate which changes. In this sense the reference is not to a phrase, but to an enonce that changes. Enonciative linguistics focuses on the paraphrase or the quasi-paraphrase, where the paradigms are the paraphrastic or quasi-paraphrastic classes, rather than on the syntactic paradigmatic relations. Thus the FDA approach to distributionalism and lexicology drifts away from the orthodox linguistic approach. Milner states that from a strictly descriptive point of view, the relation between lexis, enonce and the quasi-paraphrase is clear – the lexis permits the capturing of common properties of members of a quasi-paraphrastic paradigm, while the enonce permits the seizing of the differential properties. Conversely, with reference to lexically and morphologically identical material, all the enonces obtainable by calculable combinations of enonciative operations starting from the same lexis are in a relation of quasi-paraphrase.

Since the theory of the enonce and of enonciative operations deals with differential properties, it recovers part of the functions which other perspectives fix in the theory of the lexis. However, it is also evident that it is incorrect to speak of a theory of the lexis, and that the theory of the enonce and of enonciative operators overturns the orthodox delimitation between syntax and lexicon. Milner offers the following argument:

1 the members of a paradigm, (i), are distinguished from one another by reference to different enonces;
2 an enonce is distinguished from another by the enonciative operations that it puts in play;
3 there are lexico-morphological materials which contribute to distinguish certain members of (i).

He thus concludes that there are lexico-morphological material whose presence is the effect of an enonciative operation. In contrast, the theory of the lexis recovers part of the functions of the syntactic structure, but in a much more complex way, and their representations are more abstract than in other linguistic theories. Clearly, enonciative linguistics does not negate syntactic theory, it merely addresses other things.

A new system of representation is not only preferable, but necessary. The differential predicate used by syntactic and enonciative theory are fundamentally the same, thus the new system should integrate certain results from earlier theories. Grammatical analysis or syntactic analysis is nothing other than a manner of treating syntax. It involves the hypothesis that the attribution of a 'badly formed' global predicate is justifiable on the base of the resolution of the entity predicated in segments, to which a nature is attributed. Assuming that the attribution of the 'badly formed' predicate to an entity of language depends upon the nature of the segments that constitute the sub-parts of that entity, it is presumed that the syntax rests on an analysis. Reciprocally, that analysis is called syntactic. The nature of a segment of language is held to be the object of that which one generally calls grammar. Thus the nature of segments of language is grammatical by definition. Consequently, the analysis is referred to as grammatical rather than syntactic. Enonciative linguistics refers to other things which are not treated by recourse to a judgment of analysis of the order of 'that segment to that nature'. In other words, it does not rest on an analysis. Therefore, it does not propose a procedure of analysis, nor does it construct a list of acceptable grammatical possibilities. However, the enonciative linguist can set the limits to recover that which has been established earlier by other theories, including notions of the type 'nominal group', 'subject', 'accord', 'singular', 'plural'. Evidently the theoreticians and the practitioners of enonciative linguistics must examine their terminology closely and determine where there is synonymy or homonymy between their notions and notions which appear in syntactic theory. Again we find the debate shifting in the direction of the relationship between problematic and concepts.

Milner proceeds to make the point that all formalist linguistics revolves around a paradigm of analysis which is of little value to FDA. In a sense this point is much like that which one could make concerning language planning, or indeed any kind of planning, since it is premised on the idea of rational subjects who can draw upon their reason as clairvoyants capable of predicting the future. In this respect, what Milner is warning against is the danger of incorporating a kind of logical formalism into FDA, simply in order to sustain a logical elegance. In all formalised theory, the lexis is treated as a minimal formal entity which is inserted in the form of a linear and ordered suite of abstract positions, represented by symbols. However, neither those positions nor the symbols have a separate existence. Any lexical item is obtained through the working of an operator on the initial suite. Thus it is possible to claim that these suites are ordered in lines of derivation, the lexis being the 0 line, a particular lexis, line 1, etc. Thus, what the theory calls operators are those entities which facilitate the passing from one line to another according to an order which is both linear and intrusive. The extrinsic is entirely missing.

To claim that the lexis is the minimal formal entity is merely to restate, in another way, the claim that the theory is not an analysis. In effect, the 'parts' of the lexis cannot be put in a simple and direct relation with the constituent parts of any configuration of natural language. Milner's point is that if one considers the 'parts' of the lexis, they exist in non-geometric positions and are unable to respond directly to the question of the place occupied by any unit recognisable by lexico-morphology. If one considers a collection of lexis, they do not have the ability to allocate status to a maximal syntagm that one calls proposition or phrase.

248

One can say then that in enonciative theory, there are no apparent limits of effacement and of adjunctions of the formal entities of the theory. This situation is reversed with reference to lexico-morphology. While one does not insert lexical entities, neither does one suppress them. That is, to treat a given enonce, the enonciative linguist works on constant lexico-morphological material.

That material constitutes the highly visible, which Chomsky refers to as the surface structure. Thus we conclude that in enonciative linguistics the observable surface configuration of an enonce X only feebly reflects the structural configuration of X. This is easily explained since the structural configuration has the function of explaining the enonciative properties of X and not of representing an analysis of X. The enonciative properties permit an explanation of certain observable characteristics, but only by reference to some critical points, irreducible to that which could grasp a syntactic analysis of X, which has its own explicit order. The distance between surface structure and enonciative structure, referred to as a 'folding', can be considerable, certainly greater than Chomsky's difference between deep and surface structure. It exists in order to emphasise that the structural configuration which is expressed in terms of operations is highly stratified and considerably more diversified than the surface configuration. However, the enonces themselves are also an observable form, constituted by lexico-morphological material. In contrast to most syntactic theories, where the focus is on the relation between a lexical entity and a position, enonciative linguistics insists that the lexico-morpho-logical material is treated as an effect, as a perceptible trace of enonciative operations. As such, lexico-morphological material comes under the juris-diction of enonciative linguistics, being part of the objects that it treats. Any lexico-morphological entity is the trace of enonciative operations.

It should be evident that FDA has a quite different approach to lexicology and distributionalism than that presented in orthodox linguistics. I shall return to this difference in the concluding chapter. For the moment, I would like to present, in an elementary form, some of the methodological approaches used in FDA.

8

METHODOLOGICAL ISSUES

Post-structuralism and method

It is essential to recognise the point made by Pécheux early in his career, that within modernism methodology plays a very specific role. The discussion of problematic in Chapter 3 makes it clear that within orthodox epistemology there is a link between theory, concepts and measurement or conceptual implementation, even if many social scientists lean towards a methodological eclecticism. The epistemological imperative involves an essentialism wherein the general conception of object is an entity, the effects of which are given in its concept. This, in turn, links with a realism involving a claim for the existence of a reality that exists independently of discourse. Frequently, it also integrates truth and reality, where truth is the correspondence of thought and reality. Thus the role of methodology is to enable the analyst to achieve closer proximity to truth and reality. Thought is materially and formally separated from truth. Deleuze (1964:115–116) states: 'From a certain point of view, the research on truth is natural and very easy; it merely requires a decision and a method capable of overcoming the external influences which cast aside thought from its vocation and it takes the false for the true'. He (Deleuze, 1968) has argued for separating sense and non-sense from truth and reality on the grounds that, instead of treating truth as the highest order, it is necessary to introduce differences within truth between the basic truth of exact recognition, and the high truth of the positions of problems. He argues that submitting the truth/reality dichotomy to the same criteria as the true/false dichotomy is to introduce different levels into the element of truth or the true/false distinction. The thought object is less a discovery than a recognition of an externality which is presupposed and thereby achieves a form of transcendence. The model of recognition is where the idea of adequacy appears, presupposing the pre-existence of an object which thought places at the same level. At a higher level, 'truth' qualifies the act of positioning a problem, while 'false' no longer designates a missing recognition or a false proposition, but a non-sense or false problem, which corresponds to a state that is not an error, but a stupidity. Thus he concludes that 'truth is not the element of truth. The element of thought is the meaning and the value' (Deleuze, 1962).

250

Clearly, the denial of modernist epistemological principles in post-structuralism gives method a quite different function. The objective is no longer the revelation of truth, and the focus shifts to the issue of meaning. Thus methodological issues relate to the resolution of ambiguity in the construction of meaning, to the possibilities of meaning, and to the effects of meaning. In this respect it seeks to resort to techniques which will be of assistance in highlighting the issues inherent in the construction of meaning. The focus is not on the possible and the impossible of orthodox linguistics, with its preoccupation with the grammatical, but on the forbidden, the probable and the improbable; on the effect of operation in specific situations, rather than their link to principles and possible situations. The objective is a consideration of the local organisation of a particular discourse. It is perhaps for this reason that the range of methodological techniques in FDA is broad.

There is also the issue of the relationship between the investigator as subject and that which is studied as object, or even of the actor as subject (Boltanski, 1990:55–57). As we have maintained more than once in the preceding reflections upon the customary sociological position vis-à-vis language, there is a tendency for the investigator or the sociologist to be ignored, as also is her/his role in discourse relative to the language of sociology as discourse. In modernist sociology, this relationship involves agents who tend to be treated as if they held stable attributes, with inscribed dispositions, capable of engendering objective, unconscious intentions which are deployed to explain their action. An asymmetry is maintained between researcher and actor, with the researcher having access to the legitimacy of science.

Thus, those who look to a book such as this one, or even a chapter such as this one, in order to encounter a method which they can attach to their existing battery of methodological techniques for the analysis of discourse will be disappointed. Indeed, such a quest for a methodological blueprint assumes a particular relevance in much of sociolinguistics. It is the consequence of a tendency to focus upon the analysis of language, with little reference to, nor interest in, philosophy and theory.

It should be evident that much of the emphasis in FDA is on methodological issues, and relates to those problems which are thrown up by the consideration of theoretical positions that relate to the construction of meaning. It is also evident that the methodology itself has a dynamic quality, and cannot be seen as a static blueprint which will facilitate analysis. This link between theory and method is sometimes lost on those who, in considering discourse analysis, for want of any alternative, resort to ethnomethodological work after a consideration of the theoretical concerns of post-structuralism. They fail to recognise that methodological issues address specific theoretical problems associated with particular philosophical positions. Thus, it is not to be expected that the ethnomethodological emphasis upon the phenomenological, with its particular reference to the rational subject within interaction and communication, will generate the same methodological perspective as FDA. On the other hand, this link between theory and method is by no means clear cut and, as I shall discuss in the concluding chapter, there is a tendency for both materialist and idealist positions to resort to similar linguistic processes in their discussion of how meaning takes its effect. Perhaps this is the starting point of our discussion.

It should be clear that Foucault served as a major influence on FDA despite his seeming reluctance to enter into the technical debate surrounding language and discourse. What he did do was to develop a perspective from which discourse analysis was possible. In this respect he emphasised the need to annul that which 'naturalises' any discourse by a process of 'reversing'. This involves denying the explanation of the centred author and the discipline or the will to truth, by 'recognising the negative play of a dissection and of a rarefaction of discourse' (Foucault, 1971:54). It also involves discontinuity. Rather than searching for coherence in 'a great unlimited, discourse, ceaseless and silent which finds itself . . . repressed or suppressed' (Foucault, 1971:54), one should treat discourse as 'discontinuous practices which cross, sometimes playing, but also ignoring and excluding'. In this respect he is close to some of Bakhtin's ideas on dialogism. He also refers to 'specificity' in terms of the rejection of 'the disorder of discourse in a play of previous signification', which, in contrast, is conceived of as 'a violence which we do to things, always treating them as a practice which we impose on them; and it is in that practice that the events of discourse assume their principle of regularity' (Foucault, 1971:55). This specificity is the non-transparency of language that imposes its discursive organisation. Morey (1989:146) claims that Foucault fails to develop a method-ological discourse of post-structuralism because his discourse is incapable of being employed within an epistemological field other than locally. Finally, he refers to exteriority, which 'is not going against the interior kernel and hiding place . . . but . . . against its external conditions of possibility, against that which gives place to the hazardous series of these events and which fix the limits' (Foucault, 1971:55). In relation to these four notions, Foucault adopts four principles: event, series, regularity, and condition of possibility, and proposes to study them by the alternation of critical description (*désinvolture studieuse*) and genealogy ('happy positivism') (Foucault, 1971:71–72). Thus Foucault's discursive perspective involves a history of ideas 'which consists of treating discourses as a regular and distinct series of events rather than as the repre-sentations which seem possible behind discourses' (Foucault, 1971:61).

FDA and methodological models

Models of how to proceed with analysis have been offered by Achard (1987) and Fairclough (1992), both emphasising how there is no blueprint that can be applied to all analyses. Thus Bonnafous' (1991:18) analysis of the French press, which I draw upon below, clearly states that her choice of method is marked by an eclecticism because of the nature of the problematic which she develops. Michard-Marchal and Ribery (1982) similarly reject resorting to linguistic theory and an associated method on the grounds that their concerns were not of that order. None the less, Achard regards the introduction of a rudimentary outline of the methods of FDA as a matter of urgency if the social sciences are to escape the disciplinary focus which treats the analysis of language as marginal to their concerns. The social sciences are closed to the idea that social, psychological, economic and other processes are facts of language practice which are only put into operation across the symbolic and formal processes of language. Furthermore, he emphasises that the analysis must encompass two disciplines – linguistics and one other (e.g. sociology, economics or psychology). It is not possible to restrict discourse analysis to linguistics since the object of linguistics involves operations and formal marks rather than the conditions of use. However, the conditions of use can refer to the positions of a variety of disciplines, including psychology and sociology. Indeed, if we follow Foucault there is every reason to consider the disciplinary programme as the effects of the role of disciplines within modernism, leading to an awareness that analysis might best proceed by ignoring disciplinary boundaries. This is not an argument in favour of multi-disciplinarity but rather in favour of non-disciplinarity.

It should be evident that FDA implies assuming a specific posture in linguistics, with a focus on the field of semantics on the one hand, and distributionalism and enonciation on the other, while also rejecting the notion of 'content' and the communication model. Similarly, it involves a commitment to a particular perspective on the social. The work of Michard-Marchal and Ribery (1982) focuses upon the specific notions of 'male' and 'female' in three social-science texts written respectively by Bourdieu, Godelier and Clastres. They isolate all cases of these notions within the three texts, beginning from an awareness that the properties attributed to notions can vary from situation to situation in accordance with the play on the predicative and enonciative operations. This means that it is through the analysis of referential values constructed in the enonces that the properties are to be discovered. Furthermore, the role of enonciative linguistics is to uncover the general operations sustaining the production and the recognition of signification, the conditions of language use being inscribed in the language itself. On the other hand, the linguistic categories of person, tense, modalities and determination only achieve value in relation to the referential dimension of the message.

Where pragmatics ignores signification in assigning meaning to its pragmatic effect, the focus in FDA is very much on signification. In pursuing this focus, it divides lexemes into two categories: 'functioning lexicals' and 'functioning indexicals'. The former include substantives, adjectives, certain adverbs, etc., where the signification contributes to use. Such words are conceived of as a sort of accumlator of references and properties. These contrast with 'functioning indexicals', where signification relies upon a relationship to (1) context, and involves anaphoric pronouns such as 'it', 'in', 'which', and (2) situation, and involves the personal pronouns such as 'I', 'you', 'one', verbal tenses, passives and actives, spatial terms such as 'here' or 'there' and modal verbs such as 'must'. The signification of such terms cannot be represented by the properties of the referent. Linguistics has tended to viewed functioning lexicals as normal, while treating the functioning indexicals as deviant or exceptional. On the other hand, the linguistic functioning of terms where signification implies a relationship between enonce and situation, or what Culioli calls 'the formal aparatus of enonciation', is central to FDA. This distinction is crucial in understanding how the practitioners referred to below have undertaken their analysis.

In what follows it is my intention to present the outline of what has been proposed by Achard (1987) as a minimal framework for the analytic procedure before proceeding to consider various examples of how the facets of this framework have been approached by two analysts. These examples derive from Achard (1987) and from Bonnafous' (1991) work on the French press. However, before proceeding it is useful to remind ourselves of the manner in which FDA conceives of the relationship between the linguistic and the social in that it is this conceptualisation which has to be kept in mind when considering the various facets of the method and what it seeks to achieve.

The central thrust involves the manner in which the individual is constituted as a subject. This occurs through the relationship between interpolation, signification and the taking in charge of discourse. Thus, signification inter-polates an enociataire into meaning when the enonciateur takes charge of the discourse. This, in turn, implies an overlap between an act of language, which is supported by the construction of meaning, and the enonciateur who takes the discourse in charge.

This taking in charge derives from the marks in discourse and involves the various deictic markers of space, time and person, with the oposition of the pronouns 'I', 'you' and 'we' setting out the range of a field with specific boundaries. When the individual identity changes, then so also does signification. An importance is also placed upon indexically functioning words and upon indexical designation when an understanding of an enonce requires information about the situation, e.g. when it is essential to know who 'I' and 'you' refer to. However, signification in itself is not akin to meaning but must be accompanied by the real effect of discourse. Thus the act and the event involve the relationship between signification and the real effect, involving how the enonciateur is transformed into the locuteur occupying a real social place. The formal aparatus of enonciation operates when locuteurs are taken in charge, implying a social interaction premised upon shared meaning and the implication of a relationship between the enonce and the situation. This designates the position of the subject with respect to the situation and/or the enonce produced in this situation. There is an attempt to show how the subject is the support for his/her enonce and for the set of subjective effects which underlie what is enonced. The other feature which links the constituted subject and the situation is, of course, the modalities.

This relationship between the enonicateur (formal) and the locuteur (real social place) involves the unwinding of the enonciation internal to discourse and the social actions of which discourse is the support. These social actions are either carried by the enonce, or can run aground when taking in charge does not occur.

The model

The model which Achard presents in his 1987 paper argues for a qualitative typology involving an inventory of forms and a minimum of semantic hypotheses. In considering his outline, it must be emphasised that, for him, it is no more than a minimal element rather than constituting an exhaustive methodological grid. Indeed, much of his analytical work extends far beyond what is discussed below. In this respect, any analysis should encompass most of the issues alluded to in the preceding chapters. His outline was based on the three stages described below.

The delineation of the discourse object and the constitution of the pattern

This stage only makes sense as a consequence of the researcher offering correct questions vis–à–vis the analysis. It will only make sense if it becomes the object of a predetermined written description on the part of the researcher. Thus, discourse analysis becomes a method for conducting research into questions which are defined outside of it. If I am interested in analysing a corpus by reference to how objects relevant to nationalism, for example, are socially constructed, I must begin with a consideration of those objects, seeking to ascertain which are the relevant objects. I might thereby focus upon objects such as nation, country, or specific forms such as Britain, Wales or Scotland.

Description of the discourse in terms of an enonciative typology

The general relevance of such a description for all discourse analysis, whatever its final objective, is generally recognised, even if its central character is not necessarily underlined. Thus the basic topologies such as the explicit presence of 'tu' or 'vous', whether or not they correspond to the allocutaire, the use of tense and aspects, modalisation, etc., at least when they are explicit, are what allow us to consider certain discursive characteristics and to objectify the discourse as evidence. Considering the distinction between the enonciateur and the enonciataire in the text or conversation allows us to consider how discourses appear to be 'natural'. It might involve the inclusive 'we', or how the conference or scientific paper achieves an objectifying position by avoiding the personal pronoun. While they may appear 'natural', they also reveal the presuppositions of the social relations that they construct. Furthermore, these considerations facilitate the 'guiding' of the construction of the text.

What is clear from enonciative linguistics is that language is conceived of as an activity between subject enonciateurs, those who produce an enonce and construct a signification, and those who recognise that enonce and reconstruct a signification. In a sense, form consists of an abstract relationship which can use places in order to be materialised. The central question concerns which operations associated with the production and the recognition of significations can be generalised? That is, which are the language operations that are manifested in the language under the forms of specific agencies. It focuses upon how the linguistic categories of person, tense, modality and determinants cannot assume value other than in relationship to the referential dimension of the message so that the conditions of language use are inscribed in the language itself. Consequently, the rules of the conversion of language into discourse involve the study of the linguistic system.

Given that the enonciative subjects are constitutive of the linguistic system in so far as they recall the origins of the operations of referentiation, the relation of reference is necessarily indirect, involving the mediating relationship between the enonce and the referent that is constructed and reconstructed by the subjects. Since an enonce is not a transparent transfer of an extra-linguistic event in the broadest sense, but, of necessity, includes the subject's perspective on that event through the construction of referential values, the possible diversity of interpretation is inscribed at the heart of the same language system and, as a consequence, is capable of producing misunderstandings. It is the inscription of subjects at the heart of the linguistic system that prevents it from being conceived of as a code that links a form with meaning.

The starting point involves the orderly relationship between two terms, one being conceived of as the source and the other as the goal of the relationship. For example, if one considers the two terms 'driver' and 'driven', the linguist will take the term 'driver' and not 'driven' as the point of departure within the predicative relation. These are sometimes referred to as primitive relations (Michard-Marchal and Ribery, 1982:16), which are claimed to be held by everyone in an implicit way. Without this orderly relationship, neither the production nor the recognition of meaning, in the sense of the construction of signification, is possible. Thus, for example, the enonce:

Gruffudd and the football, they are never apart.

establishes a relationship between two terms – 'Gruffudd' and 'the football'. The terms of such a relationship are the notions or expressions that return to their organised representations and are defined by a collection of properties which articulate that which is language and that which is not. These notions are more abstract than lexical units and are therefore not categorised from a morpho-grammatical standpoint. In positing relationships between notions, one derives certain operations concerning orientation and positioning. We discuss this in detail in the following section.

Description of the discourse in terms of constructing the notional functioning

Culioli (1990) has conceptualised notion by reference to linguistics. Replacing 'act' by 'meaning', the latter being that which privileges the predicative act, leads to a conception of the meaning of a notion in terms of an attractor. A notion is predicated on a referent, this predication carrying a 'value', such values being topologically organised and partially ordered in that any value is relative and facilitates a comparison with other values. Such a conception of notion is capable of supporting the operations which convey modal values. The enonciative operations which mark the extent of taking in charge of the predication by the enonciateur, return to establish the breaks, together with their topological effects, in the field of their modal values.

The enonciative operations operate on indeterminate modal values. From a linguistic standpoint, that indetermination is inevitable, referring to the situation of the average speaker. The placing of language in discourse, by reference to a use of language that carries a social effect, serves to concretise the notion. The notion 'Welsh' lacks a legal definition and revolves around a statement such as 'Rhodri is Welsh' in relation to concrete social circumstances – in relation to the concrete individual 'Rhodri' (the referent), and by reference to concrete social circumstances, that is, in relation to the concrete individual subject, Rhodri (the referent), to the extent to which it is practically revealed by the notion. It might be claimed that Rhodri is more 'Welsh' than someone who is 'treated as Welsh', that is, as a 'typical Welsh person' which becomes the central norm. This means that, at first, the discursive value of 'Rhodri is Welsh' can be assimilated into the collection of situations where he is treated as Welsh, or where he behaves as if he is Welsh. The totality of situations organises the abstract modal values of the linguistic dimension as discursive value. It is not a matter of considering the situations as a series of isolated points that are incapable of comparison, but as a series of mutually related points. Thus, it is akin to responding to the question 'In this situation is Rhodri considered Welsh?' by removing the deviant cases and recognising a stable situation. Thus, a number of constraints are imposed on the relationship between situation and discursive value. It is a matter of an epistemological means of thinking of notions in discourse.

Clearly, given the preliminary nature of the work, at this stage it is not possible to consider all of the notions involved. None the less, for the researcher such a step does have the value of assisting him/her to reflect on the formulation of his/her main interest. The simplest way of implementing this facet of the work involves creating a lexical entrée: a representative term and a certain number of terms which the researcher judges to be equivalent.

Constructing a corpus

It is with reference to corpus that Foucault's concept of 'archive' becomes relevant (Foucault, 1969:127). In so far as it is possible, it involves the entire discursive practice, both contemporary and historical, which is relevant for the research in question. Evidently this involves reference to the issues of inter-textuality and homogeneity, as well as to the understanding of the discursive domain under investigation by the investigator. It is necessary to ascertain whether there is a homogeneity in the unity of its enonciation, what is the nature of the intertextuality in terms of its integration into intertextual chains associated with a series of text types? This in turn conditions the nature of the corpus selected and the persons responsible for selecting the corpus. It is conceivable that the investigator will consult others in the selection of a corpus in order to try to obtain a typical and representative sample. By the same token, Bonnafous (1991:14) suggests that the corpus should be accessible to other researchers, if only for comparison and for facilitating other work.

There is an inevitable link between the selection of a corpus and the task selected by the investigator. Thus, Bonnafous (1991:14) states that her interest in the interaction between 'political' discourse and common discursive practice involved the question of where one encounters the effects of discourse expressed by a society about that part of itself that it regards as 'strangers'. They can be found in spontaneous 'street talk', through interviews, in statements made by politicians or by partisan organisations. In seeking to encounter the interface between the constituted 'political' discourse and ordinary or common discursive practice, she chose to use the press, claiming that it is a source which stands between oral discourse which is not meant to be preserved or retained, and the reflection that exists in the discourse of politicians.

What is required in discourse analysis is a set of tools which, in multilingual situations, facilitates the collection and listing of all the terms employed, vis-à-vis the issue at hand, tools which relate to some practical situation where actors would agree with the nature of the reference, if not with the meaning. This is achieved by creating a corpus consisting of texts which might, for example, link 'nation' with 'we'/'they' as a constitution of groups. This is necessary because the notions in one language, for example English, may have symbolic equivalents in other languages, even if there is no semantic equivalence. Clearly the existence of a corpus which will gather texts which link concepts such as 'nation' with the equivalent identity components of 'we' and 'they', which serve to constitute groups in and through discourse, is central. Evidently, given FDA's position re a focus upon the possible, the probable and the resolution of ambiguity, the concern is not with a corpus or texts which conform with some idea of what is the correct position vis-à-vis concepts, but rather with texts which contain a position or action in relation to the problem in hand.

Once the definition of the problem has been achieved, the problem of collecting a large corpus of text for the objective in hand can be confronted. That is, the problem must be defined before the nature of the corpus unit, or the issue of whether literary, oral, etc. sources are involved. Initially, rather than narrowing down to phrases or full articles or paragraphs, it is best to begin by considering the largest constituent unit, for example, all of the newspapers on a particular day, even if only a small part of it is relevant to the problem. This should then be sampled in order to develop a body of material that can be handled by computer. Thus the initial research process involves gathering and sampling the corpus. This in turn involves reflecting on the hypotheses which relate to the homogeneity of the corpus. Achard suggests that it is useful to produce a synopsis of ten lines on these points.

In a sense there is a claim that the corpus constitutes a sample of discourse register. Thus the aim is to establish which hypotheses concerning the discourse register exist in order to constitute it as a register. Thus in Bonnafous' (1991) work on immigrants and the French press, there is a unity in the recourse to the press as the basis for the corpus, with the various articles included in this sense being related. If the corpus is homogeneous, it will have a common enonciative origin for the entire corpus. For example, with reference to newspapers, the position of 'reader' represents a zero point from which other values are calculated. Thus, homogeneity is represented in the coherent structure of enonciation, which means that an evaluation of the structure of enonciation precedes any decision concerning homogeneity/ heterogeneity. This use of enonciation in evaluating the homogeneity of a discourse is primarily a tool for criticising the initial assumption for which we have created a ten-line summary.

Restricting one's corpus to the 'quality' press may well increase homo- geneity and can thereby lead to making false assumptions about the press in general. The extent of the task of investigating the entire structure of enonciation would appear to be daunting until we recognise that whoever proposes a corpus has social knowledge in the sense that a degree of intuition is inevitable in the selection of a corpus. Thus, for example, no one would propose a report of a soccer match and a professional paper on theoretical mathematics as the basis for the formation of a corpus unless they had some hypothesis concerning what kind of homogeneity might include both of them. Since the discourse analyst is looking for something, that something is already elaborated as a social object. This does not mean that a corpus is not entirely adequate for a given goal, nor that the corpus might be a corpus of a discursive formation which did not entirely rely on the kind of intuition that the investigator initially had.

Clearly there are constraints on the selection of a corpus. One such constraint concerns what sociolinguists refer to as 'appropriate data', involving the denial of the investigator's right to choose, on an *a priori* basis, that which is a good or a bad use of a term. Therefore the corpus must be broad enough not only to accommodate this issue but also to be systematic in approaching this problem. In sociolinguistics, the issue of appropriate data tends to have a statistical referent, and involves ensuring that typical or appropriate samples of specific practices are collected from within the universe. On the other hand, in discourse analysis, the corpus is not a closed entity but can be enhanced at later stages.

Thus there are three stages which have to be considered:

- thinking about the source of the concept – even if that text is not accessible, it is important to know of its existence;
- creating an inventory of all the relevant identity categories;
- rely on intuition in order to identify what is a relevant category, while also recognising that the investigator is involved in the process of corpus selection.

With reference to this last point, one frequently discovers that a snowballing effect occurs wherein the frame can be enlarged or narrowed. Thus, for example, with regard to the issue of the link between the inclusive 'we' and 'nation', one asks: 'Which are the contexts of "nation" which relate to this narrowing or enlarging of the frame – are there statements such as "the X are a nation which . . ." or "it has been difficult for the X to obtain recognition of their national status", which create the nation while expressing a degree of ambiguity about its existence?' Thus one scans the corpus for all the terms that take the same position as 'nation', this being the first layer of the snowball. This is then followed by searching for the context of these equivalent terms. It is then necessary to return to the corpus in order to discover why X is eligible for nationhood, even if it consists of nothing more than the denied form, where 'X is not a nation'.

Once the definition of the problem in hand has been clarified, and the unit of study, such as newspapers, which satisfies the research objective has been decided upon, the investigator will begin with the entire universe – e.g. entire copies of newspapers for a specific period, before sampling that universe in order to scan specific texts, thereby creating a computerised data file. Thus in Bonnafous' (1991) study of racism in the French press, she selected ten newspapers which represented the spectrum of political opinion in France, and incorporated the entire production of these sources over the period 1974–1984 into her study. From this body of material she selected every article which made reference to immigration, giving a total of 7,576 articles, which served as her corpus. Similarly Michard-Marchal and Ribery (1982) drew upon papers written by three French anthropologists – Clastres, Godelier and Bourdieu – as the corpus for their analysis of sexism in human-science texts.

Achard (1987:48) proceeds to suggest that a list of between one and five notions which are considered as defining the object of the research should be outlined. For each of these, a list of lexemes which, in the opinion of the researcher, are indicative of the notion should be drawn up. Clearly this is merely a preliminary step, and the analysis of substitutions may well reveal further lexemes which initially may not have been evident to the researcher.

Since much of the analysis that follows would not be possible on a large scale without recourse to computer analysis, a word is in order about the role of computer programming in discourse analysis. This must be kept in mind in reading the following pages. A recent publication entitled *Statistique textuelle* (Lebart and Salem, 1994) is an invaluable source in this respect. It will become evident that key-word analysis, which reveals the incidence and localisation of the occurrences of specific lexemes within their context, is an important element of the analysis. The pole-form allows the regrouping of the contexts. Thus, for example, it is possible to specify a lexical item such as 'nation', to discover all cases of occurrence within a specific corpus and to list these occurrences by putting the lines of concordance in alphabetical order. The ability to reorganise the text in this way permits a far more synthetic reading than that which occurs sequentially. It allows the study of the relationships which can exist between different contexts of the same form. It is a method which is widely used by Achard in much of his work and which Bonnafous draws upon extensively in her work (see the example on p. 262). It is particularly effective in pursuing the issue of notion elaborated below.

In some respects a simpler task involves the listing of lexemes in terms of the frequency of their occurrence within a text or corpus. It is particularly useful in terms of comparison, allowing the frequency of lexical items in specific texts, such as the various newspapers analysed by Bonnafous, or by reference to different parts of the same text. It allows a recognition of those forms which are over-used and those which are under-used. It allowed Bonnafous to distinguish between the various newspapers sampled, noting that, for example, one newspaper under-utilised first person pronouns, class vocabulary, designations of 'racism' and governmental and legislative lexemes. This in itself is an invaluable entrée into further analysis. It allowed Bonnafous to focus upon specific terms which were over- or under-represented in seeking to establish the contextual nature of the associated notions.

Description in terms of enonciation

Inventory of persons and verbal diatheses

The next step involves a description of the corpus in terms of enonciation. This will include an inventory of persons and of their verbal diatheses, as well as an inventory of tenses, aspects and verbal modes. In some texts, such as the brochure of the SNCF (French Railway Authority) which Achard considers in his example, the mark of person might be restricted, as in this case where it is restricted to the second person plural. Other texts will have a complete range of persons and enonciative places. Bonnafous' (1991) analysis indicates that whereas a total of thirteen forms were encountered in her corpus, over half were first person plural 'we' and 'our', with the pronoun 'we' being particularly prominent, and that the distribution of the various forms varied

```
L  561   ones. It is disappointing for Welsh rugby but commercially good. We j
L  129   pell out services provided for Welsh speakers was promised in the Hous
L 3277   pell out services provided for Welsh speakers was promised in the Hous
L  140   eness and improve services for Welsh speakers, would be put on a statu
L 3287   eness and improve services for Welsh speakers, would be put on a statu
L 1629   words are taken straight from Welsh, which may have been pinched from
L 1820   eve in the principle of giving Welsh equal status with English, at lea
L 2289   eve in the principle of giving Welsh equal status with English, at lea
L  984   me," he said." This is a good Welsh team to play for because we all k
L 2301   blic sector at least, granting Welsh equal- status with English-- a pr
L 3389   statue as a tribute to a great Welsh poet- this is a send- up of the D
L  853   n' s comparison with the great Welsh sides of the Seventies. The secon
L 3385   ns to Wales to write the great Welsh novel and be interviewed on Welsh
L 1816   ate on Welsh affairs, said his Welsh Language Bill would oblige counci
L 1356   am in a revival of fortunes in Welsh rugby. It will take a long time t
L 2567   ca Jones samples the latest in Welsh honey truffles. PATRIOTIC chocoho
L  957   y the most difficult player in Welsh club rugby to stop on the drive.
L 1627   English but being preserved in Welsh." It was used in Bristol and Here
L 1300   with, if not a renaissance in Welsh rugby, at least a renewed sense o
L 1288   far more to the introspective Welsh than he ever did to the English,
L 2574   he promises that everything is Welsh. The tasty delight is being launc
L  388   st year Neath ruled the little Welsh world of rugby. Having already cl
L 3248   ment continue to allow so many Welsh members? Maybe fifteen or so woul
L 2281   e tongue under plans for a new Welsh Language Act announced by Secreta
L 3136   rwhelming majority who are not Welsh speaking." Those were the passion
L 1973   the taxpayer. The Assembly of Welsh Counties condemned the plan, sayi
L 2271   Labour- dominated Assembly of Welsh Counties, said he was disappointe
L 2244   welcomed by the Association of Welsh Districts, which had campaigned f
L 2267   Labour- controlled Council of Welsh Districts, said:" Mr Hunt has acc
L 1532   ns, welcomed by the Council of Welsh Districts, which had itself propo
L 1965   was welcomed by the Council of Welsh Districts, which had itself propo
L 2264   r Hunt favoured the Council of Welsh Districts' proposal of having a"
L 3256   e Llandrindod Wells. Survey of Welsh Business Opinion BUSINESS CONFIDE
L 2423   to marshal." The chairwoman of Welsh Labour MPs, Mrs Ann Clwyd, told M
L 3063   invited the grand committee of Welsh MPs to move out of Westminster fo
L 2474   re in 1979: tying the hands of Welsh MPs in Westminster; nationalism;
L  836   ct. during the worst period of Welsh rugby history, this much vaunted
L 3121   the authority and the power of Welsh Parliamentarians. Our hands would
L 1609   Lewis, emeritus- professor of Welsh, says the derivation is not obvic
L 1521   page 24 Hunt aims to bring old Welsh counties to life TWENTY- three lo
L 1816   . Mr Hunt, opening a debate on Welsh affairs, said his Welsh Language
L 3386   sh novel and be interviewed on Welsh- interest TV chat shows about con
L  126   olitics, page 5 Hunt pledge on Welsh language' A WELSH Language Bill t
L 3274   on consumers?' Hunt pledge on Welsh language A WELSH Language Bill to
L  170   onger' s shop. Not an ordinary Welsh shopper-- but then. this is no or
L 1833   gives English precedence over Welsh where there is a dispute over a t
L 2296   recedence to English text over Welsh in cases of dispute. Mr Hunt admi
L 1619   in mawoor)-- the mawr is plain Welsh for big-- carries the meaning sil
L 3374   k farmstead." The professional Welsh have avoided being depicted on sc
L 1034   arly." Dewi Morris, England' s Welsh- born scrum- half, will join in s
L 3101   ing their seats at to night' s Welsh Labour Party conference in Swanse
L 3051   of government. At the party' s Welsh conference this weekend several c
L  853   s of the Seventies. The second Welsh golden era extended from 1969 to
L 2252   usions for England. The shadow Welsh secretary Barry Jones, said:" Thi
L 1840   icly." Barry Jones, the shadow Welsh secretary, welcomed a bill, and s
L  133   r in Wales would have to speak Welsh." For the first we will be placin
L 3281   r in Wales would have to speak Welsh." For the first time we will be p
L 1829   here those who wanted to speak Welsh would be able and free to. Mr Hun
L 1580   y will have a bash at speaking Welsh. Next day, back to English. Well
L 2352   o wishes to contiunue speaking Welsh. The Welsh Language Society react
L 2291   ublic sector." A new statutory Welsh Language Board will help devise p
L 1622   He' s a bit didoreth straight Welsh word, is what you say if you mean
L 3326   elegation of Plaid Cymru,, the Welsh nationalist party, held talks wit
L 3243   their special needs. Even the Welsh language would have its problems
L 1585   The French have Franglais: the Welsh have Wenglish. The difference is
L 3433   rule in Wales. David Hunt, the Welsh secretary told journalists that t
L 1932   eral election. David Hunt, the Welsh secretary, said yesterday. The ei
L 1526   Broom notes). David Hunt. the Welsh secretary, said yesterday that th
L 1689   ad of those saying no; and the Welsh threw the Bill out by 5: 1. Where
L 2156   Radnor, says he approached the Welsh Office for cash, but in vain." If
L 2238   der proposals announced by the Welsh Secretary, David Hunt, yesterday.
L 1814   th English was promised by the Welsh Secretary, David Hunt in the Comm
L 3309   European Centre- set up by the Welsh Development Agency, the Universit
L 3367   its subjects, in this case the Welsh, whose foibles it plays up. The r
L 2748   overnment is essential for the Welsh identity to survive into the new
L  455   sort of deeds required for the Welsh dragon to reduce St George to a c
L 2727   itain," The first step for the Welsh to take towards the realisation o
L 1606   n"( prounouned tootee from the Welsh word for small) for crouch. And c
```

262

significantly across the ten newspapers. Since 'we' can designate a number of different people – locuteur + locuteur, locuteur alone, locuteur + allocutaire, locuteur + third person, locuteur + allocutaire + third person – and since it serves to indicate factors of cohesion and differentiation characterising 'us' and 'them', it can involve the locuteur as member of a group. This may involve activation as:

- an agent group where 'we' is the subject;
- a group where 'we' is object;
- a group which is referred to in terms of its properties and possession where 'our' is used.

In Bonnafous' work the tendency to present the locuteur as a member of a group in this way was most characteristic of the newspapers she had classified as 'extreme right wing' in her selection of a corpus.

An issue of *Mots* (No. 10) was devoted to the political 'we' and, as Bonnafous notes, political discourse is characterised by an extreme variety of referencing for each type of 'we', the frontier moving from one to another. In that issue of *Mots*, Geffroy (1985:89) claims that this was the means whereby the political subject tries to 'escape' the enonciative responsibility of the subject as a constantly shifting collective form.

The next step involves identifying the semantic effect of enonciation by referencing the syntactic function. As we have noted, 'we' might exist in subject form or as a direct or indirect object position. Achard lists all such syntactic relationships. They include the relationship of 'you', 'your' in terms of marks of verbal flexion – 'book your ticket' or 'order your meal' – it may mark 'you' as reflexive, referring to 'you' as the subject of the taking in charge. He notes the way in which the absence of 'I' or 'you' singular relates to politeness in French, their being restricted to reported discourse or marked operations. He notes the absence of 'one' while reserving judgment as to whether or not it is a rule of genre. The absence of 'we' has the effect of magnifying the presence of 'you', constructing the enonciation as an objective process, interpolating the allocutaire without personalising the locuteur. He notes the existence of two cases where the alternation of actives (where the notion-source is 'you') and passives or impersonal modalities (where 'you' refers to the beneficiary): 'the reductions . . . apply in the TGV by reference to the same conditions as in other trains' and 'a local surtax is applied to the price'. The frequent use of the passive diathesis relates to the absence of 'one' and 'we', and contributes to the objective value of the enonciation. There is a complete absence of 'they' in the text.

Bonnafous adopts a similar listing by reference to 'we' and 'our'. She notes that it is the right-wing newspapers which are the only ones to assign positive specificity to 'us', this primarily involving an 'editorial' 'we' and a 'partisan' 'we', and, second, a 'national 'we'.

Inventory of tense, aspect and verbal modes

Clearly this leads to an inventory of tense, aspects and verbal mood. Achard notes that the text of his TGV corpus was in the present indicative except for seven cases of the future indicative and one case of past tense (*passé composé*) in the context of subordination to a future principle. These temporal-aspectual changes in the mode of enonciation occur only in order to mark the exceptional nature of the process referred to: 'in the case of non-withdrawal of the fixed delay, the seat reservations *would be* automatically annulled'. There is also an example of the composed past in capitals which has the effect of placing the allocutaire in an abnormal situation.

The general function of taking in charge has the effect of interpolating the allocutaire in the formal situation that corresponds to the described process. This is achieved via signification and implies an overlap between the act of language and the taking in charge of the enonciation. It is the taking in charge that activiates the deictic structure in that it only occurs through indexically functioning lexemes.

This process is also taken on board by Bonnafous, who notes, among many similar references, that the adjective forms of 'we', and 'our' relate to the inversion of the relative importance of the 'editorial' and 'partisan' and 'national' 'we'. One newspaper has a complete absence of the qualifying or propositional development of nouns. There is a complete absence of the subjective adjective which constructs the enonciateur as the explicit or implicit evaluative source of an assertion, e.g. 'I found that wallet'. She claims that the use of the adjective underlines and stresses the emotional value of many uses of 'our', and relates to the appearance of 'our' + noun forms. This was often revealed by reference to that which a statement is opposed to, e.g. 'our existing president' is opposed to a future president or 'our national community' is opposed to a community of thought or a familial community.

Thematisation

To recap, one of the main aspects of the key-word method is that it defines the 'themes' associated with the key terms as a consequence of a knowledge that is external to the functioning of the discourse under consideration. We have already seen how Courtine (1981) took on board the question of how, in and through the discourse, a determined element can be characterised as a theme of discourse. That is, in relation to which structures and linguistic forms is it thus characterised, assuming that it is linguistic structure rather than historical knowledge that furnishes these themes. Such thematisations are ambiguous, but they also reveal a thematic order. As such, Bonnafous (1991:237) refers to them as 'the forms and segments whose appearance is directly linked to the choice of a subject' – an article on rent strikes generates a certain number of occurrences of 'price', an article on the murder of a child gives rise to a certain number of occurrences of 'violence'. These forms relate to the 'referent'. In pursing this goal, Bonnafous created a list of 400 items uniting 'the terms where the surface is particularly disequlibriated by reference to the parts or groups of connected parts' (Salem, 1988:130).

Bonnafous begins her work on thematisation by reference to two terms, 'racism' and 'immigration'. She compares the incidence of these terms over time across the newspapers of the right and the left, establishing a difference between the vocabularies of the two political extremes, a difference that is constant across time. Having run the frequency count, she then proceeds to contextualise the terms as well as others, including 'entry', 'departure' and 'expulsion'. Clearly, these are particularly interesting in that they and their converse, departure/entry, for example, have different referents. In assuming this task she relates the themes associated with these lexemes to the form or the structure of the phrase, showing for example how 'work' exists as a comple-ment at the interior of nominal syntagma as in 'the admission to work' and the 'market of work' (labour market), or as the complement of a direct object when 'work' is 'given' to 'immigrants', who are presented as beneficiaries of a right reserved for the 'French'. Work appears as a State or 'national' property. This contrasts with the use of 'work' in terms of 'immigrants' who 'seek' or 'find' work. The viewpoint of the locuteur is never that of the economic theorist.

Evidently, thematisation is used in order to highlight the text at the interior of the topographic organisation. Achard has a long list of examples in his analysis of the TGV brochure: 'For your comfort, on the TGV', 'For your journey on the TGV', etc. He notes that they almost all appear at the beginning of paragraphs. Thus the considerable frequency of thematisations and their ranking, together with the fact that they relate to topographic procedures, is interpreted as a context in which the 'real', singular allocutaire is invited in some way to filter his/her real situation in the maze of descriptive conditions which signals the text in such a way that s/he does not have to take in charge that with which it is concerned. That is, thematisation pre-frames the situation of enonciation while conveying an impression of complexity in the process of making a seat reservation.

While this takes care of most of the cases, Achard is at pains to focus attention on the deviant cases – the limited number of cases which do not occur at the beginning of paragraphs, those involving spatial localisation, a thematisation which involves the intervention of another locuteur and which also involves the predicative, internal thematisation, the fact that 'should' always has 'you' as the notion source, the use of the adverb 'only', which only occurs by reference to nominal phrases, the existence of modal verbs. He notes the tendency for the modal verb 'power' to be used in relation to the subject 'you' as notion source, using the following example: 'A place can be reserved in the first-class carriage for a handicapped person who wishes to travel in his/her wheelchair. That person pays a second-class tariff'. This assimilates the allocutaire to the position of 'handicapped' while creating the implicit place reserved for her/him. That is, it creates the handicapped in a dependent place while also avoiding the formula 'if you are handicapped'.

Localisations

He then proceeds to the spatial deictics, noting that they do not exist in the SNCF document. Neither is it possible to recover a spatial and temporal localisation either in thematisation or in the adverbs of phrases. Also there is only one temporal deictic – 'beforehand' – which intervenes immediately after a title – 'before your departure'. This confirms that the document constitutes the origin of the point of view of the range of situations constructed by the enonciataire rather than emanating from the place of the enonciateur. The spatial references involving 'to', 'in', 'on', and 'between' all pertain to the space of the company SNCF – the station, the train – and never to the space of the allocutaire.

Bonnafous' work, on the other hand, has considerable reference to localisation, and especially to the manner in which an exercise of closure is accomplished by reference to geographical and political space, and how this relates to enonciative subjects. General terms of belonging such as 'the country' or 'the nation' are usually ambiguous, this ambiguity being resolved by reference to the preconstructed. In this respect they are different from specific territorial localisations or terms of particular auto-designation such as 'France' or 'Britain'. They also relate to general terms which designate the converse of that which the spatial referent includes, that is to the 'they' or 'them' that opposes the inclusive 'we'. Bonnafous draws upon an analysis that serves to heighten such differences. Thus she demonstrates how 'country' is often linked with 'our' as an affective and diffuse nationalism that pertains to a property, the locuteur seeking to include the reader through the inclusive 'we':

> The immigrant workers contribute to enriching the patrimony of the
> working class. As such, and for all such reasons, they are called to play
> a very important role in the changes that we want for our country.

She claims that various different contexts produce the same impression, involving a community of interest between the enclosed space that constitutes 'country', the locuteur and the destinataire of such enonces. This is true even where 'country' is preceded by a definite article, either alone or as a propositional construction – 'au pays' or 'du pays' – the syntagm has the meaning of a stylistic variant of 'our country'.

She shows how in some newspapers, particular terms of localisation such as 'France' are valorised as the country of the locuteur and of 'the French' without the motifs of that valorisation being precise, and without the inclusion of any metaphor or original personification, by simply speaking of 'countries such as France' or 'the attachment to France'. She concludes that particular terms of localisation tend to be a vocabulary that sets frontiers and boundaries while also being prone to sliding and recovery – the generic 'France' is presented in a nationalist context by linking to the adjectival and nominal forms of 'French' and, when associated with 'immigrants', it serves to establish the implicit boundaries of inclusion and exclusion as they pertain to locality. This kind of opposition fixes groups by reference to space, seeking to establish the boundaries of legitimacy between people and territory.

It is important to distinguish between localisation and the concept of place. One goal of the enonciative analysis is to indicate the origin of a point of view vis-à-vis the enonciateur, thereby establishing the place of the discourse and the founding topography of the discourse. It links with the claim that an archive cannot enonce in a valid manner except by reference to this place. Of course, this is not merely a geographical location but links localisation with the other elements of deixis in establishing the social topography of speaking subjects . In this respect it links with Foucault's claim concerning the position which can and must be occupied in order for an individual to be the subject of a discourse. It locates the point at which the subject appears at the instance of enonciation. For example, the notion of nation can be described by reference to the political enonciateur and involves the place of the observer in relation to the place from which the political discourse is enonced. It may involve a base as the enonciateur of the law, or in relation to precise debates. This may lead to the political discourse being envisaged as deploying a presupposed legitimacy within an open space. It may involve the intervention within the discourse of the political enonciateur as enonciateur. It takes into account the fact that modern politics derives its power from a group, and involves the use of 'us' or 'we' as a conceptual value, involving what Benveniste referred to as the *je expansé*, the extended 'I' or the inclusive 'we'. Thus in the example 'There is a means . . . it is to invite most of the millions of immigrants who constitute our home [chez nous], many as foreign slaves to return to their home [chez eux]' (Bonnafous, 1991:161), 'we' is given the function of prepositional complement, with the preposition 'home', serving to denote the intimacy of the family within its home. Used as a complement to 'their home', it pertains to the argument of 'each one to his home'. Of course, it also runs the risk of equating family and blood, and the explicit racism that relates to the relationship. The point which Bonnafous makes by reference to the use of 'we' is that since 'we' can designate a variety of combinations of persons and enonciative subjects, they must all be listed and analysed by reference to the variety of references to which they relate.

Indirect discourse, free indirect discourse and indirect enonciateurs

The relevance of these forms for enonciation is diverse. In indirect discourse there is the literal reproduction of a cited remark. Indirect free discourse involves two voices or enonciateurs – the voice of the enonciateur who reports the remark, and that of the individual whose remark is reported. The statement cannot be attributed to one or the other.

Bonnafous (1991:175), referring to the journalistic genre, indicates that a high proportion of the first person singular are in fact cases of reported discourse where the immigrant is the referent. The concrete evocation of the experience of immigrants allows the journalist to deliver the message through an interposed person:

> 'Upon my arrival at the Citroën building, the first person who greeted me was the "interpreter". Yes, a boy whose only . . . is that of being an "interpreter", of spying on those of one's country. That would not pertain to **me. I** speak French well. But it is their method. He demanded of **me**: "What do you think of the Trade Union?" **I** replied: "Nothing, it does not interest **me**."'

She elaborates on this in claiming that the discourse on immigration is, first of all, that of others, emanating from precise persons or from an indefinite 'one'. She notes the frequent cases of the direct style marked by quotation marks, of the remarks reported in indirect style or indirect free style, titles such as 'the secretary of state for immigration', etc. that is, the enonces which the enonciative context interprets 'as the echo of an enonce or of a thought' (Sperber and Wilson, 1978:409). She cites the following example:

> 'July 3rd, last, the government, with considerable pomp, announced "a new politics of immigration". A large series of measures in favour of immigrant workers . . . And to begin immediately, with the goal of (establishing) "greater power to undertake a census of that mobile population", the government has decided to stop immigration for three months.'

She contrasts this with the enonces where the locuteur takes charge.

Manifest heterogeneity (*hétérogénéité montrée*) involves 'the presence of "the other" within the thread of discourse' (Authier-Revuz, 1984:98). It involves identifying how every word is 'occupied' by those of 'other discourses' which are like a memory deposited within them (Authier-Revuz, 1992a:21). It is appropriate to recall that constitutive heterogeneity fits neatly with Achard's perspective in that, according to Authier-Revuz (1982:140), it allows the linking of Bakhtin's dialogism and Lacanian psychoanalyis as viewpoints external to linguistics. She also claims that there is a form of negotiation between the speaking subject and constitutive heterogeneity, the 'normal' form of which involves the mechanism of denegation. She proceeds:

> The explicit marks of heterogeneity respond to the menace which represents the desire to master the speaking subject, the fact that it

cannot escape the grasp of a *parole* which is fundamentally heterogeneous. Across these marks the subject exerts itself in designating the
localised other to comfort the status of the one.

(Authier-Revuz, 1982:145)

It is in this context that Bonnafous seeks to demonstrate how 'immigrant'
serves as a privileged point of anchorage for manifest heterogeneity. This tends
to involve each newspaper criticising the abusive generalisations of the
adversary, constructing the 'immigrant' as the source of comments which
reveal that which each locuteur seeks to present about the discourse of the
other: 'Because, you see, the professional's defence of the immigrant in the
petition, using the process of the juicy "Pleven Law" is inconceivable unless it
is inscribed within a very precise political viewpoint' (1991: 208). Statements,
comments or cases are constantly used, both to deny a position and to sustain
the opposite position, thereby imposing an interpretation upon the represented
discourse. This might involve directly quoting the represented discourse as in
Bonnafous' (1991:208) example:

> From the outset of the campaign the National Front has shown that
> the arguments in favour of immigration are completely false. In
> particular, we have explained that the equation 'immigrant worker =
> a worker employed in jobs which the French don't want' is radically
> false.

Interestingly, in this case the statements appear to involve direct discourse,
while the represented discourse does not make the author explicit, even
though it purports to reproduce the exact words. This serves to accentuate
general polarisations involving the locuteur and the adversary. She also refers to
examples of discourse representation which makes direct reference to another
author, that is, it involves direct discourse:

> Georges Marchais wrote in *L'Espoir au Présent*: '. . . also for this
> immigrant, and with them, we affirm the right to "live, work and
> decide which is your country".'

This affirms the solidarity of the French people with the immigrant workers by
using specific nouns and syntagma while also identifying a particular author
with the general process of affirmation. However, the ambivalence of the
indirect discourse, especially the ambivalence of the enonciateurs, is lost in this
example. The reporting clause is missing and the represented discourse assumes
the form of a clause that is grammatically subordinate to the reporting clause.
Furthermore, the tense and the deictic structure involve focusing upon the
locuteur as the subject in charge. Yet the distinction between what pertains to
two locuteurs (reporter/reported) is confused in the sense that the demarcation
between the two is unclear.

269

From manifest heterogeneity Achard selects two types of indirect discourse: indirect discourse and indirect free discourse, intending to build an inventory of indirect enonciateurs. To recall, direct discourse inserts an enonciative situation in another, each one having its point of reference. It reproduces in the sense that it repeats the discourse of another. Indirect discourse involves an interpretation rather than a reproduction of the cited discourse; there is only one source of enonciation. Free indirect discourse lacks a reporting clause and mixes the voices of the two discourses, leading Authier-Revuz to claim that it pertains to non-marked forms of the autonomous connotation (1982:96). Indirect discourse contains only a single enonciative frame, that of the citing discourse, leading to the reference system being exclusively constituted in relation to itself and all the deictics and to the cited discourse being transposed in that enonciative frame. Within the SNCF brochure, only the situation where the machine or the booking office performs an action can be interpreted as a free indirect discourse. Rather, the abundant vocabulary of verbs or substantives means that 'demands' or 'reservations' appear as effective acts rather than as speech processes.

Part of the exercise involved in the analysis of intertextuality and heterogeneity involves how subjects, in this case the indirect enonciateur, are constituted within texts. Given that indirect discourse involves the possibility of enonces corresponding to different versions of the 'real' *parole*, this is no simple task. In the following example (Wisard, 1994:101), the enonciateur circles with precision the social and professional identity of the second enonciateur, then comments on his remark, which is reported in indirect discourse:

> 'One of my neighbours in the country, a fireman called upon to work
> in a factory, described how his colleagues would hide his tools, so as
> to prevent him from working at speed, and thus breaking one of the
> unwritten rules of the workshop. There, in real life, a terrible act of
> indictment.'

The use of inverted commas often signals a rejection by the enonciateur of what the enclosed purports – what Fairclough (1992:119) calls 'scare quotes' – thus placing an ideological distance between the two enonciateurs – the rejection of words may convey a rejection of those who use them. This merely underlines the difficulty of establishing the meaning of an interpreted discourse without reference to how it functions and is contextualised within the representing discourse.

In the following statement, Wisard (1994:107) seeks to identify traces of the second enonciateur:

> 'Whom among us did not encounter, between the queues of evacuees
> on the road, groups of firemen perched on the local water pumps? On
> announcement of the enemy's advance, they ran to safety with their

possessions. Officially, I would dearly like to believe it. Everything over there could easily have perished in the fire, provided that the tank of water was preserved, far away from the embers, with which to extinguish. . . . Glorious public servants some would call them. Alas! The suffering was more profound.'

The spatial mark 'over there' is linked with 'firemen', the marks of exaggeration — 'Everything . . . provided that . . . far away' indicate that caution must be applied to the sense of exasperation that the enonciateur displays in the specific context: the syntactic order allocates priority to the person over the function, something that contradicts the professional ethic of the fireman — 'they ran to safety with their possessions' — the exclamative marks of resentment — 'Alas!'. This indicates how the indirect free discourse carries both the traces of the enonciateurs of the cited discourse and the external point of view of the reporter on the cited discourse. Furthermore, the use of the pronoun 'us' serves to assimilate the destinataire to his viewpoint.

Intonative or gestural marks of enonciation

This is only relevant for oral discourse, and is therefore missing in both Bonnafous' and Achard's discussion.

Nominal phrases, typographic marks, titles and subtitles, etc

Nominalisation pertains to the truth value of an enonce. It also carries the potential of agency deletion so that the taking charge is once again in question. The enonce 'It is urgent to develop the production of steel' differs from the enonce 'The development of steel is important' in that the first enonce has a clear taking in charge whereas the second does not. Nominalisation may also eliminate other participants, thereby serving to make the enonciative context ambiguous. Furthermore, all acts of enonciation imply an attitude of the enonciateur in relation to that which is said. An enonce simultaneously plays on two closely linked registers: on the one hand, it states something about something; on the other, that relationship makes it the object of a taking in charge by the enonciateur. In either case, one cannot separate that which is said from the manner in which it is said. The analysis of a phrase permits the retrieval of these two elements — what is said and the modality.

Nominalisation links with the preconstructed within discourse, which means there is no taking in charge as with verb forms. The absence of the series of marks of person and modality means that the taking in charge and agency are preconstructed.

Bonnafous takes the analysis of nominalisation in French newspapers considerably further than Achard intends in his rudimentary framework. She begins by organising a series of terms such as 'country', 'Arabs', 'French', 'nation', into three categories:

- the general terms of belonging or membership: 'party', 'front', 'nation', 'national', 'race', etc.;
- the particular auto-designating terms: 'France', 'French', 'french', 'Europe', etc.;
- the general terms of alternates which confirm the identity by reference to setting boundaries – insider/outsider: 'strangers', 'immigrants', 'émigrés', etc.

She then undertakes a computer sorting analysis which indicates frequency of occurrence of the various terms and groups of terms by reference to each of the newspapers and their particular political position on the left–right spectrum.

This, in turn, leads to a detailed consideration of the general lexical items in the three categories. By reference to the membership category, the newspapers of the extreme right and the extreme left use these terms freely, whereas the other newspapers use them in a banal way, bereft of positive specificity. Thus, the notion of 'country'/'pays' is presented as positive, and is preceded by the possessive 'our' ('notre'), thereby participating in the expression of a diffuse and affective nationalism, a mixed sentiment by reference to property and appearance which the locuteur seeks to convey to the reader by the use of the inclusive 'we':

> The immigrant workers contribute to enriching the patrimony of the working class. As such, and for all these reasons, they are called to play a very important role in the changes that we desire for our country.

The 'country' is presented as a community of interest linking the locuteur and destinataire of these enonces. Bonnafous identifies a series of forms where this effect is achieved, especially those involving syntagma where affective connotation is strong, and the meaning of the term is vague. Furthermore, this effect links with the identification of 'country' with the territory of France, where the other newspapers tend to use 'country' to refer to territory external to France.

The use of 'nation(s)' and its derivatives, the adjective 'national', for example, is at the interior of syntagma, e.g. 'national office of' 'national education', etc., where the adjective denotes an extension of a level of action or of reality. 'National' denotes a determination – 'of the nation' – marking a frontier that designates France and Stranger, external or internal:

> Confronted by such a problem, it is derisory, we repeat, to speak of racism. It is an issue of sociology. AND SECONDARILY OF NATIONAL SURVIVAL.

All such uses presuppose the existence of a single nation. Furthermore, the numerous uses of the adjectival form or derivative draws upon a preconstructed notion to which the locuteur assigns specific meaning.

In contrast, the other newspapers, those which do not exist at the extremes of the political spectrum, display different characteristics. Thus, for example, the adjectival and derivative forms of the extreme right are evident in the newspapers of the extreme right. Bonnafous contrasts this highly adjectival discourse with a highly nominal discourse. Nominal terms tend to correspond to the designation of human communities. 'Country' now refers to 'country of origin' or 'country of birth' of the immigrants, to 'countries of the Common Market', 'countries which provide the labour force', 'western countries', etc., taking into account the 'source' of the other and enlarging national perception to European or Western dimensions. This difference between the nominal and the adjectival discourses Bonnafous extends to encompass the difference between a theoretical discourse that is capable of generalisation, and an auto-referential and defensive discourse. This links with the different uses of direct or indirect discourse.

A word is in order about the computer side of this analysis. Because of its size, the corpus used by Bonnafous can only be handled by recourse to computer-based analysis. Even then, she selects a representative sub-corpus for lexicometric analysis which is subjected to computer analysis. The first goal is that of achieving frequency counts of specific lexical items relative to parts of the corpus. This serves as a basis for comparison with other parts. She begins by focusing upon those items which display an annual incidence of 1,000 occurrences or more per newspaper. This allows her to recognise which terms are over- and under-employed respectively. She then proceeds to undertake a further analysis on the basis of 'repeated segments', allowing her to survey the relationship between simple forms and repeated segments. Repeated segments are defined as sets of forms which appear more than once in any corpus. Thus, for example, Bonnafous encounters 196 cases of the segment 'immigrant workers' ('travailleurs immigrés'). This analysis allows Bonnafous to list the repeated segments in order of incidence within the corpus and also according to the various newspapers and their respective political positions. In this way she is able to characterise the discourses of the various newspapers as 'relatively coherent lexical systems' (Bonnafous, 1991:142). This constitutes an expression of part of the construction of the various publications.

The construction of the publication is a central feature of the TGV brochure. It has a first part that consists of text and a second part that consists of tables. Headed titles always take the form of a nominal phrase except for the adverts on the last two pages. This serves to identify the headings as authored by the enonciataire while the nominal phrase manifests the withdrawal of the locuteur by reference to its enonciation. Most of the headings are in the nominal phrase form, with the exception of three assertive headings – 'you could', 'you do not have' and 'arrange your departure prior to arriving at the station' – which represent a linking of a simple paraphrase to another. This confirms that the preoccupation is with the organisation of the departure.

Use of deixis and anaphora

This topic is dealt with in detail, with specific examples, on pp. 240–245.

Descriptive synthesis of the discourse type insisting on the absence of each one of the dimensions

The enonciative structure of the TGV text consists of centring the origin from the viewpoint of a particular situation of the allocutaire – 'you', always by reference to the present – situated within the space of SNCF. Two temporal situations follow – 'prior to departure' and 'on the train'. Certain situations are modalised as of little value in relation to the first temporal situation. The largest problem seems to consist of allowing the singular enonciataire to reconstruct the reduced discourse to that with which s/he is concerned, while ignoring the remainder. Thus the model of reading is not one of sequentiality that is argumentatively organised.

From the standpoint of the social relationship induced by the discourse, the enonciataire is the only one invested with decision-making power – 'you' is the only source or the exclusive beneficiary of modalisations. Its 'interlocuteur' is present as a situation of fact and the verb 'power', which is the principle modality used, relates to the 'possible' rather than the 'permitted'. The term 'obligatory' functions as a non-negotiable pre-supposed. A further conse-quence of such an enonciative structure is that the traveller-enonciataire is considered in advance as one who has already taken the decision to use the TGV. The highly marked syntax of the title of the brochure – 'TGV Travel Guide' – is the link point with the text.

In the work of Bonnafous, the constructive aspect of the analysis of a range of newspapers affords a greater diversity. Yet she notes a striking use of lexical items which vary only by reference to modality of use. Yet there are exceptions. One paper theorised its racism, its locuteur never expressed itself in terms of a personal claim, but rather in the name of a community of one form or another. The 'we' reference was always at an abstract and very general level. In contrast, a second paper also used 'we' exclusively rather than a specific personal reference 'I', but generated a sense in which 'immigration' was a secondary form of capitalist exploitation. The 'immigrant' is viewed as an 'émigré' in a perspective which escapes the national anchorage of the locuteur. In yet another paper, the locuteur is constructed both as an individual and as a member of a collectivity, while in the absence of either 'I' or 'we'/'us' the locuteur does not appear to have the power to define her/his own identity and seems to have lost the power to use civic and patriotic vocabulary. In the absence of definitions of 'nation' and 'citizen' or 'people', the sliding of designation produces an essentialisation of 'la France' and 'Français'. The humanist, non-racist slant of one journal means that the 'we' enonciateur balances the national reference in terms of an indefinite reference. The weak

274

nominal designation – 'country' and 'French' being the only positive forms – is accompanied by a weak designation of the Other – 'immigrants', 'migrants', 'strangers'. The context of use of these forms none the less reveals a very negative representation.

Description of the notion

Inventory of notions

This obliges us to return to the list of notions created at the outset. To recap, Culioli's concept of notion involves that which supports the operations that convey modal values. Also, enonciative operations that mark the degree of taking in charge by the enonciataire are activated in the field of modal values. It is this that Achard seeks to explore at this stage. The first step involves making an inventory of the primary terms designating the notion. At the outset, we created a list of between one and five notions which defined the object of the research, for each of which an indicative list of lexemes was constructed. Achard produced a list of seven words. Of these, only 'comfort', which occurred once, and 'service', which occurred thirteen times, are discussed.

'Comfort' occurs in relation to assuring the needs of the passengers, and doing so through everyone undertaking to pre-reserve their seat. 'Service' has thirteen references that are listed, ranging from a reference to 'services' aboard the TGV, the 'free-service' that facilitates rapid booking, the quality 'service' that is guaranteed, to the special 'service' offered to juveniles travelling alone.

Bonnafous, on the other hand, organises her terms into three groups, as we have already discussed above. The computer analysis allows her to isolate each notion and place it in context for subsequent analysis.

Operating characteristics

This inventory is followed by a consideration of the operating characteristics. Achard begins with a consideration of the complementary places that are opened by the notion, noting that only the phrase 'an autocar service' explicitly opens a place, a place that is exclusive in the sense that it cannot be generalised to any other use. The term 'service' does not have an operator function, nor does it have any implicit reference to places where the explicit reference is missing.

He proceeds to ask the question of whether the notion can be considered as a regular nominalisation of a verb form where it exists in nominal form. He notes that in the text the notion 'service' derives from the verb 'to serve', having a variety of possible constructions. In pursuing this task, he draws upon the work of Blanche-Benveniste (1975:381–382). Those possible constructions he lists are related, without being synonyms. Only that which refers to relating something to someone involves three places. He concludes, therefore, that there is a need to focus upon these three places in order to examine the extent to which the possible interpretations of 'service' relate to this organisation. He outlines four organisational forms:

1   He begins with the case 'X serves Y to Z', noting that deletion leads to 'X serves Y' and by passivisation to 'Y is served' – with 'to Z' being optional – but 'X serves to Z' is not optional. The constraints exist where X and Z are human and Y is non-human. From an interpretative viewpoint, he notes that the places which are not mentioned continue to function as in 'the coffee is served', assuming that something is doing the serving and that someone is the beneficiary of that action. Since the non-mentioned places are tautologically mentioned – the coffee is served by those who serve to those to whom it is served – it is the taking in charge that allows the attribution of value in situation to the empty places. That is, they play a deictic role. He notes that 'Y is served' has an accomplished value which introduces a supplementary dissymmetry between X and Z – 'to be served' is considered part of its result, with X being indifferent or irrelevant. In contrast, that result continues to exist for Z, who is the beneficiary.

2   He then proceeds to consider how the change in construction facilitates 'X serves Z', from which 'Z is served' derives. The implications of this construction for Y involve the constitution of a class as part of the extension, without that construction being in any way autonomous – according to context, one could consider the construction as linking with (1) as a paraphrastic relationship or as a simple etymological relationship.

3   It is also possible to construct a context from (1) in which X = Z, giving 'Z *se sert* Y', a construction which employs a partitive instead of Y making the construction ambiguous by reference to (4) 'Jean serves himself (*se sert*) the butter' can be interpreted as Jean himself taking the butter or that he uses the butter to make a sauce.

4   The form 'Y serves to Z' derives from (1) under the condition X = 0, which signifies that 'to serve' ceases to be a social relationship between X and Z. It is not a transitive construction and cannot be passive. This allows the construction of 'Z *se sert de* Y', where the preposition *de* can be interpreted etymologically as a sort of introduction to the complement of a facilitating agent. In contrast to the passive, where the absence of an agent is the rule, it is obligatory in this construction.

Achard emphasises that the derivation of the construction (1) to (4) is not a paraphrastic relationship – Y in (4) cannot be instanced by the same objects as in (1). If Jean serves the coffee to Paul, one cannot infer that the coffee serves to Paul. What can be claimed is that the passage from (1) to (4) results in the identification X = Y, which is paradoxical since the constraints on X are contradictory to those on Y. Construction (4) opens the possibility of a loose link introduced by 'for' – 'Y serves to Z for T'.

The existence of T (anything other than X, Y or Z) is presupposed even if not explicitly mentioned.

5   The implications for Z in (4) allow us to complement T by re-entering under the form 'Y serves to T'. The implication of T allows us to construct the form 'Y serves'.

6   The form 'Y serves to U [to Z]' allows the entry of a new place in the verbal system (where U is anything other than X, Y, Z or T). A natural paraphrase would be 'S serves to Y as to U' or once more 'Y serves to Z for T to whom U always serves'. This form puts in play a condensation of construction relevant to (4) and to (5) concerning the relationships between Y/Z and U/Z respectively.

In relation to these constructions, the nominalisation 'service' can be interpreted in a number of ways:

1   By reference to 'Y is serving to Z': 'the service of Y to Z' involves the referencing of Z as a class with an extension, as in 'The serving of breakfast to those travelling is guaranteed until nine o'clock'. Nominalisation by reference to the active is possible, as in 'the service of that waiter is impeccable'. In the absence of a complement, there is an ambiguity.

2   By reference to 'Z is served' one can construct 'the service of Z', which is frequently used in the locutional form *au service de* . . . or 'at your service'. It is this form which has the greatest affinity with modalisations, and it is by reference to this form that one interprets 'a service of quality'.

3   From the form 'Z is serving to Y' ('Z serves himself Y') can be interpreted 'self-service' or 'free-service'. It is assumed that this nominalisation does not refer to the action of serving, but to a disposition which allows such an action. The relationship between (3) and the substantive then becomes etymological and discursive rather than being paraphrastic.

4–6 Apart from some lexicalisations involving rhetorical operations, the meaning of the verb 'to serve' in (4) to (6) cannot be nominalised.

Having proceeded through such an analysis concerning the extent to which the notion is furnished by the demander in nominal form, Achard then moves to consider all of the diverse occurrences of 'service' in the text. He reveals the extent of ambiguity and its resolution, the possible and the impossible. In so doing, he focuses distinctively upon the construction of the subject. He is, of course, also seeking to uncover the effects of preconstruction.

Where there is a regular nominalisation of the verb form, there is a need to discover the distribution of the associated verb form. It leads to considering the determination of the notion source and of agency, together with their enonciative status. The passive allows the verb 'to serve' to be constructed by reference to 'you' as the object and with the deletion of agency.

This leads to an inventory of the constructed notions as notion source of the notion. In the preceding analysis, the notion source of the process is X, which would appear always to be the enonciateur. This is often implicit, and, as a consequence, objectifies the standpoint where the taking in charge is by the allocutaire from the position constructed by the enonciataire. This is always presented or presupposed as a notion beneficiary.

This investigation of different discursive organisations and its focus upon notion and the deictic is taken up by Bonnafous, and, as we have suggested above, pertains to what we have outlined of her work above (see pp. 271–273). What she achieves is a description of the manner in which subjects and objects are constituted within the different organisations. Different newspapers construct subjects and objects independently and in relation to each other in different ways. Such constructions involve stabilisation and the setting of boundaries. Stabilisation involves removing deviant cases of a notion, while the setting of boundaries involves the point of distinction between 'us' and 'them', or 'French' and 'stranger' or 'foreigner'. This corresponds to Achard's query concerning the relationship between the notion and the nominal form, and the need to list an inventory of the effects of preconstruction in relation to the regular nominalisations of the verb form. It extends to a consideration of the source notions and the agency and its enonciative status.

Object characteristics

This part of the analysis begins with a consideration of the determinants of the notion – articles, possessives, demonstratives, etc. In Achard's corpus, the term 'service' is singular throughout the text, apart from where it is used as part of a title, where it is plural, or as the name of a service. Thus the structure involves presenting the class by the sequence in the titles, extracting the services one by one by reference to the classes in the text, and using the notion separately from any reference to certain namings.

The term 'service' can be determined by a localisation, e.g. 'on board the TGV' or 'to the place'; by an adjective or a postpositional adjectival locution, e.g. 'of quality', 'particular'; by a complement of a noun, e.g. 'of carriages'; or by a nominal group, e.g. 'young travellers'; or by a prepositional adjective, e.g. 'free'. It does not appear without determination, which contrasts with the absence of any example of the term preceding the single, definite article.

The term is only given in nominal form when it is constructed as a post-positional qualifier, e.g. 'reservation service' or 'free-service . . .'. Similarly, a consideration of the position of the notion in the predicate indicates that it departs from the nominal phrase on five occasions, while on four occasions it is the subject or element of a subject group, three times the object or element of an object group, and once in a prepositional complement of the nominal phrase.

Finally, there is a need to consider the relationship between the notion presented and the notion studied, which involves two processes:

- the distributional substitutes in relation to the context of the preconstructed and the predicate;
- and the notions which function in lexical anaphora in relationship to the term that is considered.

Achard failed to discover any reference to other terms or substitutes constructed in the same context. Indeed, the entire text is devoid of any anaphoric use. Rather, it is the term 'service' which plays the role of classifying in relation to the notions that are most often expressed in verb form, e.g. 'welcoming you', 'offering to travellers', 'a hostess takes charge of the children', 'to reserve a seat'. These different notions constitute the description of 'services'.

Bonnafous takes a somewhat different stance, devoting an entire chapter to this aspect of the analysis. She plays on the distinction between signifier, signified and referent. For each notion the modalities of 'to state' – citing, illustration, space occupied, subtitles, etc. – constitute the signifier; that which is stated, the signified or the meaning; and that which the discourse presents as the object of reality viewed by the stating and the stated, the referent. As a consequence of her position vis-à-vis centring, she is not happy with the distinction between signified and referent, but claims that the referent which she identifies is the 'object' of the discourse in question. The question which she seeks to address involves the relation between the signified and the referent: 'what is there in the infinite field of reality that motivates an article on immigration in any journal?' Do they have common referents, and, if they do, how are they given value in the different newspapers? In this respect, she reverts to Foucault's concepts of 'events' (1969:12), which he defines as a rupture or discontinuity rather than the trace. These 'events' may be covered by all the newspapers, whereas some may be treated as non-events by some newspapers. Her objective is to consider the different *a priori* orientations of the various newspapers as collective locuteurs.

From her corpus she develops a descriptive fiche consisting of two elements:

- one indicating the referent of the article;
- the other consisting of a summary description of the agency of the writing which she summarises.

Referring to various aspects of the article – the type, subtitles, space, illustrations, position, etc. – she builds up a value across all of the cases for each newspaper by reference to her key notions of immigrants and immigration. This she represents by circles of different radii for each summary description.

Examples of referents which she draws from the newspapers are:

- the suspension of immigration;
- a bomb explosion in the Algerian Embassy;
- a subway cleaners' strike.

279

She then analyses the different ways in which these referents are dealt with in the different newspapers by reference to interpretation (the why?), to appreciation (the how?) and to evaluation.

Different though this method may be from that used by Achard, it does serve to highlight the relationship between referent and argumentation, while also demonstrating how the referential construction is linked to the opinion about the referent. Bonnafous maintains that the referents are constructed as a measure of their capacity for integration into the newspaper's argumentation. In this respect, she shows how the same objects are differentially constructed by newspapers of different political persuasions.

Equivalent lexemes

The objective here is to examine the lexemes which the analyst has presented as equivalents, for example, 'the Principality' for Wales. The examination proceeds by reference to the same process as has already been undertaken in terms of operational and object characteristics for 'service' in the preceding discussion.

In his analysis, the only equivalent notion encountered by Achard is 'comfort'. It does not relate to any nominalisation and never operates as a direct substitute for 'service', where the distributional constraints are entirely different. 'Comfort' is never constructed as an article of service. It is not the 'service' that leads to the 'comfort', the latter being a feature of the TGV in general: 'For your maximum comfort, all travellers are seated on the TGV'. This, together with the following sentence – 'Since there are no more passengers than there are seats, reservation is obligatory' – leads to questioning the difference between 'you', 'passenger' and 'traveller'.

The absence of other terms, and the absence of a discursive relationship between 'comfort' and 'service', the two terms from his initial list of notions, shows that the 'semantic field' constituted in that search does not function in the analysed text.

Interpretation

Three steps are involved in undertaking an interpretation:

1   That part of the preceding discussion which pertains to the description by reference to enonciation is employed in order to evaluate the homogeneity of the corpus, the adequacy of the hypothesis formulated by the investigator by reference to that homogeneity and by reference to the place of the intertextuality in the enonciative construction of the entire corpus.
2   The work undertaken on the description of the notion is used to examine the construction of the representation of notions, their ambiguities and their referential stability, and the categorisation operations to which they are submitted.

3   The deictic valence of the notions studied is evaluated by examining the position of elements revealed in that part of the analysis associated with the description of the notion (see above, pp. 275–280) in relation to enonciative structure that was uncovered in the analysis (see above, pp. 276–277).

Achard considers each of these in turn:

1   With reference to the TGV handbook, Achard claims that the enonciative analysis leads to distinguishing three distinctive parts to the document: a part which is concerned with external advertising, which does not involve a taking in charge on the part of the principal enonciateur; the main text; and the part devoted to the timetables.

The first three pages constitute a form of meta-text, with a title, a presentation of the contents and tables of materials. The remainder of the text presents the brochure as an autonomous text which appeals to a minimal intertextuality. It does not adopt a position in relation to any competition, while supposing that the 'TGV traveller', if s/he is not a 'passenger', is already located in the space of having decided to travel. It shows how to do it, not why it should be done.

The complexity of the enonciative structure in relation to reservation indicates that this problem is crucial to TGV. It is here that Achard insists upon the specific nature of discourse analysis by reference to text, claiming that discourse cannot be analysed without a reflection that is determined by an externality, rather than as a constructor of an independent imaginary context. In this respect, the discourse of the brochure is more than a simple presentation of reservation procedures; it takes part in the procedure. But it is not the only element. In this respect, one is obliged to consider the essential interdiscourse in relation to which the judgment of the effect of meaning occurs, and leads to judging the effect of meaning of the analysed text by reference to the reservation procedure in its entirety. A deeper study would involve a study of the unwinding of effective interactions involving such elements as the booking office, rapid reservation service, etc.

In some sense the procedure of TGV reservation is no different from that of making a reservation on any other train. However, in another respect it is different in that the reservation can be made until the time of departure. The detailed presentation of the first part as well as the second part focuses upon the obligatory nature of the reservation. Achard raises the question of whether such an obligation should be re-evaluated after six years of experience.

The linking of making a reservation and paying a supplement suggests that the obligatory nature of reservations would not apply where there is no supplement, where a statistical analysis would allow one to judge that the train would not be full. It might be possible to restrict the obligatory nature of reservations to those trains carrying a supplementary payment and not to charge the supplement except for late reservations. If this was adopted, Achard suggests that it would lead to a change in one of the characteristics of enonciation of the document – that part which gives the reader the impression that it has a purely mechanical function for the interlocuteur. It would also lead to separating the reservation of services which are optional from the wider reservations.

Such a suggestion cannot be evaluated without observing the inter-actions at the ticket office. It is not impossible that the impersonal character of the reservation procedures has positive effects upon the interaction at the ticket office by channelling the aggressiveness of an unsatisfied customer across the system.

2   Achard has little to say in this section. He notes that the dimension 'comfort', which existed in the list of notions, is not mentioned in the brochure. It appears as a term only once, as a general presupposition. Thus he concludes that the brochure is not a publicity brochure. Similarly, the term 'service', apart from two contexts – 'free service' and 'carriage service' – concerns the localisation 'aboard the TGV'. The catering element is modalised as 'of quality'.

3   The notion of 'service' is implicitly constructed as the enonciateur source and as enonciataire beneficiary. From that viewpoint it is no different from the general enonciation throughout the brochure. In contrast, the notion of 'comfort' appears in a thematised part of the brochure and is involved in putting the enonciative frame in place.

Achard emphasises that the preceding analysis is intensive, with the analysis of forty pages taking thirty hours of work.

In considering the way in which Bonnafous draws her analysis together, it is important to consider the nature of her goal. Her initial hypothesis involved the claim that a scrutiny of the French press over a ten-year period would reveal that the discourse on immigrants and immigration had indicated a shift to an affirmation of the theses of the extreme right on the subjects and processes: 'the closing of ranks among the extreme right and the extreme left on the question of immigration derives from the fact that they integrate in a coherent way with their view of the world and its social relations' (Bonnafous, 1991:13–14). She is particularly keen to establish how a small minority from the extreme right have been able to impose a view on public opinion. Whereas it is possible to follow the enonciative structure intuitively in establishing this claim, she emphasises that FDA treats enonces as scientific objects. Thus, a primary focus of her conclusions involves a summary of the respective newspapers of both the left and the right by reference to lexicality and designation, as well as enon-ciative structure. She shows how the use of personal pronouns exercises closure, while also implicating alternative subject positions in the social construction of objects. The work undertaken allows her to characterise the respective newspapers, highlighting the similarities and differences across the various sources.

The treating of enonces as scientific objects which influence the analysis of other objects, together with a rhetorical analysis of the discursive production of the far right, leads her to assess how a relatively small minority imposes some of its problematic on public opinion. Furthermore, it leads to a discursive and ideological explication of the oscillating shifts that animate the discourse on immigration and how they involve a blurring of the right/left division.

This analysis includes how the designation of self and other operates. In pursuing this part of her conclusion, Bonnafous asserts that political discourse is constituted at two levels. The first involves the perception of self associated with self-identity and its relationship to social groups, and the associated perception of others. The second involves the 'positions', assertions, declarations, argumentations on some point, be it education, immigration or some other issue. The perception of self may be solidly established and the positions organised in a coherent way but, equally, it might shift from day to day.

Her methodological process is clarified in that the analysis of designative modalities leads to a defining designative frame that expresses the currents of majority opinion in France. The failure to define national groups of reference, the effacing of collective enonciative marks, the confusion of the use of 'strangers' and 'immigrants', the absence of direct argumentation around the issue of migration, all constitute the trace of an empty identity, of a lost sense of belonging. Her analysis allows her to indicate how this trend crosses the range of newspapers. It leads her to the conclusion that this analysis of the designation of self and other relates to the manner in which the removal of social-class representations from socio-political representations results in the construction of what she calls 'formless individuals', and how this, in turn, leads to a fear of the other.

She summarises the discursive materiality in terms of how ideas are stabilised in terms of rubric, lexicality and the temporal organisation of discourse. Her corpus leads her to recognise that the issue is not one of how there is an explicit argument revolving around an evaluation pertaining to strict definitions. Rather, it pertains to how 'immigration' is essentially ambiguous, even though information concerning the 'political' rubric is framed in specific ways, to how diversity is effectively discussed by reference to the use of designatives as presupposed elements of segregation. By the same token, 'nation' as an object seems to be unrelated to any sense of inclusive boundary definition. Furthermore, the use of banal, preconstructed notionals in terms of the French/immigrant dichotomy is crucial for the understanding of how ideas are defined. Most of the enonces that mark the extreme right are only available as a common-sense view. Yet they seem to indicate the direction and the result of a logic which locks in the implicits.

Conclusion

This chapter has sought to present the methodological approaches of two analysts. In this respect it has shown how the issues discussed in preceding chapters have been put to use within an analytical context. However, by following Achard's framework and considering how Bonnafous deploys the elements of that framework I have forced the latter's analysis into that framework. Misleading though this may be, it does serve to show how a common framework is unnecessary, if not impossible. The comparison also serves to show how two quite different copora can be equally revealing. However, it also reveals two different approaches to analysis. Achard's analysis is politically benign, largely because he has deliberately chosen a corpus which does not reflect explicitly political subjects and objects. In this respect, it contrasts with Bonnafous' corpus. On the other hand, there is another difference. Whereas Achard does not adopt an explicitly epistemological approach, but rather expresses a concern about how any analysis reveals the effects of discourse, Bonnafous adopts a much more conventional and direct orientation. She emphasises that she operates within a scientific framework within which discourse analysis assumes two forms. The first is a demonstration form which provides proof for affirmations capable of verification; and the second leads to discovery by revealing that which a simple reading of text cannot reveal. This distinction leads us to some of the issues discussed in the concluding chapter.

9

POST-STRUCTURALISM, NORMATIVITY AND THE ONTOLOGY OF BEING

Foucault and normativity

In many respects, Foucault's work can be seen as focusing upon normativity. His preoccupation was with how the actions of norms in the life of human beings determine the kind of society in which they themselves appear as subjects. He referred to 'event' in terms of the way a situation is placed within a field of social forces. It was not conceived of as the causal of change, but as a locus of chance reversal, the discontinuous moment when a transformation is evident. In some respects, it overlapped with the concept of epistemological break. However, it is perhaps closer to the Nietzschean idea of the event as a reversal of a relationship of forces, the usurpation of power, the approbation of a vocabulary turned against those who had once used it, leading to the entry of a master 'Other'. It thus appears as a critique of modernity or as the *raison d'être* of post-structuralism while differing from post-modernism as critique. Event also has relevance for an understanding of how specific points of conflict involve meaning, and in relation to which social practices are transformed. In this context, event refers to the reversal of discursive practices.

The relationship between Foucault's concept of event and normativity involves how we pass from one conception of the norm and its action to a different norm, and the different social relations associated with it. It raises the question of the links between normativity, social relationships and the insertion of individuals in the networks which these relationships constitute. It involves the different definitions of subjects and objects and the relationship of these definitions to the constitution of meaning. Of course, there is no such thing as norm in itself, there is no pure law, it is a socio-historical condition. The norm is not external to its field of application, and the focus must be on its application and the way in which it thereby produces and reproduces itself. The question shifts to one of what legitimates it.

Thus, event can be seen as analysis in the sense of a criticism which serves to reveal the taken for granted or normative; it focuses upon what arguments and presuppositions hold the normative together, or it can serve to reveal the process whereby the non-normative is constituted as deviant. Indeed, what Foucault sought to do in his genealogies was to delegitimise ideas by showing them to be deeply implicated in multiple relations of force. He displaced the participant's perspective with an externalist perspective from which the claims of reason are not engaged, but are observed at work in the constellation of power in which they function.

In contrast to the modernist discourse premised upon reason, normativity is not seen as a preordained form which relates to social order, but, rather, as the effects of a discourse which establishes a norm of knowledge expressed as 'truth'. Within the praxis philosophy of modernity, society appears to be an objective network of relations that is either set, as a normative order, above the heads of subjects with their transcendentally prior mutual understandings, as in the work of Schutz, or is generated by them as instrumental orders. Castoriadis (1995) relates social practice to a normative content by viewing action not expressively, but as the originless creation of absolutely new and unique patterns, whereby each of them discloses an incomparable horizon of meaning, a position which would appear to overlap with Bakhtinian dialogism. Whichever position we consider, we return to how the Young Hegelians critique of idealism had resulted in a disempowering of philosophy, and how Heidegger's critique of Nietzsche involves returning to philosophy its lost plenitude of power. In this position, the historical destiny of a culture or society is determined by a collectively binding pre-understanding of the things and events that can appear in the world at all. This ontological pre-understanding depends upon horizon-forming basic concepts which, to a certain extent, prejudice the meaning of any being. That is, the normative remains clearly defined. The benefit which Foucault derived from his reading of Heidegger's work is evident.

Foucault's concern was with the question of how one passes from a negative conception of the norm and its action, founded upon a juridical conception of exclusion in relation to a permitted and a defended, to a positive conception which, in contrast, focuses upon the biological function of inclusion and of regulation – regulation in the sense of regularisation. This is referenced in terms of the distinction between the normal and the pathological as they have been established by the social sciences. He argued that these two conceptions lead to quite different social relations and the mode of insertion of individuals in the network that they constitute.

The problematic which directed Foucault's work involved, first, the relationship of the norm to its 'objects', that is, norm in its juridical sense, where a landmark or boundary is established, or to a limit, as in the case of the biological norm; and, second, the relationship of the norm to its 'subjects' where certain subjects are excluded or integrated in relationship to how the norm separates or distinguishes. The norm can be negative and restrictive/ divisive and relates to domination. In this respect it sets boundaries which are related to judgment about the merits of inclusion and exclusion. Thus normativity is treated as a discourse which not only sets boundaries in constructing subjects and objects in relation to each other, but also institutionalises or stabilises certain discourses as normative. The productivity of the norm for Foucault is involved in the same process of knowledge and power by reference to its productivity in exposing the action of a norm, as subject of knowledge or as subject of power, in accordance with a line that separates the licit from the illicit, and also in that which constitutes being itself in the form of thinking subjects. Being a subject is being subjected, not merely in the sense of submitting to some external order that supposes a relation of pure domination, but in the sense of the insertion of individuals in networks which are homogeneous and continuous. This involves a normative disposition which reproduces them and transforms them into subjects.

In referring to the disciplinary society, Foucault was referring to how a collection of practices that focus upon the norm transcends a collection of social bodies such that it creates a sort of common language across all sorts of institutions. In this respect it becomes the effects of the discourse of normativity, involving the stabilisation of specific relationships between social subjects in relation to specific objects. It is the diffusion of disciplines that homogenises social space. The norm is that whereby, and across which, society communicates with itself. Thus, what orthodox sociology has studied as patterned behaviour, social norms, institutions, etc., as things which transcend individual behaviour – *conscience collective* – are now seen as the effects of the normativity. The norm is the link, the principle of unity and of communication of individualities. That is, it is the reference point that institutionalises so that social groups assume objectivity in the form of the individual. What Foucault's perspective does is to recognise the norm as a principle of communication devoid of origin and devoid of a subject. He denies the rational basis of the norm. Thus, normative individualisation happens without reference to a nature, nor to an essence of subjects. There is not a specification which declares the qualities which the individual possesses in itself and which characterises its genre or nature. In this respect, normative individualisation is purely comparative in the sense that it individualises, without ceasing, at the same time, to instigate comparison around the common measure which is instituted in the pure reference of a group to itself. By the same token, the normative involves the manner in which the local links with the global. Similarly, normative space does not acknowledge an outside, the abnormal not being merely another nature of the normal – the exception confirms the rule but in so doing it is also part of the rule.

It becomes evident that the normative involves the modality of objects while also being presupposed as progress. What is normal involves the effect of the complex practices of normalisation and leads to confusing the normal with the moral. This being the case, it is also clear that if a philosophical discourse cannot enonce without affirming some norm, then it also is implicated in the process of normativity. Evidently, we can make the same claim for sociology and linguistics. Thus, sociology becomes a particular order of discourse. Yet it is a discourse which does have a subject in the sense that all discourses have a subject which carries the enonce and which is inscribed in its structure. It is also a discourse which seeks to present the 'real' or the 'true'. It begs the question of whether it was this which prevented Foucault from developing an epistemological stance, either by reference to theory or method, and whether the acceptance of FDA as the method of post-structuralism strikes the same impossibility.

It is also clear that Foucault's work draws heavily upon Hiedegger's claim that being takes its concrete form, in practice, in the language and the institutions of a given society, thereby crossing all individuals who live in that society. These common practices which rule social life constitute the background plan which permits us to comprehend the value that is assigned to an object, to being human, thereby constituting or constructing the real, which is the essential prerequisite of directing our actions against objects and particular individuals. It returns to Foucault's concern about how human beings appear within an ambiguous position within which they are both the object of knowledge and the object that knows, becoming the sovereign that submits, the spectator that views, etc. It is a reiteration of the manner in which Kant constructed human-kind as the source of the signification of objects and as an object operating within the world, thereby transforming philosophy into an anthropology. Anthropology becomes the science which interprets humankind, while all the time knowing what humankind is. In many respects Heidegger's reference to the totalising effect of what he called 'total mobilisation' has its equivalent in the manner in which Foucault deals with normativity.

FDA, ideology and the normative

The appeal of Foucault's concern with normativity as a controlling, defining and valorising force for Pécheux, who was, without doubt, the most influential force in FDA, should now become apparent. In a sense, Pécheux's initial concern with developing a means whereby the nature of ideology can be revealed also takes us in the direction of normativity in that Marxism's pre-occupation with the normative revolved around the issue of the taken for granted, of common sense, and the way in which this conditioned the ideological order à la Gramsci. This is not to deny that there has been a tendency for ideology to be conceived of as a conspiratorial entity which is constituted before the act. Such an approach was dominated by a pre-occupation with the true/false dichotomy, with false consciousness being seen as the 'false' comprehension of 'truth' by a constituency whose interests are not served by such a comprehension. In a sense, 'false' is equated with an illusion. However, denying this hermeneutic position was a central contribution of the work of both Althusser and Pécheux. Once the conspiratorial nature of ideology was resolved, it became possible to think of ideology by reference to social practice, as something which does not require the intervention of the centred, rational, human subject. It allows the understanding of ideology as a totalising, determining, force without recourse to the principles of modernity. Ideology is no longer a prefigured, rational construct that pre-dates the act, but is to be seen as the effects of discourse. What remains, of course, is the social engineering that links to Marxism's own conception of the good life, a position which Foucault sought to avoid in his reluctance to problematise that which characterises the social world, knowing that to do so would make it difficult to differentiate his position from that of Kant.

A Gramscian approach, coupled with a delayed awareness of the significance of the work of Laclau and Mouffe (1985), who worked closely with Pécheux and Gadet at the beginning of the 1980s, has taken the study of ideology in a direction that overlaps with the concerns of FDA. The focus is less upon the epistemological than upon the function of ideas within social life. Not that this theme has been entirely absent from Marxism in the past. It involves a shift in the conception of ideology as the medium in which social struggle is realised at the level of signs, meanings and representations. Ideology equates with the manner in which the power processes which serve to sustain social orders relate to signification (Eagleton, 1991:11). Some Marxist principles are retained, and, despite the objections of those such as Callinicos and Norris, the work of some post-structuralists, most notably Michel Foucault, is also drawn upon. Ideology becomes conceptualised as discursive practice in the sense of being a form of practical action. It obliges a reassessment of the base–superstructure relationship, leading to the claim that discursive practice as ideological practice is not distinct from other social practices. It also argues for the local nature of political practice, involving how alliances are forged out of political ideology in formulating identities and subject positions. This, in turn, obliges a reassessment of the primacy of social class and an awareness of the multiple bases of subject formation. In a sense, this work involves retracing many of the steps taken by FDA during the 1970s, albeit that the input of linguistic form into method and analysis is almost non-existent.

The second problem of Marxism – functionalism – was also resolved by recourse to Althusser's work. The problem involves the conspiratorial argument in the sense that the superstructural system exists in order to sustain the economic infrastructure. Thus, we encounter a functionalist relationship between superstructure and infrastructure, a relationship which sustains particular interests and deploys ideology to that end. As such, it is an argument which seeks to demonstrate how both order and change derive from the same conditions. It also substitutes a universal rationality for the rationality of the individual. Social order derives from a coercion which relies upon consensus. Althusser drew upon Gramsci's claim that, to an extent, the superstructure can be regarded as distinct from the infrastructure. This is not the place to outline the details of this development, suffice it to say that it did allow FDA to focus upon a conception of ideology as social practice which was not constrained by the kinds of functionalist arguments which inevitably draw upon the centred rational human subject.

It is relevant here to mention the manner in which Horkheimer and Adorno rejected Heidegger's appeal to authenticity on the grounds that it represented an asocial, bourgeois reversion to an empty individualism (Hoy and McCarthy, 1994:129). Instead they refer, somewhat surprisingly, to Durkheim and his reference to social categories of thought as an expression of social solidarity, but they interpret it in terms of the inscrutable unity of society and domination. 'Domination lends increased consistency and force to the social whole in which it establishes itself' (Horkheimer and Adorno, 1972:21). That is, domination is not thought of as something that some particular people do to some other people, but as what people do to themselves though it is not in their real interest to do so. Two points emerge. First, that people can do something without recognising the consequences. That is, consequences are the result of rational preconception, but such a rationality is not necessarily part of social behaviour, even though it can be. Second, that rational preconception involves serving self-interests, either as individuals or as social categories. Thus there is a link both to the rational subject, whether as individual or as collectivity, acting in his or her interest, and to action or practice as non-rational and as, it would seem, the effects of discourse. These ideas lead to seeing society as a self-perpetuating machine, the appearance of which is the source of the misguided 'ideological' belief in both the necessity of the system as well as the value of the system's historical realisation. Indeed, they cite Nietzsche as the one who sees that Bacon's utopian dream of the enlightened spread of power into everyone's hands has the inverse effect of spreading power more efficaciously over everyone. However, unlike Heidegger and Nietzsche, whom they bracket together, they resort to the economic dimension to explain rather than to denigrate the lack of self-comprehension of the masses. In coming to depend upon either social welfare or the success of the economy for their survival, the masses come to identify with the forces that oppress them. As an oppression it is against their real interests. Conformism is interpreted as the symptom of the necessity of the spread of power and domination into all aspects of society.

Much of this debate bears a remarkable similarity to that which Althusser and Pécheux were locked into during the 1960s and 1970s. The self-reflective nature of their thinking, and the manner in which they recognised that ideas and thought are limited and contextualised by reference to their historical conjuncture, not only led them close to Foucault's concept of event, but also led them away from the conception of philosophy as a domain which advanced new substantive theories about truth and reality. This, in turn, leads to a focus upon methodological questions about how philosophy is possible as anything other than a meta-theoretical enterprise concerned with method. The limit here involved the commitment to Marxism and, in Althusser's case, was conditioned by the claim for historical materialism as the only relevant method.

While this was also true of Pécheux, in that Althusser's work retained a particular relevance for his own, his willingness to pursue methodological issues raised a number of different questions. It was these questions which largely resolved themselves during the early 1980s when the relationship with Marxism changed. However, it is not inconceivable that the way in which these developments touched upon post-structuralism led to an awareness, and even a despair, that the link to orthodox politics was broken. This is expressed by Laclau (1988:23):

> there is nothing that can be called a 'politics of poststructuralism'. The idea that theoretical approaches constitute philosophical 'systems' with an unbroken continuity that goes from metaphysics to politics is an idea of the past that corresponds to a rationalistic and ultimately idealistic conception of knowledge.

There is something of a parallel with Adorno's work in that Pécheux was clearly sensitive to 'the discontinuous, chaotically splintered moments and phases of history' (Adorno, 1979:320), this leading him to a sympathy with Foucault's concern with event. However, as in the case of Adorno, his unwillingness to abandon materialist historical explanations led him away from any direct advocation of discontinuity. It is significant that the references made to the work of Foucault in Pécheux's *Les vérités de La Palice* involve a mixture of admiration and a resounding condemnation for not alluding to the claims of Marxism. This was partly the product of conviction, but was also linked to a commitment, both to Althusser as master, and to the French Communist Party. The break with this economism and its link to rationality was complete in FDA by the beginning of the 1980s, when Pécheux left the PCF. Thereafter ideology was akin to the normative as the effect of discourse constructed out of infinite possibilities of meaning. Both the implication of the rational subject in conspiratorialism, and the idea of a structure external to discourse, disappears. It links with a removal of the evolutionism of historical materialism and its concern with inevitable progress constructed out of reason. It raises the question of the interdiscourse and its relationship to normativity.

The current neo-Foucaultian thrust of studies of ideology persists in alluding to a diluted form of Marxism and betrays a reluctance to concede that 'there is nothing but discourse', or that every account is an ideological account (Wetherell and Potter, 1992:62). It focuses upon the same struggle over the nature of 'truth' as that found in the earlier work of FDA – Foucaultianism denies its existence whereas Marxism subscribes to a particular form of truth in that it constitutes a form of relativism, its account being privileged on epistemological grounds. It leads to the need to separate discursive practice from other social practices, seeking to separate the ideological from the social. This occurs despite the fact that current studies of ideology resolve the issue of agency through the concept of subjectification and leads to retaining the agency of the social world. There is an evident tension between Marxism's essentialism and Foucaultian anti-essentialism. There is a great deal which those ploughing this furrow can stand to gain from a reading of FDA.

In contrast to these approaches, there is a sense in which it might be argued that FDA has abandoned the concept of ideology, replacing it with the concept of discourse. That is, discourse is seen as something social which has an effect upon social practice, much as ideology was conceived of. In this respect, it follows Foucault in insisting that since a sign and signification are material entities and processes, discourse itself is material. However, that materiality exists in form and not in content. The importance of effect rests partly in the manner in which closure is implicated in the manner in which certain signifiers are fixed or stabilised, while certain forms of signification are excluded.

The understanding of ideology that is an implicit feature of FDA derives from an amalgam of the ideas of Althusser and Foucault, although the input of others cannot be denied. Althusser's conception of ideology was as a representation of the manner in which people 'live' their relations to society as a whole. In this respect, it was a particular organisation of signifying practices whereby the human subject is constituted. His retention of Marxist materialism was in terms of how ideology produced lived relations by which subjects are linked to the dominant relations of production. As such, this conception departs from any rationalist theory of ideology wherein reality is distorted. Rather, his concern was with how we become inextricably entwined with social reality. Thus ideology 'expresses a will, a hope or a nostalgia, rather than describing a reality' (Althusser, 1969:234). This related to language in the sense of discourse as a code which only seems to be describing the way things actually are. Its essence involves enonciations which have effects and in that respect get things done. In this respect it was very much an affective conception of ideology.

This not to deny that for Althusser ideologies contain a kind of knowledge, but it is, essentially, a pragmatic knowledge which serves to orientate the subject to its task in society. It is here that the denial of all 'truth' and 'falsehood' enters in, this being the essence of Foucault's position. For Foucault, power is a pervasive, intangible network of force inextricably linked with social practice. The consequences of this for ideology is that ideology tends to recede in its orthodox meaning and it is for this reason that one is tempted to suggest that FDA has incorporated a specific conception of discourse in its place. The emphasis upon the ambiguity of meaning, together with the claim for a process of meaning construction devoid of rationalism, leads to a focus upon the effects of meaning which are not linked to any sense of interests. It is this that has led more orthodox materialist thinkers to claim that this position should be rejected since it fails to accommodate any conception of domination (Thompson, 1990). Yet, as we have seen, this is not correct, since one of the effects of discourse is domination. That is, discourse establishes the enonciative relations between places, which are social relations. Perhaps the result is that the epistemological is collapsed into the ontological, but if the epistemological is denied, this should be no surprise.

The question of meaning has always been at the centre of FDA. The critique of meaning as 'always already there' in the expressions of language led to the idea of meaning as constituted in historically situated discursive formations. The issue of meaning was returned to an externality in being linked to the conditions of production that determined the discursive materiality. The associated analysis involved establishing the lexical items, and the systems of paraphrase or of substitution that were constitutive of meaning. Linked to this was the claim that meaning was given by a relationship with an exterior ideology. In many respects this approach was characteristic of a period when structuralism prevailed, leading to a claim that two structures were in a situation of permanent confrontation. On the one hand, a language structure, and, on the other, the ideological formations which translated the relations of power. Meaning was constructed from a meta-discourse and language was not involved in meaning other than in relation to a theory of ideology.

From the critique of this position there emerged a new orientation towards meaning. It focused attention upon the interpretative resources of texts. Meaning is not given as an *a priori* but is constructed in each step of the description. Furthermore, it is never achieved in a structure, but derives from the materiality of language and the archive. In that sense it is constrained and open.

If one recognises that representations have a direct relevance for ideology, in the sense that they are not neutral but are tributary, and that different representations of the same object are ideologically different, we begin to recognise the relevance for the link between discourse and the production of meaning. In this respect, the notion of the implicit, and its relationships to prior discourse, has direct relevance for representation once we recognise that the implicit pre-exists discourse. Central is the reconstitution of the implicit. That is, prior discourse is crucial for the understanding of the production of meaning. Whereas, as we have seen, Foucault's early work placed emphasis upon the production of discourse, the shift in his work to emphasising the production of social meaning is highly relevant.

The production of meaning is not akin to the individual submitting to some social aggregation, but, rather, it is a directly collective process, being the diversity of responses and their eventual meeting in relation to the problems of the implicit that constitutes the meaning of enonces. Thus the central shift is not towards conditions of production of meaning as some external fixed source, but in relation to the notion of situation. There is thus a shift in the understanding of ideology from one where the world of social acts and the world of ideas are separate, to one where they are systematically and locally associated. Instead of seeing external conditions of production in a global relationship with internal constraints on the logic of a discursive domain, each enonce, pertaining to the situation in which it is plunged, is modified, and its meaning is nothing other than its modification of that situation.

Thus, both a metalanguage and a meta-discourse are eliminated in that the enonce/situation pair continues to distinguish between form and meaning, not merely in terms of reference, but because form contributes to meaning itself. The enonciative-modal apparatus of language, with categorisations anchored in the situation, has a direct affectivity in that it outlines the act of social relations. We are thus led to a situation at the heart of the production of meaning and away from any form of meta-disciplinarity.

Sociology and normativity

Given that both Althusser and Foucault have had an enormous influence on sociology during the last quarter of the twentieth century, it is pertinent and necessary to consider the relevance of FDA for the discipline. Evidently, in purporting to be a method that relates to the social, it should have a significant contribution to make to sociology. On the other hand, its focus extends way beyond the customary boundaries of sociology, thereby seriously criticising the orthodox integrity of sociology as a strictly defined field of study. It is obvious that sociology has had a strange relationship with language. While sociologists have studied language, they have tended to be unaware of sociology's own use of language. Sociology's emergence as a feature of modernism was responsible for the separation of language, mind and reality. This meant that it was possible to study reality without reference to language. It also meant that reality was reflected in language and that a consideration of evidence, as language, implied an introduction to truth. In the same manner, language and nature were separated, involving the separation of representation and fact. This meant that society could become something to study, as something separate from language. In a sense language was excluded from proto-sociology.

In treating discourse as the use of language in practical situations, that is, as an affective act linked to other acts, discourse becomes an object of knowledge rather than some 'natural' object. This, in turn, leads to discourse becoming conterminous with a particular view of sociology wherein effective action and practical context are viewed by reference to social structuration. In some respects, this is merely another way of claiming that it is essential, within sociology, to consider the role of language in social process, something which mainstream, modernist sociology has systematically avoided. Viewing language acts as social acts is to consider its stability within a ruled system of social relationships that involve shared meaning across locuteurs. On first sight, this would appear to involve some form of ruled system that is independent of discourse. As we shall see, this is far too simple a view. However, I would first of all like to turn to a more general consideration of sociology.

The relationship between normativity and social order and their relationship to law in the work of Hobbes lead us towards a consideration of the emergence of the modern State, premised upon these very ideas, and of sociology as the discipline which sought to study the laws of social development. A normative social order premised upon reason was the *sine qua non* of the modern State. It was this which became the context for the equation within sociology of society and State, society itself being addressed as a dynamic normative order. The concept of society was politically constructed in relation to the setting of spatial and social boundaries. The link to reason and the focus of cumulative knowledge were the elements which gave rise to social evolutionism as the transcendental form which explained the dynamic of the socio-political being of the State. The normative was defined in terms of a constitutive difference in which the non-normative was viewed not only as different, nor merely as deviant, but as atavistic. Society was discussed by reference to a typology based upon a binary opposition between two social forms, the modern dynamic form and the traditional, static, atavistic form. In this respect, it was characteristic of the human sciences in consisting of a discursive practice which simultaneously established a norm of knowledge which enonciates the criterion of truth, whose value is restrictive or constitutive, and a norm of power which socially constructs the subject by reference to his/her liberty. Even while proclaiming the goal of studying the deviant or the pathological, sociology was actively involved in its construction (G. Williams, 1998b).

This Hobbesian emphasis upon law and social order contrasts with that of Spinoza, who refuted any attempt to install a rupture between the state of nature and the state of society. He emphasised that in society it is always nature which dominates, and that society should be understood by reference to the laws of nature. Thus, reason and nature, or humankind and nature, were not diametrically opposed. Power was not vested in some sovereign body. Rather, Spinoza referred to micro-power revolving around the manner in which the complexity of relationships is resolved by the sharing of common notions, or notions which, of necessity, are acquired in common, and which express that which is common to all things. Thus, whereas Hobbes formed a politics on an anthropological base linked to a theory of human passion, Spinoza developed a conception of humankind subjected to the laws of nature. Norm differs from the arbitrary and artificial of Hobbes' conception. It is a view shared by Foucault.

Foucault's emphasis upon the disciplinary society places considerable emphasis upon the idea of society, with the disciplines constructing society as a form of common language between all sorts of institutions. Disciplinary society becomes a society of absolute communication. It is the normative which permits the transformation of the discipline blockade into a disciplinary mechanism, the matrix which transforms the negative into the positive, thereby permitting a disciplinary generalisation, as that which is institutionalised through that transformation. The normative is precisely that whereby, and across which, society communicates with itself. It articulates the disciplines of production, knowledge, wealth, finance, making them interdisciplinary, and homogenising social space even if it does not unify it.

Prior to the turn of the nineteenth century, things operated in relation to a principle of power according to a logic of individualisation, the discipline fabricating the individual; it was the specific technique of a power which gave individuals both as objects and as instruments of its exercise. However, that axis of individualisation was not the only one, and could not be the only one, since the norm was simultaneously the link, the principle of unity, of communication of these individualities. The norm was the reference which institutionalised so that the group took its objectivity in the form of the individual. The norm is the principle of a communication without origin and without a subject. Within normative space, the gaze makes itself invisible, while those who are submitted to it are obliged to be visible. It contrasts entirely with the manner in which the sovereign displayed power, named the associated places, and gave to each his/her identity.

Normative individualisation is achieved without reference to a nature, to an essence of subjects. That is, it does not have the form of a specification, it does not declare the qualities which the individual possesses by itself and which would be characteristic of its genre or its nature. It is a positive individualisation devoid of a metaphysical being, an individualisation without substance, resembling how an opposition of signifieds never returns, other than as differences, and without which one could rely on a substance of the signified. It is a pure relationship, but a relationship without a support. Normative individualisation is purely comparative, and individualisation is not achieved through categories, but at the interior of categories. It has no appeal to any knowledge external to that which it makes visible. Normative knowledge makes no appeal to an external to that on which it works, to that which it makes visible. Thus, the norm is that measure which, while individualising, does not cease, at the same time, to render it comparable. The individualisation is never more than an expression of an indefinite relationship. Thus the norm is a principle of comparison, of comparability, a common measure which is institutionalised in the pure reference of a group to itself, even though that group only has itself as support.

This relates to the idea that the normative space of individualisation does not recognise an externality. The abnormal is no more than another nature of the normal. It is not merely that the exception confirms the rule, but that it is also in the rule. However, normative space lacks a process of valorisation; the normative practices are not relativist. If society is normative, it is because the institutions relate one to the other. Modernity, according to Foucault, is the appearance of a normative age. It is evident that society is no more, and no less, than the effect of normativity. Thus any social analysis must focus upon uncovering the nature of the normative. This, in turn, means that disciplines do not exist to be used as a feature of an analytic method.

One of the concerns that is clear in Foucault's work concerns the manner in which the analyst intervenes in the analysis – accountability. A philosophical exposé where the philosopher enonces does not merely relate to the analytic position of philosopher, but also to philosophy as a discourse. The philosopher as subject of a philosophical discourse takes in charge the enonce of that position and, in so doing, becomes part of the normalising process. As such, the philosopher is constituted as pertaining to a 'we' which marks the distinction between the collectivity of those who are involved in a particular action from those who are not. This is something which emerges with Kant in posing the question 'Who am I now?' and 'What is it that we pertain to now?' It is this that leads to the idea of the productivity of the norm in that it defines the subject by reference to a human community constituted by its relation to a right in both a moral and judicial sense, to a legal context. However, the point of reference for Kant is not a human order but a natural order, a necessary order of things which is expressed from the point of view of nature. That is, the legal pertains to the laws of nature and not to the legal system of human nature, that is, in a physical and not a juridical sense.

The modernist creation of sociology as the means of achieving access to truth or reality by reference to a social world, as the basis for understanding that truth or reality, relates to the issue of sociology as the basis for the construction of meaning. Of course, this status has never been denied by modernist sociology, which would have justified its construction of meaning in terms of the construction of reality, and of the justifying role of objectivity in that hermeneutic process. However, if such legitimisation is undermined, where does it leave sociology? Is it anything more than discourse, unworthy of its privileged status? Does society, its central concept, retain any relevance, if that concept is, itself, a product of the sociological discourse? Is the separation of language and society a serious starting point, even if we accept that society does retain some relevance? I will now turn to one attempt to consider such issues.

Discourse as society

The focus in FDA on the global, on a universalism of being, acknowledges the existence of a normative order which is locked in a process of constant change which is seen as social change. However, a system which merely analyses the nature of discourse and its effects is incapable of drawing upon a prefigured social structure for explanation. Thus it would seem that the limits of FDA focus upon changes in the effects of discourse and do not seek to encompass any reference to causality in the modernist sense. Yet, viewing society as universal explains nothing, leaving society itself to be explained. Thus, viewing FDA as a method raises the question of its effectiveness in reaching this goal.

The normative nature of sociology seen as discourse is not in doubt. Its focus upon patterns of human behaviour which are conceived of as institutional-isation, or the taken for granted, is an expression of the normative which is only recognised by reference to its difference from the deviant. It often reduces to the idea of a normativity internal to rationality itself. It is this which was the main thrust of Achard's attempt to reconceptualise FDA as a sociology of language. In that work he sought to relate the idea of the institutionalisation of modernist sociology to the idea of discursive marking. He also conceived of sociology as a description of a system of places defined by their mutual relationship and allowing a description of social processes which are not reducible to the sum of individuals. In this respect there is an implication that norm and normativity implies a shared meaning, not merely between individuals but, in some way, across individuals, being something which generates that which has become known as society. If the concern is therefore with the norm, it implies the existence of this entity which creates or constitutes society. Furthermore, the systems which sociology describes constitute a materiality which Achard seeks to relate to discursive materiality. Since language production puts both the social structure and the associated social places, as well as the individual dimension of personality, in play, the effect of discursive materiality is to be found in the production of meaning which constitutes this structure. It implies the pre-existence of a social structure and of the same conception of interaction as that of orthodox sociology except by reference to rationalism. However, this is qualified by the claim that it is in the discursive materiality that social places are defined and not in an analytic meta-discourse of a sociology external to discourse. But how can this be if the conception of a sociology and its constituent parts and its ultimate goal derive from a preconstituted metaphysics? Is it possible to take concepts from one problematic and place them in another in the hope that they hold together in the same within a different metaphysical context? Achard's response to these questions is that the social places are opened up by the materiality of discourse and not in the analytic meta-discourse external to its object. He also insists that the stabilisation of the use of enonciative operators is not necessarily retaken in the form of a lexical designation, so that social structure does not necessarily derive in the form of lexical terminology and classifiers. This, presumably, means that he did not view social structure through the prism of orthodox sociology. If not, then what does it consist of? He is of course quite right in implying that social actors cannot conform with the vision of society contained by sociology, and that in this respect sociology constitutes a shorthand, an ideal type, in Weber's words. In this respect there is a sense in which a phenomenological input devoid of centrality emerges. His concern was with how the effects of meaning organise and permit the understanding of the dimension of physical inscription of the social processes. It involves two dimensions: (1) the organisation of the enonciation in relationship with social placing, which is a relationship resting on the deictic dimension and is motivated synchronically; (2) the effect of interdiscursive accumulation which constitutes the horizon of memory of the notional functioning.

In seeking to develop a sociology which does not privilege the centred, rational subject, there is a collapse of the distinction between the social and discourse. Discourse is treated as 'the use of language in practical situations' (Achard, 1995). Evidently, it is not just linguistic knowledge which permits the language act – social knowledge is also involved. Furthermore, the relationship between language and discourse involves the point of intersection characterised by signification. The rejection of the manner in which orthodox linguistics treats the formal structure on the basis of normativity leads to locating meaning firmly in the discursive. Thus the social construction of meaning involves three central assumptions:

1   The Benvenistean principle which claims that the meaning of a statement is not reducible to the elements that compose it and put syntactic organisation into play: 'the meaning of a phrase is other than the meaning of the words that compose it'.
2   The production and interpretation of statements are the result of the cognitive activities of subjects in interaction. Of course, a fact is not psychological, sociological, etc. except where it achieves meaning in relation to language. As we shall argue below, there is a sense in which Culioli's enonciative linguistics shares with ethnomethodology the claim that the social world is constructed in and by verbal interaction. Culioli would of course refer this to an intersubjective space in elaborating the systems of referencing, or of co-ordinates, from which the interpretations are calculated, these being non-symmetrical in the sense that the receiver does not operate as a centred, rational subject, calculating or decoding what the speaker has produced. This hinges on the non-univocality between the linguistic mark and a referential value. Consequently, the statements of any language act are necessarily plurivocal and ambiguous;
3   The activity of the construction of meaning is a social activity. Evidently it is on this last point – the social construction of meaning – that our attention must focus. Consequently, the object of sociology is a signification, and any sense of scientificity that relates to the discipline is only activated through interpretation, this interpretation conventionally involving a hermeneutic order. The sociologist must of necessity be involved in a normative basis of scientificity.

As we have seen, the Althusserian concept of interpolation, in which the individual is interpolated as subject of discourse, implies that any language act involves an interdiscursivity of constructed or preconstructed places which the individual can or cannot be interpolated into. In this respect, it is important to consider the manner in which Benveniste distinguished between objective reference and reality, between reference and the instance of discourse. The references of terms such as 'I' or 'here' are not entities such as the speaking subject, or the place where s/he speaks, but are language entities – the instances of discourse containing the linguistic signs. Culioli similarly claims that the subject as a human being is not the same as the linguistic subject, and should not be the object of linguistic description, other than to the extent that they are represented in the enonces by the linguistic categories of tense, person, determination or aspect. This being the case, interpolation involves the linking of the human subject as individual with these constructed or preconstructed places. Furthermore, the notion of situation of enonciation is a theoretical representation of the researcher, a system of referencing that permits the construction of enonciative predictive values.

Two heterogenous elements are discussed: on the one hand, the linguistic, which sets constraints on forms; on the other hand, the social, which involves meaning. It is for this reason that Achard insisted that discourse analysis must involve two elements: on the one hand, the linguistic, and, on the other, some disciplinary focus such as sociology. It is in Wittgenstein's language play, and his insistence that language games are a form of life, that we encounter the shift from one to the other. Wittgenstein referred to the signification of a word as its use in language. It is in what Milner (1978) refers to as the 'real of language', where a language has a material existence, imposing its ambiguity on speaking subjects, their consciousness and their experience, that the social is most evident. We are obliged to focus upon Milner's difference between signification (linguistic) and meaning (the real effects and pragmatic understanding). Signification involves a systematic structure of places in relationship to the formal dimensions of person, place and time, or of diverse modalities. In connection with effective situations, it allows language to perform the role of operator of interaction, situating the discourse in relation to a series of places of enonciateurs where the taking in charge of the discourse by the locuteurs has the effect of carrying the effect of the system along. That is, signification is put in play by the relationship between the notional functioning and deictics. Referentiation, as one of the operations which place notions in discourse, implies the operationalisation of the deictic by situating the referents in the situation, whereas phenomena such as anaphora, which are conditioned by syntactic constraints, give a partially autonomous co-reference to the referentiation. Social interaction occurs where the locuteurs, in taking the enonces in charge, establish a relationship between the enonces which conforms with those relationships which the formal apparatus of enonciation implicates between the enonciateurs. Social life is premised on form. Between the signification which interpolates the enonciateur, and meaning, which constitutes the real of the allocutaire, are the act and the event which are constructed by the internal structure of the enonces. In this respect, the 'putting in discourse' is conterminous with the 'putting in action'.

What is at stake here is the manner in which the language act takes its signification in the subject. It outlines how the specificity of the linguistic system produces interactions, it focuses upon the surface marks and their agencies, it explores the dialogical space where they are being enonced. This leads to exploring the dynamic between the 'selves' and understanding their interrelationships. It is clear that the insistence on the materiality of language and the integration of linguistic form and their functioning in social interaction is the cornerstone of the social construction of meaning.

Treating sociology *à la* Durkheim within an epistemological context as the description of a system of places defined by their mutual relationship, leading to a description of social processes that are not reducible to the psychological orientations of the individuals occupying those places, inevitably leads to the assumption that the system which it describes constitutes a materiality. On the other hand, this same materiality is conceived of within FDA as a dialectic between two types of simultaneous and complementary inscriptions – that in the physical environment which is fashioned by the social processes, and that in the language (discursive materiality) which, despite its abstract nature, is no less material. Discourse is viewed as language process as a social process such that the social/language distinction does not exist. Thus language production puts in play not only the social structure, but also the elements of the individual personality which occupies that social structure. Thus, one is obliged to seek the effect of discursive materiality in the social production of meaning of discourse and not in the production of discourse. This social construction of meaning of discourse has a consequence for the physical environment as well as for the effects of discourse relations. That is, there is a rejection of the reduction of the material to the physical world. This means that language, rather than carrying a symptomatic value, assumes a central and active role in sociology (Achard, 1989).

It is in the discursive materiality and not in the analytic meta-discourse of a sociology that is external to its object that the social places are defined. However, to assume that one can retrieve all of the relations of places of any society in the form of lexical items is to fall into the trap of assuming the conscious mastering of the subject over the social. Sociology cannot be of that order.

Within this framework, Achard seeks to conceive of the fundamental sociological concept of institution in a somewhat different light from its orthodox conception. Institution refers to the stable structure of types of acts, and the places with which they are associated. The individual cannot be drawn into these places other than through signification, and this interpolation of actor-speakers into the categorised places is a performative act. Language becomes a system of referenced forms which are directly, but not mechanically, linked to social acts. In taking in charge of the constructed or preconstructed, the subjects who are interpolated as actors, accept, either partially or totally, the social places that are constructively marked, as well as the presupposed situation of origin. Thus, in discursive interaction, any enonce only has virtual meaning, but this virtuality is presupposed and taken in charge by all the participants in the processes in a non-marked way. Not taking in charge is viewed as an explicit process of refusal. The explicit process (marked) can be actualised in the form of language acts (enonciation), or non-language acts (non-co-operation in the act). That is, the sociological concept of institution, and the associated concept of institutionalisation, are treated in terms of the relationship between the places that relate to the stable structuration of action, and the manner in which individuals are interpolated into these places. Even though the account of these concepts differs from their initial conception, there remains the assumption that the original sociologists were correct in identifying the relevant structures. In effect, what Achard maintains is that the institution, viewed as a stability of structure, is the main object of sociology as a discipline.

However, discursive materiality rests upon the functioning of language. From the outset, one of the goals of FDA was to discover regularities as form and structure within discourse. The concept of discursive formation was of this order. Indeed, we can go so far as to realise that if the meaning of a word changes from one discursive formation to another, and if the goal of FDA is to establish the relationship of the social construction of meaning to enonciation and place, then the starting point of any analysis must be to establish the different discursive formations. By reference to the social, a discursive formation is conceived of as the structuration of social space by the differentiation of discourse. Evidently, what we have is the discursive formation differentiating discourse, and thereby structuring localities, on the basis of regularities. These regularities are akin to legitimisation, involving unmarked discourse. From the point of view of signification, there can be no difference between the language act and its enonciateur; the legitimacy is presupposed. Whether or not the locuteur takes the discourse in charge, the place of enonciateur is external to signification, and is a matter of meaning. In speaking, the locuteur, on the other hand, operates an act of pretension to legitimacy, and this is carried in the traces of the operation. The allocutaires who are in a non-marked position accept the legitimacy of the locuteur, in so far as it is not questioned. The absence of mark in the taking in charge implies that the signification is the material face of an effectively accomplished language act.

The concepts of register and genre are linked to discursive formation in specific ways. Register refers to types of text defined by their external characteristics or their social function, while genre refers to the type of use of language. Thus, Achard (1992:87) defined discursive register by reference to language play in that it is language play that gives the regularity that constitutes a register in its social existence. It is the discursive register that creates a correspondence between the enonciateur – formal component – and the locuteur – real social place. From this initial articulation, analysis develops in two directions:

- exposing the internal unwinding of the enonciation;
- the social action which the discourse supports.

These actions are carried by the enonce and not by the intentions of the locuteur, but they can also run aground. Register thereby constitutes the local materiality of an interpolation that assumes an institutionalised consistency and that is supported by stabilisation and repetition. It functions on the base of relatively independent regularities that are independent of its operationalisation. It is in this respect that the analysis of language play cannot be linked to anything of the order of a 'grammar'.

Genre, on the other hand, refers to the type of discourse normally associated with a register. It is conceived of as a collection of enonciative elements which are constitutive from the internal standpoint of the register. In this respect, a genre is a type of use of language, as in the example of the way in which scientific discourse uses 'we' or 'one' or even 'I', but never 'you'. However, a genre in itself cannot constitute a register. The example of the novel, where the 'I' is interpreted as pertaining to the principal person of the novel and not to the author, is a case in point in that it derives from the elements associated with the novel rather than with the internal elements of any particular novel. Thus, genre is defined, not only by the range of enonciative operators that it displays, but also by reference to the initial situation associated with a broader context. That is, they are forms whose internal characteristics pertain to a discursive tradition that is linked to register. In this respect, it pertains to Foucault's archive effect, involving recurring discourses which relate to specific socio-institutional environments. There is an inherent link between register and genre wherein genre is seen as the internal form characterised by linguistic elements, and representing the non-marked enonciation of the domain. Where the elements that are external to the domain appear – such as 'you' in a scientific text – it will assume a marked value.

It should now become clear how the concept of institutionalisation or the 'taken for granted' relates to genre and markedness/non-markedness. It should be equally clear how Achard refers to institution by reference to stabilisation, or the embedding of discourse, and the associated interpolation which is formalised as a specific origin of the locution of a register. The relevance of interpolation, where the individual is converted into subject via the taking in charge, places the operating force firmly in the independent form of a structured discourse, and not in the rationality of a pre-formed subject.

This takes care of institution or patterned or ruled behaviour. It does so by invoking discursive structure rather than the normative context of orthodox sociology in which the individual is socialised in relation to pre-established norms and value systems. The discursive materiality imposes itself on the locuteur in organising the effects of position and disposition. The concept of interpolation is pivotal but assumes a social rather than a psychological con-notation. In this respect the above account also incorporates the concept of social groups in that the places which the individual is interpolated into are not merely individual places but also pertain to social groups. Thus a discourse on social differentiation may well open up places that pertain to gender, social class or language groups. It is also relevant that interpolation is not conceived of by reference to any form of orthodox psychologism and thereby avoids the mentalist problem of the relationship between the social and the psychological.

A 'fact' is social only when it is put in meaning, directly or indirectly, in the speech-act. An act becomes a social act through social signification, linked to its stability in the ruled system of social relations. However, it is equally evident that the social is defined by a certain type of stability – it is the shared meaning between the locuteur and others, a meaning which is manifested in analogous acts. However, in this respect, since there will be those who do not share this agreement, it is much closer to norm. 'Social actors' relate to the institutionalisation of behaviour or action and, in this respect, conform with the non-marked nature of the subject in discourse. A language act creates institutional places replete with subject places into which the individual is interpolated, taking in charge the discourse in relation to the place that the discourse assigns them. The subject clearly lies at the intersection of form and meaning. This requires a fixity or stabilisation of discursive forms and, in a sense, the social boils down to shared meanings constructed around similar subject positions.

The relationship between institutionalisation and legitimacy is accommodated by reference to the relationship between markedness and legitimacy referred to above. There ensues a stable relationship between forms and social practices. Yet this seems suspiciously like linguistic forms, except that it is premised on the deictic rather than the syntactic grammar. This suspicion is resolved by the recognition that discursive materiality is imposed on the locuteur in so far as the interpretative apparatus organises the effects of position. Signification becomes the key element in the stabilising process, and the multiplicity of possible meanings links to signification, with each enonce having the linguistic attribute of signification. Enonciative linguistics builds on the relationship between enonciation, signification and the world, without seeking to have this relationship mediated by the centred subject or a predetermined social form. Form is given to this relationship via typologies of discourse à la Simonin-Grumbach and Culioli which, simultaneously, establish elements of constraint.

There remains the issue of social interaction. This is dealt with by reference to Bakhtin's dialogism and the claim that an enonciation does not have any meaning in itself, in an already complete signification, since it consists of a multiplicity of plays of language. Evidently, it also draws upon deixis and the notion of language act. Meaning is the result of a practical confrontation of social groups around signification, and the plays of language are the products of open options at the heart of a discursive organisation. It also leads to viewing social processes as something that is not enclosed in the form of a global society. Rather, it leads to the claim that there are no natural boundaries to society. Given the manner in which society was defined from the start as pertaining to State boundaries, with each State having a single society, this should be no surprise. It involves interpretation in the constitution of meaning, and the manner in which the deictic structure involves the interpolation of individuals as speaking subjects within the language act. Each attestation as a language act does not have its particular or proper meaning in the sense that it is pre-interpreted, but simultaneously constitutes an act of appropriation of registers which it lays claim to, and an act whose interpretation is the object of confrontation between possible appropriations. The reported discourse and the relevant marks are the traces of that confrontation.

Whereas the focus of post-structuralism, indeed, its *raison d'être*, has been the decentring of the subject, and whereas this has resulted in a rethinking of the nature of sociology, we would insist that sociology as discourse has been premised on much more than rationality as the basis for action. Central in this respect is the relationship between normativity, patterned regularities of behaviour or institutionalisation, and social order. It is these concepts, and not merely the idea of the centred, rational subject, which have sustained the very idea of society. It would appear necessary to consider whether decentring is sufficient grounds for the rethinking of sociology. If sociology is itself a discourse, is there not a problem in creating an alternative sociology on the basis of the notions which derive from that discourse, even if these notions have been the defining criterion of sociology?

To summarise: what we have is the claim that the meaning of a notion in a real situation is partially determined by: (1) enonciation, (2) acts and (3) the interdiscourse. To this claim must be added an awareness of heterogeneity and the fact that dialogism enters different discourses and therefore does not have the same meaning or value. On the other hand, intervening between form and meaning is signification, which Milner regards as part of form. Yet Wittgenstein, whose work has played a central role in FDA since the beginning of the 1980s, referred to the signification of a word as its use in language. The importance of Wittgenstein is that the same enonce can be placed in different plays of language, since the structure of enonces does not indicate the play of language. This is the link to dialogism which Achard treats in the sense of meaning being created out of multitude plays of language (polyphony). Hence the linking of FDA, Wittgenstein and Bakhtin. Language play indicates that language acts are structured in the sense that they are linked to genres of life or social practices. Language play becomes akin to the product of open options at the heart of discursive organisation. In turn, dialogism indicates that meaning is never pre-given, but rather is the result of a practical meeting of social groups around signification. This is what led Achard to see language play as possessing a structure linked to social practice. Using dialogism, he showed that meaning derives from social confrontation linked to signification and language play. If meaning is essentially ambiguous, there are no fixed boundaries to language nor to society which has no reality outside of language, being as it is the effects of discourse. However, discourse has two sides to it:

1　signification which relates to linguistics in one form or another; and
2　an indeterminate side which relates to the social dimension of meaning and which is treated as sociology.

The social in this respect is faithful to its Foucaultian grounding and involves the manner in which meaning sets constraints on the social.

It is tempting to suggest that much of what is being said about the social in FDA is a reflection of modernist sociology couched in quite different terms. In this respect, there is the suspicion that what is happening is that orthodox sociological concepts are explained in a non-modernist way, or are couched in non-modernist terms. Thus discursive formation replaces social organisation, institution is replaced by the stabilisation of discourse, social norm is akin to genre, and social order is akin to stability or fixity of meaning. While this is perhaps inevitable, it does raise the question of the extent to which the meaning is carried over from sociology as a discourse. For most of those in FDA, this cannot be an issue in the sense that it has no pretensions concerning any form of hermeneutic. Since meaning is the effects of discourse, if there is a discourse on society, then society assumes meaning, and thereby exists. None the less, there is a case to answer when one recognises the importance of concepts of normativity and order which presuppose any analysis, where order is claimed to be a feature of discourse. On the other hand, if discourse analysis is simply concerned with the construction of meaning, why does that meaning have to be social if the social itself is merely the effect of discourse on society? Why does enonciative linguistics require an adjunct that itself, as discourse, constructs the social?

There is also the danger that there is a retreat to a process we are familiar with in the empirical tradition. It resembles induction in the sense that it would seem to depend upon the discovery of regularities. This is not to deny that such constructivism does not involve discovering 'facts' which suggest or indicate an 'order' in which they have their place or function. However, there is a danger that we prejudge 'order', that we establish something which is akin to the modernist view of society rather than being aware of Bakhtin's claim that although the word might be expressive, this does not mean that this expression inheres in the word itself. Rather, it originates in the contact between the word and reality under the conditions of the situation articulated by the individual enonce.

Linguistics and normativity

The same issues can be raised by reference to linguistics. Linguistics has been constructed as a normative discipline, involving the establishing of recognisable patterns of language use which can be categorised and ordered in order to discover the assumed structures which allow language to operate. The break between orthodox linguistics and sociolinguistics revolves around the relevance of the social for the constitution of language, between, on the one hand, linguistics as the description of patterns and processes, and, on the other, the social function of language as that which establishes these patterns and processes. Given that FDA has a great deal to say about both the nature of the social, and about the social construction of meaning, it inevitably leads to the questioning of the nature of both linguistics as a discourse and sociolinguistics as a discipline.

Changes occurred within proto-linguistics at the end of the eighteenth century involving the manner in which there was a shift of focus from discourse to language, from representation to a new relationship between representation and signification, from interpretation to analysis. There are transformations in the category of the word, in grammar. The development of philology, the isolation of Indo-European languages, the constitution of comparative grammar, the study of inflections, all reveal this fundamental shift. The form of the word's existence is no longer given in its representative and analytic functions. Rather, it has a form of existence that is determined by something else, by something beyond representation. Whereas in the classical episteme (Foucault, 1966), languages were distinguished from one another by the different usages of representations which they used, by the different discursive means which they had at their disposal, from the time of Schlegel different languages are characterised by reference to grammatical principles which are not reducible to discursive means, to signification. This means that each language has an autonomous grammatical space. As a consequence, languages can be compared without touching upon the issue of signification. Languages become objects that are analysed according to an internal structure, a structure that is increasingly analysed by reference to phonological structure.

The emergence of the autonomous space of language coincides with the emergence of the new political space of the modern State at the end of the eighteenth century. The overlap between these two spaces is what constitutes the political nature of language, and the argument of what is and what is not a language within the general typological taxonomy of Indo-Europeanism relates to the emerging political taxonomy of Europe. With the State languages being treated as languages of reason, and also as the defining characteristic of the people, it was necessary to incorporate the resulting frontiers into the intellectual discourse on language and languages. As with sociology, linguistics became the basis for the consecration of the modern State. Given the link between language and reason, and given the link between syntax and language, the definition of a particular language as pertaining to a single State also meant that there would be a single syntax for each State language. By default, those languages which were not State languages, even though they had to exist within State territory, were beyond the realm of reason, existing as worthless *patois* (Williams, 1998b). The claim for a link between correct language and correct thought was merely another keystone in the process of normativising a particular language over others. It was expressed in terms of:

Le français, par un privilège unique, est seul resté fidèle à l'ordre direct . . . la syntaxe française est incorruptible. C'est de là que résulte cette admirable clarté, base éternelle de notre langue. Ce qui n'est pas clair n'est pas français.

(Quoted in Calvet, 1987:74)

Corpus planning became the means whereby the State languages could be standardised as languages of reason, thereby intervening between thought and communication as the basis for good language producing good thought. All aspects of culture were subject to this standardising process, which became the basis of High Culture. Within linguistics, it was the basis for treating language by reference to the construction of well-formed sentences, the focus being upon form rather than upon meaning. This, of course, led to the Chomskyan orientation. It was also behind the work of several linguists associated with FDA during the early 1980s when they sought to 'force' language, in order to demonstrate that normativity could be broken without affecting the construction of meaning. It was, in effect, the early manifestation of formal semantics and contrasts with Pêcheux's (1975a:20) conception of syntax as the mode of organisation of traces of enonciative reference specific to a particular language. As such, syntactic constructions are a signification of that which they free.

The shift to a concern with discourse and enonciation involves a means of negating this normative influence and also involves a shift from a concern with the infinite possibilities of language to a realisation that discourse was the point of articulation of ideological processes and linguistic phenomena. It also relates to how semantic effects are bound up with syntax and with Lacan's claim that 'syntax, of course, is preconscious'. In this respect, it was closely linked with decentring and subjectivity and the manner in which the subject assumes positions as a speaking subject. This decentring he derived from the work of Lacan.

Pêcheux was very clear about the role of semantics in linguistic analysis and also of the need to subject linguistic theory to analysis. He saw that the discourse which was analysed was not a linguistic object but a socio-historical object which was subjected to an analysis using linguistics as a presupposed that was taken for granted. It was this which led to the critique of orthodox syntax as behaviourist, involving a subjectivist conception of semantics which derived from a postulation of the independence of the syntactic and the semantic. He was equally critical of the Chomskyan position according to which the semantic belongs entirely to the linguistic field, where semantics is a natural extension of the syntactic, so that meaning is a fact of language. It relied upon a conception which derived from both a theory of knowledge and a psychology of the centred subject, even if that subject was neutral. Such a position is hardly surprising given his roots in the work of Canguilhem and Bachelard and the manner in which his initial published work focused upon a critique of the epistemological bases of social psychology. It was an attempt to move away from a universal and *a priori* semantics.

The early involvement of Culiolian enonciative linguistics was the consequence of the importance of the work of Benveniste and Saussure in French linguistics. Benveniste distinguished between meaning and reference or designation at the interior of the process of signification. This emphasis upon signification linked with the Althusserian idea of the interpolation of the subject through signification. This approach clearly has strong implications for the decentring of the subject. However, for Benveniste, language was not merely a system of signs but also a means of communication where the expression is discourse. Meaning came to be conceived of in terms of the relationship between signs and references within a theory of enonciation. Yet Benveniste's work was strongly influenced by that of Husserl, and considerable work was necessary in order to disarticulate the theory of enonciation from its Husserlian influence so that it could link with decentring. It involved Pécheux's theory of the subjective illusion of *parole*. It was the key which opened the way to linking the linguistic work of enonciative linguistics with Foucault's work on the normative. The work of Foucault had always been present in FDA, in concepts such as discursive formation, the order of discourse, the order of things, etc. Granted that such concepts had been modified to conform with the Althusserian brand of the Marxist problematic, all that stood in the way of its accommodation on its own terms was the political involvement of the practitioner! The break with the PCF in 1982 opened the way for a discourse analysis which linked directly with post-structuralism and could be designated as French Discourse Analysis.

Whither FDA?

It is a strange paradox that while FDA as a field is attracting an increasing interest in Anglo-American circles, until recently its fortunes in France appeared to be on the wane. We have seen how ADELA disbanded following Pécheux's untimely death. Some members of this group have retreated into the more orthodox topics of linguistics or historical linguistics (Gadet, 1989a), while others, most notably Marandin, Guilhaumou and Conein have either forsaken FDA in favour of ethnomethodology, or have sought to span FDA and ethnomethodology. Courtine (1992) has gone so far as to launch a bitter attack against the assumptions of FDA, claiming that the whole idea of the decentred subject was misplaced, being no more than a fashion of the 1970s and 1980s. Of course, some, most notably Achard, Sériot and Robin have persisted with the initial project, but as a consequence of the lack of impetus in France, even they appear to have their doubts about the future orientation of FDA.

Of course it was inconceivable that those whose focus was linguistic would involve themselves with modernist linguistics with its focus upon the normativity of the eighteenth-century thrust for standardisation. Rather the focus has been more on the phenomenological as normative practice. It links with the current focus upon popular culture. What is evident is that much of the work that is of primary relevance to FDA continues within a linguistic orientation that focuses upon the importance of enonciation. Certainly this focus of the work has not abated. The importance of Culiolian linguistics is increasingly recognised, and many of those who were formerly associated with FDA have merely pursued their linguistic interests within a more confined linguistic frame. That is, the explicit attempt to relate these linguistic interests to an elaboration of a social orientation has been constrained. The manner in which FDA constituted a kind of movement or school, with a particular orientation and direction, has been restricted.

It must also be remarked that there does seem to have been something of a resurgence in FDA within France during the past two or three years. There has been something of a tendency to return to that work and to reflect upon it, while also making available some of the less accessible sources, as is evident in the work of Maldidier, Robin and Guilhaumou, and Gadet and Henry (Madidier, 1990; Guilhaumou *et al.*, 1994; Gadet and Hak, 1990). Some of this work derives from the establishment of a programme for the study of the history of the analysis of discourse within the more general work of the programme on the history of linguistic theory (URA), jointly between CNRS and Paris VII. The recent drive for academics in France to complete *thèses d'état* under the old regulations associated with the restructuring of higher education has also led to the drawing together of disparate pieces of work on FDA (Achard, 1989; Authier-Revuz, 1992c; *inter alia*). There have been various introductory summaries of enonciative linguistics (Maingueneau, 1991), of discourse analysis (Maingueneau, 1991), of the relevance of discourse analysis for the sociology of language (Achard, 1990). The series *L'Homme dans la langue,* published by Ophry, has given considerable attention to enonciation (Culioli, 1990, 1992; Fuchs, 1994; *inter alia*). A recent issue of *Langages* was devoted to the analysis of discourse in France (Maingueneau, 1995). There have also been individual studies such as the work of Collinot and Mazière (1997) on the dictionary and meaning.

While the accommodation of modernist discourse analysis and FDA would appear to be incomprehensible given their different orientation towards the centred subject, and their distinctive roles as methodologies, the same is not true of the relationship between ethnomethodology and FDA. It is evident from recent debates in *Langage et Société* (1992) that Achard was one person who was open to at least consider such a link. This derives partly from his belief that social process, and the place of language in it, is inextricably linked with discourse. Sociologists must recognise that without discourse, social process passes them by. Certainly there is room to consider the extent of the possibilities of such a marriage and why such possibilities should exist.

On the other hand, such an enterprise must be explicit, whereas there are cases where the linking of post-structuralist theory to ethnomethodology as a methodological adjunct appears to be little more than a continuation of the modernist propensity to attach method to theory. The problems of such a development are sometimes acknowledged (Wetherell and Potter, 1992) but are dismissed by the qualification 'but we feel that . . .'. It appears that there is an awareness of the inappropriateness of orthodox linguistic analyses for the study of discourse on account of its inability to confront the issue of discourse organisation in language use, but that for want of any alternative, recourse is made to ethnomethodology.

The most obvious thing the two enterprises have in common is a sustained critique of orthodox social sciences. Ethnomethodology has been preoccupied with the methods employed to gain access to the defining object of study – the social – which is understood as the totality of the global human order or of the autonomous parts that constitute the whole. It objects to the foundational unity of sociology with the natural sciences, the logic of enquiry and the scientific method. It is an objection to the assumption that the social constitutes a natural order which has a mathematical structure that is capable of discovery. Rather, ethnomethodologists make an argument in favour of local and contingent ecologies of *ad hoc* considerations and techniques, indicating that the application of method to measure the social is constituted in practices that distort or eradicate the indexical and contingent nature of the social. The application of *a priori* method and theory and a *post priori* manipulation of data is claimed to constitute the social rather than being a description of it.

Ethnomethodologists go about their task by making explicit the seen but unnoticed background practices which constitute human life, stating only what is observably the case without any claim for truth, and without recourse to theory or any associated epistemological claims. In many respects, there is no claim for the existence of a 'social', since any prior reference to it would imply an imposition that infringes the claim for the relevance of the local.

The emphasis upon non-imposition of any externality is sometimes at odds with the philosophical inheritance of ethnomethodology. Heidegger's emphasis upon the world as the hidden background of common practice, Husserl's transcendental phenomenology and its influence for Schutz' phenomenology in emphasising the assumed notion of intersubjectivity to account for communication between members and the resulting order are cases in point. In this respect, it can be argued that Pollner's (1987) mundane reasoning, which draws upon Merlau-Ponty, Husserl and Schutz, constitutes the kind of imposition that is denied. Similarly, intersubjectivity assumes a prior and necessary ordering between subjects in communication. It can also be argued that the recent introduction of Wittgenstein's work into ethnomethodology serves as a replacement for the phenomenological thrust. Of course, Wittgenstein blends well with Heidegger, especially in relation to the phenomenon of meaning. Certainly Wittgenstein's later work refutes mental processes, while Heidegger claims that Husserl's account of meaning as the thematic ordering of the conscious constitutes the invention of metaphysics. Both locate language in its use as a form of life, or as an articulation of discourse as the intelligibility of being, appealing to the ethnomethodological claim that language is simply one of the forms available in order 'to do' living. Commonsense knowledge can then be equated with Wittgenstein's language game and the common threads that they may or may not share. It requires only a small step to introduce Bakhtin's dialogism in relation to Heidegger's observation that meaning is already constituted before the subject's existence.

It can, of course, be argued that such developments have not been accommodated by all of those who would classify themselves as ethnomethodologists, while others would claim that they have merely undermined the principles of the discipline. This would imply that ethnomethodology no longer has any internal coherence, if it ever did have such a coherence. Be that as it may, this input from the work of Wittgenstein and Heidegger involves a decentring of the subject and a collapsing of the modernist distinction between language and the social. It also questions the relevance of any analysis of language as an autonomous system. What is undeniable, despite some degree of confusion and misunderstanding, is the increasing degree of overlap between FDA and ethnomethodology.

As we have seen, FDA is atheoretical to the extent that it aims only to describe the local discursive event. It is tempting, therefore, to equate discourse with common-sense knowledge. However, in FDA, the local legitimately includes a wider area than ethnomethodology's notion of the term, taking into account the traces of discursive statements present in discursive practice. None the less, there is a degree of overlap that lends possibility. Where the two orientations differ is in the relationships between localities. Ethnomethodology does not seek to relate the various local scenes that it studies, preferring to stake a claim for the autonomy of local systems. In contrast, FDA has a quite different orientation to the local, and in this respect is much closer to the classical sociological paradigm, at least potentially. In focusing on the circulation of discourses, it strives to describe both the local conditions of the construction of meaning and the relations that exist between such local conditions.

Perhaps a more relevant comparison involves the similarity between the concepts of indexicality and enonciation. Of course, whereas Benveniste discovered enonciation through linguistics, ethnomethodologists encountered indexicality through sociology. Like the French discourse analysts, the ethnomethodologists recognise that people do not state the meaning of the expression that they use, these expressions being vague and equivocal, lending themselves to several meanings. Where the two schools disagree is that whereas the ethnomethodologists insist on the intention of meaning being discoverable once the context of the statement is known, such intention is denied by French discursivists.

As touched upon above, for the ethnomethodologist, conversation analysis is the way of placing the focus on locality, and locality is the technique for indexicality. With reference to linguistics, Achard related indexicality to Jakobson's shifters or the 'deictic', where a certain number of terms do not hold absolute lexical signification but receive an interpretation in relation to the situation. The linguists envisage the point of view of forms – specialised for that 'infra-semantic' functioning – whereas for the ethnomethodologist it is the dimension of the act that is seen in that sub-determination. This leads the ethnomethodologists to claim that the meaning of action is necessarily a local construction. Others react by claiming that memory and institution also intervene in the production of meaning, or that the 'local' cannot be the same for all participants, and that the problem that requires resolution concerns the epistemological status of the observation. Yet this local construction of meaning by the participants seems far removed from the global statements of FDA.

Achard also gave relevance to the ethnomethodological concept of accountability. This related to how one produces discourses which are 'natural' accounts of research activities, while simultaneously being social acts. The ethnomethodologists claim that it is not possible to methodically distinguish the enonciative posture where the accounts are empty, from those where they are recovered as social facts to be analysed. This is not because the sociology or the history of science are necessarily conducted in order to relativise the universalism maintained by the scientific discourse at the interior of its constitutive role. Rather, one can also claim, at least to some degree, that ethnomethodology is tainted with positivism in that the ethnomethodologist is involved in the extension of a perspective where knowledge is produced by the ethnomethodologists themselves. To an extent, of course, this is also true of FDA in that while enonciative linguistics, and, to an extent, syntactic analysis, serve as important ingredients in the overall analysis, there is also a free part of any text that, to a very great extent, relies on the intuition of the individual analyst.

The significance of the involvement of some of those who pioneered FDA in ethnomethodology now makes more sense. The degree of mutual orientations has been established. However, it is unlikely that such an intermingling of fields will result in the retention of either field in its original form. It is already evident that it is the shift of both areas that is responsible for generating perspectives where mutuality is possible. It is also evident that those who have sought to draw upon both perspectives have generated an orientation that is unique, to the extent that it is questionable that their enterprise can be identified by reference to either label. In this respect, it collapses the distinction between disciplinary boundaries which divide linguistics and the social sciences, obliging the linguistic to confront the social and the social to confront the linguistic.

NOTES

1 MODERNISM AND THE PHILOSOPHY OF LANGUAGE

1 It is interesting that Stubbs in his work on discourse analysis (1983:10) objects to conversation analysis, not because of the theoretical input from ethnomethodology, but because of the tendency to limit the exercise to conversation.

3 POST-STRUCTURALISM

1 On this point see Norris' (1996:128) argument concerning the relationship between Althusser's work and structuralism and post-structuralism.
2 It is fair to note that many intellectuals in the French Communist Party followed Althusser in the direction of the work of Foucault and Lacan but it was often by reference to an ideological position conditioned by the primacy of Marxism.
3 In contrast to Norris (1996:170), Henry (1990:37) claims that the work of Bachelard and Canguilhem was opposed to that of Duhem.
4 Enonciative modalities are types of discursive activity which carry their own subject positions. Examples include teaching, which involves teachers and learners as different subjects; or medicine, which has a range of subjects with specific relations to one another.

4 MATERIALISM AND DISCOURSE

1 It should be noted that at this time several of those working on discourse analysis, most notably Dubois, Marcellesi and, at this time, Maldidier, wanted to use linguistics as a tool for revealing the ideology of a text, and lacked the depth of philosophical input that was evident in the work of Althusser and Pécheux.
2 It is probably this issue that lies behind the focus on the reflexive nature of language in Authier-Revuz' (1995) recent work.

5 THE STRUGGLE WITH IDEALISM

1 Authier-Revuz' (1995:95) comments on Houdebine's reaction to Voloshinov's work and how it differed from that of FDA are important because of her very orthodox Marxist position at the time.
2 Poulantzas combined Althusser's work with that of Gramsci within a Marxist-Leninist stance before proceeding to develop a form of Eurocommunism not dissimilar to Austrio-Marxism. His philosophical shift was equally broad.

3 I discuss the relationship between Bakhtin and Voloshinov in Chapter 6.
4 This increased collaboration with Pécheux and his colleagues would have led to the integration of Achard into the group had it not been for Pécheux's death in January 1984, and the subsequent disbanding of his team. Indeed, when Achard moved from Maison des Sciences de l'Homme to CNRS at the end of 1983 he did so in order to become a member of ADELA, and was, briefly, nominally a member of that team.

6 FORM AND DISCOURSE

1 Cf. *Mots* No. 10, which was devoted to the 'political we'.
2 The 'speaking subject' is the empirical being who is physically the author of the discourse, similarly the 'audiateurs' are constituted by the effective entourage in which the discourse takes place; the 'locuteur' is the person present in the enonce as responsible for the enonciation (pronoun and different marks from that of the first person); 'allocutaire' is the person presented as those to whom the enonce is addressed (vocative, pronouns and marks of second person); 'enonciateur' and 'destinataire' are respectively the person to whom the responsibility of an illocutary act is attributed and those whom that act is considered to be addressing. Cf. Ducrot (1980).
3 This work has recently been compiled in the form of the author's *thèse de doctorat d'etat* (see Authier-Revuz, 1992c) and has subsequently been published as Authier-Revuz (1995).
4 The social and linguistic grammar of Hobbes' work is discussed in detail in M.P. Clarke (1997).

7 LEXICOLOGY AND DISTRIBUTIONALISM

1 There is a sense in which the work of Boutet and Fiala, whom I discuss in relation to FDA, derives from the orientation of the Marcellesi group rather than that of Pécheux.

BIBLIOGRAPHY

Achard, P. (1967); Sciences, sciences humaines, idéologie. *Aletheia*. No. 6.

—— (1980a); History and the Politics of Language in France. *History Workshop Journal*. Vol. 10, pp. 175–183.

—— (1980b); Is Social Stratification Outside of Language? Paper presented at the 'Language and Power' Conference, Bellagio, Italy.

—— (1982); 'Sociologie du développement' ou sociologie du 'développement'. *Tiers Monde*. Vol. XXIII, No. 90, pp. 843–854.

—— (1984); Je jure – review of P. Bourdieu, Ce que parler veut dire. *Langage et Société*. No. 29.

—— (1986); Discours et sociologie du langage. *Langage et Société*. No. 37, pp. 5–61.

—— (1987); L'analyse de discours est-elle brevetable? *Langage et Société*. No. 42, pp. 45–71.

—— (1989); Quelques propositions en sociologie du langage. *Courants Sociolinguistiques*, INALF, pp. 39–53.

—— (1990); La spécificité de l'écrit, est-elle d'ordre linguistique ou discursif? In N. Catach (ed.), *Pour une théorie de la langue écrite*. CNRS, Paris, pp. 67–77.

—— (1992); Entre déixis et anaphore: Le renvoi du contexte en situation. Les opérateurs 'alors' et 'maintenant' en français. In M. A. More and L. Danon Boileaux (eds), *La déixis*. PUF, Paris, pp. 583–592.

—— (1993); *La sociologie du langage*. PUF, Paris.

—— (1994); Sociologie du langage et analyse d'enquêtes: De l'hypothèse de la rationalité des réponses. *Sociétés Contemporaines*. No. 18/19, pp. 67–100.

—— (1995); Formation discursive, dialogisme et sociologie. *Langages*. No. 117, pp. 82–96.

—— (n.d.); Linguistique et sciences sociales: Après le structuralisme.

Achard, P., A. Chauvenet, E. Lage, F. Lentin, P. Neve and G. Vignaux (eds) (1977); *Discours biologique et ordre social*. Seuil, Paris.

Achard, P., M. P. Gruenais, D. Jaulin (eds) (1984); *Histoire et linguistique*. Editions du CNRS, Paris.

Adorno, T. (1979); *Negative Dialectics*. Trans. E. B. Ashton. Seabury Press, New York.

Althusser, L.(1964/65); Freud et Lacan. *La Nouvelle Critique*. Nos. 161/162, 1964/65.

—— (1968); *Lire le Capital*. Maspero, Paris.

—— (1969); *For Marx*. Penguin, Harmondsworth.

—— (1970); Idéologie et appareils idéologiques d'états. *La Pensée*. No. 151.

—— (1971), *Lenin and Philosophy and Other Essays*. New Left Books, London.

—— (1976); *Positions*. Editions Sociales, Paris.

Anderson, P. (1983); *In the Tracks of Historical Materialism*. Verso, London.

Anscrombe, J. C. and O. Ducrot (1977); Deux mais en français? *Lingua*. No. 43.

Appignanesi, L. (ed.) (1989); *Ideas from France*. Free Association Books, London.

Auroux, S. (1992); La philosophie linguistique d'Antoine Culioli. In n.a. *La théorie d'Antoine Culioli*. Ophrys, Paris, pp. 39–61.

Authier, J. (1978); Les formes du discours rapporté – Remarques syntactiques et sémantiques à partir des traitements proposés. *DRLAV*. No. 17, pp. 1–78.

Authier, J., and A. Meunir (1977); Exercices de grammaire et discours rapporté. *Langue française*. No. 33, pp. 41–77.

Authier-Revuz, J. (1982); Hétérogénéité montrée et hétérogénéité constitutive, éléments pour une approche de l'autre dans le discours. *DRLAV*. No. 26, pp. 91–151.

—— (1984); Hétérogénéité(s) énonciative(s). *Langages*. No. 73, pp. 98–111.

—— (1991); Hétérogénéités et ruptures. Quelques repères dans le champs énonciatif. In H. Parret (ed.), *Les sens et ses hétérogénéités*. CNRS, Paris, pp. 139–153.

—— (1992a); De quelques idées reçues au sujet du discours rapporté. *Perspectives*. No. 4, pp. 15–21.

—— (1992b); Pour l'agrégation: Repères dans le champ du discours rapporté. *L'Information Grammaticale*. No. 55, October, pp. 38–42.

—— (1992c); Les non-coïncidences du dire et leur représentation méta-énonciataire. Thèse de doctorat d'état, Paris VIII.

—— (1995); *Ces mots qui ne vont pas de soi: Boucles réflexives et non-coïncidences du dire*. Institut Pierre Larousse, Paris, Vol 1 et 2.

Bakhtin, M. M. (1981); *The Dialogical Immagination*. University of Texas Press, Austin.

—— (1986); The Problem of the Text in Linguistics, Philology and the Human Sciences: An Experiment in Philosophical Analysis. In C. Emerson and M. Holquist (eds), *Speech Genres and Other Late Essays*. University of Texas Press, Austin, pp. 103–131.

Balibar, E. (1989); Foucault et Marx. L'enjeu du nominalisme. In n.a. *Michel Foucault, philosophe*. Seuil, Paris, pp. 54–77.

Balibar, R. (1985); *L'institution du français*. PUF, Paris.

Barrett, M. (1991); *The Politics of Truth: From Marx to Foucualt*. Polity, Cambridge.

Barthes, R. (1964); *Essais critiques*. Seuil, Paris.

—— (1966); Introduction à l'analyse structurale des récits. *Communications*. No. 8, pp. 1–27.

—— (1976); *Le plaisir du texte*. Seuil, Paris.

—— (1979); *Sollers écrivain*. Seuil, Paris.

Barthes, R. and F. Flauhaut (1980); Parola. In *Enciclopedia Einaudi*. Einaudi, Torino.

Baudrillard, J. (1975); *The Mirror of Production*. Telos, St Louis.

Bell, D. (1974); *The Coming of Post-Industrial Society*. Harvard University Press, Cambridge, MA.

Benton, T. (1984); *The Rise and Fall of Structural Marxism*. Macmillan, London.

Benveniste, E.(1966); *Problèmes de linguistique générale*. Gallimard, Paris.

Berman, M. (1983); *All that is Solid Melts into Air*. Verso, London.

Blanche-Benveniste, C. (1975); *Recherche en vue d'une théorie de la grammaire française – Essai d'application à la grammaire des pronoms*. Champion, Paris.

Boltanski, L. (1990); *L'amour et la justice comme compétences*. Metailie, Paris.

Bonnafous, S. (1983); Le congrès de Metz du parti socialiste. *Langages*. No. 71.

—— (1991); *L'immigration prise au mots*. Kime, Paris.

Borutti, S. (1991); Lieux philosophiques de l'hétérogénéité. In H. Parret (ed.), *Le sens et ses hétérogénéités*. CNRS, Paris, pp. 275–285.

Bouchard, D. (ed.) (1977); *Language, Counter-Memory, Practice*. Cornell University Press, Ithaca.

Boudon, R. (1986); *L'idéologie ou l'origine des idées reçues*. Fayard, Paris.

Boutet, J. (1989); *Construction sociale du sens dans la parole vivante*. Thèse d'état, Paris VII.

—— (1994); *Construire le sens*. Lang, Wien.

Boutet, J. and P. Fiala (1986); Les télescopages syntaxiques. *DRLAV*. Nos. 34–35, pp. 11–126.

—— (1991); Approches diachroniques et synchroniques du télescopage syntaxique. In H. Parret (ed.), *Le sens et ses hétérogénéités*. CNRS, Paris, pp. 81–93.

Boutet J., P. Fiala, J. Simonin-Grumbach (1976); Sociolinguistique ou sociologie du langage? *Critique*. No. 344, pp. 68–85.

Boutet, J., M. Ebel, P. Fiala (1982); Relations paraphrastiques et construction de sens. Analyse d'un formule dans le discours xénophobe. *Modèles Linguistiques*. Vol. IV, No. 1.

Boyne, R. and A. Ratansi (eds) (1990); *Postmodernism and Society*. Macmillan, London.

Burger, P. (1992); The Disappearance of Meaning: Essays at a Postmodern Reading of Michel Tournier, Botho Strauss and Peter Handke. In S. Lash and J. Firedman (eds), *Modernity and Identity*. Blackwell, Cambridge, pp. 94–11.

Callinicos, A. (1976); *Althusser's Marxism*. Pluto, London.

—— (1982); *Is There a Future for Marxism*. Macmillan, London.

—— (1990); Reactionary Postmodernism? In R. Boyne and A. Ratansi (eds), *Postmodernism and Society*. Macmillan, London, pp. 97–119.

Calvet, L. J. (1974); *Langage et colonialisme*. Payot, Paris.

—— (1987); *La guerre des langues*. Paris, Payot.

Canguilhem, G. (1966); *Le normal et le pathologique*. PUF, Paris.

—— (1967); Mort de l'homme ou épuisement du cogito. *Critique*. 242.

—— (1977); *Idéologie et rationalité de l'histoire des sciences de la vie*. Vrin, Paris.

Castoriadis, C. (1995); *Psychoanalysis in Contexts*. London, Routledge.

Chiss, J. L. and C. Puech (1990); Le cours de linguistique générale et la 'représentation' de la langue par l'écriture. In N. Catach (ed.), *Pour une théorie de la langue écrite*. CNRS, Paris, pp. 47–57.

Chomsky, N. (1957); *Syntactic Structures and Issues in the Theory of Language*. Mouton, The Hague.

Clarke, J. (1991); *New Times and Old Enemies: Essays on Cultural Studies and America*. Harper Collins, London.

Clarke, M. P. (1997); *Language, Grammar and Being*. Unpublished Ph.D. dissertation, Lancaster University.

Collinot, A. and F. Mazière (1997); *Un prêt-à-parler: Le dictionnaire*. PUF, Paris.

Conein, B., J. Guilhaumou, and D. Maldidier (1984); L'analyse de discours comme contexte épistémologique. *Mots*. No. 9, pp. 25–33.

Courtine, J. (1981); Analyse du discours politique: Quelques problèmes théoriques et méthodologiques en analyse du discours, à propos du discours communiste adressé aux chrétiens. *Langages*. No. 62, pp. 9–127.

—— (1992); Une généalogie de l'analyse du discours. *Discours Social/Social Discourse.* Vol. IV, Nos. 1–2, pp. 19–35.

Courtine, J. J. and J. M. Marandin (1981); Quel objet pour l'analyse du discours? In B. Conein *et al.* (eds), *Matérialités discursives.* PUF, Paris, pp. 21–35.

Culioli, A. (1990); *Pour une linguistique de l'énonciation: Opérations et représentations.* Vol. 1, Ophrys, Paris, .

—— (1992); Ouverture. In A. Culioli, *La théorie d'Antoine Culioli.* Ophrys, Paris, pp. 3–17.

Culioli, A., C. Fuchs, and M. Pécheux (1970); Considérations théoriques à propos du traitement formel du langage. *Documents de Linguistique Quantitative.* No. 7, pp. 1–49.

Culler, J. (1976); *Saussure.* Glasgow, 1976

Deleuze, G. (1962); *Nietzsche et la philosophie.* PUF, Paris.

—— (1964); *Proust et les signes.* PUF, Paris.

—— (1967); *Nietzsche et la philosophie.* PUF, Paris.

—— (1968); *Différence et répétition.* PUF, Paris.

—— (1972); *Une nouvelle archiviste.* Fata Morgana, Paris.

—— (1989); Qu'est-ce qu'un dispositif? In n.a. *Michel Foucault, philosophe.* Seuil, Paris, pp. 185–196.

Deleuze, G. and F. Guattari (1977); *Anti-Oedipus: Capitalism and Schizophrenia*, Viking, New York.

Derrida, J. (1967a); *De la grammatologie.* Minuit, Paris.

—— (1967b); *L'Ecriture et la différence.* Seuil, Paris.

Dreyfus, H. L. and P. Rabinow (1982); *Michel Foucault: Beyond Structuralism and Hermeneutics.* Harverster, Brighton.

Ducrot, O. (1980); *Les mots du discours.* Minuit, Paris.

During, S. (1990); Literature – Nationalism's Other. The Case for Revision. In H. K. Bhaba (ed.), *Nation and Narration.* Routledge, London, pp. 138–154.

Eagleton, T. (1991); *Ideology: An Introduction.* Verso, London.

Ebel, M. (1986); Apport des écrits du cercle de Mikhail Bakhtine à une analyse du langage comme pratique sociale. *Travaux du Centre de Recherches Sémiologiques.* No. 50, pp. 1–13.

Ewald, F. (1989); Un pouvoir sans dehors. In n.a. *Michel Foucault, philosophe.* Seuil, Paris, pp. 196–203.

Fairclough, N. (1989); *Language and Power.* Longman, London.

—— (1992); *Discourse and Social Change.* Polity, Cambridge.

Fiala, P. (1984); Le consensus patriotique, face de la xénophobie. *Mots.* No. 8, pp.17–43.

—— (1986); Polyphonie et stabilisation de la référence: L'altérité dans le texte politique. *Travaux du Centre de Recherches Sémiologiques.* No. 50, pp. 15–46.

Fish, S. (1989); *Doing What Comes Naturally.* Clarendon, Oxford.

Flahaut, F. (1978); *La parole intermédiaire.* Seuil, Paris.

Foucault, M. (1966); *Les mots et les choses.* Gallimard, Paris.

—— (1969); *L'archéologie du savoir.* Gallimard, Paris.

—— (1971); *L'ordre du discours: Leçon inaugurale au Collège de France.* Gallimard, Paris.

—— (1972); *Folie et déraison: Histoire de la folie à l'âge classique*, 2nd edn. Gallimard, Paris.

—— (1973); *The Order of Things.* Vintage, New York.

—— (1975); *Surveiller et punir: Naissance de la prison.* Gallimard, Paris.

—— (1976); *Histoire de la sexualité: La volonté du savoir.* Gallimard, Paris.

—— (1977); Power and Sex: An Interview with Michel Foucault. *Telos.* No. 32.

—— (1980); *Power/Knowledge: Selected Interviews and Other Writings 1972–1977,* ed. Colin Gordon. Harvester, Brighton.

—— (1985); Final Interviews. *Ravitan.* Eté 1985.

Fowler, R., G. Kress, T. Trew, R. Hodge (1977); *Language and Control.* Routledge and Kegan Paul, London.

Frank, M. (1989); Sur le concept de discours chez Foucault. In n.a. *Michel Foucault, philosophe.* Seuil, Paris, pp. 125–136.

Freud, S. (1973); *L'interprétation des rêves.* PUF, Paris.

Frow, J. (1986); *Marxism and Literary History.* Blackwell, Oxford.

Fuchs, C. (1980); *Paraphrase et théories du langage.* Unpublished Ph.D. thesis, Paris VII.

—— (1981); Les problématiques énonciatives: Esquisse d'une présentation historique et critique. *DRLAV.* No. 25, pp. 35–60.

—— (1982); *La paraphrase.* PUF, Paris.

—— (1991); L'hétérogénéité interprétative. In H. Parret (ed.), *Les sens et ses hétérogénéités.* CNRS, Paris, pp. 107–121.

—— (1992); De la grammaire anglaise à la paraphrase: Un parcours énonciatif. In n.a. *La théorie d'Antoine Culioli.* Ophrys, Paris, pp. 221–226.

—— (1994); *Paraphrase et énonciation.* Ophrys, Paris.

Gadet, F.(1977); La sociolinguistique n'existe pas: Je l'ai rencontrée. *Dialectiques.* No. 20.

—— (1981); Tricher la langue. In B. Conein *et al.* (eds), *Matérialités discursives.* PUF, Paris, pp. 117–127.

—— (1987); *Saussure.* Heinemann, London.

—— (1989a); *Le français ordinaire.* Colin, Paris.

—— (1989b); Après Saussure. *DRLAV.* No. 40, pp. 1–40.

—— (1991); La distance syntaxique dans les ruptures deconstruction. In H. Parret (ed.), *Les sens et ses hétérogénéités.* CNRS, Paris, pp. 69–81.

Gadet, F. and T. Hak (1990); *Por uma analise automatica do discurso.* Unicamp, Campinas.

Gadet, F. and J. M. Marandin (1984); La linguistique comme contexte de l'analyse de discours? *Mots.* No. 9, pp. 19–25.

Gadet, F. and M. Pécheux (1981a); *La langue introuvable.* Maspero, Paris.

—— (1981b); *La lengua de nunca acabar.* FCE, Mexico. (Spanish translation of *La langue introuvable.*)

Gadet, F., J. Léon, D. Maldidier and M. Plon (1990); A presentacao da conjuntra em linguistica, em psicanalise e em informatica aplicada ao estudo dos textos na Franca, em 1969. In F. Gadet and T. Hak (eds), *Por uma analise automatica di discurso.* Unicamp, Campinas, pp. 39–61.

Gadet, F., J. Léon and M. Pécheux (1984); Remarques sur la stabilité d'une construction linguistique. La complétive. *Linx.* No. 10, pp. 23–51.

Geffroy, A. (1985); Les NOUS de Robespierre. *Mots.* No. 10.

Glucksman, A. (1989); Le nihilisme de Michel Foucault. In n.a. *Michel Foucault, philosophe.* Seuil, Paris, pp. 395–399.

Graham, J. (1992); *Onomatopoetics: Theory of Language and Literature.* Cambridge University Press, Cambridge.

Grize, J. B. (1992); Linguistique de l'énonciation et logique naturelle. In n.a. *La théorie d'Antoine Culioli*. Ophrys, Paris, pp. 61–72.

Guespin, L.(1984); Analyse du discours en France: Acquis et tendances. In C. Kebrat-Orecchioni and M. Mouillaid (eds), *Le discours politique*. Presses Universitaires de Lyon, Lyons, pp. 131–164.

Guilhaumou J., and D. Maldidier (1979); Courte critique pour une longue histoire. *Dialectique*. No. 26, pp. 7–23.

—— (1981); 'L'affaire Fiszbin': Un exemple de résistance. In B. Conein *et al.* (eds), *Matérialités discursives*. PUF, Paris, pp. 75–93.

Guilhaumou, J., D. Maldidier and R. Robin (1994); *Discours et archive*. Mardaga, Liège.

Habermas, J. (1979); *Communication and the Evolution of Society*. Heinemann, London.

—— (1990); *The Philosophical Discourse of Modernity*. Polity, Oxford.

Hall, S. (1988); The Toad in the Garden: Thatcherism among the Theorists. In C. Nelson and L. Grossberg (eds), *Marxism and the Interpretation of Culture*. University of Illinois Press, Urbana.

Halliday, M. A. K. (1970); Language Structure and Language Function. In J. Lyons (ed.), *New Horizons in Linguistics*. Harmondsworth, Penguin.

—— (1978); *Language as Social Semiotic*. Arnold, London.

—— (1985); *Introduction to Functional Grammar*. Arnold, London.

Halliday, M. A. K., and R. Hassan (1978); *Cohesion in English*. Longman, London.

Haroche, C., P. Henry and M. Pécheux (1971); La sémantique et la coupure saussurienne: Langue, langage et discours. *Langages*. No. 24, pp. 93–106.

Harris, Z. (1952); *Discourse Analysis*. Mouton, The Hague.

—— (1969); Analyse du discours. *Langages*. No. 13.

Hassan, I. (1985); The Culture of Postmodernism. *Theory, Culture and Society*. Vol. 2, No. 3.

Hawkes, T. (1977); *Structuralism and semiotics*. Methuen, London.

Hegel, G. W. F. (1966); *Phenomenology of the Mind*. Allen & Unwin, London.

Heidegger, M. (1959); *Unterwegs zur Sprache*. Neske, Pfullingen.

Henry, P. (1975); Constructions relatives et articulations discursives. *Langages*. No. 37, pp. 81–99.

—— (1981); Wittgenstein et la double-négation. In B. Conein *et al.* (eds), *Matérialités discursives*. Presses Universitaires de Lille, Lille, pp. 105–115.

—— (1990); Os fundamentos teoricos da 'analise automatica di discourso' de Michel Pécheux (1969). In F. Gadet and T. Hak (eds), *Por uma analise automatica do discurso*. Unicamp, Campinas, pp. 13–39.

Henry, P. and S. Moscovici (1968); Problèmes de l'analyse de contenu. *Langages*. No. 11.

Herbert, T. (1966); Réflexions sur la situation théorique des sciences sociales et, spécialement, de la psychologie sociale. *Cahiers pour l'Analyse*. No. 2, pp. 174–203.

—— (1968); Remarques pour une théorie générale des idéologies. *Cahier pour l'Analyse*. No. 9, pp. 74–92.

—— (1969); Les sciences humaines et le moment actuel. *La Pensée*. No. 143, pp. 62–79.

Herder, J. G. von (1966); *Essays on the Origin of Language*. Trans. J. H. Morou and A. Gode. University of Chicago Press, Chicago.

Hobbes, T. (1839–1845); *The English Works of Thomas Hobbes of Malmsbury*. Vols. 1–11, Bohn, London.

Hodge, R. (1990); *Literature as Discourse*. Polity, Cambridge.

Hodge, R. and G. Kress (1988); *Social Semiotics*. Polity, Cambridge.

Hodge, R. and D. Tripp (1986); *Children and Television*. Polity, Cambridge.

Horkheimer, M. and T. W. Adorno (1972); *Dialectic of Enlightenment*. Trans. J. Cumming. Seabury Press, New York.

Houdebine, J. L. (1976); Les vérités de La Palice ou les erreurs de la police (d'une question obstinément forclose). *Tel Quel*. No. 67, pp. 87–97.

—— (1977); *Langage et marxisme*. Klincksieck, Paris.

Howells, C. (1992); *The Cambridge Companion to Sartre*. Cambridge University Press, Cambridge.

Hoy, D. C. and T. McCarthy (1994); *Critical Theory*. Oxford, Blackwells.

Irigaray, L. (1969); L'énoncé en analyse. *Langages*. No. 13, pp. 111–122.

Jackson, L. (1991); *The Poverty of Structuralism*. Longman, London.

Jakobson, R. (1963); *Essais de linguistique générale*. Minuit, Paris.

Jameson, F. (1972); *The Prisonhouse of Language*. Princeton University Press, Princeton.

Kant, I. (1946); *What is Enlightenment? Introduction to Contemporary Civilisation in the West*. Vol. I., Columbia University Press, New York.

Kress, G. (1985); Ideological structures in discourse. In T. Van Dijk (ed.), *Handbook of Discourse Ananlysis*. Vol. 4, Academic Press, London.

Kristeva, J. (1969); *Semiotike*. Seuil, Paris.

—— (1975); *La traversée des signes*. Seuil, Paris.

—— (1980); Word, dialogue and novel. In L. S. Roudiez (ed.), *Desire in Language: A Semiotic Approach to Literature and Art*. Columbia University Press, New York, pp. 64–91.

Krizman, L. (1988); *Michel Foucault: Politics, Philosophy, Culture*. Routledge, London.

Kumar, K. (1978); *Prophecy and Progress*. Penguin, Harmondsworth.

Lacan, J. (1966); *Ecrits I*. Seuil, Paris.

———(1978); *Le séminaire: Livre II*. Seuil, Paris.

———(1981); *Le séminaire: Livre III*. Seuil, Paris.

Laclau, E. (1988); Building a New Left: An Interview with Ernesto Laclau. *Strategies: A Journal of Theory, Culture and Politics*. No. 1.

Laclau, E. and C. Mouffe (1985); *Hegemony and Socialist Strategy*. Verso, London.

Lawson, H. (1985); *Reflexivity: The Post-modern Predicament*. Hutchinson, London.

Lebart, L. and A. Salem (1994); *Statistique textuelle*. Dunod, Paris.

Lecomte, A. and J. M. Marandin (1984); Analyse du discours et morphologie discursive. In M. Charolles, J. Petofi and T. Sozer (eds), *Research in Text Connexity and Text Coherence*. Buske Verlag, Hamburg, pp. 61–100.

Lecomte, A., J. Léon and J. M. Marandin (1984); Analyses du discours: Stratégie de description textuelle. *Mots*. No. 9, pp. 143–167.

Lecourt, D. (1975); *Pour une critique de l'épistémologie (Bachelard, Canguilhem, Foucault)*. Maspero, Paris.

Lemert, C. C. and G. Gillian (1982); *Michel Foucault: Social Theory as Transgression*. Columbia University Press, New York.

Lenin, V. I. (1947); *Materialism and Empirio-Criticism*. Progress, Moscow.

Lévi-Strauss, C. (1950); Introduction à la œuvre de Mauss. *Sociologie et anthropologie*. PUF, Paris.

—— (1962); *La pensée sauvage*. Plon, Paris.

—— (1963); *Structural Anthropology*. Basic Books, New York.

—— (1976); Preface to R. Jakobson, *Six leçons sur le son et le sens*. Paris.

Lipset, S. (1981); *Political Man*. Johns Hopkins University Press, Baltimore.

Lyotard, J. F.(1984); *The Postmodern Condition*. Manchester University Press, Manchester.

McGee, V. W. (Trans.) (1986); *Bakhtin, Speech Genres and Other Late Essays*. University of Texas Press, Austin.

Machado, R. (1989); Archéologie et épistémologie. In n.a. *Michel Foucault, philosophe*. Seuil, Paris, pp. 15–32.

Macherey, P. (1978); *A Theory of Literary Production*. Routledge and Kegan Paul, London.

Maingueneau, D. (1976); *Initiation aux méthodes de l'analyse du discours*. Hachette, Paris.

—— (1987); *Nouvelles tendances en analyse du discours*. Hachette, Paris.

—— (1991); *L'énonciation en linguistique française*. Hachette, Paris.

—— (ed.) (1995); Les analyses du discours en France. *Langages*. No. 117.

Maldidier, D. (1990); *L'inquiétude du discours*. Editions des Cendres, Paris.

Maldidier D. and R. Robin (1974); Polémique idéologique et affrontement discursif en 1776: Les grands Edits de Turgot et les remontrances du Parlement de Paris. In R. Robin (ed.), *Langage et ideologies: Le discours comme objet de l'histoire*. Ouvriers, Paris.

Marandin, J. M. (1979a); Analyse de discours en linguistique générale. *Langages*. No. 55.

—— (1979b); Problèmes de l'analyse du discours. Essai de description du discours français sur la Chine. *Langages*. No. 55.

—— (1983); Le système de programmation DEREDEC. *Mots*. No. 6.

—— (1984a); Mais qu'est-ce que Socrate a au juste à voir avec la sagesse? *Linx*. No. 10, pp. 51–57.

—— (1984b); Miniatures sentimentales. Syntaxe et discours dans une description lexicale. *Linx*. No. 10, pp. 75–97.

—— (1986); 'Ce est un autre' l'interprétation anaphorique du syntagme démonstratif. *Langages*. No. 81, pp. 75–91.

Marcellesi, J.-B. (1971); Eléments pour une analyse contrastive du discours politique. *Langages*. No. 23.

Marcellesi, J.-B. and B. Gardin (1974); *Introduction à la sociolinguistique: La linguistique sociale*. Larousse, Paris.

Martinet, A. (1960); *Eléments de linguistique générale*. Colin, Paris.

Marx, K. (1970); *Theses on Feuerbach*. In C. Arthur (ed.), *The German Ideology*. Lawrence and Wishart, London.

—— (1976a); *Capital*. Vol. 1, Penguin, Harmondsworth.

—— (1976b); *German Ideology*. Lawrence and Wishart, London.

Michard-Marchal, C. and C. Ribery (1982); *Sexisme et sciences humaines*. Presses Universitaires de Lille, Lille.

Miles, R. (1982); *Racism and Migrant Labour*. Routledge and Kegan Paul, London.

Milner, J. C. (1978); *L'amour de la langue*. Seuil, Paris.

—— (1979); La voix publique. *DRLAV*. No. 21, pp. 76–84.

—— (1984a); La linguistique, la psychanalyse, et la science. *Spirales*. No. 32–33, pp. 20–21.

—— (1984b); La constitution du fait en linguistique. In P. Achard, M. Gruenais and D. Jaulin (eds), *Histoire et linguistique*. CNRS, Paris, pp. 177–190.

—— (1989); *Introduction à une science du langage*. Seuil, Paris.

—— (1992); De quelques aspects de la théorie d'Antoine Culioli projetés dans un espace non-énonciatif. In n.a. *La théorie d'Antoine Culioli*. Ophrys, Paris, pp. 19–39.

Moeschler, J.(1985); Dialogisme et dialogue: Pragmatique de l'énoncé vs pragmatique du discours. TRANEL. No. 9.

Morey, M. (1989); Sur le style philosophique de Michel Foucault. In n.a. *Michel Foucault, philosophe*. Seuil, Paris, pp. 137–150.

Morson, G. S. and C. Emerson (1990); *Mikhail Bakhtin: Creation of a Prosaics*. Stanford University Press, Stanford.

Nietzsche, F. (1969); *The Genealogy of Morals*. Random House, New York.

Normand, C. (1970); Propositions et notes en vue d'une lecture de F. de Saussure. *La Pensée*. No. 154.

—— (1985); Le sujet dans la langue. *Langages*. No. 77, pp. 7–20.

Norris, C. (1990); Lost in the Funhouse: Baudrillard and the Politics of Postmodernism. In R. Boyne and A. Ratansi (eds), *Postmodernism and Society*. Macmillan, London, pp. 119–154.

—— (1991); *Spinoza and the Origins of Modern Critical Theory*. Blackwell, Oxford.

—— (1996); *Reclaiming Truth*. Blackwell, Oxford.

O'Neill, O. (1989); *Construction of Reason: Exploration of Kant's Practical Philosophy*. Cambridge University Press, Cambridge.

Parret, H. (ed.) (1991); *Le sens et ses hétérogénéités*. CNRS, Paris.

Pateman, T. (1981); *Linguistics as a Branch of Critical Theory*. UEA papers in Linguisitcs, Norwich.

Pavel, T. A. (1990); *The Feud of Language: A History of Structuralist Thought*. Blackwell, Oxford.

Pécheux, M. (1969); *Analyse automatique du discours*. Dunod, Paris.

—— (1975a); *Les vérités de La Palice*. Maspero, Paris.

—— (1975b); Introduction. *Langages*. No. 37, pp. 3–6.

—— (1976); Position syndicale et prise de parti dans les sciences humaines et sociales. *La Pensée*. No. 187, pp. 53–66.

—— (1979); Un exemple d'ambiguité idéologique: le rapport Mansholt. *Technologies, Idéologies et Pratiques*. April–June.

—— (1980); Remontemonos de Foucault a Spinoza. In M. Nonteforte Toledo (ed.) *El discurso politico*. Neuva Imagen, Mexico, pp. 181–201.

—— (1981); L'étrange miroir de l'analyse de discours. *Langages*, No. 62, pp. 5–8.

—— (1982a); *Language, Semantics and Ideology*. Macmillan, London.

—— (1982b); La place de l'informatique dans la recherche en sciences humaines et sociales. *Temps Réel*. No. 27, pp. 29–33.

—— (1982c); Lire l'archive aujourd'hui. *Archives et Documents de la Société d'Histoire et d'Epistémologie des Sciences du Langage*. No. 2, pp. 35–45.

—— (1982d); Sur la (dé-)construction des théories linguistiques. *DRLAV*. No. 27, pp.1–24.

—— (1983); Ideology and Discursivity. *Canadian Journal of Political Science*. Special issue, pp. 24–31.

—— (1984a); Sur les contextes épistémologiques de l'analyse du discours. *Mots*. No. 9, pp.7–17.

—— (ed.) (1984b); *Analyse de discours: Mots dans l'histoire*. Special issue of *Mots*. No. 9.

—— (1984c); Matériel en vue de l'article 'Complétives/infinitifs/infinitives'. *Linx*. No. 10, pp. 7–23.

—— (1988); Discourse: Structure or Event? In. C. Nelson and L. Grossberg (eds), *Marxism and the Interpretation of Culture*. University of Illinois Press, Chicago.

—— (1990); Analyse de discours: Trois époques. In D. Maldidier, *L'inquiétude du discours*. Cendres, Paris, pp. 295–303.

Pécheux. M. and C. Fuchs (1975); Mises au point et perspectives à propos de l'analyse automatique du discours. *Langages*. No. 37, pp. 7–81.

Pécheux, M., C. Haroche, P. Henry and J. P. Poitou (1979); Le rapport Mansholt: Un cas d'ambiguité idéologique. *Technologies, Idéologies, Pratiques*. No. 2, pp. 1–83.

Plante, P.(1981); *DEREDEC: Manuel de l'usage*. University of Quebec, Montreal.

Pollner, M. (1987); *Mundane Reason*. Cambridge University Press, Cambridge.

Propp, V. (1958); *Morphology of the Folktale*. Indiana University Press, Bloomington.

Raglan, Lord (1956); *The Hero: A Study in Tradition, Myth and Drama*. Methuen, New York.

Ricouer, P. (1974); *The Conflict of Interpretations: Essays in Hermeneutics*. Northwestern University Press, Evanston.

Robin, R. (1971); Histoire et linguistique: Premiers jalons. *Langue Française*. No. 9, pp. 47–59

—— (ed.) (1973); *Histoire et linguistique*. Colin, Paris.

Rorty, R. (1982); *Consequences of Pragmatism*. University of Minnesota Press, Minneapolis.

Salem, A. (1988); Le temps lexical. *Mots*. No. 17, pp. 105–131.

Sartre, J. P.(1964); *Les mots*. Gallimard, Paris.

Saussure, F. de (1972); *Cours de linguistique générale*. Payot, Paris.

Sériot, P. (1983); *Préliminaires linguistiques à une analyse du discours politique soviétique: Les relations prédicatives non verbales*. Thèse de 3 cycle, University of Grenoble.

—— (1985); *Analyse du discours politique soviétique*. Institut d'études slaves, Paris.

Silverman D. and B. Torode (1980); *The Material Word*, Routledge and Kegan Paul, London.

Simonin-Grumbach, J. (1975); Pour une typologie du discours. In J. Kristeva, J. C. Milner and N. Ruwet (eds), *Langue, discours, société: Pour Emile Benveniste*. Seuil, Paris, pp. 85–120.

Sinclair, J. M. and R. M. Coulthard (1975); *Towards an Analysis of Discourse: The English Used by Teachers and Pupils*. Oxford University Press, Oxford.

Smart, B. (1983); *Foucault, Marxism and Critique*. Routledge, London.

Sperber, D. and D. Wilson (1978); Les ironies comme mentions. *Poétique*. No 36.

Stubbs, M. (1983); *Discourse Analysis*. Blackwell, Oxford.

Tamine, J. (1979); Métaphore et syntaxe. *Langages*. No. 54.

Tavor Bannet, E. (1989); *Structuralism and the Logic of Dissent*. Macmillan, London.

Taylor, C. (1986); Foucault on Freedom and Truth. In D. C. Hoy (ed.), *Foucault: A Critical Reader*. Blackwell, Oxford.

Therborn, G. (1980); *The Ideology of Power and the Power of Ideology*. Verso, London.

Thompson, J. B. (1984); *Studies in the Theory of Ideology*. Polity, Cambridge.

—— (1990); *Ideology and Modern Culture*. Polity, Oxford.

Thompson, S. (ed.) (1953); *Four Symposia on Folklore*. Indiana University Press, Bloomington.

Todorov, T. (1981); *Mikhail Bakhtine, le principe dialogique.* Seuil, Paris.

Touraine, A. (1992); *Critique de la modernité.* Fayard, Paris.

—— (1994); *Qu'est-ce que la démocratie?* Fayard, Paris.

Urry, J. (1981); *The Anatomy of Capitalist Society: The Economy, Civil Society and the State.* Macmillan, London.

Voloshinov, V. N. (1973); *Marxism and the Philosophy of Language.* Seminar, New York.

—— (1977); *Le marxisme et la philosophie du langage.* Minuit, Paris.

Wetherell, M. and J. Potter (1992); *Mapping the Language of Racism.* Harvest Wheatsheaf, Brighton.

Williams, G. (1992); *Sociolinguistics: A Sociological Critique.* Routledge, London.

—— (1998a); Modernity, Normativity and Social Order: The Problem of Ethnicity. In R. Bombi and G. Graffi (eds), *Ethnos e Comunità Linguistica: Un Confronto Metodologico Interdisciplinare.* Forum, Udine, pp. 517–539.

—— (1998b); Language and Ethnic Identity: The Sociological Perspective. In J. A. Fishman (ed.), *Language and Ethnic Identity.* Oxford University Press, Oxford.

Williams, R. (1973); Base and Superstructure in Marxist Cultural Theory. *New Left Review.* No. 82, pp. 3–17.

—— (1977); *Marxism and Literature.* Oxford University Press, Oxford.

Wisard, F. (1994); *L'énonciation d'un témoignage: L'étrange défaite de Marc Bloch.* University of Lausanne, Lausanne.

Wittgenstein, L. (1958a); *The Blue and Brown Books.* Blackwell, Oxford.

—— (1958b); *Philosophical Investigations.* Blackwell, Oxford.

—— (1961); *Tractatus logico-philosophicus.* Gallimard, Paris.

—— (1969); *On Certainty.* Blackwell, Oxford.

—— (1978); *Philosophical Grammar.* University of California Press, Berkeley and Los Angeles.

—— (1980); *Grammaire philosophique.* Gallimard, Paris.

INDEX